India Studies in Business and Economics

The Indian economy is considered to be one of the fastest growing economies of the world with India amongst the most important G-20 economies. Ever since the Indian economy made its presence felt on the global platform, the research community is now even more interested in studying and analyzing what India has to offer. This series aims to bring forth the latest studies and research about India from the areas of economics, business, and management science. The titles featured in this series will present rigorous empirical research, often accompanied by policy recommendations, evoke and evaluate various aspects of the economy and the business and management landscape in India, with a special focus on India's relationship with the world in terms of business and trade.

More information about this series at http://www.springer.com/series/11234

Anand Kulkarni

India and the Knowledge Economy

Performance, Perils, and Prospects

Anand Kulkarni
Victoria University
Melbourne, VIC, Australia

ISSN 2198-0012   ISSN 2198-0020 (electronic)
India Studies in Business and Economics
ISBN 978-981-13-9377-8   ISBN 978-981-13-9378-5 (eBook)
https://doi.org/10.1007/978-981-13-9378-5

© Springer Nature Singapore Pte Ltd. 2019
This work is subject to copyright. All rights are reserved by the Publisher, whether the whole or part of the material is concerned, specifically the rights of translation, reprinting, reuse of illustrations, recitation, broadcasting, reproduction on microfilms or in any other physical way, and transmission or information storage and retrieval, electronic adaptation, computer software, or by similar or dissimilar methodology now known or hereafter developed.
The use of general descriptive names, registered names, trademarks, service marks, etc. in this publication does not imply, even in the absence of a specific statement, that such names are exempt from the relevant protective laws and regulations and therefore free for general use.
The publisher, the authors and the editors are safe to assume that the advice and information in this book are believed to be true and accurate at the date of publication. Neither the publisher nor the authors or the editors give a warranty, expressed or implied, with respect to the material contained herein or for any errors or omissions that may have been made. The publisher remains neutral with regard to jurisdictional claims in published maps and institutional affiliations.

This Springer imprint is published by the registered company Springer Nature Singapore Pte Ltd.
The registered company address is: 152 Beach Road, #21-01/04 Gateway East, Singapore 189721, Singapore

Preface

This book has been in the making for many years. It is focussed on India's performance, perils and prospects in relation to being an innovation, knowledge based economy, and suggests a number of strategies and policy recommendations for taking the country forward.

While being data rich, the book is not a detailed statistical exercise, nor is it theory centric, except where pertinent, especially in the early chapters. The book is however, strongly a 'debate starter', an agenda setter, hopefully providing thought leadership, often provocatively to chart a new course of action for India.

Any errors are the responsibility of the author. This book represents the author's opinions entirely.

Melbourne, Australia Anand Kulkarni
May 2019

Acknowledgements

I would like to thank profusely my wife Kavita, and our daughters Nikita and Priya, for all their assistance, but even more importantly their ongoing loving support and encouragement, and providing the strength for me to conclude this journey when climbing up the mountain has been particularly hazardous and strenuous. I am forever grateful. I would like to acknowledge my parents, Rangnath and Shashikala Kulkarni, who sadly passed away before this undertaking commenced, but have always been with me during its development. My parents' famous saying was 'The river only flows in one direction'. How apt for a book about knowledge and progress, continually looking ahead.

I would also like to thank Springer staff both past and present, for the opportunity to write this book and for their assistance, especially Stephen Jones, Ambrose Berkumans, William Achauer, Lucie Bartonek and Vishnu Muthuswamy.

Contents

1 **The Knowledge Economy Framework** 1
   1.1 Introduction 1
   1.2 The Importance of Innovation 3
   1.3 Definition of Innovation and Knowledge 4
   1.4 Theories and Frameworks of Innovation 4
      1.4.1 National Competiveness Theories 5
      1.4.2 Firm-Based Innovations 6
      1.4.3 Meso Theories 7
      1.4.4 Inclusive Innovation 8
   1.5 Implications of Theories for India 9
   1.6 Limitations of Theories 10
   1.7 Planning in Practice in India 11
   1.8 Techno-Nation Building 11
   1.9 Techno Nationalist Phase 12
   1.10 Techno Integrative Phase 13
   1.11 Bifurcated Phases 15
   1.12 Current Era 16
   1.13 Planning Impacts and Weaknesses 17
   1.14 Planning Legacies 19
   1.15 Premises of This Book 19
      1.15.1 A Broad-Based Approach 20
      1.15.2 Theoretical and Practical Premises 20
      1.15.3 Connected to the World 22
      1.15.4 A Solutions Approach 23
      1.15.5 Institutions 25
   1.16 Towards a Framework 25
   1.17 Enablers 26

	1.18	Education	27
	1.19	Engagement	28
	1.20	Entrepreneurship	28
	1.21	Empowerment	29
	1.22	Environment	30
	1.23	Proposed Intervention Schema	31
	1.24	What This Book Is and What It Is Not	32
	1.25	Conclusion	33
	References		33
2	**Enablers**		**39**
	2.1	Introduction	39
	2.2	India's Experience of Statism	40
		2.2.1 A Different View of the State	42
		2.2.2 The Market Mechanism	42
		2.2.3 The Enabling State	43
	2.3	Elements of the Enabling State	43
		2.3.1 Market Establishment Policies	44
		2.3.2 Market Conforming Policies	44
		2.3.3 Some Policy Reforms	45
		2.3.4 Modi Administration Performance in Relation to Market Conforming/Market Establishment	47
		2.3.5 Market Augmenting Policies	47
		2.3.6 Market Adjustment	49
		2.3.7 Market Linkage Policies	51
		2.3.8 Market Adjunct	51
	2.4	The Nature of the Enabling State	52
	2.5	Types of Instruments	53
		2.5.1 Newer Policies	54
	2.6	Paradigm Shifts	57
	2.7	Business Environment	59
		2.7.1 World Bank Doing Business Index	59
		2.7.2 Governance Data and Global Innovation Data	60
	2.8	Deficiencies and New Approaches	61
	2.9	Towards a New System of Government	62
	2.10	A Commission for Government	64
	2.11	A New Era of Decentralised Planning	66
	2.12	Knowledge Advantage Plans	67
	2.13	Planning and Governance	67
	2.14	Other Support Structures	68
	2.15	Rural Areas	69

	2.16	Other Institutional Features	69
		2.16.1 Collaborate India	69
		2.16.2 Innovations in the Bureaucracy	71
		2.16.3 Judicial System	72
	2.17	Democracy	73
		2.17.1 Composition of Parliament	74
		2.17.2 Parliamentary Process	75
		2.17.3 Conduct of Elections	75
	2.18	Corruption	77
		2.18.1 India's Performance on Corruption	77
	2.19	Anti-corruption Measures	78
		2.19.1 Demonetisation	80
	2.20	Inequality	81
		2.20.1 What Are Solutions to Rampant Inequality?	82
		2.20.2 UBI for India?	83
	2.21	Critical Challenges	84
	2.22	Health	84
		2.22.1 Model for Health Care in India	86
		2.22.2 Funding of the System	87
		2.22.3 Collaboration and Partnerships	87
	2.23	Housing	89
		2.23.1 A Comprehensive Approach to Housing	90
	2.24	Food and Agriculture	92
		2.24.1 Global Hunger Index	93
		2.24.2 Key Factors in Agriculture and Food	94
		2.24.3 Towards a Food Policy	96
		2.24.4 Governance and Reform	97
		2.24.5 Leading Practice	99
	2.25	Conclusion	100
	References		100
3	**Education**		107
	3.1	Introduction	107
		3.1.1 Studies	108
	3.2	Higher Education in India: Structural and Other Features	109
		3.2.1 Concerns About Indian Higher Education	109
		3.2.2 Structural Issues and Legacies	111
	3.3	Institutional Flaws	113
		3.3.1 The State in Retreat?	115
		3.3.2 Access and Opportunity	117

	3.4	Quality, Diversity and Innovation	122
		3.4.1 Diversity	122
		3.4.2 Quality	125
		3.4.3 Innovation	128
	3.5	Resourcing	132
	3.6	Internationalisation	133
	3.7	Labour Market Linkages	135
		3.7.1 Jobs Crisis	135
		3.7.2 Employment by Skill	137
		3.7.3 Vocational Sector	140
		3.7.4 Employability	140
		3.7.5 Labour Market Orientations of the Future	141
		3.7.6 India and the Fourth Industrial Revolution	142
	3.8	The Future of Indian Higher Education	147
	3.9	Reform Agenda	148
		3.9.1 Solutions/Mission-Based Cluster Details	149
		3.9.2 Diverse Specalisms	150
	3.10	Departure from the Present	151
	3.11	Distribution of Funds	154
	3.12	Regulation and Oversight	155
	3.13	A New Pedagogy	156
	3.14	Research Capability	156
		3.14.1 Funding Particulars	157
	3.15	Education, Training and Employment Brokers	158
	3.16	An Internationalisation Plan for Higher Education	159
	3.17	The System in Its Entirety	160
	3.18	Road Map	161
	3.19	Conclusion	162
	References		162
4	**Engagement**		167
	4.1	Parameters of Engagement	167
	4.2	Approach to the Chapter	168
		4.2.1 Exports	168
		4.2.2 Entrepreneurship	169
		4.2.3 Environment	169
	4.3	Knowledge Footprint	169
	4.4	Footprint Methodology	170
	4.5	Domestic Knowledge Footprint	171
		4.5.1 Domestic Knowledge Access and Opportunity Sub-pillar	171
		4.5.2 Domestic Knowledge Supports and Platforms Sub-pillar	171

	4.5.3	Domestic Knowledge Capability Development Sub-pillar	172
	4.5.4	Domestic Knowledge Resourcing Sub-pillar	173
	4.5.5	Domestic Knowledge Relationships Sub-pillar	173
	4.5.6	Domestic Knowledge Translation and Transformation Sub-pillar	174
4.6	Global Knowledge Footprint		174
	4.6.1	Global Knowledge Access and Opportunity Sub-pillar	175
	4.6.2	Global Knowledge Supports and Platforms Sub-pillar	175
	4.6.3	Global Knowledge Capability Development Sub-pillar	176
	4.6.4	Global Knowledge Resourcing Sub-pillar	176
	4.6.5	Global Knowledge Relationships Sub-pillar	176
	4.6.6	Global Knowledge Translation and Transformation Sub-pillar	177
4.7	Overall Findings of Footprint Analysis		177
	4.7.1	Classifying Economies	178
	4.7.2	Key Further Analysis	180
4.8	Trade		196
	4.8.1	Exports	197
	4.8.2	Services Exports	203
	4.8.3	Imports	205
	4.8.4	Global Value Chain Linkages	206
4.9	Foreign Investment		207
	4.9.1	Greenfield Investments	208
	4.9.2	Favoured Destinations	209
4.10	Investment and Knowledge Intensive Industries		210
4.11	India's Engagement Policy		210
	4.11.1	India's Policy Stance	211
	4.11.2	The Importance of Entrepreneurship	214
	4.11.3	Entrepreneurial Issues	215
	4.11.4	The Missings	218
	4.11.5	What Is to Be Done?	231
4.12	The Environment		245
	4.12.1	India's Situation	245
	4.12.2	Policy Suggestions for India	249
4.13	Conclusion		252
Appendix 1: Knowledge Footprint Methodology, Metrics and Sources			253
References			277

5 Empowerment ... 281
5.1 Introduction ... 281
5.2 Literature Review ... 282
5.2.1 Institutional Studies ... 282
5.2.2 Social Norms ... 285
5.2.3 Labour Force Participation ... 287
5.2.4 Entrepreneurship and Industrial Sphere ... 289
5.2.5 Value Chains ... 291
5.2.6 Health ... 291
5.2.7 Knowledge Economy ... 292
5.2.8 Financial Inclusion Studies ... 295
5.3 Gender Knowledge Footprint ... 297
5.3.1 Three Variations on the Footprint ... 297
5.4 Scores and Discussion for India: Males Versus Females ... 300
5.4.1 Detailed Discussion ... 302
5.4.2 More Detailed Score Breakdowns ... 303
5.4.3 Gender Knowledge Footprint in BRIC Countries ... 305
5.4.4 Results: Males Versus Females for BRIC Nations ... 306
5.4.5 BRIC Intra-gender Comparison ... 307
5.5 Policies ... 309
5.5.1 Gender Knowledge Footprint ... 309
5.5.2 Institutional Change ... 309
5.5.3 Women in Knowledge Program (WIK) ... 311
5.5.4 Work–Life Balance ... 312
5.5.5 Attitudinal Changes ... 313
5.5.6 Employment and Security ... 314
5.5.7 Financing and Funding ... 316
5.6 Conclusion ... 316
Appendix 1: Case Study on Mahila Samakhya ... 317
Appendix 2: Gender Knowledge Footprint Methodology ... 321
References ... 331

6 Conclusion ... 335
6.1 Introduction ... 335
6.2 Vision for India ... 336
6.2.1 Enlarging India's Knowledge Footprint ... 336
6.2.2 Problem Solver ... 336
6.2.3 Building 'Conbundance' Capabilities ... 337
6.2.4 Institutions of the Future ... 338
6.2.5 Returning to the 'E's ... 338

List of Tables

Table 2.1	Policy orientation	58
Table 3.1	Institutional and enrolment growth 2011–2012 to 2017–2018	113
Table 3.2	More bureaucracy	114
Table 3.3	Gross enrolment ratios: higher education (UNESCO data includes Vocational sector)	118
Table 3.4	Scenarios for expansion of higher education	119
Table 3.5	Percentage of the population aged 25 and above that have reached (but not necessarily) completed a secondary level of education 2006–2017	121
Table 3.6	Distribution of tertiary students (non-vocational): 2016 except where otherwise stated	124
Table 3.7	Times Higher Education rankings: various years	126
Table 3.8	Times Higher Education 2019	126
Table 3.9	Subject rankings India and China	127
Table 3.10	Subject distribution of papers by top ten institutions of higher education 2013–2016	129
Table 3.11	2013–2016: citations top ten universities	130
Table 3.12	Core skills of the future	143
Table 3.13	Proposed schema for Indian higher education in the future	152
Table 4.1	Knowledge Footprint Results	178
Table 4.2	Domestic Knowledge Footprint Sub-pillars (Where countries have the same score at the one decimal level, the author uses the data at the 2 decimal level to determine country and rank. This applies across all footprint parameters)	181
Table 4.3	Global Knowledge Footprint Sub-pillars	183
Table 4.4	Comparisons with other key indicators	184
Table 4.5	Distance to frontier (Best in the World)	190
Table 4.6	Distance to average global	191
Table 4.7	Distance to average BRIC	192

Table 4.8	India distance to China.	193
Table 4.9	Breakdown by metric.	195
Table 4.10	India's share of global exports by value (based on $m U.S. current dollars).	198
Table 4.11	Share of Indian exports accounted for by industry by value (based on $m U.S. Current Dollars).	199
Table 4.12	Share of Indian manufacturing exports accounted for by category	199
Table 4.13	Composition of world manufacturing exports (shares).	200
Table 4.14	India's proportion of China's exports.	200
Table 4.15	AT Kearney index investment confidence (Rank out of 25 countries)	209
Table 4.16	Filing by Knowledge Number of Registrations (share in brackets).	223
Table 4.17	Deloitte Asia Pacific Fast 500	224
Table 4.18	Typology of businesses in India.	232
Table 5.1	Gender Knowledge Footprint One: Males and Females India.	301
Table 5.2	Gender Knowledge Footprint Score Breakdowns: India.	303
Table 5.3	Gender Knowledge Footprint for BRIC Nations: Comparing male to female in individual BRIC countries	306
Table 5.4	Intra-Gender Knowledge Footprint Comparisons in BRIC countries.	307

Chapter 1
The Knowledge Economy Framework

Abstract This chapter defines innovation and the knowledge economy and considers various theories and frameworks, from the macro level through to more disaggregated approaches. It also looks at the history of planning in India through the lens primarily of science and technology. The author posits a framework for innovation and the knowledge economy for India based on a capabilities approach, called the 'E' Framework. The E framework comprises Enablers, Education, Engagement, Entrepreneurship and Empowerment. The natural environment is also presented as closely aligned with the framework elements. A key aspect of the overall approach is that India needs to be open to, and participate in, the flow of ideas from wherever and however they originate. Further, policy and strategic action needs to be strongly oriented to providing solutions to complex challenges facing India and the world.

Keywords Knowledge · Knowledge economy · Innovation · Ideas · Planning · Science and technology · Solutions

1.1 Introduction

Located in a picturesque and secluded part of modern day Bihar is the revived Nalanda University. At its peak, Nalanda, reputed to be one of the world's oldest Universities if not the oldest, was an epicentre of global learning, with students from many parts of the world undertaking training under the watchful gaze of Buddhist teachers, in fields as diverse as medicine, physical sciences, language and literature. Training was based on inquiry, oral traditions of learning and deep intellectual underpinnings (Government of India 2016; Kumar 2011; Mukherjee 2016; Sen 2015).

Fast forward centuries to the first part of this decade, and the rejuvenation of this great Institution was mired in claim and counterclaim of mismanagement, cronyism, lack of accountability and oversight and extravagant expenditure (Devraj 2016; Puri 2015; Sharma 2015; Venkataramakrishnan 2015). The new Vice-Chancellor nonetheless is proposing a bold new and firm agenda for revitalisation of this great institution (Kumar 2017). In these two opening paragraphs, we find a summation of the conundrums, contradictions and contrariness of India: great traditions of learning, scholarship and innovation, which continue in many realms today, allied with chaos and dysfunction. How to bridge these conflicting realities, how to create a single, unified and grand destiny from disparate parts, are massive challenges.

Ancient India was replete with many home grown inventions, new to the world, including in chemical science, medicine, plastic surgery, yoga, cosmology, algebra, mechanics and atomic theory (Kalam and Pillai 2013). In the modern day, India has been the home to a unique brand of innovation and invention, displayed in large extent in the frugal or inclusive innovation realms (to be discussed shortly). Innovations have ranged from clay refrigeration based on evaporative cooling techniques, the 'youtube' education revolution of the Khan Academy, non-stick frying pans, coconut packaged drinks, bulletproof jackets for defence personnel made out of pulses, machines for processing medicinal plants, unique applications of windmills to irrigation, and a myriad of health applications such as the portable Electro Cardio Gram (ECG machine), low cost prosthetics and mass eye surgeries at very low cost and high quality (Gupta 2016). These examples should not typecast India as a provider of lower technology products. There is more to the story. India has made considerable strides in 'mainstream' realms of satellite and space technologies, pharmaceuticals (the world's largest generic producer), Information and Communications Technology (ICT) and Infrastructure design and development, while its diaspora is among the world's most regarded. Yet, there remains considerable disquiet about India's overall innovation capabilities, which we identify and address in this book, such as lacklustre R&D and patenting performance, weakness in manufacturing, a very patchy education system, a digital divide, an overall paucity of brand new product innovations and poor performance on many social indicators, including health, basic education and on environmental matters. Linking old with the new, aligning 'big science' and the imagination of small grass roots innovators, modernising the technology base, and ensuring that economic gain is translated into social benefit, are all major touchstones.

Slipping back to the past for a moment, ground breaking work (Maddison 2018) found that India's share of global GDP was 28.9% in AD 1000, holding firm to 1870, when it eventually dropped to 12.2%, and continuing on a downward spiral to 4.2% in 1950, in the wake of the British Colonial era.[1]

How can India build on its reasonably strong recent economic performance and attempt to reclaim some of these glories of the past? This book examines in detail India's recent economic performance and prospects through the lens of a knowledge or innovation-based economy, as a key means of driving economic and social outcomes. What role does innovation play in this future? What kinds of innovation and knowledge are pertinent to India, given its strengths, competitive advantages, constraints, problems as well as potential? What is India's role in global innovation?

---

[1] Author calculations based on Maddison's work.

1.2 The Importance of Innovation

A threshold question is why is innovation important to India? In a general sense, it is hard to argue with the proposition that for a modern economy innovation and knowledge is more and more integral to its destiny, not just in developed economies as has traditionally been the case, but also for emerging or less developed economies, including India. The importance of innovation for countries is reflected in the following range of ways, especially over the last two decades, with various perturbations depending on economic contexts (OECD 2007, 2008–2018[2]; UNESCO 2015): R&D intensity of economies has been on the rise, as has patenting activity, including in fields such as artificial intelligence; investment in knowledge based capital, e.g. design, marketing and software has grown, and more broadly investment in knowledge has grown faster than in machinery and equipment; advanced manufactures and services, with ever shrinking product cycles and rampant technological change, are standard bearers of a modern economy; employment in knowledge intensive industries and occupations is much sought after and growing; fragmentation and integration of value chains around the world, linked by specialist capabilities and know-how, has become the norm; innovation is becoming more global and collaborative; challenge areas abound for innovation in the environment, energy and health among other things; while the Fourth (Schwab 2016, 2017) Industrial Revolution, comprising Artificial Intelligence, robotics, the 'internet of things', additive manufacturing and myriad others, including biotechnology and nanotechnology, based on fusion of technologies and convergent sectors is, and has, the potential to, transform economies in an unprecedented manner. At the same time associated with these developments is severe structural change and economic and social dislocation. Moreover, inequality is on the rise as we shall see in the course of this book, with many jobs now at serious risk associated with new technology.

At the more academic level, a vast array of studies confirm the importance of knowledge. A few examples of many are presented here. Improvements in skill enhance productivity growth, investment in software produces stronger business performance, and investment in R&D is linked with high rates of return (OECD 2007). Other work points to the positive relationship between standards of living and innovation (patent stock) in OECD and non OECD countries[3] (Ulku 2004), while the importance of national innovation systems (enrolment in science and technology, Government R&D expenditure, high technology exports) for growth in Brazil, Russia, India and China (BRIC countries) is highlighted (Sessay et al. 2016). The significance of entrepreneurship for employment and economic growth, especially in spatial contexts (Braunerhjelm 2010) has been demonstrated. For India, innovation has been the most important driving force for economic growth between 2006 and 2013, according to one source (Fan 2018), while another analysis contends that an innovation-based future for India has the potential to transform its economy, to the

---

[2]OECD 2008–2018 refers to the same name of the publication which is refreshed every two years.
[3]Note the effect of R&D stock on innovation is significant only in OECD countries with large markets.

tune of 9% growth in GDP per annum over the next two decades, to reach $U.S10.4 trillion by 2034. This would require a further major lift in R&D spending, as well as investment in new processes and business models (ASSOCHAM 2014).

With this backdrop in full view, innovation and knowledge will be critical to add value to natural resources and manage scarce resources in clever ways, build and sustain competitive advantage in a flexible manner, raise living standards, secure well paying, meaningful, interesting and challenging jobs, raise masses out of poverty, and address complex economic, environmental and social challenges through innovation, creativity and the development and deployment of knowledge. However, the innovation path and possibilities will differ from country to country, depending on resources, size of economy, skills and technology base, openness to domestic and global flows of ideas, and historical, institutional and cultural factors.

1.3 Definition of Innovation and Knowledge

For all this what is innovation? A variety of definitions and constructs can be found. We take a deliberately broad brush approach based on the development, deployment and diffusion of new and improved technologies, know-how, business and organisational models and social practices, for the pursuit of commercial and/or social gain. In this book, innovation, knowledge and the knowledge economy are used more or less interchangeably.

Our definition owes much to the Oslo Manual, as reprised in Tiwari et al. (2017, p. 17) in which innovations are described as 'the implementation of a new or significantly improved product (good or service) or process, a new marketing method, or a new organisational method in business practices, workplace organisation or external relations'. In using this broad-based approach, we recognise the interplay of scientific and non-scientific applications of know-how, of formal research and development and more informal acquisition and deployment of knowledge, and broader design features and parameters. Our approach also recognises the various 'tiers' of innovation, including scientific endeavour in prominent national laboratories and the know-how and creativity of grass roots innovators at the village level in India, for example. Further, our approach encapsulates innovation in policy as well, including new thinking, and novel design and implementation of public policy.

1.4 Theories and Frameworks of Innovation

There are a variety of theories, frameworks and applications of innovation. In this brief section, we identify various approaches, which in our view are pertinent to India. There are four broad classifications of innovation approaches that are germane. A select few examples are provided.

1.4.1 National Competiveness Theories

The first of the four broad approaches is what we describe as national competitiveness approaches which bear particularly on an emerging country such as India. These theories go to the heart of the emerging challenges that developing countries pose for developed countries in terms of inroads into products, processes and technologies.

1.4.1.1 Reverse Innovation

One of these approaches is reverse innovation (Govindarajan and Trimble 2012) which is innovation developed and adopted in the developing world, that is then transmitted and deployed in the developed world. It reverses the conventional wisdom of flows of innovation from the developed to the developing world, in which products developed for more advanced markets are modified to suit local conditions and the needs of developing economies such as India. Reverse innovation works on the premise that products and processes initiated in the developing world become attractive to the developed world, either through marginal markets (e.g. low-income segments of developed countries), or eventually as a mainstream market, as needs and demands of richer and poorer economies converge. There are five drivers of reverse innovation in developing countries: performance (making significant sacrifices in product performance at the right, affordable price); Infrastructure (new needs of emerging economies and infrastructure under construction); sustainability (developing economies face very significant sustainable/environmental challenges); regulatory arrangements (regulatory systems in emerging economies can often be less onerous, developed or stringent, providing opportunities for bringing products to market including in timely fashion); and preferences and taste (e.g. food preparations in developing economies which eventually find favour in developed economies).

With these drivers in mind, over time, these products and services become attractive to developed economies. For example, developing country preferences for products and services, and associated technological improvements, influence consumers in the developed world through the process of globalisation while sustainability issues prominent in the developing world, are of growing concern in the developed world. Further, budget constraints facing households in richer countries means that they are often open to ultra-low price options that are available in the developing world, and innovations in infrastructure in the developing world can influence the developed world when it comes time to replace ageing infrastructure (Govindarajan and Trimble 2012). A variant on this kind of approach is the indigenous innovation school in less developed economies, which is the interplay of foreign R&D and domestic capabilities, where the latter includes absorptive capacity, i.e. skills, R&D and technologies to capitalise on overseas technologies, which can provide the springboard to exports, especially for middle-income economies similar in technological and factor conditions (Brem and Wolfram 2014).

1.4.1.2 Invisible Innovation

Another interesting approach is that of 'invisible innovation' (Kumar and Puranam 2012). Looked at largely with India in mind, it focuses on the absence of well established, reputable, high profile final consumer goods, and brands originating from India. It is founded on the question of where is 'the Indian equivalent of Google'? It turns this argument on its head by pointing out that Indian innovation is invisible in the sense of being *embedded* in research, technology, design, skills and processes associated with end consumer goods, not apparent to final consumers. A number of dimensions of this are articulated: multinational corporations that establish captive innovation and R&D centres in India; outsourcing innovation to Indian firms to drive new product development for consumers in advanced economies; process innovations in India which result from the interplay of lower wages and higher skills, leading to the assignment of over qualified people to routine jobs, giving rise to highly effective and novel process innovations which become embedded in products marketed to the world (e.g. analytical and predictive tools in call centres that add value); and management of globally distributed delivery models, involving formerly physically co-located activities being broken into sub tasks and performed elsewhere on the basis of cost, time, skills and other advantages, and then integrated across different locations, time zones and cultures. India has been at the centre of managing, coordinating and integrating such disparate work, particularly in the IT sector.

1.4.2 Firm-Based Innovations

Next we turn to firm-based approaches to innovation pertinent to India. One such model in our brief consideration of innovation theories is the disruptive approach originated by Christensen (1997). Disruptive technologies and innovations have occupied the minds of theoreticians and practitioners over the last decade or so.[4] The key premises behind disruption are as follows: incumbents sustain innovation by improving performance in technology and other characteristics; in improving products and services (usually for their most demanding and profitable segments), firms 'overshoot' the performance needs of low-end customers and many mainstream ones, and in so doing open the door for disruptors to provide 'good enough' products for lower end customers, or create new markets which did not previously exist; while incumbents have the ability to react they often fail to do so, and end up faltering and failing as new entrants take over (Christensen 1997; Christensen et al. 2015).

Application of this disruption to India is possible, especially in the 'Bottom of the Pyramid' segments,[5] where new markets can emerge, or for lower end existing

---

[4]Christiansen's original theory focussed on technologies, later widened to include broader innovations encompassing business and organisational models.

[5]Bottom of the Pyramid pioneered by Prahlad (2005) describes firms who target customers in the least well off segments, tailoring products and services specifically to their needs and circumstances.

customers, who due to affordability constraints, would be receptive to lower prices with reasonably good performance (Ramdorai and Herstatt 2017). Products created for the lower end segments, or new markets, can be applied to the higher end thus disrupting the latter. Non or low end consumers disregarded, for example, by multinational corporations, i.e. the Bottom of the Pyramid segment, can provide the impetus for the disruptive innovation process.

1.4.3 Meso Theories

There are a range of approaches to innovation which focus on the 'meso' sphere of the economy. The best known of this is the idea of innovation systems. Systems literature captures the linkages, complementarities and interdependencies of relationships between actors, focussing on flows of knowledge, information, technology and ideas (OECD 1997, 1999, 2002). These theories are important in identifying points of leverage for government (and other players) action to improve innovative performance and to identify critical bottlenecks in the entire system, which impede the flow of ideas, information and knowledge. There are four types of flows of knowledge: among enterprises (collaboration, joint activities); relationships between firms, public research bodies and universities (joint research, co-patents, publications, informal connections); diffusion of knowledge and technology to firms, including through embodied means (e.g. plant and equipment); and mobility of personnel between public and private sectors. Typically included in the system are firms, research bodies, universities, regulators and financiers (OECD 1997, 1999). There are a variety of innovation system approaches, which can encapsulate regions, sectors and even international dimensions.

One recent manifestation of this, arguably, is the concept of innovation districts. Innovation districts are compact and core areas in cities which house and attract clusters of leading-edge institutions (anchors), start ups, business incubators, accelerators and are linked by retail, housing and transport (including bicycle paths). Innovation districts embody new technologies, the development and commercialisation of ideas, new firm generation and convergence of disparate sectors and technologies. They operate on the basis of connections, collaboration, shared and proximate spaces and amenities for ideas exchange and testing, open source innovation, and draw on pools of specialised labour, among other things. The interplay of physical, economic and networking assets is key (Katz and Wagner 2014).

Unlike traditional approaches to urbanisation which have concentrated on the commercial aspects of development such as housing, retail and facilities, industrial districts focus on innovation and value chain enhancement. Moreover, they eschew the model of building isolated science parks which can tend to produce 'silo' based approaches (Katz and Wagner 2014).

Three types of industrial districts have been observed (Katz and Wagner 2014): anchor plus (centred around major institutions, e.g. universities, or hospitals and a rich base of firms, entrepreneurs and spin-off companies); re-imagined urban areas (physical and economic transformation of industrial or warehouse districts); and urbanised science parks (where historically separate sprawling areas of innovation are transformed and urbanised through integrated new activities, including housing and other amenities).

Less a theory or model of behaviour but more a framework based on observation and need is the ASSURED approach put forward by the eminent Indian scholar, scientist and innovator Mashelkar (2018). This describes innovation to reduce inequality in India, perhaps more aspirationally rather than actually, positing an important role for the private sector in making profit through pursuing social objectives, 'doing well by doing good'. The ASSURED framework is *Affordability*; *Scaleability* to ensure broad reach of innovations; *Sustainability* in its many dimensions of economy, environment and society in which the market plays a vital role in competition, producing high-value goods and with less reliance on Government assistance; *Rapid*, which involves speedy movement from the 'mind to the market'; *Excellence* in technological and non-technological innovation, product, and service delivery and quality; and *Distinctive* products and services.

1.4.4 Inclusive Innovation

Finally, for consideration is the broad class of what can be described as 'Inclusive Innovation'. These have at their core in varying degrees the following: a focus on local problem solving for grass roots challenges; providing goods and services for under-served markets, especially lower income groups (Bottom of the Pyramid); environmental and sustainability considerations on a whole of value chain basis; maximising consumer and social value at lower, affordable prices; innovation around resource and other constraints; and social enterprise and community engagement in the development and diffusion of know-how (Brem and Wolfrem 2014; Herstatt and Tiwari 2017; Tiwari et al. 2017; Tiwari 2017; Nair et al. 2017; Ramdorai and Herstatt 2017; Radjou et al. 2012).

Among the relevant applications that are aligned with the above and found in (Brem and Wolfram 2014) are:

- *Frugal innovations* (the ability to do more with less which places high value on sustainable solutions across the value chain; collaborative behaviour with a range of partners; working with and immersing with consumers and co-creating products with consumers (pro-consumers), utilising new production processes such as decentralised manufacturing, sharing resources, local sourcing, new and efficient use of materials and production to produce goods and services that are affordable, sustainable and have due regard for quality);
- *Jugaad* innovation which focuses on improvised innovations and innovating around constraints;
- *Gandhian innovation* (building, modifying and linking internal and external technologies and capabilities from abroad);

- *Catalytic innovation* (with a focus more on social change, social entrepreneurship and volunteering, for under-served needs); and
- *Grass roots innovation* (similar to Jugaad but more reliant on networks among local players).

The hallmarks of these approaches is that they are increasingly linked and intertwined with emerging features of the modern economy, especially frugal innovation, in terms of crowd sourcing of ideas, the sharing economy (less emphasis on ownership but on renting and resource sharing), distributed, decentralised productions through, for example, 3D printing, micro factories and tinkering by individuals, including the 'do it yourself' movement (Radjou and Prabhu 2015). Also at play are the circular economy (cradle to cradle approach to resource use and complete and continuous recycling), spiral economy (adding value through sustainability, for example, by creating and designing high value, innovative, multi-purpose products from waste) and co-creating collaborative products and services, e.g. consumers increasingly co-design and co-produce products and services in concert with firms (Radjou and Prabhu 2015).

1.5 Implications of Theories for India

The theories and approaches that we have briefly considered bear on India in many ways and senses. The reverse and invisible innovation sectors have implications for India becoming a stronger, more global player in innovation, by drawing on its unique attributes, capabilities and advantages in cost, skills and know-how.

We have already mentioned how the disruptive innovation approach bears on the Bottom of the Pyramid segment. Beyond this, we argue for a much more profound, collaborative approach in India, including the way public policy is conducted, consistent with innovation system and inclusive genres. This book has a very strong emphasis on the support institutions required for an innovation-based economy and society and argues for a much more systems orientation to innovation, which captures flows of knowledge across sectors, technologies and spatial areas. The systems approach can play an important role in India in overcoming fragmentation and disconnects between research bodies and industry, and between education, training institutions and the labour market, for example. The industrial districts work, although embryonic, and geared more to U.S. spatial areas, nonetheless has application to India's cities as they seek to develop, diversify and modernise, and meet the complex challenges of ever-expanding urbanisation in a manner which can more effectively leverage public assets, and promote social cohesion. The Indian Smart Cities agenda could draw inspiration from this literature.

The inclusive innovation school has particular significance for India, given the richness of local knowledge, traditions of austerity, longer term orientation of society traditionally (as opposed to short term rampant consumerism), budget constraints facing firms and individuals, and the presence of large markets. In addition, a range of social needs can be serviced by frugal type innovations. The incremental nature of many Indian innovations, allied with cost advantage, awareness of sustainability factors, emergent technical capabilities and quality consciousness, are important factors lending themselves to inclusive innovation (Tiwari 2017).

Our approach, to be illuminated in subsequent chapters, calls for robustly tapping into India's vast reservoir of talents, innovative capabilities and ideas that emanate from its villages, from towns and from its people in all walks of life, reflecting in many ways the primacy of the inclusive innovation agenda.

1.6 Limitations of Theories

Yet, to be sure, there are limitations of the various theoretical approaches that have been put forward. The disruptive innovation theory has come under fire for its lack of predictive value and absence of definitional rigour and limited application, e.g. it has been focussed on very few sectors, and 'so-called' disruptions did not necessarily conform to a number of the basic tenets of the theory. Broader factors such as legacy costs, scale economies in some cases, mass competition in others, and changing social conditions better explain industry outcomes and firm-level failures (King and Baatartogtokh 2015; Lepore 2014).

While jugaad, as a key to the inclusive genre, has been lauded as an expression of Indian uniqueness, with applicability around the world, a number of concerns can be raised (Gupta 2016; Krishnan 2010; Tiwari et al. 2017). Jugaad represents a temporary and ad hoc resolution to constraints and challenges, often leaving the root cause of the problem untouched, which in the end is self-defeating. Moreover, jugaad innovations can lack design rigour, precision engineering and wider manufacturing capability. They are characterised by the absence of systematic approaches and processes, and can often raise quality concerns, and even legality issues. Jugaad can be inimical to the creation of a sustainable innovation culture, and it is more about means than outcomes as such. Further, such innovations are often local and context specific, hindering wider applicability.

The reverse innovation (and invisible) approaches hinge necessarily on the willingness of overseas developed countries to embrace products and services from the developing countries, including India, which could be problematic, especially in an era of emergent trade protection. Moreover, it is not entirely clear that all of the dimensions of the approach holds. For example, it is not necessarily the case that infrastructure developments or sustainability pressures in the developing world will necessarily influence the developed world. In addition, innovations can just as easily succeed in home markets alone or in few countries, including other developing ones, rather than developed ones per se (Tiwari et al. 2017). The invisible innovation model, in some senses, seems like a 'cop out' reducing developing countries to just one of the players in the global game rather than as leaders through bold and original final products.

The national innovation system innovation approach, while clearly having merit, arguably has an 'open ended' feel to it in the sense of leaving somewhat unfulfilled what exactly is in a system, where are its boundaries, and what does the most optimal policy design and use of instruments look like to promote a fully fledged system, and overcome deficiencies within it. The driving forces behind a system developing and evolving, especially in developing economy contexts, can often be 'hazy'.

The ASSURED framework is more about what best practice or even next practice could look like for India, and is thus an important and relevant framing of principles. However, it says less about the underpinning capabilities, knowledge and skills required to give expression to the framework.

1.7 Planning in Practice in India

Turning from theory to practice, this section examines India's innovation experience in the post-independence era, through the lens primarily of science and technology, including the five year plans and other related policies. In our view, there have been five main phases broadly.

1.8 Techno-Nation Building

The first phase is what we call *techno nation building*, straddling roughly the first four five year plans from approximately 1951–1974 (Government of India 1952, 1956, 1961, 1970). The plans emphasised the establishment and development of public scientific research institutions, technologies for national purpose such as energy, and supporting and building up of heavy industries and capital goods as 'feeders' to the rest of the economy. The objectives were to be facilitated by public investments (or public support for investments), manpower planning and technical skills development at the elite level as a basis for national economic development. The emphasis was on building domestic capabilities, underpinned by import substitution (although Aggarwal (2001) argues it was actually quite liberal where imports and capital from abroad were deemed important for the national effort). The consumer goods sector was based on reservation for smaller enterprises, for example, household enterprises, with only factory production permissible in the absence of such household capability (Datta 2017).

The approach was heavily influenced by the Soviet model of economic development, the need to develop a more independent approach to throw off the yoke of colonial exploitation, suspicion of the profit motive (except in some consumer goods), national security and to create mass employment. The idea of nation building through science and technology was reflected in the Second Plan, in noting that 'While in the first five year plan attention was chiefly devoted to the building up of national laboratories and other research institutions, the primary object in the second plan is to develop the existing facilities and to bring the work of scientists in the national laboratories and of research workers in universities and other centres to bear as closely upon important problems in different fields of national development' (Government of India 1956, Chap. 24, para 1).[6] This period also encompassed the Scientific Policy Resolution of 1958 which emphasised the vital role of technology in overcoming deficiencies in natural resources and reducing the demands on scarce capital (UNESCO 1964). The economic model in India after independence, to promote capital goods and heavy industry, was influenced by the need to mobilise large savings through public sector activities since the capacity of the private sector was limited, and that large scale investment decisions with long lead times could not rely on market forces. This in turn meant that the State was both a mobiliser of savings and investment and owner of capital (Jalan 2017).

The Government did also establish the National Research Development Corporation (NRDC) and the Council of Scientific and Industrial Research (CSIR), ostensibly as attempts to link research with industry, yet the development and diffusion of broader industrial capability did not occur, with planning and wider industrialisation proceeding on different tracks (Aggarwal 2001). It is also significant that research in the planning context tended to focus on short-term payoffs, which often adapted foreign processes for Indian contexts (Aggarwal 2001). In our view this is paradoxical, given that stated aspiration was for independent national identity.

1.9 Techno Nationalist Phase

In our consideration, the Fifth Plan, beginning in the early 1970s, marked the second phase or what we describe *as Techno Nationalism*. This is the period characterised very strongly by the more insular, inward-looking lens on policy, much more than before we argue, in terms of deliberately creating barriers to engagement with the rest of the world in the guise of overt self-reliance. This was the era of very significant strictures on technology imports, extremely stringent foreign investment guidelines, constraints on industrial and enterprise outputs, industry reservations and all manner of licenses, giving rise to rent-seeking activities. The bank nationalisation programme needs also to be seen in the overriding policy context of the day. As such, the technology policy and science and technology aspects of the plans continued to move in line with these sentiments. The starkest examples of this are reflected in the Technology Policy Strategy of 1983 (Technology Policy 1983) and the Sixth Plan (Government of India 1981). For example, the Sixth Plan (1980–1985) states very explicitly and starkly, more so than earlier plans, that 'Hence self-reliance must be at the very heart of S and T Planning and there can be no other strategy for a country of India's size and endowments' (Government of India 1981, Chap. 19, para 8). The Techno nationalist phase reflects concerns about the periodic foreign exchange crises beset-

---

[6]The quotations for the plans are indicated by chapter and paragraph, since page numbers are hard to discern in the documents, especially the early plans.

ting the country, continued fears about economic vulnerability, and exploitation of the nation if left to the whims and fortunes of other countries' policies and activities of overseas corporations, while the uncertain global economic environment, and mistrust of the private sector, added to the mix. As Aggarwal (2001)[7] states, this period approximately coincided with the 'growth with self-reliance and social justice' era, concerned more with 'sharing the pie' rather than growing it. This sentiment aligned neatly with even greater attempted control of the economy and society by public authorities. Undoubtedly also, domestic politics and the crackdown on dissent can be seen in the light of the greater government direction of the economy.

However, it should be noted that the Sixth Plan does in some senses mark a turning point. There is some recognition of the need for more linkages between academic and national scientific agencies (a partial, tentative, innovation system if you wish), foreign collaboration under the strictest of terms and the involvement of states in science and technology, an early decentralisation push.

The upshot of the policies pursued in the first two phases, especially the second, was poor total factor productivity, lack of competition both internally and externally, lack of scale, poor quality, technological obsolescence and rampant corrupt practices (Aggarwal 2001). As such, these poor outcomes led to somewhat of a 'sea change' in the orientation of policy.

In addition, the approach led to increased capital-output ratios associated with public investment, inefficient use of capital, lack of linkage between sectors, and an inability (and unwillingness) to forge export capabilities, when in fact the world was opening up to trade. Exporting from developing countries including with greater skill content was becoming more prominent (Jalan 2017). The lack of export orientation and focus on import substitution meant that consumption was emphasised at the expense of savings and investment (Puri 2017). We further examine weaknesses of the entire planning approach in Sect. 1.13.

1.10 Techno Integrative Phase

Some of the signs apparent in the Sixth Plan manifest themselves into what we call the third phase of Indian innovation beginning roughly in the Seventh Plan (Government of India 1985) and much more forcibly beyond, in what we call the *Techno-Integrative phase*. It is recognised that integration has multiple dimensions, including stronger relations between science and technology and other economic and social domains, and engagement with the rest of the world. This phase predates and anticipates, but largely encapsulates the post-1991 general liberalisation phase, and even the earlier reforms (e.g. reduction in licenses and reservations, opening up the economy to more technology imports and rise of foreign equity in the 1980s), while continuing to pay

---

[7] Aggarwal in a similar vein speaks of three phases: the growth phase of independence to the 1960's; the growth with self-reliance and social justice phase from 1960s onwards; and the liberalisation phase from the 1980s onward.

lip service to self-reliance. The Seventh Plan recognises the integration of the science and technology system with productive sectors by saying that 'For science and technology to be effectively applied, there is need to complete the total innovation chain consisting of basic research, applied research, design and development, prototype fabrication, upscaling, extension, awareness building, production engineering, design and consultancy and production and services' (Government of India 1985, Chap. 17, para 44). It more explicitly began the development of a broader-based capabilities approach, beyond the narrower science and technology frame of reference. In a similar vein, the Seventh Plan also spoke of linkages between different sectors of education, scientific research, technology development, and productive activities in agriculture and industry, and also the mobility of science and technology personnel between universities, research laboratories and industry (Government of India 1985). The Eighth Plan (Government of India 1992) reinforces and strengthens this notion of an integrative approach by highlighting the importance of science and technology as an essential part of all sectors of national activity, and recognised the growing and important role of the Indian diaspora, while also being critical of the lack of R and D from within industry. The 2003 policy statement on science and technology builds on, and reinforces this integrative phase (Government of India 2003).

The Tenth Plan extends the integration phase, and almost for the first time, consciously and explicitly gave emphasis and regard to exports, a vital component of global integration. For example, the Tenth Plan claims that 'The Indian export basket does not have a significant amount of technologically intensive products, this situation needs to change. Therefore, emphasis would be on the export of high tech products and export of technology' (Government of India 2002, Chap. 10, para 4). The plan also reinforced the need for new institutions, calling for incubators and enterprise and technology parks to link firms, and firms and technology providers. In addition, it also called for, and reiterated organisational reforms, for the Council of Scientific and Industrial Research (CSIR) to become responsive to the market place and customers, and stimulating intellectual property management, as part of the modernisation and international competitiveness agenda.

The Eleventh plan 2007–2012 (Government of India 2007), embellished this integrative thrust by emphasising systems, institutions of collaboration, and importantly multi-disciplinary research, including IT and biotechnology, and cross-disciplinary technology areas, encompassing health care, advanced computing, advanced manufacturing, robotics, sensors and integrated IT systems or a '…common denominator of cross disciplinary areas, where building core expertise and competence will have far-reaching consequences in the development of science-based technologies for societal benefit, economic competitiveness and national security' (Government of India 2007, Vol. 1, Chap. 8, para 27).

This phase of innovation and knowledge reflected a much greater awareness of the impact, importance and possibilities of markets at home and abroad, and the need to break out of the 'silo based', fragmented approach to activity. It also countenanced the beginning, in our view, of the 'managerial' approach to science, technology and innovation, emphasising intellectual property management and organisational reforms to CSIR. It should not be lost that a great deal of impetus for this era came

1.10 Techno Integrative Phase

from the crises and pressures in the economy generally, leading to the liberalisation era, and the weaknesses that the previous planning eras gave rise to. This was in many senses planning to correct for earlier plans. Interesting also is that the Eleventh Plan had two chapters, one on science and technology, the other on innovation, a growing recognition of the importance of innovation beyond narrower science and technology confines.

1.11 Bifurcated Phases

We argue that commencing around 2010, but becoming more apparent in the Twelfth Plan (Government of India 2013a) and subsequent policy statement on innovation in 2013 (Government of India 2013b) and the Decade of Innovation Statement (National Innovation Council 2013), *was the emergence of two distinct parallel phases*.[8] The first is the *Techno-leadership* phase, consistent with the thrust of the overall inclusive growth phase which began with the Twelfth Plan. Interestingly, this Techno leadership phase, has had two clear domains: the first to promote India as a global leader in innovation aiming for it to be among the top 5 global scientific powers by 2020, double the global share of publications and number of papers in the top 1% of journals and increase R&D spending to 2% of GDP (Government of India 2013b). Building global centres of Excellence, including in the university system, and clusters of world-leading industries, has been a priority of this phase. This phase viewed India not just content with being internationally competitive per se, as envisaged previously, but explicitly taking a global leadership position, concomitant with India's overall growing influence in the global economy. It also reflected a belief that India's growing capabilities and core advantages in costs, skills, technology capabilities, market size and sophistication and attractiveness as a destination for knowledge-based investment, as well as its unique jugaad type innovations, could drive India to becoming a global powerhouse. However, as we shall see in the course of this book, rhetoric and reality often do not match. Whether this is, and was, misplaced confidence or some attempt to exhort the public to greater effort, or a belief that India was genuinely on the threshold of being a global powerhouse, is hard to disentangle. In our judgement, the foundations have not been strong enough to warrant this kind of enthusiasm.

The second parallel phase is what can be described as *Innovation Inclusivity*. There has been a marked break with the past by emphasising, supporting, nurturing and promoting the growth of *grass roots innovation*, recognising the need for, and importance of, frugal innovation, open source discovery, and consideration of the broader remit and context for innovation beyond pre-occupation with large scale technology. The Twelfth Plan (Government of India 2013a) reflected the uniquely Indian approach to innovation via the Indian Inclusive Fund to support local enterprises in health, education, agriculture, handicrafts and handlooms. The Twelfth Plan empha-

---

[8] The fourth and fifth phases.

sised the need to tap into local history and ecology and encourage talented children at school level who think creatively, laterally and innovatively. Subsequent policy measures continue this thrust, for example, through the ATAL innovation mission which includes among other things, Grand Challenge Innovations, ATAL tinkering labs to encourage experimentation, and working with design and fabrication facilities (ATAL Innovation Mission 2019).

Undoubtedly, the discourse in the Twelfth Plan reflected the fact that growth had not been shared equally in society, and that many became disconnected from processes of decision making. For example, the 12th plan explicitly recognises this when it stated 'Ours is a diverse society and also an argumentative one. We are suspicious when decisions that affect us are not taken transparently and we resent too much centralisation of decision-making.... We respect the views of others, and although we may disagree, we admire and learn from those who work together to offer any vision of a better India' (Government of India 2013a, Vol. 1, Chap. 1, para 19). In the Twelfth Plan, there is a clear clarion call for new mindsets, an emerging role for community, and a breakaway from a purely elite view of India which drove planning in earlier eras.

1.12 Current Era

Finally, is the current era, representing the end of formal centralised planning as such, as exemplified by the abolition of the National Planning Commission and its replacement with the NITI Aayog. The National Institution for Transforming India (NITI Aayog 2019), formed in 2015, is a core think tank to provide strategic policy advice, direction and inputs, research and thought leadership, for the Indian Government, and technical advice to the centre and states. It has two core aspects: Team India and the knowledge and innovation hub, where the former is about the centre working with the states, while the latter is the broader-based advice.

The perception is that for India to embrace the opportunities that are within its grasp, including in the global economy, requires a more flexible and market-based approach, strengthened national-state and inter and intra government relations, and broadened and deepened engagement with the community.

The remit of NITI Aayog, is among other things, to serve as an agent of change or catalyser of activity by government agencies and others, promote a new era of cooperation between national and state governments as part of 'Team India', and develop a more accountable notion of public policy and service delivery through greater emphasis on performance benchmarking and evaluation among government agencies.

NITI Aayog is very much a work in progress. However, in our view, primarily as an advisory, think tank body which undertakes research, analysis and dissemination of information, it lacks real 'teeth'. Its agenda appears to lack real cohesion or strategic overlay and its work tends to be on an issue by issue basis, often in seemingly unrelated manner. Its plethora of reports, although valuable scholarship, arguably has limited tangible impact. Some go even further in suggesting that the NITI Aayog has no influence over public and private investments and seems to overly and uncritically support the government's agenda, which raises concerns about its perceived lack of independence. In addition, its work misses some crucial and urgent issues confronting India such as the lack of sustainable employment (Kumar et al. 2018).

The recent strategy report by NITI Aayog on modern India turning 75 years of age, in our view, confirms some of the limitations of the body, in terms of it being a statement of problems and a 'wish list' of possible actions with little attempt at prioritisation or sequencing, rather than a truly cohesive, well-articulated whole of India strategy. Moreover, it glosses over some of the major challenges facing India, including especially rampant inequality (Kulkarni 2018; NITI Aayog 2018).

Thus, while the 'jury is out' in many respects in terms of what the NITI Aayog is and could become, there is in our judgement a void in strategic planning in India. We are not by any means advocating a return to the old days of planning in India, but rather are suggesting in this book that a new form of strategy is required, taking a holistic view of the economy, environment and society, *and importantly constructed through the lens of the knowledge economy.*

1.13 Planning Impacts and Weaknesses

How then do we sum up India's innovation performance in policy terms? A number of broad observations can be made, especially linked to the period from post-independence to the 1980s. Firstly, India's science and technology performance and policy thrust mirrored that of the general development effort, even if not necessarily explicitly as part of a comprehensive, integrated approach to policy: an initial focus on nation-building, followed by strong protectionist measures through an insular, inward-looking agenda, and in the post-liberalisation era, a more nuanced approach to competitiveness, through integration, and latterly with a renewed emphasis on inclusive innovation.

Second, in the early post-independence period India pursued a narrow research and science agenda while other emerging countries, such as Korea, pursued a broader technology capability path. In this context, the developmental agenda (the 'D' of R&D) was underplayed, and there was little attempt to absorb, adapt and mesh any foreign technologies with domestic capability, and therefore not contributing to any broader learning in the economy (Aggarwal 2001). India did not foster the linkages with industry and broader community in the development, deployment and diffusion of science and technology. In fact, a number of the early plans lay some implicit blame on the private sector for not pursuing research and innovation, preferring to import technology from abroad. That the Indian authorities preferred to conduct its policies for science and technology in the rarefied air of public sector research agencies, through public bodies and a highly regulated private sector, rather than supporting, nurturing and encouraging a cadre of potentially innovative small medium-sized business sector, was a missed opportunity. Developing the private sector and harnessing its potential and latent capabilities in a coherent, meaningful way was not taken up, while the various reservations and licensing arrangements led to sub-optimal scale and lack of competition, with consequent adverse productivity impacts. Rather than address perceived weaknesses in the private sector by building and support capability development, the public sector sought to essentially replace private sector activity. Further, a common refrain of critics of the Indian model development model is that the public sector led model across a number of industries, meant resources were directed to activities that the public sector ought not to have engaged in at the cost of priorities in areas which it should have been more visible in, such as foundational education and health (Paul 2017).

Further, a telling aspect was the lack of any real focus on exports until the Tenth Plan, quite distinct from the approach and aspirations of other developing economies. With its focus on import substitution and supposed self-reliance, little attempt was made to develop a robust export base. Nor was there any real attempt to use any know-how or capability garnered in the course of import substitution as a springboard to exports, which would have been a tonic to address capital constraints, expose India to demanding world markets, realise scale and further foster an entrepreneurial mindset. Indian policymakers were influenced by 'export lag theorists' who believed that primary producing export countries in the developing world tended to fall behind world trade and developed countries (Jalan 2017).

Further, the whole approach lacked flexibility and adaptability, which did not lend itself to responding in timely fashion to changed circumstances, new technological developments, or emerging industrial opportunities and possibilities.

Additionally and significantly, we contend that there was a significant disconnect between the aims and objectives of the S&T, especially early on with its focus on heavy industry, capital goods and large science, vis a vis broader societal challenges, including poverty, women's rights and community uplift, although noting that agriculture was a priority. To be sure, there were many vague statements in these areas but it is harder to find concrete actions at least in so far as the science and technology agenda pertained to them. In fact, some argue that India's science and technology agenda mimicked what was done around the world rather than address critical problems faced by Indians (Ramaswami 2016). Others contend that whatever innovation was done, mostly ad hoc, in the pre-independence era, was simply to serve British interests, and that the British had little opinion of Indian capabilities, believing they lacked sophistication (Surie 2014). This left an indelible legacy on Indian innovation. There was not much emphasis until recently on identifying, harnessing, leveraging, unlocking, supporting and nurturing the innate talents, creativity and innovation capabilities of the citizenry. The elite view of science and technology prevailed.

The plans were dominated by the 'science push' approach rather than for example, 'demand pull' or one that canvassed broader forms of innovation, e.g. organisational practices. A manifestation of this was the emphasis on science and technology in the plan chapters rather than on innovation per se. It is only in the Eleventh Plan that there has been a specific (but separate) chapter on innovation, finally reflecting that innovations occur beyond narrower science and technology domains to encompass organisational change, process improvement, service dimensions and the like. In the Twelfth Plan, science and technology is subsumed by innovation according to chapter headings and orientation.

1.14 Planning Legacies

Although looked at in later chapters in more detail, there are many legacies that remain from the past. While India has been improving in the Global Innovation Index to reach 57th place in the report, out of 126 countries, its input performance and rankings for quality of institutions remains a challenge, reflecting the fact that many foundational aspects of India's economy are still below par (Cornell University, INSEAD, WIPO 2018). It is generally weaker on technology absorption and diffusion, including both within the economy, and from abroad, reflecting the insular, closed mindsets of the past. Moreover, India lacks a broad core of strong educational institutes below the elite ones, e.g. Indian Institutes of Technology, as reflected in higher education rankings, highlighting the attention that these elite institutes have received over time, at the expense of broader-based education. The generally poor performance of Indian manufacturing, lacking scale, size, productivity and an export orientation, is also a legacy of numerous restrictive laws and regulations, and a protectionist mindset, which in many ways remains today. Further, is the extremely poor performance on many health and social parameters, to be discussed in the course of this book. Even when allowing for level of economic development, it reflects the misplaced priorities and resource allocation of yesteryear.

To be sure, there are, and have been changes, reforms and improvements. For example, India is a leading exporter of information and communications technology (ICT) services, a testament to initiatives to support its development some two decades ago, and its performance in terms of numbers of science and engineering graduates (although not a quality measure) is among the world's leaders, while the improvement in the World Bank Doing Business Index has been pronounced (World Bank 2018). India is home to a vibrant space sector, and a number of its innovations convey real value. *The achievements however, in our judgement, have been a patchwork quilt of successes embroidered on a rug of failures.*

1.15 Premises of This Book

This section outlines the key tenets of this book.

1.15.1 A Broad-Based Approach

This book is founded on a number of premises. Consistent with the broad definition of innovation we have employed in this book, our approach does not necessarily focus on particular narrow sectors, subsectors or 'winning' technologies. In a modern innovation/knowledge-based economy, with rapid, unpredictable and unprecedented technological change, fusion of technology, rapidly shrinking product cycles, convergence of sectors and multiple applications of technology, a narrower specific sectoral or sub-sectoral approach is less pertinent, relevant and helpful. As just a few examples of the fluidity and dynamism of the current environment, it took 75 years for the telephone to reach 50 million users, just 4 years for the internet, 3.5 years for facebook and just 35 days for angry birds (video game) to reach the same number of users (Frey, Osborne, CITI GPS 2015).

In any case, from a policy point of view, the era of long-term, heavy-handed support for narrow sectors and subsectors, or even firms, as part of infant industry development and fostering of national champions, has passed. Our approach is based instead on a broader capability building one which is more appropriate in responding to rapid change in a flexible and adaptable manner, and even where possible anticipating the future. These capabilities embody the development, diffusion and transferability of broad skills and know-how, the ability to connect disparate sources of knowledge and with end users, and continually nourish these capabilities. However, as we shall soon see, interventions can occur in many different ways, and at many different levels of economy and society.

1.15.2 Theoretical and Practical Premises

Further, is the premise that ideas occur anywhere, anytime, anyhow and by anyone, which in turn is consistent with the broader-based framework. This approach recognises that ideas and know-how emanate from elite research institutions fuelled by research and development of highly qualified personnel, as well as from villagers seeking local solutions to local problems, and enterprises who develop products and services to under-served markets and areas. A key challenge in this context is to link the various types of innovation and sources and flows of ideas. This has application both in theoretical and practical terms.

At the theoretical level, the importance of ideas, and unlocking them from multiple sources owes in part to the premise of them being non-rivalrous, leading to increasing returns. Unlike with physical resources, subject to diminishing returns, ideas can be shared and re-used at near zero cost and that the accumulation and creation of new ideas lead to almost boundless opportunities for growth in a dynamic momentum, as espoused by new economic growth theories (Cortright 2001).[9] It is further claimed

---

[9]In addition to the New Economic Growth School is the increasing returns approach led by Arthur (1996) from the business school perspective focussing on high technology industries.

1.15 Premises of This Book

that 'societies that generate and tolerate new ideas, and that continually adapt to changing economic and technological circumstances are a pre-condition to sustained economic growth' (Cortright 2001, p. ii).

Other related theories highlight the importance of path dependency and evolutionary economics associated with knowledge and ideas-history, past actions, policies and institutional frameworks matter-in the way economies evolve in terms of technologies and industries (Cortrght 2001). Schumpeter's work is also highly relevant in respect of the continuous nature of ideas generation.[10] Economic dynamism and change is spurred by individual entrepreneurs who continually develop new products, services and technologies, displacing older and often less efficient ones. There is only a limited period of reward for these entrepreneurs and innovators (note the nexus between entrepreneurship and innovation) as imitators come onto the arena. However, for a time innovation and growth in these and related areas is high because innovations can induce other innovations in a dynamic manner. Thus, economies are characterised by continual creative destruction. The importance of institutions should not be ignored in the Schumpeterian view since there is a constant struggle between visionary individuals and inert social contexts (Cortright 2001).

The notion of ideas from all sources at the practical level is amply demonstrated in the Indian context by the Honeybee Network, and its associated support structure Shristi, Incubation facility (GIAN), and National Innovation Foundation, the funding arm. The Honeybee Network is a group of individuals, innovators, farmers, schools, academics, enterprises and policymakers, who identify, scout, and document, validate, link, share, scale up and add value to ideas from the grass roots (Gupta 2016). Information gaps are ameliorated and ideas are translated into sustainable products and services as appropriate, with recognition and proceeds returning to originators. The process is facilitated, in part, by the unique Shodhyatra, a 'walking class,' in which ideas and solutions to local problems are identified through a long march in villages by volunteers, and includes sharing what has been previously learnt in the journey, creating a continuous momentum of ideas generating more ideas. Sharing ideas, listening, learning and 'unlearning', openness and breaking out of inertia, and thinking in unorthodox fashion, are all keys to the Honeybee network in the vein of cross-pollination by bees. Also not to be understated is the process of 'discovery' of one's self and others in Shodhyatra (Gupta 2016).

In commenting on lessons from the Honeybee experience, it is suggested that the 'spirit of cross-pollination of ideas across sectoral, social and temporal boundaries, reinforces the idea of learning from anyone, everywhere' (Gupta 2016, p. 343), even from unlikely sources, and that what is vital is '…. the building of bridges between the formal and informal systems of science, technology, manufacturing, services, agriculture and rural and urban development' (Gupta 2016, p. 331). In short, what is important is the ability of grass roots innovators to shape the research of scientists,

---

[10]Schumpeter's later theory focussed more on large firms, rather than smaller individual entrepreneur of the earlier design, and was more pessimistic about bureaucracy and inertia associated with larger firms.

technologists and firms and vice-a-versa in the manner of 'land to lab and back to land approach' (Gupta 2016, p. 58).

In a similar vein, Mahatma Gandhi gave great priority to village level industries, local artisan capabilities and community-based solutions to holistic health, diet, and sustainability issues, and disavowed the modern economic system with its emphasis on materialism and exploitation. To further embellish the notion that ideas emanate from multiple sources, in 1921, Gandhi established a prize to attract innovators from all around the world to develop more efficient khadi (cotton) products, and called for scientists and engineers to work on a voluntary basis to meet village needs, and to promote indigenous industrialisation, but also respecting knowledge from the rest of the world where that could be applied in a non-exploitative manner (Kulkarni 2012). The chakra (spinning wheel) and khadi were powerful symbols in a number of ways: unlocking village level capabilities and providing employment; and as a national movement to bring together disparate parts of the nation in a unified, collective whole (Kulkarni 2012).

1.15.3 Connected to the World

Additionally, a key premise of our book is that India should be open to ideas and know-how from the rest of the world. This implies an *interdependent* approach,[11] in which India is inextricably connected to the world of ideas. It is about India being open to the global world of ideas, both codified and tacit, exemplified by people movements, collaboration, including open source ventures, embodied ideas in new technologies, imports and foreign direct investments, and linkage into global centres of knowledge, including value chains. This is not in any sense to imply that India is subservient to knowledge created elsewhere, or should simply mimic it, but rather it is much more about meshing and moulding know-how from elsewhere, with India's own capabilities, which in turn reinforces India's (and the world's capabilities) in a dynamic manner. Further, it is a far cry from shutting off India from the world of knowledge in the mould of the past, even in the face of growing protectionist sentiment around the world. Moreover, in this internationalist view that we present, we see India as a major player in the global development and diffusion of ideas, know-how and technology in pursuit of global solutions to global challenges, and more narrowly through the export of Indian know-how.

The importance of interdependence with the world is underscored by the fact that knowledge created by nations has significant spillovers that transcend national boundaries. This means, in effect, that countries contribute through their actions to their own development as well as the global store of knowledge, and participate in, and access knowledge derived elsewhere, provided they are open to the movement of ideas. Recent work looked at nations' 'contributory' versus 'detractor' policies

---

[11]The notion of interdependence has also been used by Bound (2007) in the analysis of Indian Innovation.

1.15 Premises of This Book

(Ezell et al. 2016), where the former are policies that contribute to the global stock of knowledge and innovation, and the latter are policies that harm global stocks of knowledge. Contributory policies are deemed to be pro-innovation taxation, human capital investments, R&D and technology transfer policies, while detractor policies are protective barriers to trade in goods and services, foreign investment restrictions, local content provisions, weak intellectual property management,[12] currency manipulations and export subsidies. Importantly, there is a strong observed correlation between countries' policies that contribute to the global store of knowledge and their own domestic innovation success. According to an index which measures the relative emphasis given to contributory and detracting policies, India scores and ranks poorly, some 54th out of 56 countries, i.e. India has more of a predisposition to detracting policies (Ezell et al. 2016). As such, drawing on this analysis, India needs to move much more fully to contributory policies, including being open to ideas and know-how from abroad, to benefit itself and the world, which is also particularly important in the context of global problems requiring global solutions.

An inspiring address by former Prime Minister Vajpayee to the Indian diaspora echoes loudly the sentiment that we ascribe to. 'We do not want only your investments. We also want your ideas. We can gain from the breadth of vision that your global exposure has given' (Jha 2003). Of course, our vision pertains to India being open to all ideas from all nations and people from all walks of life.

1.15.4 A Solutions Approach

The next premise of our approach is that of a solutions orientation to innovation and policy, i.e. developing tangible, practical solutions to complex challenges in the manner of missions. These challenges offer the prospect for entrepreneurship, commercial exploitation of ideas and social innovation, giving expression to the notion that 'necessity is the mother of innovation'. Thus, the idea of India is as a solutions-based economy, addressing complex and often wicked challenges, not only for India but for the rest of the world, while being mindful of India's level of economic development and its capacities. We point out that there are considerable challenges confronting India and the world in terms of energy requirements, natural resource and environmental management, urbanisation and population growth, food security, personal and national (and global) security, major health concerns, inequality, economic and social dislocation, as well as arguably, growth of materialism at the expense of spirituality. Our approach is to develop and promote national and global solutions in the vein of mission mode (noting that India does have some missions) and for India to develop tangible, practical and workable solutions, based on broad capabil-

---

[12] Our view of intellectual property diverges somewhat. It is about less inclination to protect IP per se but to be more about diffusion of IP naturally seeking a balance though to reward originators.

ity development, and drawing in ideas, insight and expertise from home and abroad. The policies and strategies developed in this book are based on this standpoint.

The solutions approach has also gained currency in the management literature based on finding solutions to social problems, while maintaining and enhancing private gains (profits) in the manner of the ASSURED framework discussed before.

According to Eggers and Macmillan (2013), there are six main tenets to the Solutions Revolution: wavemakers (change agents who bring creativity and resources to problem solving including investors, convenors, citizens and business who look to social impact approaches); disruptive technologies (cloud computing, mobile telephony, analytics and social media); business models that scale (franchising, online commercial platforms that connect problem solvers, citizen sourcing to perform small tasks, 'freemiums', i.e. firms that provide products and solutions for free by selling complementary products at a premium); 'currency' (time banking, information, data use, and reputation); public value exchanges (e.g. prizes for challenges, crowdfunding, pay for success for example through social impact bonds); and complete ecosystems (bringing together all the key players and constituents).

While this approach has similarities with what we are proposing, in terms of connected ecosystems for example, there are sharp differences. Our approach is based more on identifying and driving capabilities that are needed for innovation broadly, albeit from a solutions lens, rather than the focus on particular players or agents, which the 'solutions revolution' is about. Further, the 'solutions revolution' is based more on observed current examples from around the world, rather than a framework which is based on a coordinated, cohesive policy agenda, allowing for identification of core priorities, fundamental changes to institutions, or explicit articulation of the roles of government versus other agents, which is what our book proposes. It also goes without saying that our approach is specific to India outlining its opportunities, problems and constraints, recognising the strong nexus between the past and the present in shaping the future, but also noting India's potential interface and engagement with the world in truly global game-changing initiatives. History matters when looking at innovation and knowledge, which a focus on current examples of innovation cannot do full justice to.

As alluded to in the foregoing discussion, institutions matter greatly in the knowledge and innovation economy. Institutions around knowledge and information sharing, linking grass roots innovators with elite researchers, bridging and connecting global and local innovators, and promoting knowledge collaboration and joint discovery, are keys. Reforming and revamping India's institutions to enable the nation to tap more fully into its vast reservoir of potential and overcoming current and legacy impediments, is a key in this book. This also implies a role for government in India which is different from its traditional narrow subsidy mindset tailored to the perceived needs of a few, to a much more all-embracing nature.

1.15.5 Institutions

That institutions matter, and matter a great deal, is reflected in theoretical and practical ways. Broadly, institutions are the rules of the game, and the associated organisations (players), laws, regulations, property rights, informal constraints (conventions, norms of behaviour, culture, values) and encompass the key players such as political bodies, economic bodies (e.g. firms, trade unions etc.), social bodies (e.g. community groups), education institutions and Government Agencies (North 2016).[13]

In his seminal work, Douglas North outlines the weaknesses in neoclassical economics, which focuses on resource allocation at any moment in time, and that efficient markets can only operate in the context of costless transactions and complete information in which institutions matter very little (Cortright 2001; North 2016).

In practice economies are replete with transaction costs, information imperfections and other impediments to activity, as well as boundless opportunities. Reducing transaction costs, addressing information imperfections, establishing the incentives to invest in skills and knowledge, fostering competition and building accumulated learnings, are shaped, influenced and mediated by institutions (North 2016). Echoing North's work (2016), institutions need to evolve and adapt (adaptive efficiencies) to reflect new realities, markets, technologies and create the incentives and conditions by which those in the economy and society can create, take risks, innovate and experiment and develop knowledge (Cortright 2001). Analogously, is the tolerance (and indeed encouragement) of new ideas in the adaptation process. As Thurow indicates and quoted in Cortright 'As technologies change and economies grow, our institutions will need to devise new arrangements and solutions for economic problems, from allocating the electromagnetic spectrum to refining the law governing patents' (Cortright 2001, p. 18).

In the practical realm, and in the Indian context, appropriate institutional arrangements are required to further identify, promote and link (grass roots) innovations. For example, in relation to environmental sustainability and particularly sustainable design, it is claimed that 'if teaching is a word, institutions are like grammar and culture is a thesaurus' (Gupta 2016, p. 26). All are needed. Further, it is the interplay of robust institutions with other capabilities that enable the full flowering of the knowledge economy. Krishna (2017) also takes this up in the Indian context by calling for institutional reform to better link talent with opportunity, especially for those disempowered, disenfranchised members of the population.

1.16 Towards a Framework

Having considered the various types of innovation in theory and practice, and examined India's past actions, we now turn to our framework of innovation and knowledge which serves as the basic parameters and framing for subsequent chapters. It is based on 5 key capabilities or 'E's. 'E's are those broad capabilities, which in our view shape, drive, harness and promote innovation and knowledge, and in turn, are shaped by these factors in an iterative manner. The 5 'E's are captured in Fig. 1.1.

---

[13] Reproduction of North's original paper.

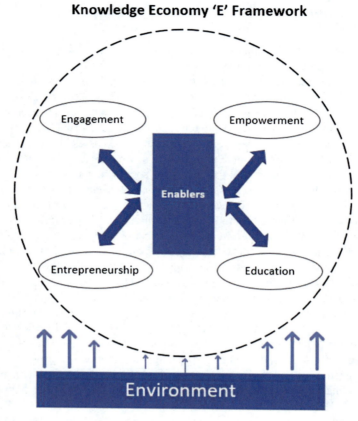

Fig. 1.1 Knowledge economy 'E' framework

1.17 Enablers

If we think of the 'E's as body parts, then the enablers are the 'spine' of innovation. As such, they are represented as a pillar of the innovation system in Fig. 1.1. There are two interrelated features of enablers. The first element is a more fundamental, foundational one, which goes to the heart of the role of the state, and in particular, its relationship with the market, honing in on the Indian context. We argue that an efficient and effective Enabling State would have a symbiotic relationship with the market and its actors, embodying partnership and collaboration, drawing on complementarities, but also correcting each other's penchant for excess.[14] The appropriate balance and relationship between the State and the market is fully explored in Chap. 2 in driving, nurturing, and shaping innovation and knowledge. The Enabling State, also in our judgement, calls for revamped institutional arrangements and newer

---

[14]Our approach is thus aligned with Nayyar (2017) as we shall take up more fully in the next chapter.

policy constructs centred on facilitation, brokerage and referral in harnessing the collective capabilities of citizenry and from abroad. In the Indian context, it marks a major departure from the traditional Indian state instruments of subsidy, protection favouring special interests, cronyism and rent seeking.

The second and related element is a narrower meaning of the term in the sense of a stable, supportive and predictable business environment for firms to innovate, invest and plan with reasonable certainty. It is about the cost structures, regulatory arrangements and legal, political and institutional supports that allow firms to create, innovate, and derive and sustain competitive advantage, balanced against other needs of society.

1.18 Education

Education, and associated capability in research, is vital for providing the foundational core skills and capabilities that underpin knowledge, innovation and ways of doing things. In the context of the human body in our representation, it is akin to the 'feet' upon which the innovation edifice rests. Education is the basis of a learning economy, to continually add to the stock of knowledge that has been garnered over time, to unlearn as well, and discard old and outmoded ways of thinking and doing. More specifically, a strong education system is a conduit to the labour market, providing skills in a flexible manner for the 'now and beyond', particularly in the context of rapid change, fuelled by new and often disruptive technologies, and changing labour market contexts and requirements. It is also about the pursuit and application of new knowledge through research and research skills obtained in the education system. Education of course, in its various dimensions and at various levels, has a broader purpose, providing access and opportunity for advancement for all in society, building civil society, challenging the status quo, strengthening democracy, promoting benefits in health, and awareness of rights.

In Chap. 3 we take a comprehensive look at the formal Indian education system (recognising though that education takes place in many different non-formal contexts), compared to other countries, focussing on tertiary education, but reaching down into the lower levels of education, as appropriate, which serve as the pipeline of the knowledge economy. Before it is thought that the education system in this book leads us necessarily to an elite model of innovation, it should be borne in mind that education serves many broader purposes as outlined, including important elements of societal enhancement.

Education is critically also a means of reaching into villages and local areas, and helping to work with local innovators through assisting with technology, research and knowledge, and absorbing and advancing ideas garnered from grass roots personnel. It is also a means of uplifting those in straitened circumstance. It should also be noted that a recent study found a positive correlation between the number of years of formal education, and the prevalence of grass roots innovations, although this was less pronounced for those with Higher Education qualifications (but still apparent) (Nair et al. 2017).

1.19 Engagement

Engagement can be thought of as the 'eyes and ears' of the knowledge economy to continue the theme of innovation aligned to the human body. It is about being open and alive to the opportunities for innovation and creativity that abound in India and the world. Engagement is about the extent to which an economy is connected, both within, and to the rest of the world, how much, and to what extent it is a participant in the local and global flows and development of knowledge. From such engagement abroad and locally comes benefits in terms of access to markets for products and services, access to critical capabilities from abroad which can be absorbed, and meshed with domestic capabilities, exposure to leading-edge customers, and participation in value chains. It also canvasses the critical collaborations, process of discovery and synergistic knowledge development, deployment and diffusion which propels individual economies and the global economy. People flow through skilled migration and the presence of a vital, vibrant diaspora are key elements of engagement, as are trade, industry and value chain participation and associated policies.

Engagement is consistent with the approach outlined earlier about needing to be an interdependent player in the global world of innovation and knowledge. Chapter 4 covers India's engagement with the rest of the world.

In relation to the foregoing discussion, a major part of Chap. 4 is to unveil an original and novel concept of Knowledge Footprint which identifies and measures the extent to which knowledge is developed, deployed, diffused and accessed in India, and the extent to which its knowledge capabilities are **projected** onto the global arena. A comprehensive approach to measuring the Knowledge Footprint and its components, is articulated for India compared to 14 other economies.

The engagement chapter also encompasses detailed analysis and discussion of trade and investment as important drivers of integration into the world economy, and focusses on India's export performance, which is an area of considerable weakness, requiring attention by policymakers and businesses.

1.20 Entrepreneurship

Entrepreneurship is the 'lifeblood' of innovation and knowledge—it is the risk taking, bold, daring 'can do' people in society who create wealth and jobs in the knowledge spheres through their vision and dynamism, and in the case of social entrepreneurship, address specific community-based challenges.

Entrepreneurship is a difficult concept to define with exactness. Two notions are presented here for comparison. The Global Entrepreneurship Monitor (GEM) defines it as 'Any attempt at new business or venture creation such as self-employment, a new business organisation or the expansion of existing business by an individual, a team of individuals or an established business' (Global Entrepreneurship Monitor Consortium 2019, p. 1). The Global Entrepreneurship Development Institute (GEDI) defines

1.20 Entrepreneurship

it as 'the dynamic, institutionally embedded interaction between entrepreneurial attitudes, entrepreneurial abilities and entrepreneurial aspirations by individuals, which drives the allocation of resources through the creation and operation of new ventures' (Acs et al. 2017, p. 32). In this latter framing, entrepreneurship, which in essence is to 'create new things or find new ways to do things' (Acs et al. 2017, p. 26) is closely aligned with innovation (of both technical and non-technical forms) and quality of entrepreneurship. Thus, in the Schumpeterian tradition, entrepreneurship is the key to spotting innovation opportunities and possibilities and acting upon these impulses. The range of necessary capabilities, embedded in wider ecosystems and institutional supports, including opportunity identification and perception, skills, business set up activities, product and process innovation capabilities, risk taking, networking, cultural support, growth orientation and the like, are those that individual entrepreneurs draw on to succeed (Acs et al. 2017). Our view of entrepreneurship aligns more with the GEDI framing, although recognising that at times, the broader entrepreneurship concept, not so specifically linked to innovation, espoused by GEM, is canvassed, especially in developing our knowledge footprint.

In this book we develop a comprehensive typology of Indian entrepreneurship, based on drivers of competitive advantage, opportunities, prospects and constraints, to highlight the distinctive nature and rich diversity of entrepreneurship in India as a frame of reference to drive policy action to addresses weaknesses and capitalise on strengths. This typology identifies a multitude of entrepreneurs and classes of entrepreneurs in India in the knowledge sphere, who through their innovative capabilities, drive change, produce new and improved goods and services and business models, and develop solutions to pressing problems confronting India and beyond. Our approach also enables us to break out of the 'one size fits all' approach to entrepreneurship policy, and to provide a more nuanced framing of policy.

Both for convenience and the fact that entrepreneurship has a strong relationship to engagement, through, for example, firm-level links to the market place at home and abroad, entrepreneurship is discussed in Chap. 4. Engagement though canvasses the wider set of inter-connections and relationships, and integration of knowledge activities within the domestic economy, and internationally, including for example, people flows, people to people connections, institution to institution linkages, and overall trade and investment policies. Compared to the more individual and firm level oriented lens of entrepreneurship, engagement is more concerned with the overarching economy wide contexts both at home and abroad.

1.21 Empowerment

Empowerment is the 'heart and soul' of innovation and knowledge—the extent to which, and manner in which, individuals and social groups can participate fully in the knowledge-based economy, as originators of ideas and beneficiaries of the utilisation of ideas generated elsewhere by others. Empowerment reflects the access and opportunity, the wherewithal and support that members of society have to participate in the knowledge economy, both individually and collectively. In many senses it goes to the heart of inclusivity, identity and freedom with respect to decision-making.

In this book, our attention is focussed on female empowerment. The concept of female empowerment is multifaceted and can comprise economic, social (including familial and community), political, educational, legal and psychological domains. One broad definition which has found favour is that empowerment is 'The expansion in people's ability[15] to make strategic life choices in a context where this ability was previously denied to them' (Malhotra et al. 2002, p. 6). This definition conveys both process and change from previously constrained situations, as well as choice. The European Institute for Gender Equality (2019, p. 1) captures similar sentiments when it suggests that empowerment is the 'process by which women gain power and control over their own lives and acquire the ability to make strategic choices'. Thus, freedom to choose looms large in these definitions, as does access to opportunity to influence social change and power to control their lives (European Institute 2019). Education, training, awareness, confidence and institutional change are keys.

Drilling down, in our context, female empowerment is vital as suppliers of labour, as researchers and innovators, as consumers and drivers of social changes, and more broadly as significant contributors to GDP. However, it is also the case that females bear a burden in large measure of inequality, inequity, injustice and disenfranchisement. The latter issues are taken up in the book in Chap. 5 viewed from the perspective of the knowledge economy. A comprehensive literature review is undertaken, noting that in general female empowerment and knowledge and innovation is under-done in the literature.

To give greater expression to access and opportunity and participation of females in the knowledge economy, we develop and introduce a Gender Knowledge Footprint. For the Gender Knowledge Footprint we compare Indian females to Indian males, and also males compared to females for BRIC nations, and females compared to females and males compared to males also for BRIC nations. The metrics canvassed are similar to those in the overall Footprint of Chap. 4, but tailored to gender specifics. A suite of policy recommendations is put forward to promote greater female empowerment, especially in the knowledge economy context.

1.22 Environment

It is worth reflecting briefly on the natural environment. Although not included explicitly as an 'E', as in our judgement it is less a generic broad-based capability or attribute when referenced against the others, being more specific in meaning and context, it certainly is impacted by, and does impact on knowledge. For example, the development and deployment of research and new technology in clean and new forms of energy, drives more sustainable outcomes while environmental challenges bring forth pressures to innovate and deliver new solutions. Further, learning from environ-

---

[15] We apply the general framing to the female empowerment.

mental management can shape innovation priorities going forward. However, in our judgement, the environment and its management, while a vital issue, is more derived from the process of knowledge discovery and development rather than a foundational capability as such.

As such, the environment appears in Fig. 1.1, but not in the dotted line enclosure, which represent the main capability tenets in the framework. Nonetheless, the environmental aspects associated with the knowledge economy, appears in multiple chapters, e.g. in relation to pricing in the enablers chapter, in priorities for education in Chap. 4, and even in Chap. 5 in empowerment, since issues around environmental and resource management, and environmental concerns, often bear disproportionately on females. A somewhat more detailed discussion, including recommendations to better manage the environment in India, is found in Chap. 4, to underscore links between environmental management and economic and industrial development at home and abroad.

The importance of the overall framework is exemplified by the fact that elements are highly interconnected. Diagrammatically, it is difficult to display all the multi-faceted connections in Fig. 1.1, however, a few examples would suffice. Empowerment and education are closely aligned since empowerment is heavily influenced by access to educational opportunities, engagement is linked to entrepreneurship in the sense of building and sustaining connections to the market place, while enablers make the whole system operate. Enablers reach out to all the other dimensions and in turn are shaped by them.

The choice of 'E's is deliberately broad to allow for policy and strategic action on a flexible and interconnected basis, building and nurturing broad capabilities which draw on existing capabilities, to capture the breadth and depth of factors that influence, and are influenced, by knowledge and innovation, as opposed to more narrow constructs.

1.23 Proposed Intervention Schema

The 'E's are a centrepiece of this book. They reflect the fundamental capabilities which ultimately drive solutions to complex challenges. As Fig. 1.2 demonstrates, to give expression to these capabilities, interventions by government (and indeed actions by other players), is and needs to be, flexible to realise solutions. Thus, intervention in developing 'E's can be at various levels, such as at the project, industry, firm, clusters of industry or at spatial level. The type, nature and extent of intervention, depends on benefit/cost assessments, need, circumstance and 'best fit'. In this way, our approach is flexible and a circumstance warranted one, which does not pre-determine winning sectors as in the past. It seeks ultimately to produce winning solutions with various means to achieve this.

Fig. 1.2 Proposed intervention schema

India has had missions in various areas from time to time, such as in solar energy and climate. Our approach is different in a number of ways. It is about a whole of economy solutions mode, not just on ad hoc topics. Further, our approach is accompanied by revamping fundamentally institutional architecture, and developing newer forms of policy. Third, it emphasises interdependence with the world.

1.24 What This Book Is and What It Is Not

This book is not a theoretical one, nor is it a technical one in the sense of incorporating mathematical modelling or regression analysis. It is though data rich, driven by benchmarking, and does provide a tentative pilot of a comprehensive quantitative Knowledge Footprint. The Footprint would require further refinement as research unfolds, either by this author or others. At this stage it is more about introducing a possible approach to considering innovation and knowledge, its measurement and impact on economy and society.

This book fills a void between the theoretical/technical and practitioner realms, the latter often found in the business school literature. This book is more by way of a 'thought and debate starter', a potential agenda and policy setter, for the knowledge economy in India, focussing on a solutions-driven approach, underpinned by different types of instruments, and a revamped institutional architecture to meet the needs of its emerging knowledge economy.

The book benchmarks India against 14 other countries. The benchmark list is at times widened slightly, depending on the issue in question. The 14 core other countries are: Australia; Bangladesh; Brazil; Chile; China; Germany; Japan; Malaysia;

Russia; South Korea; Sri Lanka; Thailand; UK; U.S. These countries comprise a solid core of developed and developing countries, to reflect India's natural competitors and those developed economy levels that India might aspire to. Brazil, China and Russia form three of the four BRIC nations, India of course being the other. BRIC countries are included against whom India is often compared, as are some regional neighbours in Sri Lanka and Bangladesh. A broad global coverage comprising most regions is intended. Where appropriate, some other countries, e.g. Philippines, Indonesia and Pakistan and Vietnam, are included in certain instances to round out analysis.

Given the lengthy period of time to put together this book and that chapters have been developed at various stages, data points do vary in time somewhat across the metrics. However, attempts have been made to include the very latest data where possible, although noting that this is not always feasible, particularly given that data provision by agencies is a 'moving feast'.

Chapter 2 is about Enablers, Chap. 3 covers Education, Chap. 4 Engagement and Entrepreneurship and Chap. 5 Empowerment. Our final chapter posits a vision for India of innovation and knowledge, gleaned from the discussion of the previous chapters. The vision is based on the unique capabilities, talents and expertise drawn from across all sections of the Indian community, and promoting and leveraging connections to the world, both in accessing knowledge and in projecting India's capabilities globally.

1.25 Conclusion

This chapter has articulated the concept of innovation and knowledge, and the various theories and frameworks that underpin them, with particular reference to India. Detailed assessments have been made of India's approach to planning and policy development in innovation and knowledge, primarily in terms of science and technology. Criticisms have been made of India's overall development stance.

A framework for thinking about innovation and knowledge, the 'E's has been developed and articulated, which guides the rest of the book.

References

Acs Z, Szerb L, Lloyd A (2017) The global entrepreneurship index 2018. The Global Entrepreneurship and Development Institute, Washington, D.C., USA

Aggarwal A (2001) Technology policies and technological capabilities in industry: a comparative analysis of India and Korea. Working paper no. 68

Arthur B (1996) Increasing returns and the new world of business. Harv Bus Rev (July–August)

ASSOCHAM (2014) Innovation driven growth in India. Report prepared by Price Waterhouse Coopers

ATAL Innovation Mission. https://niti.gov.in/content/atal-innovation-mission-aim. Accessed 12 Feb 2019

Bound K (2007) India: the uneven innovator the atlas of ideas mapping the new geography of science demos

Braunerhjelm P (2010) Entrepreneurship, innovation and economic growth: past experiences, current knowledge and policy implications. Swedish entrepreneurship forum. Research network debate working paper

Brem A, Wolfram P (2014) Research and development from the bottom up-introduction of terminologies for new product development in emerging markets. J Innov Entrep 3–22

Christensen C (1997) The innovator's dilemma: when new technologies cause great firms to fail. Harvard Business School Press, Boston, MA

Christensen C, Raynor M, McDonald R (2015) What is disruptive innovation? Harv Bus Rev (December)

Cornell University, INSEAD, WIPO (2018) The global innovation index

Cortright J (2001) New growth theory, technology and learning: a practitioner's guide. Review of Economic Development Literature and Practice: no. 4. Impressa Inc.

Datta S (2017) A history of the Indian University system emerging from the shadows of the past. Palgrave MacMillan

Devraj R (2016) Political meddling causes Nalanda University turmoil. University World News. https://www.universityworldnews.com/post.php?story=20161209184008373

Eggers W, Macmillan P (2013) The solution revolution. Harvard Business Review Press, Boston, USA

European Institute for Gender Equality Empowerment. https://eige.europa.eu/thesaurus/terms/1102. Accessed 1 Jan 2019

Ezell S, Nager A, Atkinson R (2016) Contributors and detractors ranking countries' impact on global innovation. Information Technology and Innovation Foundation

Fan P (2018) Catching up in economic transition: innovation in the People's Republic of China and India ADBI Institute. ADBI Working Paper Series 809

Frey C, Osborne M (2015) Technology at work, the future of innovation and employment. Citi GPS: Global Perspectives and Solutions, Oxford Martin School, University of Oxford

Global Entrepreneurship Monitor Consortium (2019). https://www.gemconsortium.org/wiki/1149. Accessed 4 Jan 2019

Government of India (2003) Ministry of Science and Technology Science and Technology Policy 2003. SAGE J. https://doi.org/10.1177/097172180300800105. Accessed 15 May 2019

Government of India (2013a) Planning Commission twelfth five year plan 2013

Government of India (2013b) Ministry of Science and Technology Science, Technology and Innovation Policy 2013

Government of India (2016) Ministry of Human Resource Development. National Policy on Education. Report of the committee for evolution of the new education policy

Government of India (1983) Department of Science and Technology. Technology Policy Statement 1983

Government of India (1952) Planning Commission first five year plan 1952

Government of India (1956) Planning Commission second five year plan 1956

Government of India (1961) Planning Commission third five year plan 1961

Government of India (1970) Planning Commission fourth five year plan 1970

Government of India (1976) Planning Commission fifth five year plan 1976

Government of India (1981) Planning Commission sixth five year plan 1981

Government of India (1985) Planning Commission seventh five year plan 1985

Government of India (1992) Planning Commission eighth five year plan 1992

Government of India (1997) Planning Commission ninth five year plan 1997

Government of India (2002) Planning Commission tenth five year plan 2002

Government of India (2007) Planning Commission eleventh five year plan 2007

Govindarajan V, Trimble C (2012) Reverse innovation: create far from home, win everywhere. Harv Bus Rev Press, India

References

Gupta A (2016) Grassroots innovation, minds on the margin are not marginal minds. Penguin Random House India, Haryana, India

Herstatt C, Tiwari R (2017) India's emergence as a lead market for frugal innovations: an introduction to the theme and to the contributed volume. In: Herstatt C, Tiwari R (eds) Lead market India key elements and corporate perspectives for frugal innovations. Springer Indian Studies in Business and Economics

Jalan B (2017) India priorities for the future. Penguin Viking

Jha N (2003) We don't just want your money: Vajpayee to NRI's. The Times of India, 9 Jan 2003. https://m.timesofindia.com/india/we-dont-just-want-your-money-vajpyaee-to-nris/articleshow/338869.cms

Kalam A, Pillai A (2013) Thoughts for change, we can do it. Pentagon Press

Katz B, Wagner J (2014) The rise of innovation districts: a new geography of innovation in America. Metropolitan Policy Program, Brookings

King A, Baatartogtokh B (2015) How useful is the theory of disruptive innovation? MIT Sloan Manag Rev. https://sloanreview.mit.edu/article/how-useful-is-the-theory-of-disruptive-innovation/

Krishnan R (2010) From Jugaad to systematic innovation. The challenge for India. Nevellos Graffiti

Krishna A (2017) The broken ladder. Penguin Viking, Haryana, India

Kulkarni A (2018) India's higher education sector: challenges and opportunities. Int Rev Bus Econ (IBRE) 2(1):2474–5146 (online). 2474–5138 (print)

Kulkarni S (2012) Music of the spinning wheel Mahatma Gandhi's Manifesto for the internet age. Amaryllis

Kumar A (2017) Nalanda University new VC's manta: zero tolerance of indiscipline, focus on expansion. Hindustan Times, 21 May. https://m.hindustantimes.com/india/nalanda-university-new-vc-s-mantra-zero-tolerance-of-indiscipline-focus-on-expansion/story-K6CTHQ2nKsz44emsVD46gJ.html. Accessed 21 Mar 2019

Kumar P (2011) The ancient Nalanda Mahavira: the beginning of international education. J World Univ Forum 4(1)

Kumar R, Kannan K, Mehrotra S (2018) Is NITI Aayog relevant? The Hindu, 21 Sept 2018. https://www.thehindu.com/opinion/op-ed/is-niti-aayog-relevant/article24998885.ece. Accessed 10 Dec 2018

Kumar N, Purnuam P (2012) India inside. Harvard Business Review Press, USA

Lepore J (2014) What the gospel of innovation gets wrong, The distribution machine. The New Yorker. https://www.newyorker.com/magazine/2014/06/23/the-disruption-machine. Accessed 23 Dec 2018

Maddison O (2018) A historical statistics of the world economy: 1–2008 AD. Groningen Growth and Development Centre. http://www.ggdc.net/maddison/oriindex.htm. Accessed 25 Oct 2018

Malhotra A, Schuler S, Boender C (2002) Measuring women's empowerment as a variable in international development commissioned. Paper by the gender and development group, World Bank

Mashelkar R (2018) Dismantling inequality through ASSURED innovation. Australian National University, India

Mukherjee P (2016) Like Nalanda, India must remain a melting pot of civilisations. Excerpt of a speech at the first convocation of Nalanda University, 27 Aug 2016. https://www.rediff.com/news/column/like-nalanda.india-must-remain-a-melting-pot-of-civilisations/20160829.htm. Accessed 29 Apr 2019

Nair A, Tiwari R, Buse S (2017) Emerging patterns of grassroots innovations: results of a conceptual study based on selected cases from India. In: Herstatt C, Tiwari R (eds) Lead market India key elements and corporate perspectives for frugal innovations. India Studies in Business and Economies. Springer

National Innovation Council (2013) India decade of innovations 2010–2020 roadmap. http://innovationcouncilarchive.nic.in/index.php?option=com_content&view=article&id=36:decade-of-innovation&catid=7:presentation&Itemid=8. Accessed 15 May 2019

Nayyar D (2017) The state and the economy. In: Nayyar D, Hasan R (eds) Shaping India's future: essays in memory of Abid Hussain. Academic Foundation, New Delhi

NITI Aayog (2018) Strategy for New India @ 75
NITI Aayog (2019). http://niti.gov.in/content/overview. Accessed 29 Apr 2019
North D (2016) Institutions and economic theory. Am Econ 61(1):72–76
OECD (2007) Innovation and growth rationale for an innovation strategy
OECD Science, Technology and Innovation Outlook Edition (2008, 2010, 2012, 2014, 2016, 2018)
OECD (1997) National innovation systems
OECD (1999) Managing national innovation systems. ISBN 92-64-17038-3
OECD (2002) Dynamising national innovation systems
Paul V (2017) India's big government: the intrusive state and how it is hurting us. EquityMaster Agera Research Private Ltd
Prahlad C (2005) The fortune at the bottom of the pyramid eradicating poverty through profit. Wharton School Publishing
Puri A (2015) Nalanda University: what went wrong? Bus Stand. https://www.businessstandard.com/article/economy-policy/nalanda-university-what-went-wrog-115030400031_1.html. Accessed 29 Apr 2019
Puri H (2017) India's trade policy dilemma and the role of domestic reform. Carnegie India
Radjou N, Prabhu J (2015) Frugal innovation, how to do better with less. Hachette Book Publishing India Pvt. Ltd., Gurgaon, India
Radjou N, Prabhu J, Ahuja S (2012) Jugaad innovation, a frugal and flexible approach to innovation for the 21st century. Random House Group Limited, London, UK
Ramaswami V (2016) Innovation by India for India, the need and the challenge. Siksha Publications, Chennai, India
Ramdorai A, Herstatt C (2017) Lessons from low-cost healthcare innovations for the base of the pyramid markets how incumbents can systematically create innovations. In: Herstatt C, Tiwari R (eds) Lead market India key elements and corporate perspectives for frugal innovations. Springer Indian Studies in Business and Economics
Schwab K (2016) The fourth industrial revolution: what it means, how to respond world economic forum. https://www.weforum.org/agenda/2016/01/the-fourth-industrial-revolution-what-it-means-and-how-to-respond/. Accessed 15 May 2019
Schwab K (2017) The fourth industrial revolution. Penguin Books
Sen A (2015) India: the stormy revival of an International University. NY Rev Books. https://www.nybooks.com/articles/2015/08/13/india-stormy-revival-nalanda-university. Accessed 29 Apr 2019
Sessay B, Yulin Z, Wang F (2016) Does the national system spur economic growth in Brazil, Russia, India, China and South Africa economies? Evidence from panel data 21(1)
Sharma A (2015) Amartya Sen and Nalanda University controversy all you should know OneIndia. https://www.oneindia.com/feature/amartya-sen-nalanda-university-controversy-all-you-should-know-1661314.html. Accessed 21 Mar 2019
Surie G (2014) The University as a catalyst of innovation, entrepreneurship and new markets in the Indian innovation system. In: Ramnai S (ed) Innovation in India 2014 combining economic growth with inclusive development. Cambridge University Press
Technology Policy Statement (1983) Curr Sci 65(5):1993. http://www.jstor.org/stable/24095781. Accessed 15 May 2019
Tiwari R (2017) Frugality in Indian context what makes India a lead market for affordable excellence? In: Herstatt C, Tiwari R (eds) Lead market India key elements and corporate perspectives for frugal innovations. Springer Indian Studies in Business and Economics
Tiwari R, Fischer L, Kalogerakis K (2017) Frugal innovation: an assessment of scholarly discourse, trends and potential societal implications. In: Herstatt C, Tiwari R (eds) Lead market India key elements and corporate perspectives for frugal innovations. Springer Indian Studies in Business and Economics
Ulku H (2004) Research and development, innovation and economic growth, an empirical analysis. IMF working paper WP/04/185
UNESCO (2015) Science report towards 2030

References

UNESCO Department of Natural Sciences (1964) The Government of India's scientific policy resolution, New Delhi, 1958

Venkataramakrishnan R (2015) This isn't the first time Nalanda and Amartya Sen have been controversial—it happened during UPA too. https://scroll.in/article/708750/this-isnt-the-first-time-nalanda-and-amartya-sen-have-been-controversial-it-happened-during-upa-too. Accessed 29 Apr 2019

World Bank (2018) Doing business index 2019

Chapter 2
Enablers

Abstract This chapter examines the role of the state vis-à-vis the market in the Indian context associated with the Enabling State. India needs to obtain the appropriate balance between the role of the State and the functions of individual agents in the market place, be they firms, households and other institutions, to harness complementarities and synergies, and unlock talents from right across India. In the course of this chapter, India's performance on a number of parameters relating to enablers is considered relative to comparator nations. A key focus of the chapter is on institutional revitalisation and renewal in India, in the context of a much more accountable and participatory State. The chapter closes by taking a closer look at three areas of priority, health, housing and food to provide new solutions for the pressing problems in these areas, as illustrations of the Enabling State.

Keywords Enabling state · Facilitation · Brokerage · Business environment · Knowledge advantage plans · Commission for government · Collaborate india · Corruption

2.1 Introduction

A fundamental tenet of this book is that for the process of discovery, idea and knowledge development, application and diffusion to flourish, and allow for the interconnections of sources and users of ideas, no matter where they originate from, an **enabling economy** and society is needed.

The notion of enablers has two inter-related meanings: the role of the state in enabling or broadly facilitating innovation to occur, and obtaining the appropriate balance between government and the market place; and enablers in the stricter, narrower sense of providing the most efficient, and effective business environment and social conditions within which innovation and economic activity can occur.

Both tenets, if properly applied, should allow business people and entrepreneurs to create and invest with certainty, to ply their trade and innovate without undue encumbrance, supported by the systems of government and governance that nurture and encourage all in society to express their view freely, collaborate, connect with others, and which encourages experimentation and risk taking.

2.2 India's Experience of Statism

Has India got the balance right between government and the market place? There are a number of descriptions of the roles of government in India in the post-independence period, also including the post-liberalisation phase since 1991 in which India moved away to some extent from its protective shield role of government with all its attendant patronage, subsidies, and licenses (licence, quota, permit raj)[1] to freeing up the shackles in varying degrees via import and foreign investment liberalisation, and pro-competition policies. The journey is, and has been, far from complete. For example, some contend that the process of reform in the early 1990s was conducted in stealth, focussing initially at least on trade and industrial policy, leaving large segments of economy and society untouched (Corbridge et al. 2013). This could be associated with the need to not disrupt the broader economy with rapid and far-reaching change and the need to contend with various key vested interests and constituencies. India's own economic survey of 2017–2018, speaks of a shift from 'crony socialism' to 'stigmatised capitalism' post-liberalisation, associated with all manner of governance flaws and corruption in the allocation of telecommunications spectrum licenses, for example, coal distribution and so on (Government of India 2018).

The allocation of rights to scarce natural resources among favoured interests, especially since the 2000s to the ascension of the Modi era, meant that India has also come to be known as the 'Resource Raj' rather than a License Raj. In fact, there are three types of Indian capitalism identified: those relatively corruption free and competitive sectors such as ICT, driven by technology and linked to global markets; state-owned sectors; and then those sectors, mostly resource based, replete with rent seekers, and shadowy connections to the State (Crabtree 2018). This, of course, is in addition to the very pronounced informal sector. The achievements of the Modi era shall be considered later.

India has variously been described as follows: a 'Strong Society-Weak State', in which the state role has been shaped and subsumed by familial and business ties, kinship and casteism (Das 2012); and a 'flailing state' characterised by sound elite bodies at the national (and some State) level, but that 'this head is no longer reliably connected via nerves and sinews to its own limbs' (Pritchett 2009, p. 6). The daily activities of policemen, health workers, etc., which are out of the purview, oversight and control of these elite bodies, has been marked by dysfunction, lack of coordination, capability gaps, corruption and indifference.

In a similar vein is Hirschman's 'Exit and Voice' in which individuals' and firms angst about dysfunctional politics and associated institutions lead them either to

---

[1]The licence, quota, permit raj reflects the myriad of controls, regulations and barriers to operate businesses, including restrictions on imports and foreign investment (Subramanian 2018a).

try and improve the system from within through various demands and clamour for action (voice). By contrast, as has been happening in India, in a range of services such as education and health, those same actors come up with alternatives and walk away (exit) through private provision, instead of relying on public delivery (Pritchett 2009).

Some comment that although India has opened up its economy in recent years and enjoyed economic growth, it suffers in the area of the constructive social role of the state in terms of not realising social objectives, or providing social infrastructure (education, health, environment) and indeed physical infrastructure (Dreze and Sen 2013). Others again point to India as being characterised by intrusive government in which its priorities have been, and continue to be, misplaced. The public sector has been producing goods and services which could best be left to the private sector, e.g. airlines, while neglecting activities that are typically in the State domain (Paul 2017). Subsidies, including, for example in power and other key inputs, at the behest of vested interests still continue. 'Crony capitalism' has led to, and encouraged wasteful resource usage, patronage, vote buying, corruption and neglect of basic services in areas of education and health.

Power distance, as measured by the Hofstede index (Hofstede Insights 2019), shows the extent to which there is acceptance by the less powerful that power in society and organisation is unequal. A large power distance means a great deal of weight is placed on hierarchy, authority and a 'tops down' approach to strategy and direction. India is rated among the countries with the most unequal power distance. We would argue that this power distance is inimical for innovation in which ideas, initiative and empowerment is associated with all parts and all levels of society.

An important distinction in the Indian context has been made between state and the government (Jalan 2017), where the former represents the permanent institutions of the legislature, executive and judiciary, and the latter the political party in office or the 'tenant' of the state. This dichotomy explains in some measure the failure of the state's directed national development strategy to achieve very much, since the government, representing and pandering to various sectional interests, and acting expediently has not necessarily acted in the national interest.

In a similar vein to 'flailing state' valid criticisms have been raised about the capability and resources of public administration to manage, oversee and drive the detailed aspects of each and every plan, including coordination across agencies (Jalan 2017). Even if the goals were appropriate the capacity to deliver and coordinate them, has been a huge question mark, leading to administrative failures, and multiple, overlapping, duplicative and wasteful activities.

Yet more analysis of the changing Indian state has likened it to 'Socialism with limited entry to capitalism without exit' (Subramanian 2018a). By this it means that the socialist ideology in the post-independence period constrained the entry of firms, goods and investment in the economy, but that this has given way to a situation where resources continue to be tied up in inefficient, unproductive activities, sectors and programmes. The inability to exit limits the dynamism of the economy, and in our reckoning is associated with vested interest pressures, protectionist sentiment, corruption and bureaucratic inertia.

2.2.1 A Different View of the State

In our view, what has been consistently missing has been the clarity and purpose around the boundaries of public–private activity and remit, especially in the economic context. We would consider India to be a 'lurching' state, one which lurches from one policy stance to another, overlaying one set of measures onto another and which waxes and wanes in the face of actual or perceived crises, pressures from vested interests, and the whims and 'tinkering' instincts on the part of political leaders. For example, the liberalisation efforts, although long overdue, were formed in a crisis context, while recently, there have been attempts to re-introduce protectionist measures (Panagariya 2018). One further manifestation of this is that programmes are overlayed onto other programmes. One analysis finds that about half of national government programmes were more than 25 years old and that about 90% of programmes were continuing for at least 15 years (Subramanian 2018a). Thus, while conveying some sort of permanence and stability, in fact programmes continue due to a lack of commitment and resolve to be flexible and adaptable, and pander to various pressures. New programmes simply add to existing ones in the manner of a lurching state.

While policy does needs to be flexible and adaptable in the light of changed circumstances and hence new measures should be added, they need to be framed in the context of an enduring, cohesive and integrated strategy, where costs, benefits and tradeoff's are carefully articulated and thought through, and where programmes that have passed their 'use by date' are phased out.

2.2.2 The Market Mechanism

The market is a vital allocator of resources through the interplay of demand and supply, a relatively free pricing mechanism, and forces of competition. Nevertheless, for checks and balances, to correct excesses, to ensure the provision of otherwise under-served activities, to address distributional issues, and to realise social and environmental objectives, the role of the state is still vital. In fact, as we shall see the state would need to play a strong yet different role to previous times, in an era of knowledge and innovation. The Enabling State, that we put forward, is one which respects the market but which provides an appropriate balancing and leadership role for government. The sort of role envisaged here for government does extend beyond the traditional one espoused by many economists, but which equally includes a number of these roles. To be sure, there are core activities that government must undertake, including defence, macroeconomic stability and foreign policy. There are many others, for example basic education and health, associated with merit goods, equity and social cohesion which warrant public endeavour. However, it is far from clear that government needs to be involved in *the direct production and delivery of goods and services* (Joshi 2016).

2.2.3 The Enabling State

The Enabling State is one which identifies and obtains the balance with the market place. We concur with Nayyar (2017), who claims that the state and market are complements rather than substitutes, that cooperation rather than conflict should define the engagement, and that each provides corrective checks and balances to each other's excesses, and must adapt to each other in a flexible manner. This needs to be done in a mutually supporting and reinforcing manner. It is not a case of 'either or'. The Enabling State is a key in this book.[2]

Moreover, a nuanced approach is required in the knowledge economy context. It is true that with the transformative and rapid technological change that we are witnessing, including new paradigms such as the Fourth Industrial Revolution, the parameters of 'public' and 'private' are changing and boundaries blurring: for example, new models of collaborative production and consumption, under the banner of the 'sharing economy', fuelled by new technology, are transforming traditional private assets into quasi-public ones, UBER being an important example of this. On the other hand, the continued push of traditional public functions into the private domain, through contracting out, outsourcing, the establishment of quasi markets and the like, is also blurring boundaries.

2.3 Elements of the Enabling State

The Enabling State in our assessment would comprise six main domains, capturing in essence the delicate, subtle balance between state and market place. In some ways these are the classic roles of market and Government as espoused in standard text books, but in many other ways provides a much wider and different lens, particularly as countenanced through the **knowledge economy perspective**.

- Market establishment policies
- Market conforming policies
- Market augmentation policies
- Market adjustment policies
- Market linkage policies
- Market adjunct policies.

---

[2]The term Enabling State has been used by others (Botsman 2001; Latham 2001), but in different contexts to ours, focussing on the role of community groups in delivering services. Our approach is much broader on the roles of Government and the market place in the context of the Knowledge Economy.

2.3.1 Market Establishment Policies

These are policies which, if deemed efficient and effective and address equity and distributional considerations, would impose the discipline of the market place, where this does not exist or is inadequate, for example, in respect of prices reflecting the true valuation of scarce resources. These relate strongly to the 'commons' e.g. natural resources, for which there is no natural owner as such (Joshi 2016), and which because of this, gives rise to considerable exploitation and over-use, often aided and abetted by governments. In India this would mean for example, the establishment of properly functioning resource markets, in which pricing accurately reflects demand and supply, the cost of provision and consumption. For example, water trading and a price on emissions could fall into this camp.

It would mean the establishment of 'quasi markets' where government could finance, but contract out services to private providers and/or community agencies, on the basis of competitive tender, where this can be justified on cost/benefit lines and where costs and benefits reflect, and factor in, broader economic and social benefits and costs, including equity and access provisions (Joshi 2016). These could be in areas where government has traditionally both financed and delivered services. For example, running primary care health centres along these lines could be considered. Through such mechanisms not only would efficiencies be realised, but new and innovative modes of delivery potentially attained. In so doing, it would embrace innovation in policymaking, reflecting the wider definition and context for innovation that we outlined in Chap. 1.

It would appear that despite various reforms, India has not pushed terribly hard on this front. Appropriate pricing mechanisms and the development of integrated markets, for example, in relation to natural resources, including environmental assets, has not strongly taken hold, despite some initiatives.

2.3.2 Market Conforming Policies

These are policies which recognise that a well-functioning market place is a key to the efficient allocation of resources, and that the basic parameters of structural change, as espoused by the market, need to be recognised and respected. Excessive government red tape, heavy-handed regulations, burdensome taxation arrangements and obsolete standards and norms should not encumber actors in the economy with excessive costs nor curtail creativity and innovation. Of course, these policies would need to balance carefully and explicitly the broader social value of government intervention and action. Market conforming policies would also need to identify and recognise that in the knowledge economy, as new industries emerge and old ones disappear, old regulations, norms and governance quickly become outdated and moribund. With this in mind a notion of the 'Vigilant State' as part of the Enabling State, becomes critical in identifying, understanding and removing expeditiously, outdated restrictions, e.g.

inflexible labour laws, but of course balancing this with new requirements to achieve other objectives. Such a 'Vigilant State' provides the freedom and wherewithal for individuals, households and businesses to unlock and harness their creativity, innovation and talents.

Further, as businesses increasingly operate and compete in global markets, the design of regulations, rules and taxation will need to countenance the impact on international competitiveness of existing businesses, and those that may be considering investing in a location. This does not mean some 'race to the bottom' in terms of the lowest possible taxation, for example, but rather a carefully constructed view about the optimal mix of regulations, laws and taxation regimes balancing all factors. In the spirit of Polyani, growth of the market is embedded in the regulatory and institutional mechanisms of the state (Nayarr 2017). This can also give weight to the notion that market conforming policies, for example cutting edge standards, can stimulate innovation (Porter 1990).

2.3.3 Some Policy Reforms

We present here three examples of the sorts of policies that are at the conjunction of market conforming and/or market establishment domains. The first is the author's suggestion, the other two are drawn from elsewhere.

Firstly, our idea is for an environmental footprint pricing scheme to be introduced in India. This would be **overall** pricing of resource management in India at the household and business level (water, power and land inputs and with output components including waste and emissions), based on an expected environmental footprint of a household or business of a certain size. For example, an assessment would be made of the expected usage of resources (and output dimensions impacting on the environment as mentioned) on a monthly or quarterly basis by a business or household of a certain size. For an actual footprint that falls within the expected range, pricing would be at a minimum level to cover costs of provision and usage and guaranteed access, while in situations where the actual footprint exceeded the expected footprint, prices would command a premium. This mechanism would have a number of key attributes. First, it would align prices directly with usage, and the full cost of provision and usage. Second, it would facilitate more effective environmental management, in terms of providing incentives to reduce the environmental footprint. Third, it would stimulate India's capabilities in data gathering and management, metering of power usage and the like, through the application of the 'internet of things'. Taken further, as with an emissions trading scheme, could be the establishment of an environmental footprint trading rights scheme. Those with actual footprint less than expected could trade with those in the obverse case, to buy and sell 'footprint permits'. Further, it would allow for households and businesses to receive detailed breakdowns on the contributions of water, power and land, and associated waste and emissions, to the overall footprint, allowing for switching of usage patterns where appropriate. In addition, only one footprint bill (with component information) would be provided.

Of course, in establishing such an arrangement, distributional, equity impacts and considerations would need to be assessed.

It is envisaged that such a mechanism would be implemented over time, possibly starting with larger enterprises, cascading to smaller enterprises and, then finally to households, to ensure that proper planning is undertaken, transition issues managed and ensuring learnings along the way. Similarly, the scheme would start with the impact on the environment and footprint in India, before considering the global footprint.

A variation on this approach could be sophisticated water trading, which has found favour in some countries,[3] where water rights are allocated and traded. Building on this could be a defined water envelope within which communities and businesses would have to manage and co-exist (Sivaramakrishnan 2015). One could envisage, within an overall water envelope, a basic minimum charge and guaranteed amount, and then usage above that minimum charge would command a water premium. Water trading would occur between under-users and those seeking more water.

A 'Water ATM' has been suggested (Kalam and Singh 2015), linked to a centralised water cloud database augmented by technology, to monitor usage and availability. The Water ATM would allow for withdrawal of water by households, supported by biometric data, and authentication and verification technology. This model sees free allocation for individuals/households to a certain level, with charges applying to withdrawals above the minimum (Kalam and Singh 2015).

Another interesting approach aimed at reducing road congestion based on Certificates of Entitlement (COE) has been pioneered in Singapore (Land Transport Authority 2018). Before purchasing a vehicle a COE must be obtained, which is a right to vehicle ownership and use of road spaces. Obtaining a COE is through a bidding or auctioning process with the number of certificates issued based on projections of growth in allowable vehicles linked to population growth. Such a system has the advantage of addressing congestion, providing better traffic flow and management, and enhanced environmental outcomes. Tailored to India, it (or a variation of this) could be utilised to reduce severe bottlenecks traffic in cities. Revenue from auctions could be ploughed back into infrastructure development and renewal, or handed back in the form of rebates for those among the poorer classes, or for others where mitigating circumstances prevail (Land Transport Authority 2018; Sivaramakrishnan 2015).

These are but three potential examples of how different market-based instruments can be used in an innovative way, aligned with the parameters of the Enabling State, linked to technology while allaying deleterious equity and distributional fears.

The approach that we propose is based on the use of metering, monitoring systems and the 'internet of things'.

In extolling the use of big data, analytics and social media, one should be mindful of the emergent threat of 'surveillance capitalism'. Coined by Zuboff (2015, 2019) surveillance capitalism is used to describe situations where firms offer (thrust) products and services drawing on predictive models based on observed experiences and

---

[3]For example, Australia has a water trading scheme.

behaviours gleaned from vast amounts of data. Survelliance capitalism is, and has, the power to undermine personal freedoms, autonomy and democracy (Zuboff 2015, 2019). A Vigilant State which is attuned to these factors in its approach to regulation and oversight of economic activity is critical.

2.3.4 Modi Administration Performance in Relation to Market Conforming/Market Establishment

While the Modi Administration has ostensibly made a number of reforms in areas such as single window for business, reforms to Government procurement including greater transparency, and stronger outcomes in areas relating the World Bank doing Business index (to be considered shortly), there has been disquiet about its performance. Some contend that it is stronger in project, administrative mode or smaller initiatives, rather than in coherent long-term strategy or original policy development. Implementing ideas that emanated from the previous administration such as the GST or Bankruptcy code are cases in point, with still large swathes of reform including in the labour market and land policy, and the banking sector, are still yet to materialise. It is contended that India is losing some of its lustre as a destination for investment, losing out to the likes of Vietnam, Indonesia and Phillipines and that this reflects unfulfilled reforms (The Economist 2017a, b, 2018).

In a recent Forbes article, based on expert opinion, the Modi Government received a very mixed response: only above 5/10 ratings for measures relating to non-performing loans (with various caveats around implementation), housing, fiscal discipline and significantly below 5 for rationalising and simplifying the tax regime, public investment in agricultural and rural development, new cities development, roll out of health initiatives, including especially primary health care and for manufacturing policy including investment attraction. Further, the assessment also confirms little by way of reforms in land and labour markets (Srivastava 2019).

2.3.5 Market Augmenting Policies

Market augmenting policies are those which recognise that the market undervalues and underperforms in key areas of investment in knowledge and research, because for example, the social benefits exceed the private benefits.

The market can also suffer from information gaps, under-provision of information and information asymmetries requiring government action. One manifestation of the information problem relates to longer term time horizons for many investments with markets not adequately able to determine pricing information over such a horizon (Joshi 2016).

More generally, is that the market is deficient when it comes down to the 'vision thing'. With short time horizons, questions and answers about what sort of economy and society does India want to be and can be in 20–30 years, how can India make a transition to a knowledge economy in the future, what does this mean for jobs of the future, and what constitutes civil society, including social cohesion in the context of continuous and unrelenting change, are critical domains of effective government. These sorts of long run considerations need a view about the future which well-developed foresighting can provide, calling on expert advice and tapping into stakeholder views, expertise and insights from around the nation (and beyond).

India, in our view, is currently lacking in the vision aspect. To be sure, there are certain quasi manifestations of a vision, including financial inclusivity in providing greater access for citizens to banking services, Swach Bharat (Clean India), Solar Missions and the recent Health (and insurance) measures to provide broader health coverage. Nonetheless, we argue that there is an absence of an overarching, co-ordinated, unifying vision which can bind constituent actors and the community at large and exhort activity based on shared expectations. We argue that this is certainly absent in the knowledge economy domain, save for some excitement in such areas as the space programme. In our view, the promise of the inclusive, innovation decade flagged as part of the Twelfth Plan has not particularly materialised. The abolition of the National Knowledge Commission, as a key instrument to articulate a long-term view about the knowledge economy is disheartening to say the least. The NITI Aayog, which replaced the old Planning Commission, could serve such a vision making role, but is more an advisory organ, preparing somewhat narrow expert reports in particular fields. The attempt at a vision by the NITI Aayog appears not to have gone terribly far.

Somewhat contentiously, the early post-independence five year plans, although technocratic and elite by nature, did have elements of vision making in terms of articulating a view about the kind of economy and society for the future. It was about a strong leadership role for government in the economy through advanced, heavy industry, laying the foundation for subsequent industrial development and attempting to position India as self-reliant, self-fulfilling, self-assured and throwing off once and for all the yoke of colonial exploitation. Although difficult in retrospect to justify and support, at the time it did have some underlying logic to it. Where it came unstuck, as we have demonstrated, was its lack of flexibility in the face of changing economic contexts and circumstances, its seemingly open encouragement of rent seeking and corruption, and over-reach in terms of a heavy handed government driven approach to micro management of the economy, thereby stifling creativity. Moreover, it was not inclusive of broad sections of the community.

What we call for is vision making, an outline of which will be articulated in the final chapter and through the book, based on India as a knowledge economy power, supported by ideas drawn from all over society and economy and the meshing and interplay of these ideas to generate solutions to complex challenges.

2.3 Elements of the Enabling State

The market augmenting element that we put forward, is in some senses, at least consistent with the work on the Entrepreneurial State by Mazzucato (2015). According to Mazzucato, an entrepreneurial state is one which is pro-active, creates markets by taking risks (beyond which the private sector is willing and able) and acts as a lead and catalytic investor, bringing others along with it in a networked manner. The role of the state is a visionary, strategic one and mission focussed in this reckoning, which goes well beyond the traditional notions of correcting market failures. Such a state has been instrumental, in Mazzucato's view, in driving major industries in the U.S and elsewhere in defence, pharmaceuticals and biotechnology, among others.

Our view is that elements of the Entrepreneurial State and more traditional notions of government addressing market failures can run in tandem, as seen by our multifaceted nature of government vis-à-vis the market place. Certainly, we envisage aspects of the Entrepreneurial State in arguing for a vision making approach for India, and bringing stakeholders with it, and having a more solutions/mission orientation. However, we see that the more pivotal role in India is for the government to unlock and leverage the talents across the economy and society, to solve problems, through policies of facilitation and brokerage, and development of broad capabilities (the 'E's), certainly not rejecting subsidies and other supports where they can be justified. We are doubtful, given its experience, that India possesses the sophisticated state capability, and ability to withstand vested interest pressures, to take on the strong and comprehensive leadership role as envisaged in the Entrepreneurial State.

2.3.6 Market Adjustment

Generally, and particularly with the knowledge economy, there is upheaval. New industries, technologies and business models emerge-witness the emergent Fourth Industrial Revolution—while economic activity and employment in traditional industries disappear, and whole regions can be affected through the process of structural change. Inevitably there will be winners and losers. The market can be a dramatic force for change but can give rise to much economic and social dislocation and inequitable outcomes.

As such, there is a role for government to smooth, moderate and mediate these forces without curtailing them per se but ameliorating their adverse impacts, and indeed, ensuring that wider segments of society and economy can participate in, and take advantage of the opportunities afforded by change. This implies a number of roles for government: helping to transition from declining areas of the economy to growing ones, through, for example comprehensive skilling and training; and promoting new growth opportunities in affected regions or towns, with potential income support for those harshly affected. From the available evidence, India has not developed a comprehensive approach for transitions from the old to the new, still having a great deal of its economy locked in lower value activities, for example in low productivity, low value agriculture and has rather neglected badly the needs of a modern workforce, and the huge investment in skills and reskilling that are needed. India is not equipped for the future challenges of technology and rapid change as subsequent chapters will show. Some 69% of Indian jobs are at risk according to the World Bank while on various other indices India is not prepared for the future world of work (Citi GPS, Oxford Martin 2016).

Since the mid-1980s a process of global convergence has been underway with poorer countries, including India, growing faster than richer countries. However, there are some dark clouds on the horizon for India (and others) as a late converger, such as slowing down of world trade including a backlash of protectionist sentiment from advanced economies, and major structural adjustment issues facing India (growth has not been accompanied by a great deal of transfer of resources from low productivity to higher productivity sectors (Government of India 2018). Unlike China, India's growth has not been accompanied by growth in 'good sectors' [4] while weakness in human capital formation, and the need to make rapid advances in agricultural productivity to feed the population and free up resources for other sectors, are all pressure points. There is a risk for India that resources will only move from low productivity, informal sectors to only slightly better sectors (Government of India 2018).

More broadly, policies which seek to reduce inequality and inequity in society, including among minority groups through empowerment and provision of opportunity, is the basis of a civil society. This is a society which does not leave people to the often unforgiving vagaries of the unfettered market place. However, these measures need to be determined after careful consideration of benefits and costs, monitored and evaluated to circumvent misuse. On this score there has been much criticism of successive Indian Governments, in areas such as food distribution to the poor through the Public Distribution System which has been characterised by leakage and corruption. The general absence of a safety net for those in the informal sector (and India has enormous numbers in this segment), and the prevalence of vulnerable employment, to the extent that jobs are available, are sore points. The employment situation remains in crisis as we shall see in the next chapter, but improvements have been made in other areas, including direct financial welfare transfers into bank accounts and some attention to the provision of social security to those in the unorganised, informal sector, although this is far from comprehensive or seamless (Gomes 2018). Many challenges remain in addressing the considerable income and wealth gaps and disparities in India. It is a fact that India suffers from rampant inequality.

---

[4]Good sectors are dynamic and high productivity ones, basically manufacturing, finance, telecommunications, and professional services, while less good are considered to be hotels, restaurants and transport.

2.3.7 Market Linkage Policies

We identify a set of measures called market linking policies, which are about building and harnessing connections and linkages in the economy. They are about developing a fully functioning ecosystem which identifies, facilitates and leverages the benefits of collaboration, the sharing of ideas, information and know-how, the process of joint discovery, and sharing of risks and costs. They are about bringing disparate players together for common goals, where the 'whole is greater than the sum of the parts'. Further, these policies are about linking elements of the different 'power structures' in an economy, for example, building the connections between village-level initiatives and complementary national-level efforts.

Such policies could also be thought of as market coordination, for example, the harmonisation of labour markets, product markets, financial markets and 'markets for ideas'. In such a system consistency and coordination can be realised and the balance between collaboration and competition attained. In many ways market linkage policies lend themselves to the innovation systems approach which exemplifies the deep and highly interdependent relationships between constituent actors in the system, be they financiers, firms, academia, policymakers and research bodies, although we argue that such an approach needs to be extended to other segments of the economy and society beyond the elite levels.

India continues to lack a vibrant ecosystem of innovation. Siloed boundaries between, and within public Institutions remain, as do limited linkages between public and private entities in the innovation sphere.

2.3.8 Market Adjunct

Finally is the notion of market adjunct policies, which has a strong relationship with market linkages. These are in effect the support structures for markets, the extramural institutions which underpin a fully fledged, efficient, innovative and vibrant economy and society. These are the institutions including, but not limited to, a properly functioning democratic system of government, a free press, a transparent, open and accountable bureaucracy, strong judiciary and citizen rights and access to basic rights and services, and participation in processes of decision-making. Douglas North and others have written extensively about the importance of, and link between institutions and economic and social prosperity as we saw in chapter one (North 2016; Cortright 2001). It is important to note that there is no standard check list of or 'ticking the box' exercise when it comes to institutional development and renewal (Dreze and Sen 2013). Rather, institutions need to be aligned with history, context, political features and traditions of a nation, while building for the future. Effective and efficient institutions should be about what types of institutions serve what purpose, meet what challenge, and which support the most effective deployment of resources, to harness the creativity, talents and aspirations of individuals and enterprises, while maintaining important safeguards and checks and balances.

We argue that India does not have institutions that are conducive to national prosperity, and particularly the knowledge economy. We **dwell** on this particular aspect in this chapter, as an absolutely fundamental aspect of the Enabling State. Just by way of a 'taster', the prevalence of widespread corruption as an institutional failure, the sluggish judicial system, a moribund education and training system, a disconnected research apparatus and democracy in need of improvement and reform are examples. Government agencies that are still insular and siloed in nature, which are 'turf protectors', rules and 'red tape' oriented, and fragmented in operation (despite improvements) amplify our arguments. These are just some examples of where Indian institutions are misaligned with the need to identify, unlock, harness and leverage creativity and talents of its people. We advocate for new and substantially reformed institutions and ways of doing things, as a clarion call for greater community engagement and dialogue, reforms to government agencies, a better functioning democracy, and a more effective education and training and research system, better attuned and aligned with the needs of a modern, knowledge intensive economy. As Lateef comments, many reform agendas of countries have faltered due to neglect of institutions, and that studies highlight the importance of institutions which play a '…key role in creating, regulating, stabilising and legitimising markets' (Lateef 2017, p. 204). This message is also reinforced by Nayyar (2017) in highlighting the importance of institutional interventions to set rules of the game, create regulatory frameworks and monitor the functioning of markets. To this, we would add institutions which are capable of driving an 'over the horizon' view.

2.4 The Nature of the Enabling State

Having examined the broad roles and parameters of the Enabling State vis-à-vis the market, we now turn to *the nature and characteristics* of such a State.

Ideas can originate anywhere, anytime by anyone. Identifying, leveraging and integrating ideas in a timely and needs based fashion, calls for different characteristics and policy instruments of the State. An expensive subsidy driven approach which supports pre-determined priority sectors and firms at length, can be inimical to unlocking the broader economy and society wide set of ideas and capabilities, and focuses on a narrow few chosen areas, potentially fostering an entitlement and dependency borne out of rent seeking activities. Our Enabling State approach is more concerned with the **facilitation** of activity, but interposed with direct government action, on a case by case basis, where justifiable on benefit-cost grounds in the wider sense, including social and environmental outcomes. It is also about flexibility in that interventions to develop broad capabilities as part of the 'E' framework, can, for reasons of need, circumstance, focus and limited resources be deployed where best suited, including at the project level, firm level, and on spatial and meso-cluster bases, as we explained in chapter one. Key characteristics of an Enabling State include

2.4 The Nature of the Enabling State

brokerage activities, where government plays an intermediary role linking and bringing players together in the promotion and diffusion of ideas and knowledge. The role of brokers is a key one in this book, which will be outlined in subsequent chapters. In a sense this can be thought of as a writ-large extension service for the knowledge economy. A part of the Enabling State can be described as *referral*. This is not referral in the time honoured bureaucratic tradition of 'buck passing' between government agencies, nor is it about the dubious practice in India of appointing and anointing middle persons to provide access to essential services to 'grease the wheels' (Joseph 2016). It is about fostering complementary networks of problem-solving experts, whose diverse and innovative capabilities can be deployed on a wide scale. Such networks and individuals within networks can also provide mentoring support, advice and information, to unlock and support innovative capabilities. Another key component of the Enabling State is to think of it being *vigilant* (the vigilant state as we have already mentioned), one that is attuned to constantly shifting technologies, industrial applications, significant structural change and paradigm altering education and training needs. Vigilance is a characteristic in which the state can respond quickly (and even better anticipate the future although this is problematic) to changed circumstances, and at levels of economy and society, e.g. at the grass roots and village level, where action may be most needed.

India has much to improve in this area as we shall see later in this chapter and in subsequent chapters.

2.5 Types of Instruments

It is appropriate to turn to the **particular** types of policy instruments that underpin an Enabling State. While not denying their importance, and indeed they form some part of our strategic recommendations, we argue that knowledge intensive economy policies need to be less reliant on more traditional narrower measures such as explicit and implicit subsidies and taxes and regulations and anti-competitive arrangements. While having a role, they can be expensive, foster rent seeking behaviour and pressure from vested interests, favour certain narrow interests and sectors and can be open to charges of crony capitalism, as well as being inefficient in various instances by not reaching intended groups (Joshi 2016; Panagariya and Bhagwati 2012; Ninan 2015). In addition, they distort the market place signals by encouraging over use—the classic example in India being the distortionary impacts of free power and free water (Ninan 2015). Regulatory controls can be onerous, dull creativity and innovation, and impose large costs and burdens associated with compliance, and administration. Moreover, utilising such approaches can create difficulties in keeping up with technological change, particularly pertinent in a knowledge economy where change is rapid. In our view, an all-encompassing, all-embracing knowledge economy, built on leveraging ideas from all sections of the economy and society, needs different set of policy measures and prescriptions. A narrow set of measures focussed on particular firms and sectors does not unlock the wider and broader talent pool across economy and society in an inclusive manner. New instruments are needed for new times and aspirations.

Where subsidies and tax breaks and regulatory imposts are still legitimate measures, and we don't deny their importance or need under various conditions, in our view, they should be linked to benefit-cost testing, sunset clauses and proper vetting and evaluation, and used in broader manner where possible to foster wider capabilities, rather than in specific, narrower confines.

So what are the newer types of policies that we refer to?

2.5.1 Newer Policies

First, bringing players together in collaborative ventures, partnerships and joint ventures designed to deploy synergistic knowledge, identify and capitalise on complementary capabilities, share ideas and jointly create solutions to complex challenges in a market augmenting fashion, are critical. This involves a very significant role for problem-solving in mission mode for the knowledge economy which can achieve the twin aims of commercial need and societal challenges. Two examples of this 'positive production' are demonstrated in respect of India's missile capability development and testing, the first where indigenous capability development in human resources and technology was facilitated by a collective, collaborative national effort, while the second case involved partnerships between India and Russia, based on complementary capabilities, and knowledge synergies (Kalam and Singh 2015). Positive production was characterised by openness to new ideas and experimentation, promoting enterprise, collaborative effort and taking failure in its stride. Positive production can be contrasted with negative production associated with the example, of Coco-Cola in India, in which there was a passive and undue reliance on technology from abroad, with little or no domestic value added, leading to low skill, low wage outcomes (Kalam and Singh 2015). From our perspective, the Coco-Cola example is not to deny the importance of foreign ideas, technology and knowledge, but rather there is a need to harness these and mesh with local capability and talents in an interdependent, genuine partnership approach in the pursuit of higher value outcomes.

Second, our approach is about linking across the 'influence spectrum'. For example, it means connecting 'elite science' with grass roots innovation. Projects at the national level involving large scale research projects create significant positive spillovers which are beneficial for grass roots innovators, and grass roots innovation can shape and influence national priorities and programmes. Building these kinds of linkages so that the national and local act in concert is important. One manifestation of this is the impact and importance of satellite technology on the performance of individual farmers.

Third, it also involves breaking out of traditional 'siloed thinking' and narrow discipline, technology and organisational boundaries. Recent work and experience demonstrate the importance of the fusion of generic technologies such as biotechnology, ICT and nanotechnology and the blurring of boundaries within, and between arts and humanities and sciences and engineering (STEAM agenda), and the interplay of the emerging fourth industrial dimensions including robotics and artificial intelligence. Thus policies should seek to bridge artificial discipline and technology divides.

Fourth, are sort of policies that foster mentoring support, advice and role models to harness the deep creativity and talents of individuals and provide opportunities for all to participate in, and share in the fruits of the knowledge economy and society, akin to the market linkage domain. There are many 'broken ladders' in India (Krishna 2017), including a disconnect between talent and opportunity, especially in the 'beyond 5 mile' range (i.e. 5 miles beyond the main urban centres), due to lack of information, limited access to government officials and agencies (and lack of knowledge of government programmes), poor physical and social amenities, absence of advisers, counsellors, role models and paucity of influence networks and institutions for engagement between urban and non-urban centres. There is a dichotomy between the 'dollar economy and the rupee economy' (Krishna 2017).

Fifth, are policies that are information intensive in the market augmenting mode. These include policies that overcome information asymmetries and information gaps, including in the context of technological complexity, and in some cases can address the modern problem of excessive, unfiltered and extraneous information and 'noise'. Provision of information, analysis and insight into industry, market and technology trends are key, as are institutions that address information gaps between providers and users. One manifestation of this is the growing importance of specific intermediaries who can help users to absorb, work with and deploy technologies, including for example in ICT (Dewing and Jones 2016). This would be particularly significant in India where there is a sharp divide between the digital 'have's and have not's'. These intermediary type influencers align with our notion of the referral State in which networks of experts can be utilised to diffuse knowledge capability. Similar notions are advanced in later chapters regarding education and training brokers, i.e. specialists who can guide and assist students.

While one can argue that information provision could be better provided by private providers than governments, governments can socialise this information over many users, thus enhancing efficiency, while often the private sector will be reluctant to engage in information provision as it can be easily appropriated by others without return. Further, governments can often, by virtue of their over-arching functions see connections across activities and 'fill in the dots' to form a coherent whole. In any case, where it is feasible and more cost effective to do so, governments can contract out the private sector to provide information.

Further, and as alluded to before, the emerging knowledge economy is characterised by rapid technological change, the churn of entrepreneurship, disruptive innovation and technologies, and deployment of new business and organisational models. For example, new forms of collaborative production and consumption in the sharing economy are rapidly and fundamentally transforming the way businesses are run, new ICT technologies are posing challenges to privacy and cybersecurity, while biotechnology, artificial intelligence, gene technology and associated research is bringing into sharp focus issues of ethics, safety standards and so on. What is required therefore is a fleet of foot government, in the manner of vigilance, capable of responding to (if not anticipating) such changes in the environment and context in a timely and proportionate manner. This in turn calls for a new approach to regulations, which relies on a cooperative and partnership-based approach, drawing on expertise that resides in industry and community, and use of risk-based regulations which are a more nuanced and differentiated approach incorporating stringent measures for higher risk entities. In addition, removing regulations which have passed their used by date will require vigilance and agility on the part of government, as will adoption of new ones. For India, this will require a sea change of attitudes, mindset and capabilities. A system of governance that has had entrenched input driven views of regulation needs a refresh based on outputs and outcomes.

We also argue that new approaches to an Enabling State in India should put a premium on experimentation and risk taking. Tackling seemingly impossible problems, using different lens on issues, accepting failure, experimenting with different approaches, valuing initiative and creativity and accepting difference, diversity and dissent, indeed welcoming it, should be part of the new lexicon of policy. Well targeted financial support through a national experimentation fund aimed at tacking national challenges in an innovative manner, which embraces all walks of society, is one such possibility. Another key element would be to continue to relax the constraints on failed entrepreneurship and create a culture where failure can be embraced as part of learning and unlearning among other things. In fairness, the Indian Government has moved somewhat in this direction in recent years, through for example various funding packages and measures, reductions of barriers to exit from entrepreneurship (Government of India 2016 and the India Inclusive Fund (National Innovation Council 2019) previously adopted. More is needed to be done in a consistent and coherent way, at all levels of government. *Building state capability in these and other areas is a critical challenge.*

Yet another example of the sort of new policy instruments that underpin an Enabling State is the demonstration effect-identifying and championing, promoting and publicising success stories as exemplars to others, to foster and feed learning and continuous improvement.

In addition, an important role for policy in the context of ideas, innovation and creativity is to recognise that knowledge can also be garnered from outside national boundaries, i.e. recognising and working with the global market for ideas. As such, being able to create the conditions to identify such knowledge, access it, mesh and absorb with domestic capabilities is key. In our view this has many different facets. First, is to be open to the myriad of knowledge channels, including mobility of researchers, technologists, students, imports of advanced know-how, through goods and services and technology, and foreign direct investment. It also means promoting outward mobility where appropriate to garner access to know how. One such important role is to tap into the Indian diaspora as a strategic knowledge-based asset, to ensure that the connections back home for those Indians residing abroad, remain intact and enhanced. This could be effected through collaborative projects with diaspora, further fostering mobility between home and host countries, and providing favourable terms for diaspora investment in knowledge-based industries and activities, as well as creating the conditions where diaspora can act as a conduit to other players and markets.

A key role for policy therefore is to act as an antennae or window to the world. This will in turn require the capacity, either within government or through other experts in the market place, to spot opportunities in an agile manner, identify collaborative possibilities, understand local needs and how international knowledge can assist with that, as well as participate in global projects. Too often policy concentrates on liberalisation, in the context of the rules for freer trade and mobility of resources, which although important, are certainly not the end of the story. Integration, in our estimation, on the other hand, is much more about building the connections and partnerships, forging the key linkages abroad. Integration needs to go hand in glove with liberalisation.

These considerations also mean providing an environment more generally in which dissent, debate and difference can be tolerated. Richard Florida's work on creativity, and in city contexts particularly, points to the importance of the melting pot of diversity, which when allied with vast talent pools and technology, can be powerful forces for innovation and prosperity (Florida 2003, 2008). Yet for example, India performs less well on the parameter of knowledge absorptive capacity compared to its overall standing, in the Global Innovation Index (Cornell University, INSEAD, WIPO 2018).

The Enabling State would also allow for, and encourage, people to build new skills and importantly transfer existing capabilities into newer contexts and sectors, as we envisaged in the market adjustment aspects of the earlier discussion. The ability to transition effectively and efficiently out of declining activities and into promising new ones through skills and training, labour market assistance, including effective job matching services, supported by specialist advisers and counsellors, should be hallmarks of modern day Indian policy. Thus, a generic set of capabilities which can be flexibly deployed in a multitude of ways, as distinct from narrower discipline specific strengths, is the way forward, but also a major challenge.

2.6 Paradigm Shifts

The following table captures some of our proposed shifts in policy from the current state to our future, preferred paradigm. Many of these proposed actions will be countenanced in this and later chapters. The differences between the dominant current paradigm and that envisaged for the future lies in new institutional underpinnings, participation and engagement across all levels of society, and less intrusive but facilitative policy instruments (Table 2.1).

Table 2.1 Policy orientation

	Current	Proposed
Relationship of state and market	Guiding the market	Symbiotic relationship of state and market working with the market and enabling it
Policy orientation	Subsidy, taxation and regulatory mindset	Seeing and building connections through facilitation, brokerage, information and networking based approaches
Stakeholder relationships	Growing importance of opening up government to public scrutiny, through for example online transparency of government procurement and citizen suggestions and input into Smart Cities	Sustained and significant participation in decision making at all levels of society, enabled by new participatory institutions
Centre-State	Some devolution from Centre to States, especially in finances, through 14th Finance Commission	Comprehensive transformation of relationships between tiers of government beyond finances, embodying co-operative and competitive approaches with a renewed focus on the third tier of government
Institutions	Traditional parliamentary democracy	Increased role for extra parliamentary institutions
Key organisations for governance	Mainstream departmental government agencies	New organisations (Commission for Government and Collaborate India)
Relationship to the world	Some liberalisation (but with a protectionist mindset never far way) and a rules, processed based approach to trade and investment	Interdependent-global collaboration in ideas and projects
Economic thrust	Reform and revitalisation of existing sectors e.g. Make in India	Creating knowledge economy solutions in mission mode to address complex problems based on complementary capabilities
Reform orientation	Gradualist and Managerial i.e. project and process driven	Fundamental re-alignment of policy, practice and institutions
Policy focus	Separate issue by issue	Vision for India as a knowledge economy power

Source Author assessment

2.7 Business Environment

The previous sections established our broader parameters and notions of an Enabling State. This section considers the closely related, yet narrower notion, of the effectiveness of the business or support environment in India, for innovation and economic activity to flourish. Regulatory and tax regimes, cost of doing business, the strength of the legal system and labour market conditions among others, all count. This section serves as an important launching pad for more definitive deliberations and recommendations to address shortcomings in India's policy, politics and institutional architecture.

There is a wealth of evidence about the importance of a strong and supportive business environment (World Bank 2018a): the positive association between efficient infrastructure and healthy business environment and export performance; the positive productivity impacts for small and young firms of lower tax compliance burdens; conversely that the positive impacts on GDP per capita of trade are negated in countries with rigid and cumbersome regulations; sound corporate governance is a key to a healthy and efficient investment environment and productivity, while protection of minority investors is vital to spur access to finance; financial and trade reforms are more effective in developing economies with sound property rights; there are positive and significant effects of improved business regulations, fewer procedures, lower levels of minimum capital on starting a business, and that where procedures are more complex or unclear, the likelihood of corruption is higher; formal registration of business activity gives rise to access to new equipment and larger scale of operations, and that conversely, excessive regulations and restrictions increase the number of informal businesses and hinders scale.

2.7.1 World Bank Doing Business Index

The World Bank (2019) Doing Business Index (World Bank 2018a) finds India moving progressively up the ladder to reach 77th place out of 190 countries, up from the 100th place in the 2018 Index. India is lauded as one of two countries to have made significant strides in two consecutive years, with particular gains in trading across borders, including single window clearance, implementation of the GST, reductions in time taken to obtain electricity, and 'one stop shop' arrangements for construction permits. Yet, there remain challenges and points of contention. With the exception of Brazil, India lags behind BRIC countries, and is also lower than a number of emerging Asian economies, such as Malaysia and Thailand, Indonesia and Vietnam. In addition, India lags the BRIC average on starting a business, registering a property, paying taxes, enforcing contracts and resolving insolvency.

Of the 10 categories that comprise the index, India has improved in starting a business, dealing with construction permits, getting electricity, getting credit, trading across borders and enforcing contracts marginally. It is the case however, that

India has lost ground by rank, in areas of registering a property, protecting minority investors, paying taxes and resolving insolvency. It is the 'dealing with construction' permits that has exhibited the greatest gain in rank, from a very poor 181st in 2018 to 52nd in 2019, and appears to have been the single most influential aspect of India's overall upward movement. So the point is that despite laudable gains, the performance is still uneven and patchy.

The Doing Business Index is typically not a qualitative one so it is hard to gain a true guage of quality of inputs and infrastructure in the main. In addition, the index covers only two cities: Mumbai and Delhi (The Wire 2018), and therefore is not representative of the diverse and divergent economic landscape in India. Others point to methodological issues rather than reforms, and additions to the number of countries being covered in the index, for changes in India's rankings (Sandefur and Wadhwa 2018) Further, by its own admission, the World Bank index does not capture broader aspects such as infrastructure performance, bribery and corruption, macroeconomic stability, tariffs, protective barriers and other aspects of trade (World Bank 2018a). Some of the measures such as labour market flexibility, important for India, are given scant attention, and only surface as part of 'reduced labour taxes and mandatory contributions by employers, or taxes other than profits and labour'. As such, some of the restrictive labour regulations, so apparent and stifling in India do not feature. Further, one must question whether reducing employer mandatory contributions in provident funds, is in the interests of a cohesive, inclusive economy.

Nonetheless, the upward movement is to be commended though.

2.7.2 *Governance Data and Global Innovation Data*

World Bank Governance data which measures 'Voice and Accountability', 'Political Stability', 'Rule of Law', 'Government Effectiveness' 'Control of Corruption' and 'Regulatory Quality' shows that over the last twenty years, India has lost ground on voice and accountability, political stability and rule of law, with slight gains in Government effectiveness and larger gains in regulatory quality (World Bank 2019).[5] On the latest data, of 20 benchmark countries (the original 15 plus Nepal, Philippines, Vietnam, Indonesia and Pakistan), India is barely in the top 50% for

---

[5] Voice and accountability measures views of the extent of citizen participation in choosing a Government and freedom of expression, freedom of association, and a free media.

Government effectiveness captures perceptions of the quality of public services and civil service, its independence and the quality of policy formulation and implementation, as well as the credibility of the government's commitment to such policies.

Political Stability and Absence of Violence/Terrorism measures views of the likelihood of political instability and/or violence, including terrorism.

Regulatory quality captures perceptions of the ability of the government to develop and implement sound policies and regulations that facilitate business and private sector development.

Rule of law measures perceptions of the extent of confidence in, and adhering to rules of society, especially the quality of contract enforcement, property rights, the police, and the courts, and the likelihood of crime and violence.

2.7 Business Environment

voice and accountability and control of corruption, and in the bottom 50% for the others, despite having higher levels of economic development than a number of countries. Interestingly, what we have seen is declines in freedom and application of law, when at face value one would expect improvements in these areas in the face of liberalisation. What we surmise is that economic liberalisation has benefited only a few and that liberalisation has been narrowly framed as a series of very specific pro-business activities, often associated with favoured interests.

The latest Global Innovation Index (Cornell University, INSEAD, WIPO 2018) also sheds light on India's mixed bag of achievements. Despite India rising from 76th place in 2014 to 57th in the latest year (out of 126 countries), it performs poorly relative to its overall performance in input parameters such as institutional performance in which it is ranked 80th and infrastructure (77th). Indeed on infrastructure, India continues to be at the weaker end of our 15 country comparator set, as it is on institutions. It should be noted that India performs above its overall performance in market sophistication, reflecting the cadre of emerging savvy entrepreneurs, and outputs (except in creative outputs). Interestingly, India performs reasonably well on innovation efficiency, 49th, i.e. the ability to translate inputs into outputs. Thus, there appears to be an 'inspite of' effect, i.e. inspite of its relatively poor performance on core inputs, including infrastructure, India is making headway on innovation. This raises two key concerns: whether further gains are possible and sustainable in the context of poor input performance and/or how much better could overall innovation performance be if the input side of the equation were to be improved.

The most recent Global Competitiveness Index (World Economic Forum 2018) captures the issues identified in the Global Innovation index in pointing to weaker than overall performance on infrastructure, many aspects of the enabling environment (e.g. transparency, corruption, property rights), product markets, trade openness, labour market flexibility and future workforce and skills, soundness of banks, administrative requirements, meritocracy, access to and use of ICT, social capital and security. However, interestingly and surprisingly, India is rated reasonably strongly on innovations in education, a point which we shall question in chapter three. Moreover, India ranks better than its overall performance on some aspects of public sector performance and checks and balances.

These indices that we have looked at in this section are not focussed on the myriad of poor social indicators which later chapters will explore.

2.8 Deficiencies and New Approaches

This section digs deeper into some of the key deficiencies in the Indian economy and body politic, which, if improved, could lay the foundation for further success in the knowledge economy, and economy and society more broadly. In particular,

---

Control of corruption measures views about the extent to which public power is exercised for private gain, including various types of corruption and "capture" of the state.

a strong focus in this section is on the institutional underpinnings of the economy and society. We argue strongly in this book that India does not have the institutional architecture to meet the needs of a knowledge economy. Institutional reform is core to an Enabling State, and to the market adjunct role of Government.

At its broadest, for example, India's education and training system does not meet the needs of industry and twenty-first-century skills; its science and technology infrastructure and capability does not overwhelmingly facilitate quality research, nor has a specific connection to commercial need and societal issues; its regulatory structures and policies, in spite of significant efforts in recent years, still leans to being cumbersome, complex, and filled with anomalies; national-state role and relationships can be improved significantly; labour laws constrain flexibility and rapid adjustment to emerging labour market needs; the judicial system is painfully slow with a backlog of cases extending many years. These are just a few of many, many examples that are on display. One recent comment, encapsulates the challenges India faces in government and governance 'Despite the advent of democracy and national independence, the Indian State has remained tiered and distant, and the process of the state remain hierarchical, compartmentalised, insular and upward looking' (Krishna 2017, p. 188).

In many and varying ways, India fails one of the key 'E' tests, that of the Enabling State. It has had a system of governance and government which has meddled and intruded in areas not required, including in the commercial world, while neglecting areas that it does have a critical role to play in infrastructure, education and health, and in many fields of scientific endeavour (Paul 2017). Moreover, a slow moving intrusive state is ill equipped to handle the challenges of a knowledge intensive economy, which puts a premium on unleashing knowledge from everywhere, and on agility and flexible responses in the face of intense global competition, as well as being able to facilitate the shifts in resources from declining to growing areas, while bringing people together in a constructive and shared manner.

2.9 Towards a New System of Government

At the outset we advocate a new path for India's system of government, including national-state relations in the context of the knowledge economy. There are a number of issues at play. While devolution has been occurring at least in the financial arena, due to the devolution of taxation revenue to the states from the deliberations of the 14th Finance Commission, and the introduction of the Goods and Services Tax (GST), there are still question marks hanging over federalism in India, particularly as we look to the future. Comments have been made about the complexity of the GST. The GST has many different (and frequently changed) rates, various implementation flaws, concerns about state's losing ability to raise revenue autonomously, including vexed issues about compensation in the event of revenue shortfalls, and concerns about methodology regarding division of revenue, meaning that some states perceive themselves to be subsidising others (Debroy 2018; Das 2017; Subramanian 2018a; World Bank 2018b). Nonetheless, there also has been praise for the exercise in terms of its revenue generation, and sheer ability to get it done even though issues have been raised about a possible loss of sovereignty for both the centre and the states, and the possibility of states 'backtracking' on agreements (Subramanian 2018a). Moreover, in other respects such as the labour market, it is contended that the national government has simply 'passed the buck' to the states to deal with this area requiring urgent reform, despite some consolidation and rationalisation (The Economist 2017a).

Despite its emphasis on Team India, involving and including states, NITI Aayog is still very much a think tank, advisory body lacking real teeth. There is a notable absence of an over-arching institution to coordinate and foster inter-government relationships on a systematic, whole of government basis. The still significant concurrent list, which involves overlapping national and state remit, requires further review and clarification, a belief shared by others (Reddy 2017). In some cases reforms to produce an integrated national market, are patchy, and require ongoing attention (Bhandari 2017), and India needs to move to a more sophisticated, 'fit for purpose' approach to public services which embodies diversity, and meets varied expectations in the country (Reddy 2017; NITI Aayog 2017). Others again point to wasteful, overlapping and cumbersome arrangements, lack of coordination, and varying reform progress, among national and state government agencies and instrumentalities, in certain key areas such as business development, power, housing, health and agriculture, just to name a few (Bhandari 2017; Center for Global Development and Accountability Initiative 2015; Gandhi 2018; FICCI and CBRE 2018; Subramanian 2018a). In a similar vein is the limited policy and decision-making and evaluation capability of states and lower tiers of Government, which reinforces 'flailing state' notions.

Additionally, in our view, even beyond the concurrent list, is the need to consider the full remit of current and future national-state relations, roles and responsibilities, in the context of the knowledge economy which is transforming the way services can be delivered, the way in which industries operate and giving rise to new business models of governance. Further, consideration of which level of government is best equipped to foster community engagement and participation in decision-making is a crucial element. The need for integrated, seamless national markets to promote efficiency and productivity, e.g. in agriculture, raises valid points also about centre-state (and local) relationships. In addition, the continued competition among states for economic activity, including from overseas, puts a premium on seizing opportunities quickly and in flexible manner, also bringing into question the most effective architecture for inter and intra-government relationships (and with the private sector). Further, are new and emerging knowledge considerations, including challenges of cyber and biosecurity, regulatory implications of research and technology, e.g. gene technology, new labour market contexts, e.g. rise of the 'gig economy', applications of robotics and artificial intelligence and climate change response. These pose questions as to which tier of government, or tiers of government in concert, are best equipped in terms of effectiveness, efficiency and innovation to address these issues.

As mentioned, one driver of change has been the establishment of the NITI Aayog, a more decentralised, devolved structure, to replace the centrally driven, 'command' approach of the erstwhile Planning Commission. Instead, through a series of working groups comprising representatives of state and national governments, a more collective approach to policymaking is being developed. However, it could be argued that the working groups have been focussed on very specific issues and topics, rather than large scale, overarching frameworks and issues, nor have come up with terribly far-reaching or innovative proposals, particularly in so far as the knowledge economy is concerned, with one or two exceptions such as ATAL Innovation Tinkering labs, mentioned earlier.

In addition, is the very vexed question of the third tier of government. In spite of constitutional requirements for the devolution of functions to local governments, progress has been stalled, as states in particular have been reluctant to cede power (Government of India 2018).[6] Moreover, are questions of the capacity for governance at the local level, and to the extent that local level decisions are made, they tend to be taken on the basis of closed shop, localised, unrepresentative networks of vested interests. (Krishna 2017). The Economic Survey of 2017–2018 (Government of India 2018) points to the state and local tiers relying more on devolved resources and less on their own (especially rural bodies) when compared to overseas counterparts, and that the bigger issue even beyond not having enough revenue raising powers is underutilisation of these powers. That underutilisation could be occurring is because of unwillingness to do so due to the potential citizen backlash against those tiers of government which are closest to citizens. A 'low equilibrium trap' occurs in which desire for control among higher tiers of government dovetails neatly with an unwillingness on the part of lower levels to utilise revenue powers (to the extent that they exist) because of proximity to citizens (Government of India 2018). In short, the ability of lower tiers of government to drive change, embrace autonomy and deliver to the citizenry has been stalled and compromised.

2.10 A Commission for Government

To this end, we call for a major reconfiguration around the role of government. At the outset, we argue for the creation of *a permanent* Commission for Government (CFG),[7] directly accountable to National and State Parliaments rather than the Government or ruling party of the day. The Commission For Government would be broad based, and subsume existing bodies including NITI Aayog, and the Finance Commission and Inter-State Council. The Commission for Government would not be at

---

[6]The 73rd Constitutional Amendment recognised Panchayat's or rural/village tiers of Government as self governing institutions, and the 74th Amendment did the same for urban local government.

[7]Jalan (2018) also calls for a new over-arching body to oversee National and State relations, although quite different from ours in scope and remit. Subramanian (2018a) also calls for a new body to address National-State relationships but more from a financial standpoint.

2.10 A Commission for Government

the behest of governments which it is currently, for example, in the establishment of Finance Commissions.

The Commission for Government, comprising independent experts and supported by advisory mechanisms, and with inputs from bipartisan Parliamentary Committees would have a wide remit. The Commission could be modelled along the lines of the Electoral Commission.

It would review and articulate the respective roles and functions of national, state and local governments, including funding and revenue arrangements, with a stronger remit for the lower tiers of government, as appropriate. This would be achieved through binding compacts between the tiers of government, with appropriate penalties for non-conformance. The proposed approach would mitigate against 'scope' creep on the part of various tiers of government. The Commission For Government would review all current aspects of inter-governmental functions, and have a proactive approach in identifying and formulating roles and responsibilities relating to emerging issues of the type mentioned previously, and the flexibility to undertake inquiry depending on need and circumstance.

In conducting these activities, the Commission would consider the following (a) which function is most cost effectively delivered by which tier of government having regard to economies and diseconomies of scale including national market integration (b) which functions can best meet the needs of its citizens in an accountable, timely and flexible manner (c) which functions can allow for the most effective citizen engagement in decision-making processes (d) which tier of government is most effectively able to leverage the ideas of its citizens, and to strengthen the knowledge economy, and its application in developing solutions to complex challenges around resource management, energy, urban development and rural development, for example (e) which functions and which tier of government can best promote international competitive advantage, noting that in an era of global mobility of labour, capital, goods and services that governments compete in terms of efficiency, quality and innovativeness of service delivery (f) which tier of government is best able to respond to emergent technological change and its implications for efficient and effective service delivery (g) consideration of the extent and magnitude of inter-jurisdictional spillovers (h) assessment of the capacity and capabilities in policy, delivery and evaluation (i) decide on optimal revenue raising and expenditure functions, and policies, including full review of grants from central to lower tiers of government.

The Commission for Government would have powers of enforcement. In addition, it could, for example, derive powers on an 'opt out' basis. Thus the Commission's deliberations, could have automatic imprimatur unless 70% of parliament opposed it, where the 70% would reflect the combined vote of national and state parliaments. In this way the proposed body would best promote bipartisanship among political parties, and reflect the deliberations of national and state arenas. In addition to the voting mechanism would be a series of working groups and advisory mechanisms across all layers of government to advise it, including from the 3rd tier of government. Further, as appropriate the CFG could have cells or chapters at the lower levels.

There are two further proposed functions of the Commission. The first would be to co-ordinate significant activity (with appropriate thresholds to determine 'significant') across and within jurisdictions in the light of its deliberations above (and having chapters of the Commission at sub-national tiers of government as mentioned). The Commission would not be an implementing body nor programme delivery or specific funding body to ensure that the lines of accountability are clear and to minimise potential conflicts of interest.

The second function would be to provide advice on the roles of government vis-a vis the private sector and community (not for profit) sector, consistent with the Enabling State, and embodying the notion of partnership and collaboration. This advice could take the form of initiating inquiries (or having referred to it inquiries into the role of government) and publishing reports (including for example, an Annual State of the Enabling State report) which provide indicative guidelines as to the role of government vis-a-vis the private and community sectors, and how new developments may alter these roles and functions.

Before a misleading impression is created that this is merely a return to the old days of 'command and control' via a reconstituted Planning Commission of some sort, there are some important considerations. The aim of the Commission for Government is to identify in a constructive, deliberate and overarching fashion the respective roles of national and lower levels of government, with an emphasis on *devolution* as appropriate. It is therefore, far removed from the rigidly defined central government determined priorities of the past. Second, is to view the respective roles of tiers of government in a flexible manner in the sense that technological change can alter optimal delivery of services by agencies. Third, is the explicit engagement of representatives of the sub-national tiers of government in the Commission's deliberations. Fourth is that the Commission itself has no funding powers, and thus does not invite the 'Plan and Non Plan' financial aspects of the previous planning era which led to confused accountabilities and creeping centralisation. Finally, is the advice on the role of government relative to the private sector, modelled along the lines of parameters that we discussed earlier in this chapter to ensure, for example, that the public and private sectors are in balance, form partnerships where appropriate and do not engage in 'over-reach'.

2.11 A New Era of Decentralised Planning

As part of our notion of the knowledge economy, we propose a fundamentally different planning approach that departs from the traditional notion of centralised planning. It would be driven in the main through a 'bottoms up' approach, giving greater expression, autonomy and freedom to innovate and create at lower tiers. This planning approach would be given the imprimatur, and be overseen, by the Commission for Government, consistent with the foregoing analysis.

2.12 Knowledge Advantage Plans

The main component of planning is the development of what we call 'Knowledge Advantage Plans'. Metropolitan areas and their disaggregated tiers, the municipalities, would develop a series of knowledge advantage plans. The process would start at the municipality level and be aggregated to the metropolitan level. These plans would be based on existing and potential location-specific advantages at the micro level with opportunities for growth and expansion based on identifying, analysing and leveraging **location-specific assets**. Location-specific advantages could be (a) historic (b) reputational (c) natural asset (e.g. port location or transport hub) (d) intellectual capital, e.g. presence of leading universities or highly developed research capabilities and skills sets and (e) cultural assets. This owes some to the emerging industrial district literature and practice (Katz and Wagner 2014).

The aims would be to identify and understand in detail *unique actual and potential advantage* possessed by locations, to create knowledge intensive businesses, industries, social enterprise, locational renewal and technological capabilities, and address economic and social challenges by providing tangible solutions. Spatial development in India has been characterised by 'coping' mechanisms to cater to expanding populations in adhoc manner, and as Sanyal (2018) says based more on physical characteristics (e.g. the building of physical facilities or the hardware rather than the software or human centric skills and capabilities), and the establishment of facilities such as education and training institutions in locations removed from the fabric of cities which represent the vibrancy of citizen activity and engagement. Further, it is important not to necessarily conflate spatial development with technology solutions. Moreover, spatial development needs to be countenanced on a more flexible basis to be able to respond to changing needs and circumstances.

2.13 Planning and Governance

These Knowledge Advantage plans would be funded jointly by state and metropolitan governments, with implementation at the local municipal level (or metropolitan area), as is economically and technically feasible, having regard to capacity and capability. In turn, this means recast and enhanced roles and powers for metropolitan (and municipal) levels of government in the context of Commission for Government deliberations. India has a very patchy record of devolution of responsibilities, functions and fund-raising powers to the third tier of government. In this model, we envisage a much stronger role for metropolitan government, through a directly elected mayor supported by a cabinet comprising representatives elected by municipal representatives (who are themselves elected by the people). India has also had a mixed experience in reforms and democracy at the lower levels of government, including various experiments with directly and indirectly elected mayors, and chief executive officers of metropolitan areas directly appointed by state governments (McKinsey

Global Institute 2010; Sivaramakrishnan 2015). There has been commentary about the intrusive nature of state government involvement in local affairs.

As mentioned, we propose the direct election of mayors as a further strengthening of democracy at the third tier, and recognition of the emerging importance of this tier of government in the context of our knowledge economy focus, as well as the greater influence of elected municipal level representatives. It is also proposed that these elections deliberately be free of party politics. Mayor and municipal elections would be conducted on the basis of personal characteristics, the strength of the proposed ideas and policies, and concrete and tangible aims for the location that candidates bring, rather than through allegiance to political parties.

The reform of this structure is important for the development of the knowledge advantage plans. It means that oversight is done by the tier closest to where such advantage resides, consistent with principles of subsidiarity, and the requirements in the knowledge era for flexibility and agility, and direct accountability and participation of the community. It would also mean however, greater funding autonomy for local government agencies. This could be through their own revenue raising powers, including raising funds in the financial markets. In addition, we argue that the recently implemented GST should explicitly build in mechanisms to support and fund third tiers of government. These matters would be canvassed by the Commission for Government, as would the most appropriate level of government to manage broader infrastructure provision, beyond specific knowledge advantage plan requirements. For example, the provision of basic and general amenities such as power and water could be overseen by metropolitan agencies with joint funding by state and metropolitan levels, while other activities could be the sole province of states where inter-metropolitan spillovers and linkages are significant.

2.14 Other Support Structures

The Knowledge Advantage Plans would be enhanced by further features: the establishment of Councils of Advisers who are specialists in their own fields, and the establishment of People's Forums. The People's Forums would be participatory bodies, constituted either on virtual (web-based communities of practice and ideas forums) or on an in-person basis, aimed at providing citizen's initial input (in the initial identification of advantages one could envisage an 'advantage competition' among citizens to help identify advantage from a raft of ideas),[8] review and feedback into the plans. In this way we envisage greater participation and involvement in planning activities throughout the entirety of the planning process. Drawing on citizen capabilities and perspectives in shaping knowledge advantage plans and identifying locational advantage would enhance both the development and results of these plans, and garner 'buy in' for implementation.

---

[8] Some of the mechanisms for community input have also been envisaged and undertaken in the Smart Cities Agenda.

2.15 Rural Areas

These reforms and development of plans, including knowledge advantage plans, would be replicated at the rural/regional/village levels through a similar apparatus. Thus, for example, mayor equivalents would be elected at the most efficient and effective tier of rural India, e.g. district level (or even a higher level of aggregation to realise scale economies and efficiencies), with the lower tier panchayat[9] (local village or agglomerations of these) leadership analogous to the municipal one in urban contexts. There is a vast array of unique advantages in village India to draw on for knowledge advantage plans, including tourism assets, traditional medicine capabilities, social enterprise, artisan industries and unique capabilities in solving problems. Panchayats could also be given enhanced powers and ability to raise funds through, for example, tapping into community banking and issuing of community knowledge bonds linked to particular projects, subject to capacity and capability.

The Commission for Government would oversee the system of decentralised planning, supported by, and working with agencies at national, state and local levels, and its own independent experts and consultative committees. It would oversee the provision of information regarding key economic, social and environmental parameters over a 5 and 15 year period to help shape the knowledge advantage plans, and would ensure coordination across, and within, tiers of government in development and implementation of these plans. For example, the Commission would ensure that states coordinate activities where multiple metropolitan activities in relation to knowledge advantage plans are in play, and similarly at the national level where multiple state activities are involved.

2.16 Other Institutional Features

This section proposes a range of other Institutional arrangements aligned to the needs of a knowledge economy in India.

2.16.1 *Collaborate India*

As part of the shift to a more inclusive, collaborative approach to economic development, we propose the establishment of **Collaborate India**. This would be a mainstream government agency, at national level, located in the Prime Minister's Department, and with counterparts at lower level tiers designed to foster collaborative activities and create a new culture.

---

[9]Panchayat is the village (or related rural area) leadership elected by the community.

It would have the functions of identifying, supporting, co-ordinating, promoting and publicising collaborative ventures. More specifically, its functions would embrace:

- Promoting public, private and community partnerships, including especially in the innovation sphere, e.g. industry and research partnerships, and act as **a referral** for collaborative projects
- Publicising and promoting collaborative ventures
- Serving as a repository of information about collaborative projects as a basis for strengthening the reach of collaborative networks for future projects
- Linking up projects at grass roots level with national level and state level projects
- Coordinating whole of government support for innovative projects
- Being an interface with existing bodies such as Sristi and the Honeybee Network—this in turn would strengthen the profile, reach and remit of these bodies without damaging their local character and attributes
- Extending into and having chapters in the villages—the purpose of which is to link in a series of physical and virtual networks, collaborative projects of all types and all sizes.

Collaborate India would be active in both the physical and virtual worlds in all its domains, e.g. social media, online coordination and support, and through the development of a 'Collaborate India app' which would alert, for example businesses, to potential collaborative projects and partners. It would aim to be a fast moving, coordinating body. In that way, we envisage one of its primary roles to be that of coordination, facilitation and linking of projects by tapping into the vast reservoirs of knowledge across the entire country. It would also have a pro-active role of opportunity spotting for potential projects and project partners. Over time, once established, we would envisage Collaborate India to have chapters abroad to more fully link up Indian ventures with overseas ones.

This new body for collaboration could have various specialist divisions relating to types of projects (based on size, scale, technology, extent of research) but which 'talk to each' other. Collaborate India would also have coverage of public-private Infrastructure projects.

Collaborate India would link closely with the Commission for Government. It would have project-specific responsibility, which would dovetail with, but also differentiate itself, from the Commission of Government which would have the strategic and coordinating role in respect of the knowledge advantage plans, and broader oversight of the respective roles and responsibilities of the various tiers of Government. Collaborate India would work closely with existing bodies at the grass roots level such as the Honey Bee Network, and draw on its database of projects and innovations (Gupta 2016).

2.16.2 Innovations in the Bureaucracy

More generally, as another innovation in public policy, we would advocate changes to the bureaucracy towards smaller ministries or government agencies (at both national and state level) which would separate policymaking and spending from regulatory oversight to minimise conflicts of interest and sharpen the focus of agencies. Also, it is argued here that national government ministry cells be instituted at the state government levels to ensure consistency and coordination in programme delivery.

Smaller ministries would in turn be supported by a network of implementation agents operating at the grass roots level to deliver and monitor programmes and adjust quickly to 'on the ground' requirements. Implementation agencies could be citizen representatives, not for profit agencies or via beefed up Panchayat bodies. In this way, delivery could be focussed at the levels closest to citizens, to understand in depth what is happening and required 'on the ground', and be able to respond in a flexible manner, incorporating local expertise. This would be in the manner of the Vigilant State as part of the Enabling State.

A variety of criticisms have been levelled at the Indian Administrative Service including the unhealthy close nexus between the civil service and politicians, the recurrent and short term postings and transfers which mitigate against the retention of expertise, weaknesses in performance management, absence of competency-based standards and lack of training and matching of required job skills with actual skills. The absence of appropriate training is also noted in agencies such as the police force (Lateef 2017).

As do others, we advocate for complete lateral entry in the civil service, from middle management level and above, to ensure that people with different talents, perspectives and insights can be brought into the service depending on need, and meshing with existing talent. Lateral entry would be conducted on a merit and competitive basis, including providing opportunity for existing staff to progress upwards. It would also mean that the system would move away from time-based mobility, which is open to nepotism and favouritism. Of course, lateral entry into the civil service needs to be accompanied by open, transparent and accountable selection processes (Kalam and Singh 2015; Subramanian 2018b). A strong cadre of policymakers, well resourced, trained and with expertise in key domains, could go a long way to address the problems of the flailing state—a sound top level with 'arms flapping' elsewhere. Further, much stronger internal performance management systems built on measuring performance against core metrics would be sought with redeployment or redundancy options canvassed for those not meeting requisite key performance indicators (Lateef 2017). The Modi Government has been moving in the direction of stronger performance measurement and accountabilities among bureaucrats.

In addition, we call for more integrated ministries. For example, we would recommend the creation of a Ministry of Innovation and Design at both national and state level, rather than the narrower current Ministry of Science and Technology. This would be to connote a wider, more multifaceted context to innovation beyond science, embracing design, design thinking and the non-technical aspects of innovation and grass roots innovation. It would represent the interface between science, technology and broader forms of innovation into a seamless whole, thus obviating needless and counterproductive 'silo' or boundary issues relating to innovation.

2.16.3 Judicial System

India's judicial system suffers from chronic overload, backlogs, pending cases, stays, injunctions and delays. According to the Indian Economic Survey of 2017–2018, the average age of pending cases is almost four years across various tribunals and has been rising, and costs of delay for various projects can be up to 52 crore rupees (Government of India 2018).[10] Others point to considerable underinvestment in the judiciary (in terms of the numbers of judges and a high number of vacancies), lack of transparency in the selection of judges and uncompetitive remuneration for them. (Lateef 2017), These impediments are exacerbated in more complex, specialised economic cases where such expertise is in short supply. One of the problems is the referral of cases to higher courts, rather than being dealt with at lower levels or in more specialised arenas. To be fair, measures have been undertaken, including more use of electronic means of administration and paperwork, alternate dispute resolution mechanisms, including a focus on mediation through Lok Adalats.[11] However, the situation is a major concern, and is reflected in the weakness in the World Bank Doing Business Index, which has India ranked 163rd out of 190 countries on enforcing contracts, well below its overall rank of 77, and below most emerging and developed economies (World Bank 2018a). It is a major source of institutional failure.

What is to be done? Some possibilities include: time-bound restrictions on length of cases, after which monetary penalties would apply depending on who is deemed to be the offending party in terms of delay; limitations on the number of appeals; much greater and rigorous enforcement of court jurisdictions to avoid 'jurisdictional creep' (which is where cases are continually referred to other higher courts) (Government of India 2018); development of more specialist advisory support for judges through panels or Councils of Specialist Advisers, especially cases involving specialist economic expertise (a variant of this is suggested in the Economic Survey 2017–2018 for Training Academies for Judges) (Government of India 2018); and fast track courts for cases deemed to be of national importance according to national interest criteria.

We argue for the use of quasi-sub courts which would involve conducting of cases, including preliminary judgements, made by post-graduate law students, which then would be referred to the senior courts. Such a system would allow for much of the leg work to be done by law students and would count towards their studies and careers, as a form of micro-credentialing through certification, and would ensure that students gain more practical experience and exposure to the court system.

---

[10] A crore is equivalent to 10 million rupees.
[11] Lok Adalats are quasi courts which rely on negotiation, consensus and mediation.

2.17 Democracy

India's democracy can be a messy affair. However, it is successful in that elections are held regularly, Government's change hands, voting is open to all in society, and the Electoral Commission does an admirable job in holding things together. Nonetheless, there is considerable angst in India over its state of democracy. Vote rigging and vote buying, criminality among parliamentarians, stalled passage of key bills, delays, disruption and disrepair in parliamentary proceedings have been the hallmark of Indian politics (Jalan 2017). In a damning statement on Indian politics, Lateef (2017) finds that on average, politicians have become very significantly wealthier while in parliament. The number of members of parliament facing criminal charges, including serious charges, has risen, while productivity has declined, as reflected in the reduction in time spent on parliamentary business (as distinct from interruptions and adjournments which have increased). In the 2014 Lok Sabha elections, more than 1400 of 8214 candidates faced criminal charges, while more than two-thirds of these were serious criminal charges (Lateef 2017). Various explanations have been put forward for political parties nominating criminals including the possibility of criminal charges levelled by opposition parties out of revenge; nomination as a reward for undertaking criminal activity on behalf of political parties; the belief that parliamentary membership offers a degree of protection for those facing conviction; and the notion that those with criminal connections can 'get things done' for the electorate (Lateef 2017; Koul 2018).

The Economist Democracy Index rates India in a category called 'flawed democracy' (The Economist Intelligence Unit 2018a). At 41st place out of 167 countries, India is in the camp of countries which, although having relatively free and fair elections and traditions of respect for civil liberties, have problems in respect of governance (functioning of government), political culture (e.g. perceptions of importance of democracy), and political participation (e.g. citizen engagement with politics, women in parliament, participation in political parties and in political NGO's).

Various proposals (and indeed some actions) have been put forward including public expenditure on elections and caps, further limits on individual contributions, and emphasis on electronic traceability of donor funds (Jalan 2018; Panda 2019a). Even beyond these useful measures and suggestions, this author suggests hitting corrupt politicians 'where it hurts'. Where violations of campaign funding guidelines have been found after careful auditing (results of the audits would be made public), votes could be deducted based on the extent of deviation from donor limits. For example, 10% extra donations beyond limits would result in 10% deduction of votes for a party in a constituency where the violation occurs. Electronic traceability of funds is key to make this work. Even further, if funds cannot be traced electronically then this would result in immediate disbarment of candidates.

Dissatisfaction with the state of democracy has led to the rise of grass roots movements, and urgent clarion calls for reform. The issue here is less about the overall conduct of elections in the sense of process but rather the practice of democracy in the way parliament and government works, its relationship to its constituents and the efficiency and effectiveness of democracy. In this context, while strictly not related to the knowledge economy in India, it is an over-arching institutional feature which shapes and influences the functioning of democracy and which underpins the passage or non-passage of legislation in the national interest. Moreover, innovations in institutional design and character are part and parcel of a knowledge economy and society.

To enhance the democratic system of government, a key part of the market adjunct domain is no easy mission. Yet there are a number of options that we propose.

2.17.1 Composition of Parliament

At the very least the composition of parliament should reflect its societal composition. As such, over time there could be changes to the way selections of candidates are made with requirements that election funding in both the public and private realms be dependent on changes in composition of potential parliamentarians. We also advocate that consideration could be given to a series of sub-parliaments, e.g. youth and female, with elected representatives of these sub-parliaments further electing members to the main parliament, via reserved seats.

Another key aspect does directly relate to the world of knowledge and ideas. While knowledge, ideas and innovation flow across national boundaries, could not the political representation reflect the opening up of India? Although highly contentious, since there is likely to be a significant element of the population who are opposed to Indians moving abroad amid concerns about 'brain drain', one possibility could be to reserve seats for Indian diaspora, elected by the diaspora.[12] This would refresh parliament, bring new ideas into the mix, and reflect the contribution that the vibrant, active and influential diaspora brings in terms of remittances, commercial ties, cultural engagement and scientific and technological know-how, among other things.

This could be achieved by allowing the diaspora regional voting blocs where the number of representatives from these voting blocs in the Indian Parliament is linked to the proportion of the population of Indian diaspora in regions abroad, or based on share of remittances originating from various regions. This would reflect a mature approach to India's 'soft power' and influence abroad and would further link Indians abroad to their county of birth. In this way relationships would be extended even beyond the valuable money flows that non-resident Indians (NRIs) bring and give rise to further change and influence. With NRIs increasingly being given greater opportunity to invest and conduct business, this would be a further extension of growing engagement with the diaspora.

---

[12] A similar notion was put forward as an idea for Australia more than a decade ago (Duncan et al. 2004).

2.17.2 Parliamentary Process

Another issue for reform is the parliamentary processes themselves. As we have seen, too often, bills are delayed or deferred. A number of possibilities can be canvassed. Firstly, an expanded role for the Electoral Commission to establish rules which mandate the passage of bills in a proscribed time frame could be considered, with penalties imposed on those blocking bills such as suspension from the parliament or some form of monetary penalty. Of course, if the rule makers themselves are at fault, how likely is that they will be open to such suggestions? One would be hopeful that media pressure, citizen movements activities and pressures from constituents themselves disadvantaged by the inaction of political leaders, could be an impetus for change. One other possibility to reform parliament is to have an elected council, separate from any political party or government, comprising eminent persons to advise political parties, hasten decision-making and mediate agreement to break parliamentary deadlocks (Murthy 2016).

Citizen drafting of bills and voting prior to being submitted to parliament is a possibility, amplifying direct citizen participation in legislative matters and decision-making, as is the use of social media to track performance by politicians against electoral promises, and more broadly the use of micro surveys via phone and online means to identify key issues at the local level (Saunders and Mulgan 2017). This would engage citizens and serve to understand the impacts of government decisions at the micro level. Such measures would break the hold that careerist politicians have on legislative matters.

Finally, we would argue for new processes regarding the confirmation of appointment of ministers and senior most bureaucrats. This could be thrown open to the public once the initial selection process has been undertaken. One method of doing so is to have U.S style confirmation hearings. These hearings could be conducted through a combination of judiciary (who would have to meet the highest standards of probity) and the public, via elected representatives of citizens groups, with broad representation reflecting societal composition. The Electoral Commission, or High Court, could, as appropriate, inviolate ministerial or senior bureaucratic appointments.

2.17.3 Conduct of Elections

Despite elections being relatively clean affairs, there is considerable scope for improvement in their conduct.

One possibility is for the Commission for Government to develop comprehensive pre-election economic, social and environmental scenarios. These scenarios would provide an important frame of reference for each political party's election manifesto, and ensure an objective basis upon which to develop and promote policies, and potentially augment scenarios. This means that political parties' manifestos and election promises would be guided by the best available publicly available information presented by experts, would have a common basis of fact, and thus reduce the potential for exaggeration and manipulation about the real state of the economy and society. Taken further, scenarios would be informed by feedback and participation from the public. Thus, the public would help to shape the parameters upon which elections are fought, and subsequently vote on policies based on the scenarios that they helped to create.

Two related features are proposed. Firstly, that costs of each party's programme, based on whatever scenario, it utilises, would be provided to and audited by the Election Commission for accuracy and would mitigate the outrageous practice of 'vote buying' by parties to reach out to various vested interests. While there may be huge questions about the extent of proposed influence by the Electoral Commission, the fact remains that the Electoral Commission in India is a body which has a good track record for being clean, effective, efficient, accountable and transparent.

The second key element is what we describe as 'trade-off' honesty declarations. Political parties would be obliged to specify in detail their priorities, and what associated tradeoffs or opportunity costs that this entails. For example, based on particular scenarios, a particular party may choose to place greater weight on environmental outcomes and environmental management. The party would need to specify what this might mean, for example, in terms of possible economic growth foregone or vice-a versa. Likewise, a party may choose to promote a stronger export stance, which may compromise on domestic consumption. These tradeoffs would need to be explicitly made, articulated and presented.

Finally, and potentially on a trial basis, is the possibility of issue-based democracy. While the population would vote for a preferred party on the basis of its overall platform, there could also be a series of micro votes related to particular issues, where the particular issues would be specified in advance. Thus, it is quite possible for the overall party of power to be different from those elected to manage particular issues. The advantage of this approach would be to drive bipartisanship and specialisation and allow for a more segmented, finely tuned democracy, in the sense of people voting for very specific issues and policies, rather than a bundle of policies which may not entirely capture their needs, aspirations and objectives. In turn, it means that political parties need to be rigorous in all of the policies that they put forward, and would need to make greater effort in developing, articulating and selling each and every policy to the electorate.

The options for reform proposed here, can be facilitated and enhanced through extensive deployment of information and communications technology. For example, one can visualise a system of voting akin to Facebook 'likes'. This of course presupposes access, utilisation and skills in ICT and bridging the digital divide in the nation.

Another possibility put forward is to have 'right of recall' (Kalam and Singh 2015) whereby elected representatives can lose their representation for misdeeds if sufficient numbers of the population call for it (by petition for example), with subsequent elections held. A change of representative should occur if a new candidate receives more votes than the incumbent.

Of course, many of the changes proposed here would require significant constitutional amendment, and these matters are beyond the scope of this book.

2.18 Corruption

Earlier, we canvassed some of the key tenets of India's business environment. One issue that we delve into further is corruption.

Corruption continues to be a significant issue in India, like a cancer eating away at the body of Indian life. Fuelled in large measure by the buying and peddling of influence associated with the 'Licence-Permit-Quota Raj' and more recently the 'Resource Raj' (with the offering of inducements in return for permits and licenses to operate), corruption in India has taken on a life of its own. There are many and varied manifestations of this we have alluded to, including the close nexus between bureaucrats and politicians, corruption in the judiciary and police force, rigged appointments in many key positions, for example in higher education, criminality among elected representatives, bribery and cream skimming in relation to government contracts, and the presence of dishonest intermediaries in agricultural and other key markets. Between October 2011 and September 2012, the estimated loss to the Indian economy from corruption reached around £4 billion (Saunders and Mulgan 2017), while other estimates have loss to GDP of 62% from corruption (Das 2019). It is also observed that there is a corruption multiplier, i.e. loss to society of 3–4 times the monetary gain for the corrupt, associated with broader deleterious impacts on productivity, efficiency and investment, project delays, loss of tax revenue and poor quality of goods and services. Indeed, it is pointed out that corruption has a negative impact on the investment to national income ratio through choice of projects that are uneconomic and subject to delay (Jalan 2018). There are further issues since lower income countries would be reliant on critical public investments, which are likely to be associated with corruption, in turn giving rise to adverse impacts on economic outcomes, thus obviating the initial intent of investment (Jalan 2018).

2.18.1 India's Performance on Corruption

How does India fare overall on corruption?

According to the Corruption Perception Index of 2018 (Transparency International 2019), which is an amalgam of a range of indices, India is in 78th place out of 180 and continues to face significant challenges. Although improving slightly in score terms and rank last year, India had been declining in rank in the three previous years. It is currently however considerably behind developed nations, as one might expect, but better placed than its BRIC counterparts and superior to its regional neighbours in Sri Lanka, Pakistan and Bangladesh. That is 'goodish' news. However, India does lag behind a number of emerging economies in Malaysia and Chile, with whom it may also naturally be compared. As the Transparency International indicates, 'Despite spectacular public mobilisation in 2011, where citizens demanded that the government take action against corruption and advocated for the passage of the comprehensive Jan Lokpal Act, these efforts ultimately fizzled and fell flat, with little to no movement on the ground to build the specialist anti-corruption infrastructure required' (Transparency International 2019, 2018, Index, p. 1). Of course, there is a view that corruption, if channelled in a strategic way, through targeted growth sectors, can be a vehicle for achieving economic growth as in China, and other parts of Asia, and that the presence of middle persons can actually raise their status and income (Crabtree 2018). However, we would suggest that the economic and societal costs of corruption would far outweigh any perceived benefits. According to the crony capitalism index (The Economist 2016), India is 9th out of 22 countries (the lower the ranked number the more cronyism), where cronyism is defined as billionaire wealth from rent heavy sectors.

Corruption Perception results from the previous year, i.e. the 2017 index, confirm that India has had a poor record when looked at against its Asia-Pacific counterparts, and also highlighted the lack of press freedoms in India, and indeed significant violence against journalists (Transparency International 2018; Salas 2018).

The deep, entrenched and systemic nature of corruption is also reflected at all levels. According to the most recent Local Circles report (Local Circles 2018), based on a survey of citizens across the nation, more than half had paid bribes, up 15% from the previous year. Bribes were most commonly paid in relation to property registration and land issues and to the police and municipal corporations. An overwhelming majority were not aware of help lines, while only one third considered that states had taken measures to address corruption, and even then this has not been effective.

2.19 Anti-corruption Measures

What is to be done? On the one hand there is the need to strengthen and reform the processes of government and governance, and political participation of citizens. We outlined a series of measures earlier to promote greater citizen input, involvement and participation in the life of the nation, which may go some way to addressing corruption. The Right to Information Act is an excellent example of an initiative to drive accountability forward. We would extend that to 'The Right to Action Act' whereby the number of requests for information which exceed a certain amount must trigger action on the issue. Public pressure and the collective weight of information requests would be required. Safeguards would need to be put in place to mitigate against 'gaming the system'. Others propose that the Right to Information should be driven by compelling institutions and agencies to release information in any case, as a matter of course, rather than waiting for requests for release (Jalan 2018).

One idea worth considering is to change or attempt to change incentive structures. For example, bonuses could be provided to civil servants, at all levels of government,

2.19 Anti-corruption Measures

linked to India's performance in the Corruption Perceptions Index or related index. Penalties for declining performance would also be implemented.

Another interesting suggestion to change 'how the game is played' is to exempt from penalties, at least for petty corruption, those who give bribes for routine tasks which should occur anyway, with penalties still for those who demand bribes. This suggestion, could at least mean theoretically that those paying the bribe will have the disincentive to inform on bribe requesters removed, possibly leading to less demand for bribes (Mundle 2017). Of course, it does go without saying that government officials, are highly unlikely to take measures to penalise themselves. The machinations associated with the Lokpal (Corruption Ombudsman) Bill is a case in point. However, when allied with other approaches, including stronger whistle blower regulations and measures suggested below, then things might change, when looked at as an integrated whole. One further issue is that legislation has focussed on civil servants malpractice, rather than the private sector itself, or the private sector's relationship with government (Debroy 2019). This anomalous situation, given that there are two players in the bribery game, the giver and the taker, has been addressed in the most recent law with bribe giving now an offence (Local Circles 2018). Nonetheless, for all this, India faces some extreme challenges in corruption.

At the institutional level, 'Corruption India' an integrated national and sub-national online database, maintained by an independent concerned citizens authority could be put in place. An associated corruption index could be established to identify, track and monitor bribery and corruption with annual public reporting against achievements (or not) made in reducing corruption, both on the taking and giving dimensions of bribery. This would mean a greater balance to the 'demand' and 'supply' aspects of corruption. Such a mechanism could have strong exhortative effects, and its purpose would be to bring external pressure to bear on public authorities. A traffic light system could be undertaken to grade corrupt activities according to red, amber and green light for the severity of the infringement and the urgency of action required. The traffic light would then guide the nature and extent of action demanded. Citizen voice, allied with media reporting and inquiry, would then help to influence the taking of appropriate action.

This mechanism could be funded and supported by citizen groups and concerned individuals through crowd source funding, NGO funds and from overseas, including concerned diaspora. In so doing, it would provide focussed effort, scale and deployment of resources in a consolidated fashion. It would be an interactive arrangement in that citizens would add their knowledge and experience of corruption at all levels of government to this database, as a means of providing an updatable register of corruption. It would be akin to the successful 'Neighbourhood Watch' programme in other nations, which is citizen led action aimed at identifying and monitoring crime action in a locality.

Another important idea calls for a Business-Community Institution (BCI), an organisation which could provide ratings of companies on corruption, starting only with publicly listed companies and then others on a voluntary basis. Only high rated companies ratings would be made publicly available, meaning some implicit pressure on those whose ratings were not made public. The BCI would be funded by a combination of non-corporate initial funding, and membership fees, and would be supported by specialist capabilities to undertake advocacy, research, media activities and outreach to like-minded corporations, individuals and institutions (Mundle 2017; Dixit and Mankar 2018).

Various similar initiatives are underway in India. For example, Janngraha is a not for profit organisation in which citizens anonymously report instances of being asked to pay bribes. Close to 50,000 reports have been filed on the website in over 630 cities across India (Saunders and Mulgan 2017). The 'I paid a bribe' (2019) movement is another example of real-time citizen reporting (I Paid a Bribe 2019).

Already measures to improve transparency of government activities through use of information and communications technology in public procurement, and other details of government contracts is promising, and should be accelerated at both national and state levels.

We propose, somewhat contentiously, to give a certain 'quasi respectability' to bribery and corruption. This is to provide some degree of legal immunity from prosecution for people and institutions to turn 'black money' into 'white money', and deposit ill-gotten gains into a fund which could be used either to further fight corruption or to be used for social development purposes. While at one glance this may appear to be tacitly 'rewarding', or at least not penalising criminal behaviour it may alter some of the thinking associated with corruption. It could also redress the drain from the real economy of significant amounts of money. The proceeds from turning 'black' into 'white' would then be used to fund critical infrastructure and basic services.

Finally, this author suggests that action around corruption needs to start at an early age. It is a long-term process to wean societies off the lure of corruption. Too easily, the culture of corruption becomes casualised, entrenched and accepted at all levels of society. As such, education and awareness in school and higher forms of learning through compulsory ethics and values courses right the way through to higher education could be implemented, as could tangible, practical projects, as part of the curricula at school level (and above), including working with the community to identify corruption, and develop solutions at local level and advocate for its redress.

2.19.1 Demonetisation

Demonetisation policy implemented in 2016, aimed at removing notes from circulation in the name of reducing corruption, has unleashed the full spectrum of views. On the one hand, the Government's own Economic Survey (Government of India 2018) claims that after an initial downturn the economy is back on the positive track, while others are critical in various degrees about the adverse impact on the poor, on various sectors, and for those dependent on cash, as well as on the informal sector which dominates the economy. Others speak of implementation flaws, and that a 'black market for the black market' has sprung up (Alam 2017; Goswami 2016; Nordman and Guerin 2018). Others again are even more scathing likening it to theft and the worst excesses of the Emergency of the 1970s (Forbes 2016). Some are more careful pointing to costs of the scheme but suggesting that the 'jury is still out' and that many inter-related factors including the almost concurrent imposition of the GST alongside demonetisation, needs to be factored in (Dutta and Kulkarni 2018). Moreover, whether it has, and to what extent it has alleviated corruption, (the core intent of the policy), is certainly open to much questioning.

Despite these views, it can be said with reasonable certainty that the policy was not an unmitigated success, which goes to the heart of the implementation issues that have so bedevilled India.

2.20 Inequality

While the foregoing analysis has focussed on the governance and public action related to corruption, there are further deeper elements to consider.

There is a strong correlation between corruption and social exclusion, with regression analysis showing that social inclusion is a significantly greater predictor of corruption than GDP per capita. There is an unfortunate cycle of corruption leading to unequal distribution of power leading to unequal wealth and opportunity and so on (Heinrich 2017). Thus breaking this cycle is a key to reform.

Corruption therefore in this judgement is tied up strongly with inequality. Of course inequality is not merely linked to corruption but has wider premises including poor standards of governance and delivery of essential services, misplaced priorities in resource allocation, lack of employment generation and other societal based discriminations facing particular social groups. According to the UN Human Development Index, adjusted for inequality in life expectancy, education and income inequality, India is 131st in the world out of 189 countries, well behind BRIC countries and various Asian countries including Thailand, Malaysia, Indonesia, Philippines, Vietnam and Sri Lanka, with among the highest levels of inequality in the world on education and very significant in the other two categories (United Nations (UN) 2018). A recent Oxfam 'Commitment to Reducing Inequality index' (Oxfam 2018a) which measures government spending on health, education and social protection (as a share of total government expenditure), progressivity of the tax system (tax collection, tax laws, e.g. anti-avoidance, tax impacts on inequality) and labour rights (minimum wage, worker and labour union rights, and women's legal right at work) showed that India was ranked a miserable 147th out of 157 countries overall, 151st on spending, and 141st on labour rights and wages. While India was placed an apparently creditable 50th on progressivity of the tax system, there are many challenges in respect of the efficiency and effectiveness of the collection of taxes (Oxfam 2018a).

Oxfam (2018b) finds that if India were to reduce inequality by one third, 170 million people would no longer be poor. Even more damning is that the increase in Indian billionaires wealth over the last year would be enough to finance 85% of all the states budgets on health and education, and that the increase in the wealth of the richest one percent (which accounted for 73% of the wealth generated in the last year) would be equivalent to the total budget of the central government in

2017–2018. Further, and staggeringly, it would take 941 years for a minimum wage worker in rural India to earn the equivalent of a top executive in a leading Indian garment company in a year and just over 17 days for the same executive to earn the lifetime income of a minimum rural worker in India (Oxfam 2018b).

Various other studies find highly uncomfortable levels of inequality in India when compared to most other countries, bar South Africa, as well as experiencing one of the largest and rapidly growing inequality outcomes in Asia. Then there is a large urban–rural divide, and inequality between States. Of course, there are many concerns with inequality including lack of social cohesion, the absence of civil society tenets, lack of consensus for structural reforms in an economy, and that pervasive inequality can lead to poorer economic growth outcomes and financial instability. This is contrary to the older notions that inequality is pronounced at early stages of a nation's development which then diminishes as countries grow and become wealthier (Crabtree 2018).

2.20.1 What Are Solutions to Rampant Inequality?

A variety of remedies have been put forward to address inequality and poverty, including wealth taxes, and globally agreed taxes on capital (Piketty 2014). The political 'saleability' of these remedies is highly problematic. One measure that has garnered increasing attention in India, including in the context of the 2019 election campaign, and abroad, is a Universal Basic income (UBI). At its simplest, the UBI is a blanket income for all in society regardless of their wealth or employment situation. There are many positives with the approach including its conceptual simplicity, guaranteed income support, allowing time to seek a job or start a business rather than attempt to 'take any job', and avoidance of the private and social costs that come with more targeted welfare programmes, including problems of how to target, leakage and corruption. In addition, there are issues such as stigmatisation of beneficiaries and the political costs when segments of the population are excluded. Further, the presence of 'gaming' to attempt to qualify for targeted assistance is mitigated. On the negative side of the equation are concerns about the cost to budget and the economy of a universal scheme, payments being usurped by dominant members of a household (e.g. males), creation of disincentives to work, and that unconditional support could lead to expenditure on 'frivolous' items. Societal angst about the richest receiving payments, and concern that such universal schemes could come at the cost of effective programmes and the provision of essential public goods, are also key points (Government of India 2017a; Khosla 2018).

2.20.2 UBI for India?

The Indian Government's own assessment of a 'nearly UBI', which would exclude the top 25% of wealthy individuals, was that it would cost 4.9% of GDP. Other proposals of a similar nature varying by levels of income support and degree of universality, have the costs ranging from 3.5% to 11% of GDP. Various alternate proposals have been put forward such as linking payments to GDP rather than fixed amounts or straight out interest loans to poorer segments (Government of India 2017a; Khosla 2018).

Pilot UBI programs run in Madya Pradesh and Delhi produced interesting results. In the former, which involved unconditional monthly benefits in addition to existing welfare arrangements, benefits were noted in respect of improved living conditions, purchase of household assets, improved nutrition and public services. In the latter case, which encompassed payments in lieu of subsidised food and which were provided to female heads of households, and thereby had a more limited remit, benefits were observed in increased expenditure on nutritional foods. No adverse impacts on calorie consumption were noted (Khosla 2018). However, from conducting small pilots to implementing an all embracing national universal effort would seem a leap too far. On the international front, a pilot scheme in Finland aimed at the unemployed, did not provide any real evidence of improved labour market outcomes, but rather, gains were observed in terms of health, lessening of stress and greater wellbeing, of themselves laudable outcomes (Kangas et al. 2019).

The author considers the UBI, on balance, to be something worth exploring in India. However, given the difficulties of implementing such a scheme, including costs and potential issues associated with dimunition or removal of other programmes, our approach is to *suggest conditional choice* based transfer mechanisms at least in the interim, linked to the knowledge economy. By this is meant providing, in effect, vouchers for targeted groups (e.g. females, minorities, those significantly below the poverty line, long term unemployed or those in particularly vulnerable employment) but with user choice in pre-determined areas such as (a) education and training (b) job ready skills (c) development of entrepreneurship capabilities and even possibly (d) knowledge-based community development projects via pooled funds at the local level, which in turn would stimulate work experience, develop skills and contribute to raised social capital.

Under this mechanism, there would be both targeted support, potentially lessening cost constraints while allowing citizens to best choose what works for them. It would also be linked to the knowledge economy to stimulate capability building in this arena. Brazil has had reasonable successful experience with conditional transfer mechanisms (Dreze and Sen 2013). However, ours is of a conditional choice based variety, with support services provided to assist recipients to make better informed choices. Of course, we do not discount the administrative complexities associated with this approach, but with tools of big data, predictive analytics and using the machinery of existing programmes, these issues and complexities may not be insurmountable.

Over time, we would envisage a 'two envelope' UBI of sorts, subject to trial and full benefit cost-analysis, including private and social benefits/costs. The first envelope would be a basic income payment, say paid to the lowest 40% or so in the community with further targeting along the lines of the conditional choice transfer mechanisms.

2.21 Critical Challenges

This section considers three particularly challenging areas for India: Health; Housing; and Food/Agriculture. It is in these three areas that we illustrate the sorts of policy reforms, innovations and initiatives consistent with the knowledge economy, and an appropriate role for government in the context of the Enabling State. These three areas could also represent the flexibility of interventions, in this case at the sectoral level, to address critical missions.

To begin with, we refer to the Empowerment Line developed by McKinsey Global Institute (2014). An Empowerment Line is the minimum required cost for a household to consume basic needs (food, energy, housing, water, sanitation, health care, education and social security), and the Empowerment Gap is the difference between current consumption and that calculated by the Empowerment Line. This gap was estimated to be 4% of GDP. Further, the Empowerment Line's minimum consumption was considered to be 1.5 times that of the official poverty line. Health, food and housing are among the key drivers of the Empowerment Gap.

2.22 Health

While noting India's improvement in relation to maternal health and child mortality, (Mor et al. 2017), massive challenges remain. According to the Health Access and Quality Index, India is ranked 145th in the world out of 195 countries, which measures a comprehensive range of diseases, including communicable and non-communicable diseases. Compared to its overall score, India performs weaker on multiple conditions, including TB, various forms of cancer, hypertension, diabetes, strokes and heart disease (The Lancet 2018). The number of Indians with diabetes has grown from 26 million in 1990 to 65 million in 2016, obstructive pulmonary disease sufferers from 28 million to 55 million over the same period, cancers have increased by 28% and the contribution of cardiovascular diseases to total deaths has almost doubled since 1990 (Horton 2018), not to mention the mental health crisis that is engulfing the nation in terms of suicides and other conditions. Higher performing countries on socio-demographic factors (a measure of income per capita, average years of education, and total fertility rates) had higher scores generally on the Health Access and Quality Index, as is to be expected. India's performance on the Health Access and Quality index is weaker than Bangladesh, Sri Lanka (by a considerable margin), the rest of the BRIC nations, and other emerging economies such as the Philippines, Malaysia, Indonesia, Thailand and Vietnam. Yet India does score higher on socio-economic demographic factors than many of these countries, meaning that in theory at least India should be able to perform better than these countries. It is also the case that in the study (The Lancet 2018), that the disparities on the index within India are among the highest in the world (as is the case with China).

In a previous analysis, the observed index score was compared with what could/should be expected given a country's socio-demographic profile. India has considerably underperformed on health relative to its socio-demographic profile and this under-performance has worsened over time between 1990 and 2015 (The Lancet 2017).

That the Indian situation is extremely challenging is in no small way linked to a number of related factors. On a comparative assessment against BRIC nations, South Asian economies, and other emerging Asian economies, India suffers from infrastructure deficiencies (e.g. beds for mentally ill patients in hospital), human resource deficiencies (physician and nursing density per 1000 population), and lower shares of government funding on health as a share of total health expenditure and overall government expenditure, and on a per capita basis. This has meant an over-reliance on the private sector, raising significant issues of access and equity, and high out of pocket expenses which has aligned with limited insurance access. An upshot of this weak public spending when compared to other nations, is that India's overall expenditure on health as a share of GDP is low when judged against other nations (UN 2018; World Health Organisation (WHO) 2019). To this can be added absenteeism of health professionals, corruption, capacity building constraints, malpractice and fraud, and lack of regulatory oversight in terms of standards (Dreze and Sen 2013; Joshi 2016; Ninan 2015).

Therefore, India confronts many stark realities. It needs to put in place reforms in a number of areas including; an integrated healthcare approach, emphasising both preventive and high quality responsive care for physical and mental health which contrasts with the current fragmented approach; a user centric 'patient first' approach regardless of capacity to pay; a stronger role for the public sector in expenditure, oversight and coordination, within the context of public–private collaboration, which we shall speak of soon; the need for balance between competition and collaboration in the health sector to achieve efficiencies, and obtain the knowledge synergies to build capabilities; a whole of India approach emphasising both urban, regional and remote areas in a planned manner; the continued introduction of innovation in the use and deployment of technology, business and organisational models; a collective approach that involves the deployment and use of existing community based skills, knowledge, insights and capabilities; and the need to consider health policy in broader and wider policy contexts such as food and nutrition policy, spatial development and climate and environmental policy.

2.22.1 Model for Health Care in India

Our model for health care in India embodies the innovation and partnership approach that we have been emphasising as part of the Enabling State. It involves an integrated healthcare approach, is patient centric, aims for analytic and evidence-based approaches with a whole of health orientation, including holistic and preventative approaches.

A core component of our health system involves integrated networks of public and private providers, operating in partnership, emphasising and building synergies around their respective complementary capabilities, addressing gaps in the system in the pursuit of complete care, in a timely and responsive manner. An independent National Health Regulator would call for bids among health provider networks who would necessarily comprise public, private and community-based health specialists, operating across the primary, secondary and tertiary segments,[13] in conjunction with alternate/traditional medicine providers. Competitive network bids would be called for using criteria of cost, efficient delivery, collaborative capabilities, innovation in healthcare (including for example use of technology such as telemedicine, mobile health care, home and community-based care), commitment to capability building (e.g. training of skilled personnel) and equity considerations. The location of networks would be driven and informed by overall detailed spatial needs and considerations in consultation with state and local governments. Networks could also include medical research and pharmaceutical representation. Compared to the traditional metrics focussed on cost considerations, this wider set of criteria would be employed to determine and measure performance of the successful network, along the lines mentioned above. The networks would operate on a for-profit basis with strict safeguards and standards overseen by the Health regulator in terms of pricing schedules (and movements), probity, quality, accountability and governance.

The other important aspect of the system that we envisage is to have initial Referral Centres or frontline first port of call mechanisms, in which patients attend in person (or online) to obtain a first diagnosis (based on e-health records available to the individual and the Referral Centres), and early advice regarding type and extent of health care required within the primary, secondary and tertiary health network. Referral Centres would operate even before the primary health care facilities are brought into play, and would operate independently of the networks. The Referral Centres would be publicly owned and managed, to provide objective, independent advice and information to patients, and in this way serve as an important 'health broker' to address information asymmetries between patients and health providers. It would be staffed by health professionals, including community health workers. On a related note is the possibility of employing information brokers to manage health records and information for individuals. The initial assessment and referral pave the way for subsequent referrals through the system.

---

[13] Primary Health Care is usually general practice and allied health. Secondary care is mostly hospital based and specialised. Tertiary is even more specialised.

2.22.2 Funding of the System

In terms of funding of the system we envisage the establishment of a commercially oriented, joint venture company, with an autonomous Board, to purchase services from the preferred network. This commercial entity would be distinct from the Health Regulator to ensure that there is no conflict of interest or blurring of boundaries. It would comprise government equity and private equity (funds for which would be facilitated by tax breaks) and purchase health care from the networks with strict performance criteria, as advanced earlier. Bonus for over-achievement would be paid to the successful networks, and penalties for under-performance would be put in place, thus incentivising the selected networks. The funding vehicle would derive income from its own separate investments, and from dividend payments from the networks (who would be allowed to operate on a profit-based approach provided equity and distributional considerations were explicitly met). The government equity component of the joint venture company would serve to meet the basic health needs of the less profitable segments of the network, usually the primary healthcare component. To support the system, we also envisage that there would be some means tested patient co-payment for the primary sector, to both assist in funding the system, and to prevent over-use of its services. Further, we would argue that network charges would move between price bands across the entire system, to contain costs and ensure stability but also provide flexibility of pricing with the overall network profitability in mind. Under certain circumstances, the joint company could also, in addition to its purchasing role, be an investor in the network (although this would need to be carefully distinguished from the purchaser role to ensure probity, transparency and proper accountabilities), as a means of injecting more capital.

We also envisage that there is an important role for insurance providers, including social insurance and micro insurance providers, to ensure greater coverage and that equity concerns are addressed, especially in regard to the more expensive and complex secondary and tertiary segments of the network. This would be through a combination of employer sponsored insurance on behalf of employees (chapter five has more detail on this), and Government funded insurance for those who cannot avail themselves of employer funded mechanisms, due to poverty, unemployment, underemployment and/or where the employer is unable to do so (e.g. businesses in the unorganised sector).

2.22.3 Collaboration and Partnerships

The envisaged system would work on the basis of collaboration and partnership. Although containing elements of purchaser-provider approaches, the emphasis here is much more on drawing together **complementary capabilities** in the network through deep partnerships to forge national health assets, rather than purely arm's-length transactions, for perceived efficiencies. The deployment of optimal health delivery drawing on the disparate, complementary and specialist capabilities of members of the network, and flexibility (e.g. skilled personnel could be deployed rapidly in parts of the network from other parts depending on need and circumstances), are hallmarks of the system. An emphasis in the system is on capability building to address chronic shortages in skilled personnel, through comprehensive training undertaken by the network, who would be specialists in health care. The capacity for, and track record, in training and skill development would be an important part of the network selection process.

Compared to the National Health Policy 2017 ((Government of India 2017b) which does, it should be said, have some common aspects to what we propose)) which calls for the private sector just to "fill in gaps" that the public sector cannot meet, we call for a much more integrated public/private/community approach, recognising complementary capabilities. Further, our approach can be distinguished from that put forward by NITI Aayog (2017) which views the public and private sectors in competition.[14]

Delivery of the networks would be through special purpose public–private partnership modes. Public–private partnerships of this kind can have significant impact and importance, but India has had a patchy record in these areas due to delays in approval, lack of appropriate risk apportionment, the need for more flexibility in responding to changing circumstances among other things, and requirement for greater institutional capacity to monitor, evaluate and establish projects (Government of India 2015: The Kelkar Committee). Development of institutional capability to manage such activities is also a key requirement as our chapter on education will address. Further, the experience and expertise of the Indian diaspora, and other foreign providers, who could bid for network selection, is also important in this light. The key to our proposed approach is that it is less of a traditional PPP where a public asset is financed and run by a private entity, but rather based on a genuine partnership approach, far less about contracting out of services, but more focussed on deep cooperation founded on the relative strengths, complementarities and synergies, of the various parties, including the private and public (and community sectors).

The networks can also be virtual in their design and delivery, particularly as they relate to more remote areas. In this case, use of telemedicine and mobile health vans with electronic connection to the nearest hospital may be considered. India is currently in the midst of a mobile revolution with the presence of education and health options available by roving specialists (World Bank 2012). New innovations, including such things as portable electro cardiograms are making this possible. These are the sorts of technologies and capabilities that need to be exploited.

In terms of inter-governmental arrangements, it is suggested that the health system be funded on a shared basis between centre and states with the amount of funding by states subject to 'capacity to pay' testing. The delivery of specific networks could be overseen by local government agencies. Oversight of the whole health system would be through the independent National Health Regulator (including oversight of the commercial vehicle that we outlined) but would be subject itself to oversight by a

---

[14] There ae also some elements of what we propose in Mor et al. (2017).

Board comprising health experts and government representatives from all tiers. In the end, the exact nature and specifications of the various tiers of government would be a matter for the Commission for Government.

The recent announcements by the Modi Government to provide publicly funded insurance for the poorest segments of society (Ayushman Bharat: Long Life India) and to implement health and wellness centres are at face value, welcome and consistent in some senses with what we propose, although there has been a mixed response. While some have lauded the announcements (Lancet Editorial 2018), various criticisms have been mounted, including doctors and hospitals being left out of pocket (low purchase prices), over-emphasis on hospitalisation, and under-emphasis on primary care, underfunding of the scheme and poor condition of existing health centres (village clinics) as well as the lack of rigorous planning on a spatial basis (Doshi 2018; The Economist 2018b; Saxena 2018).

2.23 Housing

India faces a number of challenges and issues in the housing sector. Some estimates have the shortage of urban housing in India at around 19 million houses, even higher, driven in the main by households living in congested areas and obsolescent housing, with 96% of the shortages accounted for by the economically weaker sections of the community (Palayi and Priyaranjan 2018). This requirement for housing is expected to grow significantly as the urbanisation of the Indian economy proceeds rapidly with some estimating that demand for affordable housing is likely to reach 38 million by 2030 (Palayi and Priyaranjan 2018). This is not to deny the existence also of considerable rural/regional housing shortages. In fact, some estimates have the rural housing demand to be higher than urban (Tiwari and Rao 2016). Further, the Indian housing scene is characterised by a large swathe of vacant housing (Tilotia 2015), which is out of the reach of those in lower income groups, and often fuelled by black money.

To be sure, the Government has put in place the Housing for all by 2022 programme 'Pradhan Mantri Awas Yojanna' and subsequent policies, which among other things, provide credit subsidies, affordable housing public–private partnerships, granting of infrastructure status for housing to allow cheaper access to finance, reforms to capital gains tax arrangements and the lowering of GST on affordable housing (Palayi and Priyaranjan 2018; FICCI and CBRE 2018; KPMG 2018). The Housing for All policy called for 20,000,000 houses to be built by 2022. As of August 2018, only 800,000 homes were built (KPMG 2018).

Inspite of the various initiatives the housing sector continues to face numerous challenges including: land shortage and high prices (especially in urban areas) and associated affordability constraints; bottlenecks in approval processes; need for greater capacity among agencies (and reduction in silos) in relation to planning, design and execution; overlapping, blurred responsibilities, and lack of alignment between various tiers of government; skills shortages; density and floor space constraints; and severe weaknesses in the rental market (onerous dispute resolution conditions and difficulties of eviction, capping of rents (FICCI and CBRE 2018; KPMG 2018; Palayi and Priyaranjan 2018; Deloitte 2016).

2.23.1 A Comprehensive Approach to Housing

A comprehensive housing approach in India is needed based on the **knowledge economy** precept and which again goes to the heart of the appropriate role of government. Firstly, we argue for *diversity* in housing to address the needs of the disparate demographic and social groups in Indian society. Housing should be segmented, targeted and designed around the varying needs of the community including the elderly, youth and transient populations in terms of size, facilities, structure and fit out. India could become an exemplar of multifaceted 'fit for purpose', 'fit for community', segmented and needs-based housing. For example, despite much talk of India's demographic dividend with its bulging youth numbers, it is the case that India's older age cohort is significant and growing in number. Housing with the latest facilities to suit the needs of the elderly is an important issue.

Overseas experience is illuminating. The Netherlands is undertaking a world first 3D printing of houses, for example. This involves the latest development in customised technology and use of sustainable building practices and designs. As a recent report claims "…the technology allowed it to create homes in almost any shape, and to print in 'all kinds, qualities and colours of concrete', all in a single product" (ABC News 2018).

Opportunities abound of this kind in India, relying on the synergies between research, technology, design principles, customisation, sustainability and differentiated need.

A starting point would be a comprehensive housing audit exercise conducted every five years by metropolitan and municipal bodies, to address critical shortages against need, where need is identified not only in aggregate but by type of housing. Second, is that flexibility in institutional responsiveness is needed. This has multiple dimensions, including fast approval for housing projects and the ability to efficiently identify, purchase and convert disused land and redundant property (e.g. closed down of factories) into housing possibilities. This requires institutional coordination, ability to identify opportunities for flexible land use, and a capacity to act quickly upon these opportunities including sophisticated purchasing mechanisms in the manner of the vigilant state. To give expression to this, we advocate the establishment of Construct India, a new organisation, which could be tasked with purchasing property that has become disused or redundant and in turn leased and/or sold for housing (and commercial) purposes. Where necessary, the lease price could accommodate a degree of implicit subsidy to account for distributional effects.

2.23 Housing

In addition, we envisage stimulation of the sector through a Construction Development Innovation fund,[15] a competitive fund open to public and private housing developers and community groups to jointly design and build new innovative housing, including micro housing, shared housing (and co-working in the case of non-residential arrangements), public housing for the less wealthy, modular housing, and incorporation of new materials (environmental friendly housing) and sensor capabilities to address security needs. Such innovations would include specific amenities (e.g. for the elderly), where the emphasis is on diversity and choice linked to need. More broadly, the Construction Development Innovation fund would be extended to capture climate sensitive and resilient housing and construction, i.e. buildings which can adapt to climate variability in efficient and cost-effective manner. In this way India could become an exemplar for resilient, sustainable housing.

These initiatives require a much stronger remit for comprehensive spatial planning, linking housing (construction), with transport, land use, social amenities and environmental factors.[16] One example of this could be the development in India of new integrated housing and industrial estates which link business development, technology parks, transport and entrepreneurship hubs, with housing to form fully functioning clusters of activity and accommodation. This in turn could be integrated with the unique knowledge advantage plans noted earlier and provide a basis for competitive advantage by micro-region. In addition to the housing audit describe earlier, we would suggest that Construct India be given a wider remit to identify 'whole of infrastructure' needs for India on a long-term basis, including the spatial distribution of infrastructure, and the balance between 'hard infrastructure' such as transport, and 'soft infrastructure' such as ICT needs, and social amenities including libraries and cultural amenities. Seeing the connections across the various policy spaces is an essential aspect of the Enabling State.

While the measures above would assist in stimulating the supply of housing, including varieties of different types of housing, more generally, attention needs to be paid to affordability and new finance models. Risk sharing funding vehicles between banks and public authorities for both purchasing and rental finance products could be considered, as could 'predictive' models of finance whereby rental and housing purchase loans (i.e. the amount and terms of loan) could be based on the likely lifetime labour market prospects of individuals.

One other possibility is a 'pooled' finance model based on the anticipated increased value of real estate when integrated future housing, land, business and transport developments are taken into account (McKinsey Global Institute 2014). Loans could be made to collective entities representing these clusters, either by municipal authorities or financiers, which in turn could be distributed to individuals/businesses in these clusters, with associated tailored terms and payments. This

---

[15]The Construction Development Fund could be an extension of the recently established National Housing Bank, a dedicated fund for affordable housing including priority lending and land authorisation (FICCI and CRBE 2018).

[16]McKinsey Global Institute (2010, 2014) also has important recommendations and insights into spatial development, including housing.

mechanism would help to build scale across financial products, defray transaction costs for financiers and individuals, and ensure that all can benefit from the anticipated increase in value of the cluster as a whole. This model is particularly pertinent for social housing projects.

A further potential example of innovation in policymaking is a nexus between job creation and housing. For example, an 'earn as you build' concept could be instituted whereby construction workers have the option of foregoing certain percentage of incomes which would act as a de facto deposit on housing that they themselves are building either for themselves or as landlords. This in turn, could be linked more generally to an amended Mahatma Gandhi National Rural Guarantee Act (MGNREGA (or Universal Basic Income arrangement) where, for example, part of the guaranteed income could be for a deposit or rental. These deposits would then serve as collateral for banks. Other reforms could involve micro lending as collateral for larger lending.

A further development that we propose is a strengthening of temporary housing especially for itinerant people in urban centres. Through housing apps, potential accommodation seekers could be informed of temporary housing availability including immediate vacancies, with allocations based either on sharing arrangements, lottery, mini 'on spot', online auctions (with mechanisms to ensure some form of affordability criteria is met), or allocation by authorities based on criteria related to family need and circumstance. Temporary housing could manifest in many forms, including mobile housing, use of shopping malls, which, as appropriate, could be appropriately equipped at night, with small charges imposed for maintenance. In addition, measures to address the imbalance in housing by incentivising those having multiple housing to share or rent to those in need, including through social recognition, should be considered to better match supply and demand.

Consistent with the market conforming policy suite, we would advocate the establishment of a fast track project approval process, speeding up land record digitisation and reforms to regulations in the area of Floor Space, which constrain effective space utilisation (NITI Aayog 2017).

The clarification of the exact roles of various tiers of government would need to be undertaken through the Commission for Government, as outlined earlier. However, we would envisage a much stronger role for municipalities and metropolitan areas, and their rural counterparts in the development and delivery of housing options.

2.24 Food and Agriculture

The latest Global Food Security Index (The Economist Intelligence Unit 2018b), which measures a country's ability to supply and access food and related inputs, found that India ranked a mediocre overall 76th out of 113 countries, slightly higher for affordability (73rd) and availability (=70th) but weaker on quality and safety (=79th) and 99th on natural resources and resilience (which measures aspects such as waste and water management, protection of biodiversity, ability to manage climate events and agricultural risk management but which does not contribute to the overall

2.24 Food and Agriculture

score). At 76th place overall, India is only marginally ahead of lesser developed cohorts in Pakistan (77th), and Bangladesh (83rd), weaker than Sri Lanka (67), and weaker still when compared to BRIC counterparts, and other emerging economies including Malaysia, Philippines, Indonesia, Chile, Thailand and Vietnam. India's weaker performance vis-à-vis these countries, is broadly also reflected in the affordability, availability and quality criteria, lagging even further on Natural Resources and Resilience (NRR).

India needs a comprehensive, efficient and integrated national asset management approach, which in our view should capture appropriate pricing of assets, research and development, including in food management and preservation techniques, and early warning capabilities associated with impending disaster (which India is better placed in). Of 19 sub-metrics in the Global Food Security Index (excluding NRR), India is rated as very good (top quartile) in political stability risk, urban absorptive capacity and nutritional standards. It should be noted that the former two are more generic rather than specific about food security management. India is rated as moderate (2nd quartile) and weak (bottom quartile) on 13 metrics spanning such things as food consumption as a percentage of household expenditure, poverty, R&D spending on agriculture, agricultural infrastructure, diet diversification, micro nutrient availability and food safety net. India is rated good (3rd quartile) on volatility of agricultural production, corruption and access to financing for farmers, reflecting loans and grants in recent years.

In short, it would appear from the data that a number of foundational aspects such as quality infrastructure, research and innovation to promote healthy and varied agricultural products and services, quality of food, and nutritional value are lacking. In this section, we look at some of the distortions in the agricultural market place which are behind this, reflecting our view that India has not had a fully effective functioning Enabling State, which at least in part has given rise to some of the issues in the index. When looked at over time, there are further worrying signs. Over a 6 year period from 2012 to 2018, India's scores overall and for affordability and availability have declined, while the only category in which India has improved is quality/safety, which although as we have seen, continues to lag other countries. By contrast, for the Asian Region as a whole, scores in all parameters, including overall scores, have improved over this period (The Economist Intelligence Unit 2018b).

2.24.1 Global Hunger Index

The Global Hunger Index (2018) demonstrates further areas for concern. It measures the proportion of undernourishment in the population, wasting and stunting in children under 5, and mortality under 5. This Index has India rated as 'serious' (although improving over the last 20 years approximately as have all the countries we consider). In the 2018 index, India is ranked 103rd out of 119 countries. In terms of the raw data, improvement in India is seen for a number of the metrics over an approximately 20 year period, disturbingly though, the prevalence of wasting in children has actually increased (a feature it shares with Bangladesh, Brazil and Indonesia[17]).

India currently has prevalence of wasting in children at 21%, the highest of our 12 country benchmark, which includes Bangladesh and Pakistan. For the other 3 metrics, despite improvement over the last 20 years, the incidence is stubbornly high relative to most countries that we consider. Critical to note is the importance and impact of broader factors. Child wasting is closely aligned with access to water, sanitation and maternal health, while key factors behind stunting include women's education, gender inequality, with pronounced differences by region, caste and ethnicity, despite the implementation of measures such as the National Food Security Act (Global Hunger Index 2016).

Finally, the latest Global Nutrition Report (UK Development Initiatives 2018) points to a staggering number of children who are stunted and wasted in India, of the order of 46.6 m (a third of the world) and 25.5 million respectively. Again these numbers find expression in terms of critical challenges of young motherhood, illiteracy and awareness of such factors as open defecation. Despite the laudable aims of the Swach Bharat (Clean India), various social mores prevent use of toilets, including unwillingness of non-untouchables to clean toilets (Petrikova 2018; Mitra 2018; Global Nutrition Report 2018).

The Global Nutrition report (UK Development Initiatives 2018) points to emerging issues associated with rising income levels among a number in India, including obesity, diabetes, blood pressure and that India has only made limited progress against global nutrition targets. However, others are more bullish about the success of the Swatch Bharat (Clean India) programme and India's broader health agenda in varying degrees (Pathak 2019; Kumar and Prasad 2019; Panda 2019b).

2.24.2 Key Factors in Agriculture and Food

A deeper dive into food security access, distribution, and quality reveal many weaknesses which go to the heart of the appropriate role of the state.

As the foregoing analysis has shown, a far-reaching approach which looks at the complete picture and surrounding factors behind nutrition and hunger issues is essential. A sample of the weaknesses in India underscores the issues that the country faces in terms of a state which over-reached, has misplaced priorities, and has not linked policy action with need. We focus here on the economic domain to illustrate some of the glaring deficiencies. These include:

- Presence of minimum support prices (MSP's) and associated procurement which apply to some commodities and bias production away from higher value and

---

[17]Countries benchmarked in this case are India, Bangladesh, Brazil, China, Malaysia, Russia, Sri Lanka, Thailand, Indonesia, Philippines, Russia, Pakistan and Vietnam.

nutritional products such as fruit, vegetables and towards cereals; price inflexibility that distorts supply and demand[18] patterns and has resulted in the depletion of water resources, soil degradation and deterioration in water quality, and a system of minimum support prices which discriminates against Eastern States (NITI Aayog 2017; McKinsey Global Institute 2014; Chand 2019; Subramanian 2018a).
- Targeted public distribution system which provides products to the poor (mainly cereals, wheat and rice) and is subject to considerable leakage, inefficiency and corruption, and lack of appropriate targeting (although this has improved in recent years due in part to shifts to more direct benefit transfer), while many question whether a calorie-based approach inherent in the public distribution system has been beneficial or essential for nutrition (Ninan 2015; Panagariya and Bhagwati 2012).
- Food Security Act which extends the public distribution beyond narrower targeting thus bringing into question the true distributional intent of these policies. Also, some question whether the Food Security Act provides enough emphasis on farmer income (Swaminathan 2016), while others again point out (Global Hunger Index 2016), as we have spoken of, that, 'surrounding' issues of distribution, logistics, sanitation, and income inequality among other things are a major constraint to food security.
- The presence of complex webs of intermediaries, through the Agricultural Produce Market Committee (APMC), which are highly regulated markets, means that farmers are rarely able to interact with consumers and also receive a fraction of prices as intermediaries 'cream skim' the value, and also in many cases, control logistics and charge exit/entry fees for trading (McKinsey Global Institute 2014; NITI Aayog 2017).
- Absence of complete value chains in storage, processing, transport and distribution and logistics (Gandhi 2018; Hasan 2017; McKinsey Global Institute 2014).
- Poor productivity (yield per hectare against a number of Asian competitors, and in relation to other sectors), associated with the lack of modern agriculture techniques such as precision farming, the absence of scale, presence of small landholdings and lack of support infrastructure for agriculture (McKinsey Global Institute 2014; Subramanian 2018a).
- A subsidy driven approach, for example, for fertiliser which produces an incentive for over use, distorting resource usage and agricultural performance. Similarly, the absence of appropriate water prices, has led to water intensive crops grown in water scarce areas, while power and other subsidies distort production and consumption patterns (Ninan 2015; Gulati and Saini 2017).
- The presence of 'two agricultures' in India, the well irrigated and input driven North, where challenges exist in changing the focus from price support and subsidies, and the Central, Western and Southern parts of India where problems arise from inadequate irrigation, insufficient investments in research and development, and ineffective procurement (Economic Survey 2017–2018 Government of India 2018).

---

[18]Gandhi 2018 argues that MSP have fallen however.

- Loss of farm revenue of the order of 15–18% on average, and as high as 20–25% owing to impacts of climate change in 3 main respects: increase in average temperatures, decline in average rainfall and increase in the number of dry days (Government of India 2018): This in turn means a desperate need to address the climate change impacts on agriculture.

Government policy through such measures as 'Doubling of Farmers Income' (NITI Aayog 2017), based on loan waivers and other supports again are more by way of entrenching a subsidy, 'lurching' approach, with ad hoc solutions moving from one crisis to another. This is instead of an innovative, fully integrated policy approach which carefully canvasses and links the various arms of policy together.

2.24.3 Towards a Food Policy

A comprehensive approach to food and food security is required, linked to knowledge, innovation and physical infrastructure development. In our view this has many facets. First is the need for a comprehensive food priority map for India, which would be agreed upon, participatory exercise identifying (a) key opportunities for value-added production and nutritional products based on differentiated need among various groups in society (b) determine optimal locations and mix of products given soil, climate and other conditions (c) develop a comprehensive export approach (d) identify key inputs, technology supports, and infrastructure needs to make India genuinely competitive globally in agriculture, including a seamless, national market for agriculture (e) support for research aligned to priorities in the food map (f) understand and agree key roles for respective stakeholders, including through collaborative investment (g) identify and apply key sustainability principles to farms to promote India's 'clean green' credentials (h) develop a publicly available food nutrition database. This comprehensive food priority map would be mandated by the central government, involving all states, farm groups, community groups and local villages/rural areas.

The second main element is to promote the concept of food corridors. These would be core links between farms and urban areas, aimed at complete linkages between agriculture and final consumption, consistent with the food priority map. Thus, urban area firms could sponsor or adopt a collection of farms in a series of networks in contiguous areas, adding value to raw farm produce, and further process, distribute and transport products, including to export destinations. Sponsorship could take many forms, including ownership (although contentious), contracting and serving as a lead customer driving innovation, productivity and efficiency through the entire value chain, transferring knowledge, expertise and management capabilities, but without losing sight of the two way transfers of ideas. Based on deep and traditional knowledge, farms could be invaluable sources of know-how to urban enterprises.

These food corridors, organised on specialisations, according to appropriate land and resource availability and product mix, would be supported by national, state and

2.24 Food and Agriculture

local authorities, linked to knowledge advantage plans, as appropriate, in a manner akin to Special Economic Zones. It would involve collaborative networks of farming and downstream businesses, informed by the food priority map, and facilitated by the most appropriate level of government, including cooperative inter-government arrangements, and intra-government relationships, for example, between urban and rural counterparts. In this way India would integrate its farm businesses, build scale and specialisation linked to greater nutrition.[19]

Another key measure, allied with food corridors is to have co-located farm and energy hubs, in which farms generate, use and earn income from distributed energy (including especially alternative forms of energy such as solar and biomass) linked to farming activities, provided cost and scale issues are addressed. Gandhi (2018) points to the need for incentivising consumers in rural areas to make solar energy viable. More about energy hubs and the environment is spoke about in chapter four. These initiatives enhance energy production in India, especially alternative energy, and secure additional income streams for farmers, and potentially overcome the problem of access to secure energy associated with reliance on a national energy grid. This in turn could mean 'pooling' of land (McKinsey 2014) by farming aggregators to take advantage of these opportunities, with Government taking on a role of broker in these activities. In fact, pooling of land more generally, would overcome the disadvantage of scale associated with small landholdings. Gandhi (2018) also speaks of further diversifying income opportunities for farmers, including leasing of agricultural equipment, the need for an amended MGNREGA to pay farmers for farming activity and create non-farm jobs in rural areas.

Beyond this, and established on a competitive basis, would be the designation and demarcation of exemplar farms, which would serve as demonstration effects of modern practice and application of leading edge farm techniques, including climate and pest resistant crops and use of precision productivity enhancing irrigation, among other things. One approach worth further developing and diffusing is the concept of nutri-farms, which are farms and farming practices dedicated to improving nutritional deficiencies (Swaminathan 2016).

2.24.4 *Governance and Reform*

There are many other key elements of our proposed plan. We would envisage the gradual removal of the complex set of intermediaries to allow for direct and immediate negotiation of prices between farmers (or aggregators of farmers) and downstream purchasers aided by technology and the use of online apps to provide up to the minute, real-time information on prices, weather conditions and input availability. It would transfer power and authority to the farming community.

In addition, the minimum support price must be rationalised. One key possibility for consideration would be to remove this price support and instead support farmers

---

[19] McKinsey Global Institute (2014) speaks of a similar concept around Food Parks.

through a much more sophisticated form of insurance (Manjul 2016), building on existing schemes. This could mean, for example, in our reckoning, setting insurance cover for price fluctuations from established benchmarks where the level of cover and premiums would be set on the basis of traffic light indicators. 'Red', 'amber' and 'green' represent deviations from 'normal' market prices due to adverse climate impact and other changed agricultural conditions, e.g. red could mean catastrophic loss of produce. Where necessary, government could provide assistance to support part of the premium cover, depending on farmer income, assets and so forth, or act as a guarantor of support. This scheme, if properly devised, would alleviate the distorting effects of minimum support prices. Another possibility is to reform the minimum support price to allow it to respond more flexibly to changed market conditions via price bands, within which prices can move up or down. Other proposals have been floated including a price deficiency scheme which ensures payments to farmers based on the difference between MSP and market prices, or minimum reserve pricing through auction, or government procurement designed to mop up any excess supply, thus enhancing farmer returns. Various limitations have been expressed about such schemes, including impact on farmer costs, ongoing demand and supply imbalances, and that such measures should not be in isolation from broader reforms (Rangarajan and Dev 2019; NITI Aayog 2018).

More broadly, we argue for a reduction in a range of subsidies in an orderly, planned and co-ordinated way and to be replaced with a development based agenda as identified. Some estimates have found the total food, fertiliser, power, canal irrigation and agricultural subsidies to be of the order of 4,00,000 crore in 2017 with total input subsidies on fertilisers, canal, irrigation and agricredit alone worth 188,158 crore in 2016, leaving in its wake public investments in such things as infrastructure investment. The distorting effects of subsidies adversely affects resource allocation and favour larger firms (Gulati and Saini 2017). These authors also speak of numerous restrictive regulations on the movement of commodities between states or within districts in states and limitations on stocks held by the private sector that have constrained efficiency and productivity. This has been inimical to the creation of a unified, nationally integrated agriculture market.

In the context of a development based agenda, we call for removal of such restraints, aligned with our market conforming view of the role of the state, and to ensure that agricultural produce can be transferred and traded freely on national and international markets. The absence of an integrated national market reflecting numerous barriers and national and state government anomalies, has been telling in its negative impacts on scale, productivity and efficiency. Not only must India embrace a truly national market but must do so with the world. Recent reports point to limited implementation of the electronic market for agriculture, which would be a useful tool to enhance price discovery associated with demand and supply, remove information asymmetries between buyers and sellers and give rise to greater transparency in trading, and foster the true pursuit of a national integrated market. However, only 45 lakh farmers out of 12 crore have availed themselves of the electronic market owing to lack of digital literacy and electronic infrastructure bottlenecks (Vikram 2019).

The Public Distribution System (PDS) of providing subsidised food for the poorest has been contentious. Some argue that the system has merit and has improved distributional efficiency and effectiveness over time (Dreze and Sen 2013), but on balance there has been considerable wastage, leakage and corruption, lack of proper monitoring and inappropriate definitional rigour regarding poverty (meaning many undeserving people have received benefit), and a preoccupation with consumption of calories which some argue has little to do with nutrition (Ninan 2015; Panigaraya and Bhagwati 2012). The shift towards direct financial benefit transfers is positive in overcoming some of the difficulties and is welcome in our view. If it is still deemed necessary that some elements of PDS remain, then further reform is necessary. It could be run, owned and managed by farm groups, to give greater oversight to those responsible for production and thereby reduce red tape. Farmers, on a collective basis, could be paid to oversee the PDS, thus providing alternative income streams. Alternatively, a public–private joint company arrangement could be considered. These measures would need to be linked more broadly with highly sophisticated transport, distribution and logistics capability for food associated with innovation, technology and application of knowledge to accurately track, monitor and evaluate distribution flows and implement rapid capabilities response in respect of any bottlenecks.

2.24.5 Leading Practice

There is an important role for government to support, sponsor and disseminate best practice information and research to farmers and consumers of food, especially related to nutritional food, consistent with some of the measures outlined earlier in this chapter. One interesting proposal comes from Swaminathan (2016) who calls for Community Hunger Fighters to identify and promote improved nutritional practices. This could be extended to urban areas in respect of nutritional information and awareness through a nutritional database aligned with our food map idea. An important role for various tiers of government, in our view, could be to establish multi-faceted, integrated agribrokers whose job would be to identify, disseminate and co-ordinate best practice agriculture techniques, provide information and advice on a tailored basis to individual farmers and groups of farms, and to link this with nutritional advice to individuals and consumer groups, so as to better align production and consumption with an emphasis on higher value, nutritional products. These initiatives would build on extension services that are deployed in a number of parts of India (McKinsey Global Institute 2014).

Finally, we note the plight of farmer suicide in India. The measures here towards higher value-added production, corporate tie up's, opportunities for direct selling to enhance returns through price discovery, suggestions to diversify income, and a 'two envelope UBI' advanced earlier would go some way to addressing this extremely challenging social problem. In addition, we would see a broader role for the brokers to also serve as counsellors and confidantes for 'at risk farmers', while the government and community groups could put in place reserve jobs (beyond MGNREGA), at least on a temporary basis for these farmers.[20] This would require a new role for Government, one that is attentive, vigilant and works closely with constituent groups in the true embodiment of partnership.

2.25 Conclusion

This chapter has found that India historically has not achieved the correct balance in terms of the role of government versus other players. Government intervention in economy and society has often been intrusive and heavy handed with seemingly misplaced priorities. The roles of government through a series of market associated parameters have been put forward by the author, for the knowledge economy, with a focus on the Enabling State. Key Instruments of a new approach include facilitation, brokerage and experimentation aimed at unlocking and leveraging ideas from everywhere and from anyone in collaborative fashion.

Absolutely critical is the need for revamping India's institutional structure, which in the author's judgement, is inimical to the requirements of the knowledge economy. Our proposals for the Commission for Government, Collaborate India, vehicles to address corruption, reforms to improve bureaucratic, judicial, parliamentary and election processes, and new forms of decentralised planning are among the keys in this book. We then considered three critical areas of health, housing, and food to demonstrate the sort of reforms we are canvassing in the context of the Enabling State, and founded on the basis of the knowledge economy.

Through the course of this chapter, and indeed book, comparisons between India and other nations have been made.

References

ABC News (2018) World's first 3D printed house to be built in Netherlands, 8 June 2018. https://www.abc.net.au/news/2018-06-08/first-3d-printed-homes-to-be-built-in-the-netherlands/9846574. Accessed 8 June 2018

Alam N (2017) India's demonetisation drive has boosted banks and start up's but it is still a failure. The Conversation, 21 Feb 2017. http://theconversation.com/indias-demonetisation-drive-has-boosted-banks-and-start-ups-but-its-still-a-failure-71704

Bhandari L (2017) Energising the states 2017. In: Mohan R (ed) India transformed 25 years of economic reforms. Penguin Random House India

Botsman P (2001) Master to servant state. In: Botsman P, Latham M (eds) The enabling state. Pluto Press

Center for Global Development and Accountability Initiative (2015) Power to the states making fiscal transfers work for better health

---

[20]More generally, a job guarantee scheme has been put forward by Meyer (2019). This could be directed at agriculture as required in our view.

References

Chand R (2019) MSP and farmers income. In: Debroy B, Ganguly A, Desai K (eds) Making of New India. Wisdom Tree
Corbridge S, Harriss J, Jeffrey C (2013) India today: economy, politics and society. Wiley
Cornell University, INSEAD, and WIPO (2018) The global innovation index
Cortright J (2001) New growth theory, technology and learning: a practitioner's guide review of economic development literature and practice: no 4. Impressa Inc
Crabtree J (2018) The Billonaire Raj a journey through India's new gilded age. Oneworld Publications Ltd
Das G (2012) India grows at night: a liberal case for a strong state. Penguin International
Das (2017) Some concerns regarding the goods and services tax. Econ Polit Wkly 52(9)
Das G (2019) Jobonomics India's employment crisis and what the future holds. Hachette India
Debroy B (2018) Is the world simpler than it was before GST? The Jury is in The Economic Times, 29 May 2018. https://m.economictimes.com/news/economy/policy/is-the-world-simpler-than-it-was-before-gst-this-jury-is-in/articleshow/64359881.cms. Accessed 14 May 2019
Debroy B (2019) Reducing corruption-the Modi Government agenda. In: Debroy B, Ganguly A, Desai K (eds) Making of NEW INDIA transformation under Modi Government. Wisdom Tree
Deloitte (2016) Mainstreaming affordable housing in India, moving towards housing for all by 2022
Dewing C, Jones T (2016) Future agenda six challenges for the next decade. Third Millennium Publishing, London, UK
Dixit A, Mankar R (2018) New ideas for fighting corruption in India. QRIUS, 8 June 2018. https://qrius.com/new-ideas-for-fighting-corruption-in-india/. Accessed 20 June 2018
Doshi V (2018) India's 'Modicare' a multi-billion dollar gamble on health The Sydney Morning Herald, 23 Sept 2018. https://www.smh.com.au/world/asia/india-s-modicare-a-multi-billion-dollar-gamble-on-health-20180923-p505hy.html. Accessed 6 Oct 2018
Dreze J, Sen A (2013) An uncertain glory: India and its contradictions. Princeton University Press, NJ
Duncan M, Leigh A, Madden D, Tynan P (2004) Imagining Australia: ideas for our future. Allen and Unwin
Dutta A, Kulkarni K (2018) Cash strategies and black money: a look at India's 2016 demonetization effect, one year later. Int Rev Bus Econ (IRBE) 2(1):1–6
FICCI and CBRE (2018) Affordable housing: the next big thing?
Florida R (2003) The rise of the creative class. Basic Books (Technology, Talent and Tolerance)
Florida R (2008) Who's your city. Basic Books
Forbes S (2016) What India has done to its money is sickening and immoral. Forbes, 22 Dec 2016. https://www.forbes.com/sites/steveforbes/2016/12/22/what-india-has-done-to-its-money-is-sickening-and-immoral/#1232d6f817f5. Accessed 20 Feb 2016
Gandhi F (2018) A rural manifesto realising India's future through her villages. Rupa Publications
Gomes E (2018) EPFO proposes move to create social security cover for all- all you need to know. QRIUS, 20 June 2018. https://qrius.com/epfo-proposes-social-security-cover-for-all/. Accessed 27 June 2018
Goswami (2016) Modi's bank note ban has inflicted pointless suffering on India's poorest. The Conversation, 25 Nov 2016. https://theconversation.com/modis-bank-note-ban-has-inflicted-pointless-suffering-on-indias-poorest-69157
Government of India (2017a) Ministry of Finance. Economic survey 2016–2017
Government of India (2017b) Ministry of Health and Family Welfare. National health policy 2017
Government of India (2018) Ministry of Finance. Economic survey 2017–2018
Government of India: Department of Economic Affairs, Ministry of Finance (2015) Report of the committee on revisiting and revitalising public private partnership model of institutions (Kelkar Committee)
Gulati A, Saini S (2017) 25 years of policy tinkering in agriculture. In: Mohan R (ed) India transformed 25 years of economic reforms. Penguin Random House, India
Gupta A (2016) Grassroots innovation, minds on the margin are not marginal minds. Penguin Random House India, Haryana, India

Hassan R (2017) Sustaining growth, ensuring inclusion. In: Nayyar D, Hasan R (eds) Shaping India's future: essays in memory of Abid Husain. Academic Foundation, New Delhi

Heinrich (2017) Corruption and inequality: how populists mislead people. Transparency International. https://www.transparency.org/news/feature/corruption_and_inequality_how_populists_mislead_people. Accessed 15 Feb 2018

Hofstede Insights (2019). https://www.hofstede-insights.com/country-comparison/india/. Accessed 12 Mar 2019

Horton R (2018) Offline. The new politics of health in India www.thelancet.com, vol. 392, 15 Sept 2018 (growth in cancer etc) https://www.thelancet.com/journals/lancet/article/PIIS0140-6736(18)32211-6/fulltext. Accessed 6 Dec 2018

I Paid a Bribe (2019). www.ipaidabribe.com. Accessed 2 May 2019

Jalan B (2017) India priorities for the future. Penguin Viking

Jalan B (2018) India ahead 2025 and beyond. Rupa Publications

Joseph J (2016) A feast of vultures. Harper Collins, India

Joshi V (2016) India's long road. Penguin Allen Lane, Haryana, India

Kalam APJA, Singh SP (2015) Advantage India, from challenge to opportunity. Harper Collins Publishers, New Delhi, India

Kangas O, Jauhiainen S, Simanainen M, Ylikanna M (eds) (2019) The basic income experiment 2017–2018 in Finland. Preliminary results Ministry of Social Affairs and Health 2019

Katz B, Wagner J (2014) The rise of innovation districts: a new geography of innovation in America. Metropolitan policy program. Brookings

Khosla S (2018) India's universal basic income bedevilled by the details. Carnegie India

Koul B (2018) Does India need a dictator. Vitasta Publishing

KPMG (2018) India real estate and construction: consolidating for growth

Krishna A (2017) The broken ladder. Penguin Viking, Haryana, India

Kumar A, Prasad U (2019) Reforming the health sector. In: Debroy B, Ganguly A, Desai K (eds) Making of New India transformation under Modi Government. Wisdom Tree

Lancet Editorial (2018) India's mega health reforms: treatment for half a billion, vol 392, 25 Aug 2018. https://www.thelancet.com/journals/lancet/article/PIIS0140-6736(18)31936-6/fulltext. Accessed 6 Dec 2018

Land Transport Authority Singapore (2018) https://www.lta.gov.sg/content/ltaweb/en.html. Accessed 1 Dec 2018

Lateef S (2017) India's governance challenges: why institutions matter. In: Mohan R (ed) India transformed 25 years of economic reforms. Penguin Random House, India

Latham M (2001) The new economy and the new politics. In: Botsman P, Latham M (eds) The enabling state. Pluto Press

Local Circles (2018) India corruption survey 2018 report, in Partnership with Transparency International, India

Mazzucato M (2015) The entrepreneurial state debunking public myths vs private sector myths. Revised Edition Public Affairs, New York

McKinsey Global Institute (2010) India's urban awakening: building inclusive cities, sustaining economic growth

McKinsey Global Institute (2014) From poverty to empowerment: India's imperative for jobs, growth, and effective basic services

Meyer H (2019) Five policies to deal with the loss of jobs to automation (UBI Is not on one of them). QRIUS, 15 Apr 2019. https://qrius.com/five-policies-to-deal-with-the-loss-of-jobs-to-automation-ubi-is-not-one-of-them/. Accessed 20 Apr 2019

Mitra P (2018) India accounts for a third of world's malnourished children. QRIUS, 30 Nov 2018. https://qrius.com/india-accounts-for-a-third-of-the-worlds-malnourished-children/. Accessed 4 Dec 2018

Mor N, Dhar D, Venkateswaran S (2017) Healthcare in India: a fork in the road. In: Mohan R (ed) India transformed 25 years of economic reforms. Penguin Random House, India

References

Mundle S (2017) Two aspects of governance: public service delivery and corruption. In Nayyar D, Hasan A (eds) Shaping India's future: essays in memory of Abid Hussain. Academic Foundation, New Delhi

Munjal S (2016) When will India leapfrog? In: Kumar S (ed) What will leapfrog India in the twenty-first century. Wisdom Tree

Murthy N (2016) A competitive edge. In: Kumar S (ed) What will leapfrog India in the twenty-first Century. Wisdom Tree

National Innovation Council India Inclusive Fund (2019). https://InnovationCouncilarchive.nic.in/index.php?option=com_content&view=article&id=52&itemid=34. Accessed 28 Apr 2019

Nayyar D (2017) The state and the economy. In: Nayyar D, Hasan A (eds) Shaping India's future: essays in memory of Abid Hussain. Academic Foundation, New Delhi

Ninan TN (2015) The turn of the tortoise. Penguin Allen Lane, India

NITI Aayog (2017) India three year action agenda 2017–2018 to 2019–2020

NITI Aayog (2018) Strategy for New India @ 75

Nordman C, Guerin I (2018) The shock of India's demonetisation: a failed attempt to formalise the economy. https://theconversation.com/the-shock-of-indian-demonetisation-a-failed-attempt-to-formalise-the-economy-93328. Accessed 4 Apr 2018

North DC (2016) The institutions and economic theory. Am Econ 61(1):72–76

Oxfam (2018a) The commitment to reducing inequality index

Oxfam (2018b) 15 shocking facts about income inequality in India. www.oxfamindia.org/block/15shocks. Accessed 30 Nov 2018

Palayi A, Priyaranjan N (2018) Affordable housing in India. RBI Bulletin

Panagariya A (2018) India's trade policy folly: current turn to import substitution will take economy down from turnpike to direct road. The Times of India, 25 July 2018. https://timesofindia.indiatimes.com/blogs/toi-edit-page/indias-trade-policy-folly-current-turn-to-import-substitution-will-take-economy-down-from-turnpike-to-dirt-road/. Accessed 5 Sept 2018

Panagariya A, Bhagwati J (2012) India's tryst with dynasty. Collins Business, India

Panda B (2019a) Lutyens' Maverick, ground realities, hard choices and tomorrow's India. Rupa Publications

Panda B (2019b) Nutritional health: mother and child. In: Debroy B, Ganguly A, Desai K (eds) Making of New India transformation under Modi Government. Wisdom Tree

Pathak B (2019) Swach Bharat mission lays the foundation of change. In: Debroy B, Ganguly A, Desai K (eds) Making of New India transformation under Modi Government. Wisdom Tree

Paul V (2017) India's big government: the intrusive state and how it is hurting us. Equity Master Agera Research Private Ltd

Citi GPS: Global Perspectives and Solutions (2016) Oxford Martin School 2016 Technology At Work v2.0

Petrikova I (2018) What India could learn from Ethiopia about food security. QRIUS, 29 Nov 2018. https://qrius.com/what-india-could-learn-from-ethiopia-about-food-security/. Accessed 4 Dec 2018

Piketty T (2014) Capital in the twenty-first century. The Belknap Press of Harvard University Press, Cambridge, England

Porter M (1990) The competitive advantage of nations, the free press. Simon and Schuster, New York

Pritchett L (2009) Is India a flailing state detours on the four lane highway to modernisation. HKS faculty research working paper series RWP09-013, John F Kennedy School of Government, Harvard University

Rangarajan C, Dev S (2019) Removing the root of farmer distress. The Hindu, 28 Jan 2019. https://www.thehindu.com/opinion/lead/removing-the-roots-of-farmers-distress/article26106031.ece. Accessed 5 Feb 2019

Reddy Y (2017) Union-State relations and reforms 2017. In: Mohan R (ed) India transformed 25 years of economic reforms. Penguin Random House, India

Salas A (2018) Slow, imperfect progress across Asia-Pacific. Transparency International. https://www.transparency.org/news/feature/slow_imperfect_progress_across_asia_pacific. Accessed 30 Mar 2018

Sandefur J, Wadhwa D (2018) A change in the World Bank methodology (not reform) explaining India's rise in doing business ranking. Center for Global Development. https://www.cgdev.org/blog/change-world-bank-methodology-not-reform-explains-indias-rise-doing-business. Accessed 5 Feb 2018

Sanyal S (2018) India in the age of ideas selected writings 2006–2018. Westland Publications Private Limited

Saunders T, Mulgan G (2017) Governing with collective intelligence. Nesta

Saxena V (2018) India's ambitious health insurance scheme questioned. Asia Times, 24 Sept 2018. https://www.asiatimes.com/2018/09/article/indias-ambitious-health-insurance-scheme-questioned/. Accessed 15 Oct 2018

Sivaramakrishnan KC (2015) Governance of megacities. Oxford University Press, New Delhi, India

Srivastava S (2019) Tracking the Modi-Meter in Forbes India. Pre-budget special, 1 Feb 2019

Subramanian A (2018a) Of Counsel. The challenges of the Modi-Jaitley economy. Penguin Viking

Subramanian T (2018b) Lateral entry into civil services is the reform India needs. QRIUS, 16 June 2018. https://qrius.com/lateral-entry-in-to-civil-services-the-reform-that-india-needs/. Accessed 20 June 2018

Swaminathan M (2016) Ending malnutrition and violence: pathways to a happy India. In: Kumar S (ed) What will leapfrog India in the twenty-first century. Wisdom Tree

The Economist (2016) Comparing crony capitalism around the world. https://www.economist.com/graphic-detail/2016/05/05/comparing-crony-capitalism-around-the-world. Accessed 17 Mar 2019

The Economist (2017a) India's Prime Minister is not as much of a reformer as he seems. https://www.economist.com/leaders/2017/06/24/indias-prime-minister-is-not-as-much-of-a-reformer-as-he-seems. Accessed 24 June 2017

The Economist (2017b) Narendra Modi is a fine administrator, but not much of a reformer. https://www.economist.com/briefing/2017/06/24/narendra-modi-is-a-fine-administrator-but-not-much-of-a-reformer. Accessed 24 June 2017

The Economist (2018a) Why foreign investors are losing interest in India. https://www.economist.com/finance-and-economics/2018/12/18/why-foreign-investors-are-losing-interest-in-india. Accessed 18 Dec 2018

The Economist (2018b) Modicare India's government launches a vast health insurance scheme, 27 Sept 2018. http://www.economist.com/asia/2018/09/27/indias-government-launches-a-vast-health-insurance-scheme. Accessed 8 Oct 2018

The Economist Intelligence Unit (2018a) Democracy index 2018: me too? Political participation, protest and democracy. https://www.eiu.com/public/topical_report.aspx?campaignid=Democracy2018. Accessed 10 Dec 2018

The Economist Intelligence Unit (2018b) Global food security index. https://foodsecurityindex.eiu.com. Accessed 3 May 2019

The Global Hunger Index (2016) India: making food a right for all. Wethunger Life. Case Study. https://www.globalhungerindex.org. Accessed 4 May 2019

The Global Hunger Index (2018) https://www.globalhungerindex.org. Accessed 4 May 2019

The Lancet (2017) Healthcare access and quality index based on mortality from causes amenable to personal healthcare in 195 countries and territories 1990–2015. a novel analysis from the global burden of disease study, 21 Nov 2017. http://dx.doi.org/10/016/50140-6736(17)30818-8

The Lancet (2018) Measuring performance on the health care access and quality index for 195 countries and territories and selected subnational locations: a systematic analysis for the global burden of disease study 2016, 23 May 2016. http://dx.doi.org/10/1016/50140-6736(18)30994-2

The Wire (2018) India jumps 23 places on World Bank's ease of doing business ranking. https://thewire.in/business/india-world-bank-ease-of-doing-business-rankings-2019. Accessed 31 Oct 2018

Tilotia A (2015) The making of India. Rupa Publications India, New Delhi, India, Game Changing Transitions

References

Tiwari P, Rao D (2016) Housing market and housing policy in India. Asian Development Bank Institute (ADBI), Number 565, April 2016, ADBI working paper series

Transparency International (2018) Corruption perception index 2017. https://www.transparency.org/new/feature/corruptions-perceptions-index

Transparency International (2019) Corruption perception index 2018. https://www.transparency.prg/cpi2018. Accessed 9 Feb 2019

UK Development Initiatives (2018) Global nutrition report. Shining a light to spur action on nutrition

UN (2018) Human development indices and indicators. 2018 statistical update

Vikram K (2019) Three years on, government's e-mandi project yet to gain traction. The New Indian Express, 3 Feb 2019. http://www.newindianexpress.com/sundaystandard/2019/feb/03/three-years-on-e-mandi-project-yet-to-gain-traction-1833566.html. Accessed 19 Feb 2019

World Bank (2012) World development report gender equality and development

World Bank (2018a) Doing business index 2019

World Bank (2018b) India development update, India's growth story

World Bank (2019) Worldwide governance. https://info.worldbank.org/governance/wgi/#home. Accessed 15 Mar 2019

World Economic Forum (Klaus Schwab) (2018) The global competitiveness index

World Health Organisation (2019) Health statistics. www.who.int/topics/statistics. Accessed 2 May 2019

Zuboff S (2015) Big other: surveillance capitalism and the prospects of an information civilisation. J Inf Technol 30:75–89

Zuboff S (2019) Time to curb excesses of surveillance capitalism Straits Times, 26 Jan 2019. https://www.straitstimes.com/opinion/time-to-curb-excesses-of-surveillance-capitalism

Chapter 3
Education

Abstract In the course of this chapter, the author investigates the crucial role of education for the knowledge economy in India, and critically examines India's performance with respect to higher education participation, quality, research capability, resourcing and structure and governance of the system. It is found that India's higher education performance is patchy and lags other countries in terms of innovation, quality, diversity, employability and internationalisation. Nor is it preparing students particularly effectively for the challenges of the future economically and technologically. The chapter makes a number of key recommendations for a revamped higher education system in India, including one which is connected into the global networks of innovation, and which fosters stronger relations with the labour market and society more broadly.

Keywords Diversity · Quality · Mission · Research · Access and opportunity · Resourcing · Governance · Technology

3.1 Introduction

This chapter examines the key aspect of the 'E' framework, Education, or what we could consider as the 'feet' of the innovation and knowledge economy.

Higher education and training has a pivotal role to play in the development of a nation, especially a knowledge intensive one, through its role as a: provider of skilled labour, which underpins higher living standards, developer of cutting edge research, creating solutions for commercial need and social imperatives; as an instrument of social change through promoting debate, dissent and the exchange of ideas which brings to bear different perspectives and insights, and through community engagement. In addition, Higher Education has a pivotal role in promoting access and opportunity, including those from lower socio-economic backgrounds and minori-

---

This chapter draws on a paper presented by the author in 2017 and subsequent journal publication in 2018 (International Review of Business and Economics). Some parts of the chapter are the same as the paper, however there are considerably more new sections, updated data and embellished arguments. Permission has been received from the editor of the Journal and from Springer.

ties (Government of India 2013a; Dreze and Sen 2013).[1] More recently, it has served as a crucial means of integrating into the global flow of ideas and know-how through the movement of people, knowledge, technology and institutional and personal connections, and as an export earner in its own right.

3.1.1 Studies

Mountains of theoretical and empirical work highlight the importance of human capital for productivity and economic growth, supported by the rise of the Endogenous Growth theories. Although not necessarily specifically related to higher education per se, this body of work is germane to higher education. Various transmission mechanisms of education to improved economic performance are identified, including through the human capital approach (education improving the skills and abilities of the workforce leading to higher productivity and ability to use technology); innovation approach (education to influence the development of new ideas and technologies); and knowledge transfer approach-education as a means of diffusing ideas, know-how and technologies (Tara and Kumar 2016).

Various studies have focussed on different but related aspects:

- Skill bias in technology usage, including especially in ICT, driven by investment in skills training[2] (Bhat and Siddharthan 2013)
- Higher salaries and improved quality jobs are associated with enhanced skills hierarchies (Khare 2016)
- Countries with higher education levels have faster value added and employment growth (Siddharthan and Narayanan 2013);
- Returns from human capital matter at least as much as returns from physical capital (Khare 2016); and the average private return to investment in tertiary education is 16%, however in some observed studies based on country data, the returns vary significantly by specialisation, with the highest returns from engineering and technology (World Bank 2019)
- Cognitive skills rather than education per se matter for economic growth, although education influences the development of cognitive skills (Tara and Kumar 2016), while the type, quality and efficiency of education is important for economic growth (Khare 2016); returns to work for an additional year of employment in cognitive professions is of the order of 3% compared to 2% for manual work (World Bank 2019).
- R&D has an affirmative impact on firm productivity (Kathuria et al. 2013);
- There are positive spatial impacts of human capital, including agglomeration effects (Bhat and Siddharthan 2013)

---

[1]The Planning Commission states these factors in the more general context of education.

[2]A number of studies focus on school education, nonetheless these are insightful and instructive and provide pointers to the value of tertiary education.

3.1 Introduction

- Human capital promotes social capital, in turn enhancing economic growth, with research suggesting that more educated people have greater trust of others (World Bank 2019)
- Tertiary education enhances the demand for lifelong learning, which is essential for the multiple careers that people undertake over their working lives, reinforcing the need for further tertiary education (World Bank 2019).
- The changing nature of work, with its interdependence of general and specific technical skills, is enhancing the value of, and need for, complementary capability development, facilitated by higher education and vocational education (World Bank 2019).
- The health impacts of greater education are pronounced (related more to early years) (World Bank 2019).

An Asia Development Bank study (ADB 2015) focussing on India (and China) showed that human capital has had a positive impact in terms of economic growth and labour productivity over the long run between 1960 and 2010, while another study found positive impacts of human capital on total factor productivity in formal manufacturing in India (Kathuria et al. 2013). Then there is the growing inequality in India, especially in urban contexts, associated with skills premiums (ADB 2015) while some studies have highlighted the importance of skills in facilitating Foreign Direct Investment (Siddharthan and Narayanan 2013). Interestingly, other approaches have drawn a link between human capital and environmental factors, namely that skills formation can serve as a substitute for energy usage in India, helping to reduce energy consumption and pollution (Sahu and Narayanan 2013).

3.2 Higher Education in India: Structural and Other Features

This chapter considers higher education in India from a number of parameters: structure and governance; access and opportunity; diversity, quality and innovation.

3.2.1 Concerns About Indian Higher Education

India's higher education system is a litany of woes. A multitude of authors (Agarwal 2009; Government of India 2013a, b; 2016a, b; Kapur and Mehta 2017a, b; Kumar 2015; Kulkarni 2018a, b; NITI Aayog 2017, 2018; Ramaswami 2016; Trilokekar and Embleton 2015) have commented on its endemic flaws: lack of linkage to employers and labour market needs; major quality concerns, including especially in the burgeoning private sector, but also in the public domain; handicaps of poor research performance; issues around lack of appropriate governance, transparency and accountability; undue government and ministerial influence in appointments and ministerial patronage in the proliferation of private institutions, giving rise to all manner of conflicts of interest and quality concerns; mismatches in funding relative to enrolments between elite central institutions and state based ones; gross enrolment ratios which are significantly lower than counterpart nations, meaning massive pent up demand, and lack of access and opportunity for millions; burdensome input based regulations focussed on staffing numbers and physical facilities rather than outcomes; low and inflexible fee structures in both public and private arenas, setting up incentives to seek under the counter 'capitation payments'.

A number of authors (Government of India 2013a, b; 2016a, b; Kumar 2015; Ramaswami 2016) have commented on the inadequacy of the curriculum in higher education. These concerns include: lack of practical and industry orientation; presence of multiple silos, including within academia and discipline area, and limited interaction with industry via staff mobility; outdated pedagogy based on regurgitative, rote-based approaches rather than on genuine inquiry, learning, problem-solving and collaboration; lack of a holistic approach to education with a focus on narrow 'credentialism' rather than on broader contexts of education, or nurturing of curious, inquisitive minds and providing multifaceted student experiences; traditional methods of teaching focused on lecturers providing information to students in a unidimensional manner; and faculty shortages and various administrative and regulatory burdens on hiring.

The situation is best encapsulated by the view of students themselves. In a recent survey of what matters to international students from India, including why they were attracted to study abroad, apart from the usual refrain of quality education, employment prospects, worldwide connections, and travel opportunities, a stand out factor was the wish to have a more practical orientation to learning which is absent at home. The need for greater diversity of specialisations (combining both breadth and depth), as well as independent learning possibilities, also were key factors (QS 2016).

To be fair there are some positives. Altbach (2014, p. 503) famously speaks of 'Islands of Excellence in a sea of mediocrity'. The Indian Institutes of Technology are renown the world over, and many of its alumni are distinguished in academia, the professions, and have significant influence back home in India in terms of trade, investment, research, cultural aspects and even political influence. Some of the newer private entities demonstrate positive signs in terms of teaching and interface with industry, while 'non-institutions' such as the Khan Academy are innovative efforts in providing online education to the masses. The Heritage Xperiential learning school (at the school level rather than tertiary level) is a novel approach to education based on self-discovery, relationship building, creative and social intelligence, citizenship and fostering the adaptability quotient to adapt to changing contexts (Das 2019). Nonetheless, despite the pockets of excellence, a seismic shift is required to produce a stronger education system across the board.

3.2.2 Structural Issues and Legacies

There are, and have been, significant structural deficiencies, as exemplified by the affiliated system of universities and colleges, where the university awards a degree, sets the curriculum and examinations, and colleges blindly follow these to the detriment of innovation, creativity and autonomy, or linkage to local circumstances and needs. Universities have been burdened with oversight of colleges (sometimes as many as 500–1000 Colleges per university), while the affiliation fees that colleges provide to universities establish rent-seeking activities on the part of universities (Kapur and Mehta 2017a, b; Kulkarni 2018a). There are multiple associated disconnects in the system: the absence of a research and teaching nexus, with much of the research being done only in a few elite institutions (Higher Education Institutions of National Importance such as the Indian Institutes of Technology) and public laboratories rather than in universities as a whole; and a disconnect between teaching and examinations, where examinations are set and conducted by universities, but colleges are where teaching occurs (Datta 2017; Government of India 2013b). As a result, the ability of research to inform teaching (and vice-a-versa) and new pedagogy for example, and the continuous evaluation, feedback and information flows, inherent in a nexus between teaching and examination, are lost.

It is important to recognise that the Indian system is what it is due to multiple historical legacies. The current system owes much to the legacy of the British colonial rule. The higher education system was designed to foster and facilitate colonial intentions and objectives including running the Empire as cheaply as possible (Datta 2017). Indeed, Tharoor points out, in quoting Lord Mcauley about the teaching of English that "This was designed to also teach a minority of Indians to form a class who may be interpreters between us and the millions we govern." (Tharoor 2016, p. 219). This meant that the upper reaches of the British/Indian Civil Service were filled by British educated in Britain, with lesser positions filled by Indians educated in British institutions in India (Datta 2017). Universities in India became merely examination based entities, driven by rote learning, stifling innovation and creativity and aimed at filling lesser posts in the British administrative machinery. This in large measure accounts for the examination orientation of India's university system today. Early systems of education, namely the Gurukal approach, drawing on close personal relations between the guru (teacher) and pupil in a holistic sense embodying values, service, duty, philosophy and precepts beyond a narrow curriculum, and Buddhist teachings, for example, at the eminent Nalanda University, gave way to both Muslim and later British rulers (Kulkarni 2018a).

The second legacy followed independence when 5 year central plans, allied with government control over the commanding heights of the economy, through public ownership and regulation of core 'building block' industries, was the favoured approach to development by the Nehru Government, inspired by Soviet central planning. In such an environment, a few elite national institutions (Indian Statistical Institute, Indian Institute of Science and Indian Institutes of Technology or Institutes of National Importance) were established to support such planning through the provision of engineers, scientists, statisticians and researchers (Datta 2017). Any research linked to industrial needs was handled through a network of public bodies such as the Council of Scientific and Industrial Research (CSIR). As such, any research in institutions outside these august bodies was completely marginalised, and mainstream universities became largely teaching bodies. The critical nexus between teaching and research, in the sense of Humboldt's vision for a university, was absent.[3]

A third related legacy, we argue, is that the higher education system generally has lacked the key linkages with other players in the economy including industry, small businesses and the broader community. When allied with import substitution and an inward-looking development model, critical linkages with the global flow of ideas and participation in global value chains of knowledge, and even local flows of ideas and, know-how, were not fostered. India's poor performance in inbound tertiary mobility, and less strong position in technology absorption performance, are reflections of this legacy (Cornell University, INSEAD, WIPO 2018). Of course, we recognise that as a developing country with large population, the capacity to pursue such grander global aspirations in international education is highly constrained. The point is that the model of development did not allow it to be pursued to any great extent even at later stages.

A fourth legacy is that in emphasising central planning of commanding heights, supported by a few associated elite institutions, the broad base of strong 'middle' tier institutions, providing sound education and opportunity for the wider population, has gone missing in many ways. A 'missing middle' is a recurrent theme in this book, including as it relates to enterprise, exports and other domains.

Another core legacy of the Indian education scene, in our view, has been the disavowal of Mahatma Gandhi's education precepts based on Buni Yadi Talam (Basic Education) or Nayi Talim (New Education) (Kulkarni 2012; Tara and Kumar 2016). These philosophies centred on 'Education for life, Education through life and Education throughout life' (Kulkarni 2012, p. 138). They emphasised artisan skills, vocational skills, including traditional trades and craft, work experience while learning, values-based approaches with a well-balanced curricula emphasising serving and caring, socially inclusive education and connections to local village industries. A key premise of the Gandhian approach was that teachers need to be learners themselves, including from students. Gandhi was fiercely critical of the British approach to teaching designed to prepare Indians for clerical roles, and which emphasised cramming for exams. The confluence of the British legacy and the post-independence centrally planned, elite-driven education model put paid to the Gandhian vision. While Gandhi focussed mainly on school education, it would be no great stretch in our view to argue that India's chronic weakness in vocational education (Government of India 2016a; Gupta et al. 2016; Mehrotra et al. 2014; Pillay and Ninan 2014), including poor quality, the relative absence of qualified teachers, weak enrolment rates by world standards, lack of effective linkages with industry and the absence of appropriate

---

[3] Wilhem Von Humboldt was the Interior Minister in the Prussian Government in the 19th century. The Humboltdian view is that of unity of teaching and research in a University (Datta 2017).

funding models, as well as lack of prestige for the vocational sector, are all further legacies of the failure to capture the Gandhian spirit.

3.3 Institutional Flaws

The legacy is what it is. What though of the more recent past? India's higher education scene suffers from a number of structural flaws. The higher education system has 'exploded' in terms of enrolment and institutional growth as seen in Table 3.1. As it stands, enrolment in Higher Education is over 36.5 million, up from 29.2 million in 2011–2012 (Government of India 2018a).

Reasons for the growth of enrolments in recent times (and indeed over the last quarter of a century) centre on aspiration, the growth in the age-appropriate population, including growth in secondary education as the natural pathway, and rising skills needs in the economy (Kapur 2017).

However, India's gross enrolment ratio, despite growing, is still at the weaker end of the spectrum when compared to our benchmark nations. India is only ahead of Bangladesh and Sri-Lanka among our comparator set. This points to massive pent up demand in the system, which when allied with an inability to provide jobs on a large enough scale, suggests that the 'demographic dividend'[4] is in great deal of trouble. More will be spoken of these issues shortly.

Table 3.1 Institutional and enrolment growth 2011–2012 to 2017–2018

	Enrolment growth (%)	Institutional growth (%)
Public universities (National and State including Institutes of National Importance)	20.1	23.0
Private universities	89.7	81
Public colleges	40.4	35
Private colleges	76.6	74.6
Stand-alone	20.96	−10

Note Private universities in our assessment are fully private and those aided by Government. According to the All Industry Survey of Higher Education (AISHE), Stand Alone Institutions are those not affiliated to universities, who cannot provide degrees but run diploma level programs. Further, in AISHE, colleges cannot provide degrees in their own name, and are affiliated to/recognised with universities. Only affiliated and constituent institutions of Central and State Public universities are counted as colleges

Source Government of India (2018a), with author calculations (updated version of previous paper by author)

---

[4] The demographic dividend typically relates to India's youthful population which dominates overall share of population.

The second main point to note is the massive privatisation of the system that is in train. As can be seen from Table 3.1 growth in private sector enrolment in both universities and colleges, exceeds that of public, although noting that in raw student numbers the public sector is still ascendant for universities but not colleges. Further, enrolments in private colleges outweighs that of government run colleges by a ratio of up to 2:1 and enrolment in private colleges comprises just over half of enrolments in the entire system.

Structurally, the higher education system has been focussed more on the growth in the number of institutions. For example, average enrolment per college has declined over the last six years, while there have been significant spatial imbalances when considering colleges per capita. According to the most recent data, some 18.5% of colleges have less than 100 enrolments, and only 3.6% of colleges have enrolments more than 3000 (Government of India 2018a). It would appear that institutions are proliferating, often as body shop arrangements, as 'ribbon cutting exercises' and through patronage and influence. This seriously exacerbates quality concerns and has been characterised by lack of regulatory oversight, and an inability to hire teachers. The system as a whole in our view lacks critical mass and is highly fragmented, with increasingly poor capacity utilisation (Kapur and Mehta 2017a, b; Kulkarni 2018a).

The Twelfth Five Year Plan noted this when it claimed that 'With the growth rate of Institutions matching that of enrolment, the problem of low enrolment per Institution evident at the start of the Eleventh Plan remains' and that '…further expansion should be undertaken in the context of also achieving discipline diversity and increasing capacity within existing institutions, rather than creating new institutions' (Government of India 2013a, Chap. 21, para 193). Clearly, for a variety of politically driven motives, the advice of the Planning Commission has been rejected.

The now-defunct Planning Commission also noted a large number of areas with populations between 10,000 and less than 100,000 without proximity to institutions (Government of India 2013a).

Clearly from a structural perspective the system is in disrepair and needs a coordinated, integrated approach to *enhanced* capacity utilisation, consolidation and then possibly expansion, with an explicit focus on access (and quality of course) on a spatial basis.

That the system is flawed is also reflected in what we consider a gradual departure from the central premise of education: to provide quality education for all. Instead what we have is a 'bureaucratisation' of higher education (Table 3.2).

Table 3.2 More bureaucracy

	2011–2012	2012–2013	2013–2014	2014–2015	2015–2016	2016–2017	2017–2018
Professional staff/Teacher ratio	0.64	0.69	0.72	0.74	0.74	0.85	0.94
Pupil/Teacher	23	23	24	23	23	26	29

Source Government of India AISHE various years, Author calculations and update of table from previous paper by author

According to our calculations, there has been a significant rise in the professional or non-academic staff to teacher ratio, *at the very same time that the pupil-teacher ratio is worsening*. Thus, the administration of the vast and expanding system is taking precedence, at least in human resource terms, over the academic functions, reinforcing our view about the 'ribbon cutting' nature of Indian higher education. Moreover, pupil–teacher ratios vary widely, ranging from 17 in Mizoram and 18 in Tamil Nadu to 67 in Bihar (Government of India 2018a).

3.3.1 The State in Retreat?

What we observe is that the Indian state appears to be in some form of 'retreat' in higher education, with declines in initial funding per student in tertiary education over the last five years,[5] now putting India ahead only of Bangladesh of our comparator set. This is also reflected in the declining government expenditure on tertiary education as a share of total public expenditure on education and government funding per tertiary student as a percentage of GDP per capita (UNESCO 2018). India is also ranked 40th out of 50 on resources devoted to higher education, according to Universitas 21, although when adjusted for the level of economic development its overall relative position improves (Williams and Leahy 2019).

These findings need to be contextualised in many respects. Firstly, against the backdrop of rapid growth in institutions, including public ones, a declining public outlay per student raises 'red flags' about value for money. Secondly, and as we have indicated previously, the unfettered growth and proliferation of the private sector has raised severe questions about quality, accountability, transparency, governance and issues of equity and access, Thirdly, declining public expenditure on tertiary education, whichever metric one uses, is occurring at the very same time that nearly all other countries in our comparator set are increasing their public investments. Other countries are becoming increasingly cognisant of the need to enhance public investment in a key strategic sector which promotes knowledge building capabilities, vital for long term competitiveness, recognising the positive externalities that public education confers. Of course, one could argue that the current trend is a rebalancing of the system. India has typically had a higher share of total government expenditure on education accounted for by tertiary education than other countries. Yet this needs to be seen in the light of the overall low and static share of government expenditure totally on education as a share of GDP, hovering around the 3.8% (UNESCO 2018),[6] well short of successive Indian Government aspirations of 6% of GDP (Government of India 2016b), and which is low compared to other countries. Further, the imbalance in the system is reflected in the lion share of national public funding catering to

---

[5]Approximately 2011 or 2012 to 2016 or latest year.
[6]The UNESCO reference pertains to raw data obtained by the author in 2018 from UNESCO data.uis.unesco.org accessed 20/7/2018 with analysis, inferences, conclusions and commentary from the author.

relatively small numbers of enrolees, while the state system (which caters to the great bulk of students) has seen its share of total expenditure falling (Government of India 2013b).

In addition, are questions about returns to investment in the higher education sector, when one considers the still relatively weak gross enrolment ratios, lack of employable graduates, lack of interface with industry and questionable or non-existent research performance, save for a few elite institutions. Beyond this, we point out that a historic bias to tertiary education (mostly in a few elite institutions) has come at the expense of secondary (and primary) education sectors, the **very pipeline** to tertiary education. In short, whether India has had the balance right in respect of its priorities accorded to the various tiers of education is certainly debatable at the very least. India's expenditure per student on upper and lower secondary education, for example, has been well short (despite growth in recent times) of other nations in our comparator set, including emerging economies of Asia (UNESCO 2018). Further, it should be noted public investment in vocational education, as another critical pathway to employment and further study, has been under-done as we described earlier and shall discuss in more detail later.

Nonetheless, we take the view in this book that on balance, India has to be receptive to allowing more private sector participation in the higher education system, provided that such private investment brings forth quality, productivity, efficiency in the sector and access to global knowledge. This is because of the sheer need and scale of the sector, probably beyond the scale of government. Second, private equity, apart from cash, can bring in injections of management expertise, know-how and capability. Third, at least in higher education, there are significant private returns to investment in the form of greater remuneration and job security for those investing in human capital, of the order of 16%, while others suggest up to 20% and even higher for females (Joshi 2015; Kapur 2017). For all that, a robust system needs a strong government role in higher education for a multitude of reasons: equity and access issues; as a strategic sector for the knowledge economy; and for market failure reasons such as positive externalities, including in research, for merit goods arguments and risk and uncertainty in future returns from education (and capital market imperfections) for students which may constrain participation, and information gaps and asymmetries (Chowdry 2009).

As with our approach generally in this book, the public (and community) and private sectors should be seen as synergistic, complementary and collaborative, drawing on their respective roles and capabilities, and addressing collectively weaknesses in the system. Consistent with this is the need for a carefully nuanced, coordinated and planned approach to higher education, engaging both the public and private sectors.

Some have argued that India's recent higher education policies have at least acknowledged the need for India to be competitive, to address labour market needs, and are becoming cognisant of the knowledge economy (Schwartzman 2015), but others argue that India's move towards privatisation is less about a coherent policy but more about the breakdown of the state and that the '…. Education system remains suspended between over-regulation by the state on the one hand and a discretionary

3.3 Institutional Flaws

privatisation that is unable to mobilise private capital in productive ways' (Schwartzman 2015, p. 26). Encouragement of the growth of private institutions, ostensibly to cater to growing demand, has been marked by public authorities actively participating and facilitating the process of privatisation for private gain themselves (Trilokekar and Embleton 2015). In short, commentary about Indian higher education as representing 'Half baked Socialism, Half baked capitalism' (Trilokekar and Embleton 2015) resonates with this author. So we reiterate our premise that India's higher education should not be 'either or' but rather a balanced approach between public and private provision based on carefully articulated needs and rationale and strong and rigorous oversight bringing together the complementary capabilities of the two sectors.

3.3.2 Access and Opportunity

This section assesses India's higher education sector in providing access and opportunity for its citizens.

3.3.2.1 Gross Enrolment Ratios (GER)

While it is true that India has increased its numbers enrolled in raw terms in higher education and lays claim to being among the world's largest sector, if not the world's largest sector, and has made improvement in its gross enrolment ratio, the fact remains that a great deal of the population of eligible age are simply missing out. India's gross enrolment ratio in tertiary education is seen in the following Table 3.3.

Simply put, despite growth, India is not in the same league as most nations in providing adequate access to education. With a comparable population, China is close to double that of India in its gross enrolment ratio. Therefore, it is simply not correct to say that a large country cannot afford to educate people in such large numbers. By our calculations, approximately 41% of age-relevant people in India are not working, looking for work or studying.[7]

An elite system is one in which a privilege of birthright and or talent determines access to education, corresponding to less than 15% of gross enrolment, a mass system has up to 50% GER, which reflects the preparation of the population for the technical and economic elite roles, and a universal system is one that has more than 50% participation in higher education among 18–23-year-olds, with the eventual outcome being the adaptation of the whole population to social and technological change (Trow 2007). According to the technical definition therefore, India

---

[7]This may be somewhat overstated because of inclusion of 15–17 year olds in part our calculation rather than the strict adherence to the generally accepted 18–23 year old category for the analysis. Unfortunately the labour force data on which part of these calculations are based do not totally align with population data which does relate to 18–23 year old.

Table 3.3 Gross enrolment ratios: higher education (UNESCO data includes Vocational sector)

	2012	2017
India	24.4	27.5
Australia	119.7 (2015)	121.86
Bangladesh	13.4	17.6
Brazil	45.0	50.5 (2016)
China	28.0	51.0
Chile	78.8	91.5
Germany	60.5 (2013)	68.3 (2016)
Japan	–	–
Malaysia	36.3 (2014)	41.9
Republic of Korea	96.6	93.8 (2016)
Russia	76.1	81.8 (2016)
Sri Lanka	17.2	19.0
Thailand	50.7	49.3 (2016)
U.K	59.8	59.4 (2016)
U.S	88.7 (2013)	88.8 (2016)

Source UNESCO (2019). Reproduced with permission of UNESCO

has attained the profile of a 'mass system' somewhat marginally. However, this is masking the vast number of age-relevant people not in the education system, while quality and employability issues would also suggest that India is not necessarily preparing the population for technical and elite roles. In our judgement, India has characteristics more akin to an elite model when allowance is made for these factors.

The gross enrolment ratio varies from as low as 5.2% in some remote areas to more than 56% in other areas (Government of India 2018a). Of course, enrolment is determined by a number of factors beyond the availability of institutions, including income levels, job prospects, cultural factors, student mobility, safety, and student and parental aspiration (Government of India 2013b). Therefore, in framing a response to both increasing gross enrolment ratios, and its spatial distribution, it is important to consider these all-encompassing features rather than just focus on building more institutions.

Based on population projections in the 18–23 age group, and utilising the very conservative 30% gross enrolment ratio[8] we construct the following 'back of the envelope' scenarios based on holding average enrolment per institution steady and varying the number of institutions or holding numbers of institutions constant and varying average enrolments per institution, to realise the gross enrolment ratio of 2030, as shown in Table 3.4.

---

[8] The 2030 GER that we use is in fact the Government target for 2020. To be ultra conservative we have held this same GER figure to 2030, also we consider that a 30% target will not be met by 2020.

3.3 Institutional Flaws

Table 3.4 Scenarios for expansion of higher education

	Scenario 1	Scenario 2
	Hold average enrolment steady and vary number of institutions	Hold institutions constant and vary average enrolment
Colleges	Extra 7769 colleges	Extra 128 people per college
Universities	Extra 163 universities	Extra 1645 people per university
Stand alone	Extra 2250 institutions	Extra 35 students per stand alone

Source Author calculations based on AISHE data

In reality, some combination of these scenarios, i.e. a combination of varying enrolment rates, and increasing the number of institutions will be required. These scenarios are presented as extreme ends of the spectrum. Nonetheless, whichever way one looks at it, the implications of an increase in GER in capacity terms is massive, particularly so given our conservatism. The magnitude of the task is particularly pronounced when the government sector, whose key role is to promote access and equity, is seemingly in some sort of retreat. If pushed to make a judgement, one would surmise that improving average enrolments per institution, to enhance capacity utilisation, would be a better approach.

In our view, what is required is a better-planned approach which integrates education needs with population, demographic planning, and spatial development. This would have a number of elements: better capacity utilisation in the first instance to address the particularly weak average enrolments in some colleges; consolidation of facilities to build scale, avoid duplication and wastage of resources; consideration of building new institutions where they are of a 'hub and spoke' type to service a wider area of need; the injection of further private capital where regulated, quality controlled and not driven by political interests; potentially supporting outward investment abroad in the establishment of campuses in other countries, and using this as a lever to promote greater outbound mobility of students as well, thereby promoting greater access to the global pool of ideas, knowledge and new pedagogy; integration of the vocational education sector with higher education to provide seamless education pathways; much greater and concerted use of online modes and virtual teaching arrangements; considers in a meaningful way the balance between physical and virtual investment space, which means having a wider notion of education beyond traditional 'bricks and mortar' approach to embrace virtual entities such as the Khan Academy, as part of overall planning, as novel ways of transmitting learning. However, bringing these institutions or quasi institutions under a regulatory umbrella will be challenging.

To be fair, India has been making inroads into online education, as a means of addressing access issues, through strong uptake of Massive Open Online Courses (MOOC's) and other applications. For example, SWAYAM is a government programme, which oversees free online courses by a number of institutions, and for a small fee for certification, with transferability of academic records. However, it is considered still to be subject to onerous and restrictive rules and regulations about the number, types and composition of courses allowed to be offered, and various other bureaucratic procedures, and could be more open to older age groups (Jagannathan 2018; Government of India 2019a).

3.3.2.2 Leaky Pipes

The issue of low levels of gross enrolment ratio at the tertiary end, although not necessarily in raw terms, is part of a much larger story of 'leaky pipes'. The flow of potential students into higher education is not occurring due to weakness in enrolment at lower levels.

Over the last five years, India's gross enrolment rate for both lower and upper secondary levels[9] has increased, but even now there is far from complete coverage especially for upper secondary, and well short for both when compared to our benchmark countries, with the exception of Bangladesh. India's GER in 2016 was 65.5% for upper secondary education and 87.9% for lower secondary levels respectively.

Of significance is the high levels of discontinuation (those who have completed last level of enrolment but not gone on) and to a lesser extent drop-out rates (those not completing last level of enrolment). According to surveys conducted by the National Statistical Services Organisation, discontinuance rates increased between 2007–2008 and 2014–2015, across almost all levels of pre-tertiary education. In particular, discontinuance has risen in the upper primary, secondary, higher secondary and diploma levels. In varying degrees, these are the 'feeder' tiers into tertiary education (Government of India 2010, 2016d).

According to the later survey, four key areas stand out for discontinuance and drop out: financial constraints on households; economic activities, e.g. working in home businesses, especially for males having to assume the breadwinner role; domestic activities; and 'not interested in education', more pronounced for males and females of lower ages (Government of India 2016d).

An array of forces are behind these numbers: vulnerable financial positions of families associated with lack of stable, secure employment and the preponderance of informal, insecure employment; cost of education and the tradeoff's and relative benefits and costs that households make regarding investment in education; and of course gender-based stereotyping, in relation to traditional domestic roles for females. As one would surmise, not continuing education is more pronounced for females, and weighted more heavily to engaging in domestic activities, while males

---

[9]Lower Secondary students (ISCED 2) typically enter between ages 10 and 13 (and begins after 4–7 years of primary education), and aim to provide skills from subject/theoretical curriculum and as a basis for lifelong learning. Upper Secondary (ISCED 3) is for completing secondary students to provide skills pertinent for work or tertiary education, with more differentiated options and streams, compared to ISCED 2. Upper secondary students typically enter between ages 14–16 and the programme usually is completed after 12 or 13 years after the beginning of primary (12 years being the most common). Students are typically 17–18 years old when they complete Upper Secondary Source: UNESCO International Standard Classification of Education 2011.

3.3 Institutional Flaws

are more strongly aligned with economic reasons (Government of India 2016d). An important and worrying reason is the lack of interest in education. This may point to significant weakness in pedagogy and perceived relevance of education in India at the earlier levels. More of this will be considered in the chapter on female empowerment.

While India has constituted a 'Right to Education Act' to mandate and ensure access for all 6–14-year-olds, it has been criticised for focussing too much on inputs, including facilities, hiring practices and 'having a one size fits all' approach, as well as automatic promotion of students, rather than learning outcomes (although modifications in this direction are being made). A 'Right to Learning' or similarly quality, outcome and standards approach would be of greater benefit (Dreze and Sen 2013; Government of India 2016a; Jagannathan 2018; NITI Aayog 2017).

The upshot of these factors is that India is among the weakest of all our comparator countries in terms of the population with at least some secondary education as shown in Table 3.5. The World Bank's new Human Capital Index based on probability of survival to age 5, expected years of schooling, quality-adjusted years of schooling, and health sees India in a lowly 115th place out of 157 countries (World Bank 2019).

Table 3.5 Percentage of the population aged 25 and above that have reached (but not necessarily) completed a secondary level of education 2006–2017

India	51.6%
China	77.4%
Brazil	60%
Russia	95.6%
Bangladesh	45.5%
Pakistan	37.3%
Australia	90%
Germany	96.5%
U.S	95.3%
U.K	82.9%
Japan	93.3%
Republic of Korea	95.6%
Chile	80.6%
Malaysia	80%
Sri Lanka	82.8%
Thailand	44.8%

Source UN (2018). Reproduced with permission of UN

For a country which aspires to be a knowledge economy power, these are damning portraits. Moreover, other data from the World Economic Forum (2017), points to significantly declining secondary education attainment rates at higher age brackets. Thus, in one sense it means that younger cohorts are more aware of, accessing and obtaining at least secondary education, which bodes well, but older cohorts have not had this opportunity, or if they have, are not availing themselves of this. Thus, not only does India need to focus on education at lower levels among the age-specific cohort, a priority on raising attainment across all cohorts, including older ones, is required. This means consciously planning for and providing access to education for all segments of society. It is important that India does not fall for the trap of only catering to the 'demographic dividend'. This is all the more pertinent as the numbers in the older age cohorts grow.

Further, the 'Right to Education Act' has not necessarily been accompanied by appropriate resourcing. Government expenditure on lower and upper secondary levels, on a purchasing power parity basis, has only been increasing marginally over the last few years, and currently lags all countries bar Bangladesh in our comparator set. It is thus behind Sri Lanka and other emerging economies. When assessed against the share of total government expenditure on education, India performs the weakest of all comparator countries in lower secondary but is the highest on upper secondary (UNESCO 2018). Thus while there is emphasis on upper secondary in the overall education spending budget, it is the quantum that is lacking. It also means that the foundation of lower secondary education is under-done. We have not explored primary education, since our focus is on those tiers of education more closely aligned to the knowledge economy. It should also be noted that of course tertiary education is likely to be more expensive given its greater complexity and more specialised instruction.

3.4 Quality, Diversity and Innovation

This section considers India's education performance on the related parameters of diversity, quality and innovation.

3.4.1 Diversity

By any notion, Indian higher education lacks diversity. College enrolments, driven in large measure by the affiliation system, churn through graduates in the manner of an assembly line. While having many thousand institutions in higher education, just one area of discipline, Arts represents more than one-third of total under-graduate enrolments, some 36.4% (Government of India 2018a) and three discipline areas represent close to 70% of enrolments. India is more based on the illusion of diversity. Real diversity is important for student choice, multifaceted experiences, for the interplay of different fields and collaboration and sharing of knowledge, which gives rise to innovation and new ways of doing things. The increasing importance of Science,

3.4 Quality, Diversity and Innovation

Technology, Engineering, Arts and Mathematics (STEAM) is one manifestation of this. Further, despite the importance of agriculture and veterinary sciences to the Indian economy, there is little enrolment in this area, and there needs to be much more focus on vocational education to meet the emerging needs of the economy (Government of India 2016e).

It would appear that the lower cost of homogenous degrees, their general accessibility to the population, availability (relatively) of teaching staff as opposed to more specialised areas, and the 'signalling' effect of a degree (e.g. in the labour market, and for females in terms of marriage) could all be key determinants of India's lack of breadth. The illusion of diversity is also represented at the institutional level through the presence of many single discipline organisations ostensibly on the premise of specialisation, yet lacking the breadth and connection across disciplinary areas necessary for knowledge development and flows (Kulkarni 2018a). For example, more than one-third of colleges have a single programme only (Government of India 2018a). What is needed in India is a flexible approach based on diverse specialisations.

Similarly, the narrowness of options is also reflected by the fact that nationally, out of approximately 191 courses, just ten courses cover more than 84% of enrolment (Government of India 2018a). This points to poor uptake of a number of serious endeavours, and lack of connection across programmes. Further, there is a de-linking effect between Ph.D. and postgraduate (e.g. Masters Degrees). For example, for Ph.D.'s the maximum number are in science, then engineering and technology, while in postgraduate, it is social sciences, followed by management that dominates. Thus, there appears to be no particular pathways to build, sustain and nurture excellence and elite research.

3.4.1.1 Diversity by Level

While it is true naturally in most countries, that the ISECD 6[10]or undergraduate dominates enrolment, consistent with providing mass or near-universal enrolment, it is much more amplified in India, than in other countries, including in lesser developed nations. India is at the lower end of the scale, especially in Ph.D.'s (ISCED 8) when measured by share of enrolment, but has grown in sheer number. While India performs better at the ISCED 7 (Masters) level relative to other nations in share terms, in considering the weak relative performance on Ph.D.'s this could point to ceilings associated with further learning (UNESCO 2018) (Table 3.6). Less than 4% of Colleges, the mainstay of the system, run a Ph.D. programme, and only a third have a postgraduate programme (Government of India 2018a). However, as the Economic Survey of 2017–2018 indicates, the majority of these Ph.D. students are in STEM fields which is relevant to the knowledge economy (Government of India 2018b).

---

[10]Tertiary comprises ISCED 5 (short cycle tertiary usually between 2 and 3 years and includes vocational), ISCED 6 (Bachelor Degree or equivalent usually 3–4 years), ISCED 7 (Master's level or equivalent), and ISCED 8 (Doctoral or equivalent). Source: UNESCO International Standard Classification of Education (2011).

Table 3.6 Distribution of tertiary students (non-vocational): 2016 except where otherwise stated

	ISCED 6	ISCED 7	ISCED 8
Australia	51.0	13.8	3.0
Bangladesh	76.8	17.5	0.5
Brazil	96.9	1.8	1.2
Chile	63.3	7.3	0.4
China	51.6	5.1	0.8
Germany	60.2 (2015)	33.2	6.6
India	86.5	13.1	0.4
Japan	69.4 (2015)	8.6	1.9
Malaysia	50.5	11.2	3.3
South Korea	67.1 (2015)	7.8	2.2
Russian Federation	57.1	20	1.8
Sri Lanka	76.6	14.8	0.3
Thailand	82.6 (2015)	8.5	1.1
U.K	65.4 (2015)	18.1	4.8
U.S	47.8 (2015)	12.9	2.0

Source UNESCO (2018). Reproduced with permission of UNESCO

Drawing on UNESCO (2018) data, we also observe that when comparing India to the U.S. (generally regarded as a bastion of a broad-based, liberal education system), there is a greater spread of enrolments by discipline in the U.S. compared to India at the undergraduate level.

The share of Ph.D. pass outs to total Ph.D. enrolments is approximately 20% (Kulkarni 2018a). We recognise that this type of analysis needs to be more accurately informed by tracing and tracking individual student progress, nonetheless it does contain some important messaging about throughput. Further, as a threshold point, quantity is no indicator of quality. Of course, for a number of jobs higher level qualifications are not required. Nonetheless, the relative absence of highly skilled experts as a proportion of the student cohort in India and when compared to abroad (India is at the lower end of researchers per million population compared to U.S., Israel and China according to the Economic Survey of 2017–2018), could make it difficult for India to play a leading role in the national and global knowledge economy. One further insight is that Indian Ph.D. students in the U.S. in STEM fields are far outweighed by China (Government of India 2018b).

The findings in this section have many implications, including potentially the lack of jobs in fields requiring very high end skills in India forcing these people into lower end jobs not commensurate with their skills (indeed anecdotal evidence has many Ph.D. graduates applying for lower end clerical roles (Das 2019), the unattractiveness of academia as a career destination associated with 'red tapism', absence of cutting-edge facilities, lack of research focus in all but a few elite institutions, and the greater remuneration associated with corporate careers, including in multinational corporations.

In terms of breadth of educational opportunity, the Indian education system lacks a robust vocational education and training (VET) arrangement. India is ranked 106th out of 125 countries in vocation education enrolment, in the Global Talent Competitiveness Index (Lanvin and Monteiro 2019) reinforcing the lack of diversity in the system. The Government has abandoned its target of skilling 500,000 by 2022. However, much will need to be done in terms of raising quality, access and critical linkage to Industry. The vocational education and training system has been significantly under-developed in India, among other reasons, one of the important ones being lack of prestige accorded to it.

3.4.2 Quality

This section considers various dimensions of quality in Indian Higher Education.

3.4.2.1 Internal Quality Ratings

The Indian Higher Education scene faces many challenges in quality. Some 32% of accredited universities were rated A Grade or above, 52% as B and 16% C, and out of colleges, only 10% have been rated A, 66% B and 24% C (Joshi 2015; Government of India 2016a). Many Institutions were not even accredited by the National Assessment and Accreditation Council (NAAC).

Earlier, we saw some of the issues associated with quality constraints in India, including the emphasis on rote learning, lack of innovation and creativity in pedagogy and highlighted the reasons why Indian students go abroad in large numbers.

3.4.2.2 Global University Rankings

In this context, it is useful to explore global university rankings as a proxy for both quality and reputation. Although criticised for being more input rather than outcome or even output focussed, and not addressing student experience, international rankings are an important window to the world in terms of the attractiveness and reputation of nations' institutions, particularly vital in the context of globally mobile students, staff and researchers.

The following table shows India's rankings in the Times Higher Education Rankings (Times Higher Education 2018) (Tables 3.7 and 3.8).

Table 3.7 Times Higher Education rankings: various years

	2013	2014	2015	2016	2017	2018	2019
India	3/400	5/400	4/401	17/800	31/981	42/1103	49/1258
China	9/400	10/400	11/400	37/800	52/981	63/1103	72/1258

Source Times Higher Education various year rankings and author analysis including updating from author's previous paper

Table 3.8 Times Higher Education 2019

	In top 100	101–200	201–500	501–800	800+
India	–	–	5	16	28
China	3	4	7	28	30

Source Times Higher Education rankings (2019a, b) and author analysis, updating from author's previous paper

What is important to note at the outset, is that the number of globally ranked institutions in India has grown progressively (although note the increased number of overall ranked institutions globally) and its share of globally ranked institutions has grown from 0.75 to 3.9% between 2012–2013 and 2017–2018. By contrast, China has grown from 2.25 to 5.7%. So there are some signs of promise for India.

Beyond this it is pertinent to note that India does not, and never has had any institutions in **the top 200** ranked institutions, generally considered a benchmark for an excellent university. On the other hand China has 7 in the top 200 and 3 in the top 100. Moreover, India's ranked institutions are driven by the small, elite Indian Institutes of Technology (IIT's) and Indian Institute of Science. Most of India's institutions are in the lower reaches of the rankings. In very rough terms, only 5.4% of Indian universities are ranked. This goes to the heart of a bifurcated system of some elite institutions surrounded by a lack of world-class standards generally. Seven out of India's top ten institutions are currently either IIT's or the Indian Institute of Science.

What is promising though is India's reasonably heartening position on the newly instituted Times Higher Education Impact Rankings, which measures universities' contribution to the United Nation's Sustainability Development goals. India has 12 ranked institutions overall out of 466, and these institutions demonstrate a commitment to addressing UN sustainable development goals in areas such as inequality, education, health, industry and infrastructure. However, challenges present themselves in the other UN goals of climate change, and strength of institutions, including legal ones (Times Higher Education 2019a; Kulkarni 2019).

3.4.2.3 Subject Rankings

The results of the ranking by subject are highly revealing (Times Higher Education 2019b). They reveal the narrowness of India's higher education system, both in terms of quality and diversity. Firstly, there are no institutions ranked at all in a number of subject areas: education, law, arts/humanities, psychology and very few in business and economics, and social sciences. Importantly, India has no ranked institutions by subject in the areas that dominate student enrolment as we saw earlier (Table 3.9).

Table 3.9 Subject rankings India and China

	Number of ranked Institutions India	Best placed Indian Institution	Number of ranked Institutions China	Best placed Chinese Institution
Arts and Humanities	0 out of 506		10 out of 506	Peking University = 23
Education	0 out of 428		4 out of 428	Peking University 26
Law	0 out of 187		3 out of 187	Tsinghua University 48
Psychology	0 out of 463		6 out of 463	Peking University = 56
Social Sciences	2 out of 666	IIT Kharagpur 251–300	33 out of 666	Peking University 23
Business and Economics	3 out of 585	University of Delhi 301–400	33 out of 585	Tsinghua University 18
Clinical, pre-clinical and Health	9 out of 721	251–300 JSS Academy of Higher Education and Research	31 out of 721	Tsinghua University 35th
Computer Science	20 out of 684	Indian Institute of Science 176–200	55 out of 684	Tsinghua University = 20th
Engineering and Technology	38 out of 903	Indian Institute of Science = 95	67 out of 903	Peking University 14th
Life Sciences	19 out of 751	Indian Institute of Science 251–300	48 out of 751	Tsinghua University 10
Physical Sciences	25 out of 963	Indian Institute of Science 251–300	63 out of 963	Peking University 19

Source Times Higher Education and author analysis

Second, the position is stronger in engineering, computer sciences, physical sciences, and life sciences compared to other disciplines. This is positive but also highlights the dilemma of Indian higher education-quality is associated with areas that have less pronounced numbers in student enrolment. This poses an essential challenge for India, to raise the quality levels across the board while serving the masses.

Further, though, is the narrowness by institution. As can be seen in Table 3.9, the best-placed institution is just one for the most part, the Indian Institute of Science.

There are some parallels with China. China's ranks are dominated by either Peking or Tsinghua University, although they occupy a much higher rank than India's best. There is also significantly more ranked institutions in the science and engineering fields than other fields, as is the case with India. This suggests that both countries have a much stronger disposition in these fields, either because of traditional strength areas, or legacy investments, i.e. both countries have sought to build industries relying on engineering and scientific capabilities, and to that end have focussed effort at least in research in these areas. However, there are significant differences as well. China, as we have noted though, has many more ranked universities **overall** than India, and this is reflected also in the subject areas. Second, however, China has a broader spread of subject rankings, reflecting its greater quality and diversity than India. Third, China has more ranked institutions than India in ICT, a discipline area that India is considered to be a leading player. This suggests that India's long-term foothold in this field is not as secure as is commonly thought, and that value adding and building capability through research, technology advancement and product development and diffusion is more likely to happen in China, in so far as the higher education sector is a driver of these capabilities.

3.4.3 Innovation

How Innovative is India's higher education scene? World class innovation and research is another attribute of a leading edge system of higher education. It reflects the true distinguishing feature of an institution of higher learning and is an integral part of education in the broader Humboltdian sense.

3.4.3.1 Outputs

On an analysis of the Scopus database (Scopus 2017) we found that for 2017, India produced more than 100,000 articles of which some 80% were produced by Indian higher education institutions, including especially Institutes of National Importance, such as the famed Indian Institutes of Technology (IIT's). In 2012, this proportion was

3.4 Quality, Diversity and Innovation

roughly the same although the total number of papers was around 75,000. In the main, universities and certainly colleges have limited research orientation, being largely teaching bodies, thus missing out the crucial synergies, pedagogical improvement and enriched course offerings that come from the research and teaching nexus (Datta 2017).

Our findings on outputs are consistent with Krishna and Patra (2016) who show that the share of total Indian papers produced by the Higher Education Sector has been steadily growing over time and accounts for around 70% of papers produced by Indians. Yet it is the case that the great bulk of papers produced are by only a few elite Institutions. These authors also reflect on the disconnect between research bodies and Universities, and for the need for Universities to have the dual functions of teaching and research.

3.4.3.2 Papers of Top Institutions

A closer examination of the nature and type of research undertaken by the higher education sector in India versus the powerhouses in China and the U.S. is interesting.

We use the Leiden database for 2013–2016 which measures publications in the Web of Science (research articles and reviews) and counts only those published in international scientific journals. At the outset, there are only 24 Indian higher education institutes that make the threshold in the Leiden database, compared to 175 in the U.S. and 148 in China (Leiden 2018). If we focus on the top ten research institutions in Higher Education in these three countries as representing the 'best of the best' then we find that these institutions produced 355,256 papers in the U.S. between 2013 and 2016, 244,942 papers in China and 44,058 papers in India. Hence the overall volume of papers of India's top 10 institutions lags considerably behind the U.S. and China for their best 10.

Secondly, is the type of papers by subject. This is shown in Table 3.10.

Table 3.10 Subject distribution of papers by top ten institutions of higher education 2013–2016

	U.S (%)	China (%)	India (%)
Biomedical and Health Sciences	55.7	34.7	19.9
Life and Earth Sciences	11.9	12.2	11.7
Maths and Computer Science	4.7	12.4	12.4
Physical Science and Engineering	19.4	36.96	54.8
Social Science and Humanities	8.4	3.8	1.2

Source Leiden (2018) and author calculations

In each country, sciences are dominant, reflecting these disciplines' proclivity for producing research papers. However, there is greater research diversity in higher education in the U.S. and China than in India. There is a stronger focus on humanities and social sciences in the U.S. than in either India or China, but China has a more diverse base of research papers than India among the top 10 best performing institutions by subject, including within the sciences. Apart from volume constraints, India has a narrower subject base of papers. This could militate against it taking a broader perspective on economy and society.

3.4.3.3 Citations

Table 3.11 reveals that India is still off the pace when compared with the U.S. and China on a variety of other parameters. On average, the top ten institutions in the U.S. and China (in that order) are more likely to be cited in the top most journals, display greater propensity to collaborate generally, internationally and with industry, and to collaborate over larger distances than for India. India however performs more strongly in terms of shorter distance collaboration among its best institutions. Tentatively, these data provide some interesting clues. India's top most institutions still on average have not reached the quality standards globally as measured by citations. Further, India has less propensity to collaborate, suggesting that the critical linkages with industry, at least in terms of papers, is not as well developed as in these other two countries. Of course, linkage and collaboration with industry do take other forms beyond papers. Further, these results do show that India is also not as well linked into global systems of innovation, as reflected in average collaboration internationally. However, India has more tendency than the U.S. at any rate to collaborate over short distances, tentatively pointing perhaps to some strengths in local clustering.

Table 3.11 2013–2016: citations top ten universities

	U.S (%)	China (%)	India (%)
Cited in top 1% of journals	2.2	0.7	0.5
Cited in top 5% of world journals	9.6	4.3	3.2
Cited in top 10% of world journals	17.4	9.1	7.2
Average collaboration	81.6	70.13	57.6
Average collaboration internationally	41.8	28.6	24.7
Average collaboration with Industry	7.2	3.7	2.5
Average collaboration <100 km	8.5	14.6	11.3
Average collaboration >5000 km	38.5	25.7	21.1

Source Leiden Institute (2018), author calculations

Therefore, India still has its work cut out in enmeshing itself into global systems of knowledge. More needs to be done overall for India to engage with the broader world of ideas exchange, knowledge access and joint activity from which knowledge can be harnessed, leveraged and developed further.

3.4.3.4 Patenting and Sources of Ideas

One of the parameters of a strongly functioning higher education system is its relationship to the market place, a key indicator being patents. From recent data (Government of India 2012b, 2017b) we observe that patent applications to the Indian Patent Office have increased from 43,197 in 2011–2012 to 45,444 in 2016–2017. Patenting in India is currently dominated by foreign players (70%), the top ten positions which belong to the corporate sector. Thus, there is a relative absence of domestic capability in the commercialisation end of the research spectrum. While this is arguably a primary responsibility of the corporate sector, in many countries higher education institutions are patent holders in their own right and in support for the commercial sector. Apart from the IIT's which provided 400 patent applications in 2016–2017 (itself a relatively small number), patent applications by the rest of the Indian higher education sector are far less. Further, as one measure of the global orientation of innovations, patent applications in the U.S. originating from India are dominated by U.S. firms operating in India (Kulkarni 2018a; USPTO 2017).

Thus, patenting both in India and outside India is dominated by foreign concerns. Further, the Indian higher education sector is not a strong patent performer either at home or abroad, meaning it is not connected to local (to the extent they exist) or global innovation systems. It is missing those vital connections into innovation both domestically and abroad, from which knowledge, technology and commercial orientation flow. The domination of Indian patent application by foreign residents could be leading to 'crowding out' of local capability by attracting resources, holding intellectual property (IP) closely and not diffusing capability more broadly, or simply that the inherent local capability is not there. Of course, it needs to be recognised that patenting is not the 'be all and end all' of innovative activity. Often companies and academics do not take the patenting route. The emphasis on jugaad innovation or improvisation in India further, does not often require patenting activity. However, arguably, jugaad can only take a nation so far-it is usually in local contexts responding to particular narrower circumstances and needs as we saw in Chap. 1. A wider and more diffuse context for innovation may require greater attention to patenting.

Of further relevance is the extent to which firms depend on higher education as a source of ideas and know-how. In a UNESCO survey, less than 10% of innovation-active manufacturing firms overall considered that higher education was a highly important source of ideas in India, far less than own enterprise sources of ideas, or from competitors or other firms. Further, for innovation-active manufacturing firms, some 53.3% of firms claimed that lack of highly qualified personnel was an important hampering factor, while this was the case for 44.2% of non-innovative active manufacturing firms (UNESCO 2017).

3.5 Resourcing

Turning to resourcing, what can be observed is that there has been growth in number of higher education researchers in India in recent years, but that this has been associated with declining productivity. On the basis of our calculations, papers per higher education researcher fell from 2.7 in 2012 to 0.7 in 2017. Despite the growth in the number of researchers, India still has one of the lowest researchers per 1000 full time equivalent (FTE) of our comparator countries at 0.6, although in raw numbers it is relatively high (close to 283,000), but still dwarfed by China with more than one million researchers, the U.S. and even the U.K (UNESCO 2018).

These findings also need to be seen in the context of R&D performed by sector (UNESCO 2018).[11] Only 4% of total R&D performed is from the Higher Education sector and this has in fact fallen over the last few years. India is the weakest performer of all our benchmark nations for which data is available on this criterion currently, and deficiencies are also represented in the very small share of GDP accounted for by R&D spending in Higher Education, and when considering expenditure by Higher Education measured in constant purchasing power pricing currency. Thus at the same time, as India's higher education researcher base is expanding, expenditure has been falling. Therefore, Indian researchers have been working on a declining 'shoe string' (Kulkarni 2018a). This is likely to further adversely impact productivity. While a number of countries have also experienced declines in gross expenditure performed by higher education, it has been from a much higher base.

There is however some measure of structural alignment being undertaken in the sense, that as share of gross expenditure on research and development (GERD), business expenditure is increasing, reflecting arguably a more commercial orientation to research. However, there are many cautionary tales. Firstly, India has had a declining overall share of GDP devoted to total research and development expenditure. Gross expenditure on R&D as a proportion of GDP has declined from 0.83% in 2011 to 0.62% in 2015, at a time when most countries have increased their share, consistent with driving forward in a knowledge economy (UNESCO 2018). Indeed, the latest Economic Survey (Government of India 2018b) finds that India under-spends on research and development as a nation relative to its income level and living standards, a reversal of the situation of years gone by.

By contrast, China's GERD as a proportion of GDP has grown from 1.78 to 2.11% between 2011 and 2016, and now exceeds the U.K, and is pressing hard on the U.S. Further, in India, the government sector holds the largest share of GERD at 52% in 2015 (although falling from 60% in 2011). This is the highest of any country in our benchmarking set (UNESCO 2018). Thus, large parts of expenditure and resources continue to be locked away in government laboratories and departments. Having large swathes of research tied up in government agencies is not necessarily ideal in terms of promoting knowledge-based industrial development, and is surely a legacy of the post-independence development model. To some extent, though, this could be obviated by excellent technology transfer mechanisms out of government agencies

---

[11] Data from UNESCO obtained on 20/7/2018 Author interpretations.

or strong collaborative networks with industry, yet it is not apparent that this is occurring. Further, the narrowness of research in the public domain is represented by the fact that some eight government agencies account for three-fifths of public investment (Government of India 2018b) in research and development. Moreover, nearly all of government R&D is from the central government, suggesting that India is missing local contexts, needs and connections in its research.

Despite the growth in the business R&D performed as a share of total R&D, India lags considerably behind other countries. Corporate priority for research and development is lacking. There are 26 Indian companies on the world's top 2500 global R&D spending list, as compared to 301 Chinese companies (Government of India 2018b). Further, as the Economic Survey points out, the limited nature of India's corporate R&D is reflected in the fact that 19 out of 26 companies are in just three sectors: pharmaceuticals, automotive and software. As we shall see in subsequent chapters, the narrowness of India's economic and industrial base, and its shallow pockets, is reflected not only in R&D but also in entrepreneurship and exporting.

3.6 Internationalisation

At its height, Nalanda University was a major international centre for learning with anything up to 10,000 students from abroad, including from China, Tiber, Mongolia and Hong Kong. Admission criteria for this Buddhist learning stronghold was stringent, based on interview, and instruction was in oral form, embodying tutorials, discussion and debate, as a precursor to more modern forms of learning. It was founded on close personal relations between teacher and student, and its free residential programme encompassed a broad range of disciplines, including religion, philosophy, logic, medicine and science among many others. Further, Nalanda University was characterised by close engagement with the local community (Kumar 2011).

We argue that India should endeavour to recreate those historical highs. This is more pertinent in the context of a globalised world in which ideas, know-how, people movements, capital and goods transcend national boundaries. Opening up India to the best and brightest abroad, meshing with India's own talents, will widen horizons, expand boundaries of knowledge and discovery, and lead to sharing of knowledge, insights, perspectives and development of complementary capabilities.

Indian students leave the country in droves. According to the Indian Ministry of External Affairs, there are 752,725 Indians studying abroad in 86 countries (Government of India 2018c). These students are important assets to India, either in terms of returning home armed with the latest know-how and insights, or if they choose to stay become members of a highly vibrant, successful, and influential diaspora overseas, who can, and do, retain links back to India scientifically, culturally and economically.

While recognising the value of outward student mobility, inward mobility provides important benefits for a nation in terms of access and exposure to diverse skills and talents from abroad, possible work options and opportunities, not to mention the revenue that flows from international students and associated multiplier effects.

India is ranked a lowly 102nd out of 126 on the inbound tertiary mobility of the Global Innovation Ranking (Cornell University, INSEAD, WIPO 2018). While the Project Atlas placed India as one of the emerging hubs for international students in 2017, this was based on students coming from only particular parts of the world, as we discuss below (Institute of International Education 2017).

In contrast to the numbers going abroad, latest data has just over 46,000 international students in India (Government of India 2018a). The composition of international students in India raises some important questions. Just one country, Nepal, accounts for 25% of international students in India, and the great bulk of students are from neighbouring less developed countries, including from the Middle East, and other parts of South Asia. Moreover, 15 programmes, mostly undergraduate ones, account for 78.5% of foreign students, and overall the undergraduate share is 77.4%. Thus, in our view, India lacks the critical linkages into the established mainstream knowledge hubs of U.S. (only 3.1% of students are from the U.S.) and Europe, especially in research and postgraduate student expertise. Students can bring a wealth of insights, knowledge and connections of their own. These connections are vital in terms of access to key global knowledge centres, as potential collaborative partners, and even possibly employment prospects in India. Certainly, inward student mobility is on the radar of the Indian Government. It has recently announced an International Education Plan, which is designed to double India's market share from 1 to 2% and attract 150,000 to 200,000 international students by 2020 (GK Today 2018).

However, the plan will continue to focus on students from Africa and the neighbourhood. In our view, India needs a comprehensive, integrated international plan comprising both inward and outward dimensions, to capitalise on the global and circular flows of ideas, know-how and expertise around the world. Recent work emphasises the importance of knowledge 'nomads', who are highly skilled professionals travelling the world to work on complex projects, developing and linking knowledge across national boundaries (Day and Stigloe 2009). India needs to make this a priority commencing with students from all around the world.

Another limiting factor is that just one state Karnataka, accounts for more than a quarter of international students (Government of India 2018a). Thus, the potential flow of knowledge and talents embodied in international students is spatially constrained.

Of course, we are completely cognisant of the fact that India is coming from a long way back. As we have stated, quality challenges exist in abundance, structural weaknesses are aplenty, and greater investments in student support and infrastructure are required to attract and retain international students. Catering to the domestic cohort is challenging enough. Moreover, it should be recognised though that India is playing an important role in its neighbourhood in projecting soft power through attracting international students.

Long-term reputation raising investments are needed. Some further insights highlight the challenges faced. India fares poorly on tolerance towards immigrants and minorities according to the Global Talent Competitiveness Index (Lanvin and Evans

2018). While this index is not necessarily strictly related to inward student mobility, it is somewhat symptomatic of an 'attitudinal shaping' issue. This also needs to be seen in the context of recent work which highlights the importance of talent, technology and tolerance in driving economic and social progress and innovation (Florida 2003). Further, and of more direct and immediate relevance is the strength of 'surrounding competitiveness'. India does not fare well on the measure of QS best student cities which captures desirability (liveability, safety, pollution, corruption), rankings (number of ranked Universities in a city), student view (student experiences and staying after graduation), employment prospects and affordability (where Indian does perform better). Out of 101 top global student cities, India has only one city, Mumbai in 99th place (QS 2018).

3.7 Labour Market Linkages

The relevance of the Higher Education system can also be understood in the area of job creation. We analyse briefly the labour market in India, and then consider its interface with Higher Education.

3.7.1 Jobs Crisis

By any measure and standards India has a job and labour market crisis. There are a range of data sources drawing on household, industry or government labour market schemes, none of which is consistent in methodology or assumptions used. In fact, the absence of reliable labour market data in India is a pressing issue. Whichever data source one examines, it makes for bleak reading. For example, the now-defunct Household Annual Employment-Unemployment Survey, encompassing both organised and unorganised sectors,[12] showed that between 2013–2014 and 2015–2016, employment **declined** by 13 million, with declines in manufacturing (mostly in urban areas) and agriculture, and only small increases in retail, professional, scientific and technical activities, public administration and defence, and wholesale and retail trade (Abraham 2017). Our calculations confirm this decline. While some would argue that the decline in agricultural employment is naturally associated with

---

[12]There are a few definitions of organised and unorganised sectors. The organised sector is the public sector plus private sector firms that employ more than ten workers. The organised sector is associated with workers having full social security benefits and union representation. Even within the organised sector, formal workers only receive the full social security benefits, which informal workers such as contract workers, may not necessarily receive, and where employment is less secure (Joshi 2016). Other analogous notions to organised sector relate to the formal or registered firms that use electricity and hire more than ten workers and those that do not use electricity but employment twenty or more (Kapoor 2017). For the purposes of this book, we use organised, registered, formal more or less interchangeably, and unorganised, informal and unregistered in the same vein.

productivity growth and structural change as an economy develops (The 'Lewisian' structural change), others contend that this may not be the case. The Indian situation is accompanied by slowdown in the growth of gross value added in agriculture (Abraham 2017). As an important aside, analysis shows that while the Indian economy has grown, its commensurate poverty reduction has not been as pronounced due to the poor's reliance on low wage, low productivity agriculture and weaknesses in manufacturing, including especially the unskilled, labour intensive manufacturing in the unorganised sector (Hasan 2017). Related to this is that rates of economic growth have been lower in States that have accounted for the largest fraction of India's poor.

Other analysis using employment elasticities drawn from national accounts showed overall, only marginal improvement in organised manufacturing employment between 2014–2015 and 2016–2017, limited to very few sectors: wearing apparel, textiles and chemical and chemical products (between 2014–2015 and 2015–2016). Unorganised sector employment in manufacturing grew by 1.6 million between 2010–2011 and 2015–2016 (Kapoor 2017), not nearly enough to meet the nearly one million entrants into the labour force monthly. Nor do any of these analyses say anything about the quality of jobs, as many are forced to establish own account businesses because of the absence of formal jobs (Kapoor 2017). Quarterly Employment Surveys, canvassing both the organised and unorganised sectors, confirm the stagnant or declining picture in a number of manufacturing and service sectors (Abraham 2017).

Other work highlights the parlous nature of the employment situation in India, including the possibility of job losses in key sectors associated with automation and industrial restructuring, falling employment elasticity (meaning that every 1% increase in GDP is associated with declining employment growth), people being forced to take poor income jobs to the extent that they are available, and highly restrictive labour laws which constrain the development of size and scale by enterprise. One example of the latter is that companies which employ more than 100 permanent employees need the permission of the government to lay off anyone, which has locked resources into inflexible, unproductive situations. Various other rules abound in relation to such things as changing hours/shifts, multiplicity of national and state laws, and often state intransigence on improving the terms and conditions for fixed term/contract workers. To be fair the Modi Government has attempted to simplify labour codes and improve conditions for non-permanent workers, but there is a sense that labour reforms have been simply passed onto States (Das 2019; Jagannathan 2018; Joshi 2016; The Economist 2017).

Recent analysis contends that India's unemployment rate is significantly higher than government data would countenance, and could be as high as 16% for youth unemployment, while the unemployment rate is increasing as the employment rate is declining, indicating declines in labour force participation as people simply stop looking for jobs (Basu 2019; Vyas 2018). The poor labour force participation of females is considered in detail in Chap. 5.

Another key feature of the Indian labour force in recent years has been the growing preponderance of contractual jobs in the organised sector, which tend to be less well paid and lack social security cover. This is giving rise to growing 'informalisation'

3.7 Labour Market Linkages

of the organised sector. In addition, even within the more stable and secure regular wage and salary group, more than two-thirds have no written job contract, leave alone those who are employed on less secure, more casual bases. Also apparent is the very high proportion of those except self-employed who are not eligible for social security. A further point to note is that of the significant proportion of people who are working less time than they are available for, meaning that under-employment is also a significant issue (Government of India 2016f; Kapoor 2017; Jagannathan 2018).

In the unorganised sector itself, any jobs growth has come more from own account workers, usually associated with lack of options in the labour market, rather than 'full throated' entrepreneurial zest. We shall speak more about this in the next chapter.

World Bank analysis contends that India is one of various South Asian countries whose employment rates are much lower than what is predicted given levels of development, and that to keep employment rates constant in India would require more than 8 million jobs annually. Further, employment rates are simply not keeping up with growth in working population which is increasing by 1.3 million every month (World Bank 2018a).

3.7.2 Employment by Skill

On a skills basis, data derived from the International Labour Organisation (ILO 2018), reveals that India's overall employment is significantly lower than China's, even as they have similar population sizes. This in part reflects the poor labour force participation in India, at just over 50% compared to China's over 70%. Moreover, India has the lowest labour force participation of our comparator countries, including those with lesser developed status such as Bangladesh and Sri Lanka (World Bank 2018b).

What is interesting though is that across the three time periods, as shown in Fig. 3.1,

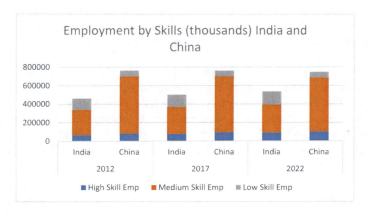

Fig. 3.1 Employment by skills. *Source* ILO Author analysis

India has a larger share of high-skilled employment and low-skilled employment, compared to China, but not in raw numbers. This reflects the significant divergences in the Indian economy, and its bifurcated nature: comprising high-end work in the service sector, aided by graduates from elite institutions undoubtedly, and a very large proportion of low-skill work, reflected in low wage, low security, low productivity jobs in the unorganised sector. At 77%, India has by far the highest rate of vulnerable employment among our comparator set (World Bank 2018b). Our calculations reveal that by industry, knowledge intensive manufacturing accounts for just 0.9% of manufacturing jobs, and 6.5% of service jobs, means that the total knowledge intensive sector accounts for 7.4% of total jobs.[13] For an economy which is aspiring to be a knowledge powerhouse, this is not reflected in the employment domain.

Unlike China, India does not have a strong core of medium-skill jobs which one would expect people to enjoy better pay and work conditions, compared to lower skills level. This in turn can be linked to a manufacturing sector which is not dynamic, large scale or a major job creator, and if anything has suffered significant reverses over the last few years. Certainly, manufacturing in India needs a massive boost, not just 'Make in India' but 'Make value in India', to drive more sustainable, better paid jobs.

It is worth considering briefly the structure of Indian industry. India has not pursued the traditional model of development, advancing from agriculture to manufacturing to services. However, this begs the question of what is the importance of manufacturing? For employment, as well as the learnings and positive externalities and linkages with services, manufacturing certainly has a place. Various work finds that for manufacturing (or any sector or sub-sector) to be an engine for growth, requires it to be productive, have both national (i.e. resources moving from lower productivity parts of a nation to higher parts) and international convergence to productivity frontiers, the ability to absorb resources and have alignment with comparative advantage of the nation (Government India 2015b). For Indian formal manufacturing, these conditions do not hold due to market distortions (land, labour and capital) and interestingly, specialisation in more skill intensive areas, inimical to India's comparative advantage in labour intensity. Further, is that India suffers from premature industrialisation in the sense of manufacturing peaking earlier and at lower levels of GDP per capita and employment, than a number of other countries, to the extent that India has industrialised at all. Services on the other hand conform to the 'engine of growth' conditions. There are however, a number of considerations, Should India attempt to be more in line with its traditional comparative advantage or move even further and faster down the skills and higher value paths? (Government of India 2015b). We come down firmly into the latter camp. To promote and sustain higher value jobs, and better living standards, this is the direction India should take, To be sure, it will be difficult and will require massive doses of skills, education and training and *transition* arrangements out of lower value to higher value sectors. This

---

[13] Author calculations drawing on data from Government of India Employment-Unemployment Survey 2014.

3.7.2.1 Graduate Performance and Outlook

Comparing new graduates with employment patterns makes for disturbing reading. By our calculations, the inflow of new graduates *alone* from India's tertiary institutions exceeded overall employment growth between 2012 and 2017 by close to 1.5 million[14] with the divergence heightened when comparing graduate inflow with growth in employment in medium and high skill occupations, where one would normally expect graduates to land. We calculate that the gap between the expected inflow of new graduates between 2017 and 2022 will exceed overall employment growth over this period by anything up to 8–10 times. This is in part due to the expected slow-down of employment growth. What these numbers demonstrate, even allowing for their 'back of the envelope' nature, is that India is not creating anywhere near enough jobs to cater for fresh new graduates and their likely entrance into the job market. This of course does not include other job seekers, apart from the fresh graduates.

Unemployment rises the more educated people are in India. This is one manifestation of an economy that simply does not create enough jobs, especially those requiring greater skill. Moreover, significant proportions of the more educated segments drop out of the workforce entirely, although not to the same extent as those with lower levels of education. From a knowledge economy perspective, these are disturbing features. Employment rates are relatively high for the most specialised segments, i.e. postgraduate and above, which in itself is challenging, since this reflects more elite rather than mass employment (Government of India 2016f).

The most dominant reason for unemployment among those with tertiary qualifications regardless of location and gender, is 'non-availability of job matching education, skills and experience', particularly in urban areas. It is simply the case that the economy is not generating jobs that are commensurate with skills and experience of its population. This in turn puts pressure on graduates to try and obtain lower paid jobs (Government of India 2016f).

There are severe disconnects in the Indian labour market exacerbated by the fact that many employers report significant skills shortages and gaps. One estimate has a skills gap in India of the order of 347 m by 2022, while other estimates suggest large skills gaps, if not of that order of magnitude (Badrinath 2016; Kumar 2016; Majumdar 2016; Pilz 2016). It is also the case that unemployment exists contiguously with skills gaps and shortages.

The parlous nature of India's labour market is amplified by the labour market outcomes by discipline for tertiary graduates. As a potential knowledge economy player, the weakness in STEM related fields in terms of employment is noted. However, the generalist arts/humanities stream fares even worse (Government of India

---

[14] Author calculations based on ILO data and Government data from the AISHE reports.

2016f). Some contend however that engineering and technology-oriented graduates have found jobs relatively more easily, than say, education graduates (Khare 2016).

Further, and despite its limitations, data from the National Career Service is interesting. It shows that as at the end of March 2018, total job seekers dwarfed total job vacancies of the order of a staggering 50:1 (Government of India 2018d). Further, as determined by the Employment-Unemployment Survey, there is a significant proportion of the workforce, who are available for 12 months of employment, but are actually working far less.

3.7.3 Vocational Sector

One of the key weaknesses is in India's vocational sector, which would be an important component of skilling and employment creation, especially in the middle skill space. India has a severely under-done and under-emphasised vocational system, lacking investment, prestige in the public eye, and integration with industry and broader higher education, as we previously indicated. For example, despite various measures India continues to rank poorly on vocational enrolment (106nd place out of 125) according to the 2019 Global Talent Competitiveness Index (Lanvin and Monteiro 2019).

Other data points to the very small share of people receiving vocational training (5.4%). Training, to the extent available, is biased towards those in employment and is based largely on informal training rather than on a modern, professional or systematic basis. Only 8 out of 23 sectors have more than 80% of the labour force receiving formal vocational training with numbers well below this is in various other sectors. Further, where formal vocational training occurs it is skewed towards wage and salary earners rather than the large swathes of contract or casual staff (Government of India 2016g).

3.7.4 Employability

Of course, there are always two sides to the equation. The fact of the matter is that while jobs might be scarce, there is the problem of employability of graduates. A vast array of studies and surveys has demonstrated that Indian graduates lack employability skills. The system is not geared to the needs and challenges of industry and employers.

A study of 40,000 Indian technical graduates covering skills of english, communication, quantitative skills, problem-solving and programming skills, found that only 38% were employable (Mehrotra 2016). Twenty-first- century skills of communication, problem-solving and analytical skills among others are lacking. Other studies show that only one quarter of engineering graduates are employable, and that only 10% of other graduates are (Khare 2016). Yet more studies find that less than 20%

of graduates from higher education institutions are rated as immediately employable and that it is time to consider a graduate employability ratio, another GER (Government of India 2016a). There are considerable gaps in the employability of graduates coming out of leading institutions and the rest, and between cities (Khare 2016). Other studies point to the fact that out of every 100 engineering graduates, only 18% were employable in IT services, less than 4% in IT products and about 40% only in the lower end of outsourcing businesses (Jagannathan 2018).

Thus, India desperately needs a comprehensive approach to the labour market including emphasising higher value, stable and sustainable jobs, with strong interface between education institutions and the labour market. The proposed features of a new and revamped Indian higher education system are proposed at the end of this chapter.

3.7.5 *Labour Market Orientations of the Future*

In terms of the labour market we propose that annual, 5 year and 15 year strategic job mapping exercises be carried out to identify promising job growth activity areas, skills required, current and expected skills gaps and shortages. Among the key elements of this exercise, drawing on inputs from stakeholders across the country, as part of the planning arrangements described in Chap. 2, would be:

- Strengthened manufacturing base with a focus on exports, as a job generators, initially concentrating on lower value segments, but moving progressively upwards over time: a more robust 'medium skill' sector would be vital as a transition to higher value jobs, and in its own right
- Development of 'skills sets of the future' programme, which emphasises not just technical skills but broad-based non-technical and 'soft skills'
- Focus on newer segments, including 'green capabilities', and problem-solving missions (more of this will be spoken about) with industrial and commercial opportunities. For example, health care, infrastructure and a myriad of design capabilities spring to mind.
- Transition plans aimed at moving out of low value, vulnerable employment to higher value employment, including through provision of safety nets especially in the unorganised sector (a process already started), accelerated and large scale training, and development of flexible skills which can be adapted to many different contexts and applications
- Stronger labour market matching services, including better predictive approaches, to connect employers with potential employees;
- Provision to remake and re-design existing jobs, in concert with employer groups, to embody more skill, especially focusing on 'at risk' jobs;
- Utilising Government schemes such as Mahatma Gandhi National Rural Employment Guarantee Act (MNREGA) giving it a more focussed skill orientation (Gupta 2016); and

- Improving the business environment for job creation, including reforming labour market restrictions on hiring and firing, burdensome labour laws and general ease of doing business.

These features would require a significant mindset shift away from focussing on preserving dying industries at all costs.

3.7.6 India and the Fourth Industrial Revolution

How equipped is the Indian Higher Education system, and economy more broadly, to meet core skills of the twenty-first century? The twenty-first century is characterised by the fourth industrial revolution, the confluence of automation, artificial intelligence, robotics, 'internet of things', 3D printing, fusion of technologies, the sharing economy, and whole new organisational and business models, often on a decentralised, distributed basis. In turn these forces, and more broadly the growing knowledge intensiveness of economies, is putting a premium on a new skills agenda, including problem-solving, team work and collaboration, critical thinking, creativity and innovation, entrepreneurship, communication, flexibility and cross-disciplinary thinking. Inequality and structural change is a major factor concern associated with these radical changes (Schwab 2016, 2017; World Economic Forum 2015, 2016).

3.7.6.1 India and the Future of Work

There is radical change underway in varying degrees around the world. More than one-third of all jobs across all industries will require complex problem-solving as a core skill in 2020, versus less than 1 in 20 jobs that will require physical strength as a core. Even more telling is that some 65% of children entering primary school today will work in completely new jobs that don't exist yet and more than one-third of skills needs by 2020 will comprise skills not yet significant (World Economic Forum 2016). The future of skills is characterised by rapid and unprecedented change. One illustration of this is that 50% of subject knowledge during a four-year technical degree will be outdated by the time of completion (World Economic Forum 2016). This places an enormous premium on the capacity of an education and training system to be highly flexible, adaptable and responsive to economic and social needs, and which can provide a broad basis of capabilities, adaptable to different contexts and applications. In some eyes, there is a 'race' between teaching needs and education system, with the latter simply not being able to keep up due to slow, cumbersome and bureaucratic processes (Frey and Osborne, CITI GPS 2015).

While some might argue that India can, and should, stand apart from the global fourth industrial revolution given its large, lower skilled workforce and poverty, the history and experience of India staying apart from global trends, including investments, and trade, in post-independence is not strong. Moreover, it is simply much

3.7 Labour Market Linkages

more difficult these days to stand apart from global trends, despite pressures from certain sectional interests do so. The opportunities, potential for productivity gains and economic growth, and the pervasive nature of technological change are transformative. What we argue is that these developments and opportunities need to be leveraged, utilised and capitalised on in India specific contexts, and to address India specific needs and challenges. This will mean being open to ideas and knowledge from abroad, meshing with one's own to develop solutions to complex challenges.

How does India fare though on matters related to the fourth industrial revolution and core skills of the future? Table 3.12 from the author, illustrates India's performance and prospects relating to the higher education sector in the context of core skills of the future.

Table 3.12 Core skills of the future

Core skills	India's higher education current capabilities and situation	Way forward
Problem solving and critical thinking	Focus on rote learning with limited application to practical problem solving	Focus of the future should be on meeting national and global challenges via solutions/mission mode
Teamwork and collaboration	Little interface with industry	More joint projects in research with industry, mobility between academia and industry
Entrepreneurship	Emerging capability but needs expansion in institutions	Entrepreneurship as a core in all courses
Creativity and innovation	System lacks research capability except for few elite Institutions and public sector agencies; absence of strong commercial orientation while quality and standing in research and research outputs needs improvement; proliferation of substandard journals and papers	Strengthen nexus between teaching and research; improve research capacity and quality, including of translational kind linked to core solutions
Cross disciplinary thinking	Siloed approach to curricula	Breaking down discipline boundaries through more cross fertilisation of subject areas

(continued)

Table 3.12 (continued)

Core skills	India's higher education current capabilities and situation	Way forward
Diverse specialisations	Insufficient diversity in course offerings, lack of course renewal and lacking pathways	Continually introduce new courses, new modes of teaching, pathways within higher education, and between vocational and higher education
Flexibility	Not meeting industry needs	Employability as a focus of higher education
Communication	Text book oriented, passive teacher driven approach to learning	Project work, facilitated learning between teacher and student emphasising discussion, debate, knowledge discovery and joint problem solving between students, and students and staff
ICT skills	Divide between 'Have and Have not's' including gender, still prevalent	Access and usage uptake to be enhanced, including across social groupings, with higher education as a driver of such learning
Highly developed and advanced data management and analytic skills	Emerging in certain sectors driven primarily by private enterprise rather than education and training institutions	More emphasis on predictive capabilities, including ability to track student progress, identifying and anticipating actions for 'at risk' students
Numeracy	Proportion of grade 3 who can do at least subtraction was 27.7% in 2016 (NITI Aayog 2017)	Emphasis on raising teaching standards towards global best practice, and focus on learning outcomes rather than inputs
Literacy	Proportion of grade three who can read a grade 1 text was only 42.5% in 2016 (NITI Aayog 2017)	Emphasis on raising teaching standards towards global best practice, and focus on learning outcomes rather than inputs
Social skills (empathy, emotional intelligence, persuasion, negotiation)	Limited focus of education and training system, concentrating mainly as a 'degree factory' based on outmoded curriculum	Needs a broader view of education and training system to link to societal change and needs, and inculcation of India's culture, heritage and values: a refashioned Gurukal system for the 21st century

Source Author views and analysis Table with inputs from World Economic Forum (2015, 2016), Berger and Frey (2015), Ramaswami (2016), Kumar (2016), Citi GPS (2016), World Bank (2019)

3.7 Labour Market Linkages 145

In our view, India is not equipped to address the needs of twenty-first-century skills. As has been mentioned numerous times in this book and chapter, the Indian higher education scene lacks creativity, innovation, industry linkages and broader economic focus. It is a system which is still very much bound by its legacy: focussing on rote learning, 'cramming' for exams, limited reform in curriculum and pedagogy, and lack of relevant research capability.

3.7.6.2 Automation Index and Production Readiness

More broadly, the recent Automation Readiness Index (The Economist Intelligence Unit 2018 which measures the ability of countries to develop and promote the capabilities required to meet the challenges of automation, including artificial intelligence, machine learning, robotics and the like is illuminating. The index comprises the innovation environment[15]; education policies; and labour market policies.

On the overall readiness index, India is ranked 18th out of 25 countries, its innovation environment 17th, labour market policies 16th and education policies at 22nd out of 25. Thus, India is in the lower reaches of the index in all its parameters, *with the weakest being education policies*. This reinforces our view that India's education policies are by and large ill-equipped to deal with the challenges of the twenty-first century.

Readiness for the future of production is based on the structure of production (economic complexity and scale, where complexity is based on diversity and ubiquity of products with more sophisticated economies producing more diverse products while there are fewer economies capable of producing sophisticated products) and drivers of production (technology and innovation, human capital, global trade and investment, institutional framework, sustainable resources and demand environment). India is regarded as a 'legacy' economy, at risk for the future, due to weaknesses in the drivers of economic performance, especially in human capital and sustainable resources, but with strengths in structure of production (World Economic Forum 2018).

3.7.6.3 Job Losses

The issue of job growth and loss, in the context of technological change, is a complex one and a hotly contested field. According to a famous study conducted (in relation to the U.S.) by Frey and Osborne (2013), some 47% of jobs in the U.S. are at

---

[15]Innovation Environment (public investment and support for private investment in research on robotics and automation, policies and regulation towards entrepreneurship, support for technology transfer and adoption, ICT infrastructure, cluster development programs, ethics and safety); Education Policies (early childhood strategy, programmes for 21st century skills, technical skills agenda, career guidance, STEM, lifelong education support, teacher training, use of technology in education delivery, school autonomy, social dialogue in education sector; Labour market policies (workforce and workplace transition agenda, research on the impact of automation, artificial intelligence and robotics, re-training programs, university and labour market dialogue).

high risk due to computerisation. In particular, it is observed that while high-skill and low-skill jobs have grown in the U.S., other types of jobs have become more vulnerable. Vulnerability in lower skills jobs in less advanced economies may be heightened. Looking ahead, some contend that by 2062, artificial intelligence will equate to human intelligence (Walsh 2018).

The advance of automation is not just pertinent to developed economies but also encompasses developing ones. It is anticipated that 69% of jobs in India and 77% in China are susceptible to automation (Citi GPS 2016). This is not just confined to manufacturing, but will potentially engulf other sectors, including various services. Of course, this needs to be looked at in the context of relative costs of labour, versus the costs of say, installing and running robots. Nonetheless, try as it may, it will be difficult and indeed undesirable for India to try and stand apart from these developments. Automation at its broadest, encompassing robotics, artificial intelligence, additive manufacturing, computerisation and the like, provide scope for efficiencies, trade, global value chain integration possibilities and opportunities, and transformative innovation across multiple sectors, businesses and organisations (Citi GPS 2016). The key for India will be to harness the employment creation potential of these activities (new professions, occupations, and sectors), and to focus on those higher order, value-added skills and capabilities which are less inclined to be automated such as creative skills, social intelligence (tacit knowledge embedded in social and cultural contexts), perception and manipulation skills (understanding the interface between physical and other domains). This in turn will put a premium on innovation, flexibility and having adaptable education and training systems as well as the ability to shift out of 'at risk' activities to in-demand areas, in an orderly fashion. The author does not underestimate the impact and challenges of these factors for India, which has large swathes of the population in lower paid, lower value, lower productivity, informal jobs. Finally, a range of sectors, with higher employment elasticities of growth, have been identified in India as job creators (Jagannathan 2018). However, many of these sectors are not knowledge intensive necessarily, which may constrain India's path towards higher value, more productive, higher paying and secure jobs.

Others are more optimistic on a global level arguing that the share of the workforce (in the U.S and U.K) that is likely to shrink is less than pessimists believe, and that new emerging fields and occupations, e.g. health care, creative sectors and new business services, allied with re-design of jobs at risk to emphasise more skill, job specialisation, product variety, task variations and complex skills (such as personal service, technology, design) will mitigate job losses. Few occupations are completely ripe for automation, and parts of jobs are more likely to be automated than entire ones (Bakhshi et al. 2017). The extent of automation depends on labour and automation costs, quality factors, technical feasibility of automation and societal and regulatory factors. Further, in the more positive vein, technology-enhanced jobs have traditionally more than offset job loss (Jagannathan 2018). Other studies by the Economic Strategy Institute in the U.S or Forrester Research, are respectively, either optimistic about job creation or conservative in respect of job losses. Others again point to an interdependence, for example, between robotics and human intelligence (Jagannathan 2018).

3.7 Labour Market Linkages

The importance of upskilling is underscored and reinforced by the view that 'Workers in jobs that require originality—that is the ability to come up with unusual or clever ideas about a given topic or situation, or to develop creative ways to solve a problem-are substantially less likely to see themselves replaced by computer-controlled equipment...' (Berger and Frey 2015, p. 5). In a similar vein, the Institute for Future Work has identified ten skills for the workforce of the future. These are: sense making (ability to determine the deeper meaning of significance of what is being expressed); social intelligence; novel and adaptive thinking; cross-cultural competency; computational thinking; new media literacy; Transdisciplinarity; design mindset; cognitive load management (ability to discriminate and filter information for importance); and virtual collaboration (Citi GPS, Oxford Martin School 2016).

While the jury may still be out in terms of the exact ramifications of technology, what is apparent is the growing importance of knowledge-based employment as a driver of sustained prosperity. This in turn leads us to explore what can be done in the Indian higher education system to give Indian students, graduates and industries the best chance of success.

3.8 The Future of Indian Higher Education

Indian Higher Education is at the cross roads. It can either pursue the path of mediocrity, churning out graduates with not particularly employable qualifications, floundering research capability, unfulfilled community objectives, or it can pursue a different approach. It is the latter that we seek to address. We propose a radical structural and organisational change in the system. These suggestions need to be read in concert with the broader labour market reforms that we canvassed earlier. A number of authors have recommended significant structural and organisational change in India's higher education system, including a multi tiered structure comprising research and varying levels of teaching (Ernst and Young, Federation of Indian Chambers of Commerce and Industry (FICCI) 2013).

Of course, we must recognise that change is underway. India's Draft New Education Policy (Government of India 2016a, b) provides some important pointers to reforms for the future, and there have been some important initiatives in recent years. Various initiatives have been mooted or are already underway in varying degrees, including a domestic university rankings scheme, new institutes of excellence, greater autonomy for worthy colleges, skills and quality frameworks and facilitating bodies, strengthened governance through the Higher Education Evaluation and Regulation Authority (HEERA), and the Rashtriya Uchchatar Shiksha Abhiyan (RUSA), the National Higher Education Mission, which provides a more effective, efficient and equitable approach to funding of states by the centre through state Higher Education Councils and development of State wide plans (Government of India 2013b; Kulkarni 2018a).

However, as with a number of things Indian, the proof will be in the 'implementation pudding', Previous policies (Government of India 1968, 1998) such as the 1968 and 1986 policies (revised in 1992) were replete with lofty goals around community engagement, fostering values in education, promotion of scientific endeavour, and access of education for all. Yet it would not be a stretch to say that many goals remain unfulfilled and that objectives were couched in vague terms so as to make their implementation problematic. Even recently, there has been criticism of the complex, convoluted approach to managing and delivering on the Government's skills agenda (Jagannathan 2018).

3.9 Reform Agenda

Notwithstanding various initiatives undertaken in the recent past, and intentions of reform, much more needs to happen of a fundamental far-reaching nature. It is to this that we turn. Seismic change is required.

We consider that the higher education and vocational education system should be oriented towards long-term solutions and missions addressing the challenges confronting India and the world, and organised **along mission clusters and problem-solving universities**, as shown in Fig. 3.2.

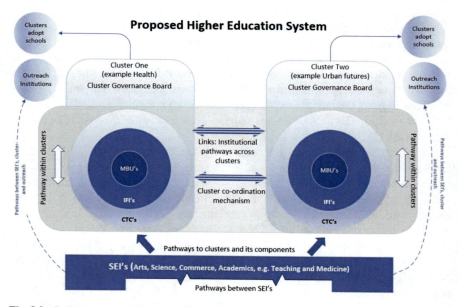

Fig. 3.2 Proposed higher education system

3.9 Reform Agenda

We envisage a series of diverse specialisms that revolve around solutions in areas such as natural resource management, environment, health and population, urbanisation, spatial development, food security and social development, among others.[16] These solutions or missions would be chosen after careful analysis, and drawing on wide stakeholder, community consultation and input. Missions would be sufficiently broad based and flexible to capture the vital interdependencies of required capabilities and to adjust Missions as required.

3.9.1 Solutions/Mission-Based Cluster Details

The clusters[17] would involve the close interplay and interdependence of a range of institutions as follows:

- Mission-Based Universities (MBU's) whose focus would be on developing cutting edge research and strong postgraduate teaching (but also undergraduate programmes) aimed at addressing complex challenges through applied, mission focussed research which has broad application across economy and society, and where appropriate, include basic research in these institutions
- Industry Focused Institutions (IFI's) which would be chartered with the responsibility of providing core linkages into industry with a focus on graduate employability, two-way mobility of academic staff between industry and institutions, research linked very specifically to industry needs associated with solutions and missions, and consultancy services. It would also allow for micro-credentialling or certification for specific competencies.
- Corporate Training Centres (CTC's) would be institutions directly focussed on the needs of individual firms.
- Specialist Enabling Institutions (SEI) provide foundational studies and curriculum, but specialised in arts/humanities, science, commerce, health and so on. Also included in the specialised institutions are Teacher Academies, for example, to provide leading edge teaching capabilities, as well as other capabilities that India is sorely lacking in, including public administration.
- Outreach Universities (OU) which are focussed on meeting the needs and challenges of villages, rural areas and community groups, including minorities, and which provide opportunity and access for rural people to participate in education and training
- Outward Institutions, including diasporic institutions, to promote Indian higher education abroad, as part of an integrated approach to internationalisation. One potential manifestation of this could be the idea of joint Indo-foreign universities, aimed at promoting collaboration between institutions.

---

[16] The Economic Survey 2017–2018 (Government of India 2018b) speaks of aligning research with Missions.

[17] Our approach is consistent with that proposed by Ernst and Young, Federation of Indian Chambers of Commerce and Industry (FICCI) (2013) in having a multi tiered, multi faceted approach by specialisations and functions.

The above diagram, Fig. 3.2, shows how the system would work. It is based on the premise of clusters aligned with finding solutions in mission mode. Two examples of clusters are provided. The clusters comprise the MBU's, IFI's, CTC's and Outreach institutions. The SEI's are foundational institutions and sit outside the cluster formation, as do the Outward institutions which would have a more general remit. Outward institutions are not showing in the diagram.

3.9.2 Diverse Specalisms[18]

Our approach fundamentally involves a shift from a generalised to more focussed, yet diverse education system, arrayed around a series of challenges facing India and the world. It also would mean more industry focussed arrangements, based on employability and industry needs.

There would be flexibility and diversity built around specialisations. This flexibility is found in many ways. Firstly, the missions are not set in concrete, but are expected to evolve and modify in scope over time. Secondly, the system is diverse. There are multiple pathways within each cluster, between each cluster, between the specialist enabling institutions, and specialist enabling institutions and clusters. For example, depending on aptitude and rigorous assessment criteria, students and staff may be able to move between Mission Based Institutions and Industry Focussed Institutions in subject and project choice, to both undertake research and visualise its application in industry contexts.

The IFI's would represent much greater opening up of the system to industry engagement, including in setting curriculum, fostering staff mobility between industry and academia, and in allowing for much greater deployment of placements, internships and project work-based learnings for students. IFI's would break down the traditional boundaries of higher education (HE) and vocational education (VE), by combining many elements of both, providing flexibility and pathways of study. In fact, we argue for dismantling the traditional and unhelpful boundaries between HE and VE. Distractions, even in naming conventions, which separate higher education and vocational education would give way to these umbrella or over-arching IFI's. While the IFI's would **focus** on solution or challenge areas, its remit could also extend across a number of other industries.

The Specialist Enabling Institutions, focussed on undergraduate studies, would be the more foundational studies, e.g. B.A. or B.Sc. Students could complete courses in these institutions before specialisation in clusters or undertake cross SEI studies to bring together the different perspectives that Arts and Science bring, for example, or even undertake SEI studies in conjunction with Cluster based Institutions. Degrees

---

[18]Our approach is consistent with that proposed by the Government in terms of Excellent Universities, but differs significantly in respect of having much stronger lower tiers of education, and co-ordination and pathways emphasising diversity and specialisation. Moreover, performance accountability is much stronger in our case.

3.9 Reform Agenda

could be granted either by the SEI's or SEI's in concert with other Institutions in the clusters, as joint degrees. Our proposed system places a very high premium on flexibility, pathways and a variety of choices.

Each Cluster would be overseen by a Cluster Governance Board, comprising national, state and local government representatives and would include industry and community representatives. Further, as our diagram indicates, there is a Cluster Coordination mechanism overseen by a joint Cluster Group (with similar representation) designed to oversee, capture and facilitate pathways between clusters to promote cross-cluster learning, teaching and research.

The system is also cognisant of the need to provide access and opportunity for rural Indians, and minority, disadvantaged groups. As such, a series of Outreach Universities are proposed, which are aligned with both (SEI's) and the cluster programme to provide education and training for those in rural India, allied with needs of these areas, for example in resource management and health outcomes.

Our system would also involve forging a stronger nexus between higher education and schools. This would aim to enhance the passage and pathways from schools to institutions by providing exposure of school students to courses and curriculum of higher education, modes of teaching and so on. To facilitate this, it is proposed that each cluster have a series of interlinked schools to manage. For school students this would involve undertaking either full or part subjects, appropriately tailored, at a higher education institution, which would count as some form of prior credit before entrance proper, and serve as a micro credential, which may also assist with job search.

3.10 Departure from the Present

The system is a major departure from the current scene. It would do away completely with the university-college affiliation system and replace it with a series of high calibre learning institutions which provide both higher education and vocational education integrated together, and teaching and research in varying degrees. The model can be thought of as 'Unicols' in this sense combining traditional aspects of universities and colleges. The approach would subsume, scale up and integrate existing institutions where threshold quality standards are met. In this sense it is not necessarily institution heavy.

The system is designed to enhance student and staff choice, creativity, collaboration and innovation, aligned with key solutions/missions focus. It essentially transforms institutions from passive learning bodies to pro-active problem-solving exemplars.

We would also advocate that the system introduces the for-profit motive explicitly but cautiously. This would give fresh impetus to allowing private capital into the system, including full foreign providers with campus establishment and autonomy,[19]

---

[19] At present foreign institutions can operate on a partnership basis with Indian Institutions.

and inject new management thinking, pedagogical approaches and perspectives into a stale system. It would also mean making explicit what is already 'under the counter' via capitation fees. As mentioned previously, with significant private benefits in higher education, then there is ample scope for private provision. However, and it cannot be emphasised enough, that this move to allow for private participation on a for-profit basis needs to be accompanied with very strong regulation and quality standards. At present, providers operate on a notionally not for profit basis, although in reality this does not quite happen.

The following table highlights the proposed schema for Indian Higher Education in the future

The system involves considerable flexibility to ensure that solutions areas can be reoriented over time, and that skills developed can be transferable.

Our approach also retains a balance between public and private funding, and is based on a collaborative model between tiers of government, and in the case of IFI's, as a tripartite arrangement. In the IFI model, the private funding would be capped at least initially to just short of majority ownership. There are still considerable market failures in this arena, for example externalities, and strong linkage to strategic and potentially sensitive elements associated with missions/solutions, to warrant not complete private ownership. There would be significant fee flexibility in allowing fees to move between minimum and maximum bands. The government funding would be to ensure that the system has financial stability and guaranteed funding. Over time, this could shift towards greater private funding. The CTC's would be based completely on private funding, being closest to corporate interests. The other institutions are variously based on public ownership and funding at national, state and local levels, as seen in Table 3.13.

Table 3.13 Proposed schema for Indian higher education in the future

Institution	Role/Competitive driver	Ownership/Management	Funding tier	Possible fee structure
Mission Based Universities (MBU's)	To provide cutting edge teaching and research aligned to problem solving contexts and core missions. Part of the missions is to have dual technology transfer centres in the MBU's to provide technology to industry for a fee and also buy in technology as part of research	National Government	National Government	Subsidised by National Government, with contributions from students

(continued)

3.10 Departure from the Present

Table 3.13 (continued)

Institution	Role/Competitive driver	Ownership/Management	Funding tier	Possible fee structure
Industry Focussed Institutions (IFI's)	To provide strong linkage between education and training and industry/economic needs, aligned with missions/solutions, but not exclusively	Joint National, State Govts and industry	National, State Govts and Industry. Industry funding limited to 49% initially at least, and on a for profit basis, with Government funding 51%	Considerable fee flexibility based initially on movement between minimum and maximum bands before moving to full market based fees
Corporate Training Centres (CTC's)	To provide training aligned with needs of individual enterprises	Private companies	Private companies	Full fees based on market
Specialist Enabling Institutions	To provide diverse but specialised foundational studies	National and State Govts jointly owned but some management could be outsourced to private providers	National and State Govts shared with ownership levels based on capacity to pay on the part of States	Largely subsidised by Government, with some cost recovery element for students
Out-reach Universities	Provide access and opportunity for regional and rural areas and for minorities, with research linked to local needs through collaborative research projects undertaken with MBU's	State and Panchayat	State and Panchayat, with Panchayat contribution based on the capacity to pay	Subsidised by Government with some cost recovery for students
Outward Institutions	To promote global linkages in teaching and research through offshore delivery, expanding opportunities for Indian students abroad	Either fully privately owned or joint public/private	Either Private Institutions or joint private/public	Subject to the rules and requirements of overseas countries

The extent of government ownership and funding (and funding sharing agreements) of the system, i.e. between national and lower tiers of government, would depend on jurisdictional (e.g. state and local) capacity to pay, training and educational needs, overall economic development and so forth.

Student contribution would vary from full fee payment as set by the market, in the case of Corporate Training Centres and differentiated student contributions in the case of MBU's and IFI's with higher student contributions from MBU's compared to the others, given their more specialist offerings and likelihood that graduates from MBU's are likely to earn more than from other institutions over a lifetime. SEI's and Outreach Institutions would have a stronger overall role for government and funding responsibility due to equity and access considerations, and the historical role for government in supporting more foundational elements of education. For SEI's and Outreach Institutions there would be some cost recovery charges for students, through minimal charges, to defray the cost of provision of education. This would be distinct from fees in other parts of the system where fees are more a direct reflection of the private returns to education. As with other countries, it is proposed that income contingency loans be put in place for student contribution.

Extensive use of **transition** scholarships to enable those from disadvantaged backgrounds and/or highly able students to move from one part of the system to another, e.g. from SEI's to MBU's, is a feature of the approach.

3.11 Distribution of Funds

There would be two layers of funding distributed to institutions in respect of the government funding component: base funds linked to achievement of minimum standards (with financial penalties for not meeting standards), and top up funds based on exceeding standards for teaching and research. More will be spoken about how the model works shortly in the section on research. Funding for teaching would be on similar lines.

Funding would be provided through the **Clusters**, and to SEI's separately outside clusters. Funding would be provided to encompass both teaching and research, but there would be separation of teaching and research funding pools, discussion of which will be undertaken shortly. Thus, as we have described previously, Cluster Boards would become important oversight mechanisms directly accountable and responsibile for strategic planning and finances, identifying priorities for learning and teaching and developing strategies for research, engagement with industry and community, and monitoring and evaluating performance of constituent institutions.

In some senses, our proposed system with respect to funding and governance is consistent with, and builds on the approach being undertaken by RUSA which is a performance-linked funding approach and is based on the creation of State Higher Education Councils, and associated State education plans (with linkage to Institutional plans) to receive funds (Government of India 2013b). Our approach differs in many respects by having a much more integrated, comprehensive approach to higher education, linked firmly to industry and community need, with a much more-broad based curriculum as we shall see shortly.

Our system would actively and explicitly bring Panchayats into the equation as the body of government most closely aligned with local needs, challenges and circumstances. This would extend to joint ownership.

3.12 Regulation and Oversight

We propose the establishment of Quality India (QI) as the overall regulatory oversight body, including over private players. QI would have responsibility for setting, monitoring and enforcing curriculum and research standards and ensuring financial probity across the system. It would have strong powers of enforcement. Quality India, although a national body, would have cells in each state to ensure coordination across the system. The Modi Government has mooted the establishment of the Higher Education Evaluation and Regulation Authority (HEERA) which would integrate higher education and vocational training, have strong powers of enforcement, and work with the sector to raise standards (Kulkarni 2018b).

The focus of standards would be on learning, teaching and research outcomes rather than an input based approach and encompass employment, community engagement outcomes, and metrics associated with achievement of solutions/mission-centric goals. How standards are reached, staff hiring decisions, and deployment of resources would be up to individual institutions, thus providing greater autonomy than has traditionally been the case.

A differentiated mechanism is proposed to monitor and enforce risk, facilitated by specialist divisions in QI, for example, a division for MBU's, IFII's, etc. Risk ratings would guide the nature and extent of regulatory oversight and monitoring, with greater oversight for more risky institutions, where risk is measured by financial risk, reputation, risks of not realising standards of teaching and education or obtaining mission/challenge goals. Risk ratings would be made publicly available on an annual basis. Compulsory accreditation would be required for all institutions, not just based on whether they receive funding from public authorities.

As with the Modi Government initiative for HEERA, funding and grant giving would not be part of QI's charter, unlike the University Grants Commission (UGC) which has had overlapping responsibilities of governance, standard setting and regulatory oversight as well as grant allocation. This has given rise to blurred lines of accountability, conflicts of interest and lack of focus. There is a need to ensure that the focus of QI, is as a setter and enforcer of standards, which is not diluted by grant giving, to ensure greater transparency and accountability.

We concur with the view expressed that India needs a focussed, dedicated, Indian Education Service (IES) to oversee the system of education (Government of India 2016a). In our reckoning, such a body could either replace the Ministry for Human Resources and Development (MHRD) or be a specialist part of it. It would have oversight over the cluster model to ensure consistency, coordination and develop an over-arching strategy and drive a vision for the future. It would comprise education specialists (including via secondees from institutions and sector themselves) and broader policy personnel, and would be 'open' to having lateral hires from outside the civil service, based entirely on merit. The IES at national level would have cells in state governments to ensure inter-governmental consistency and coordination. We would also advocate that the IES be supported by an independent Board of Advisers. Further, and over-time, we envisage that there would be an interface and tie up's between IES and like-minded bodies abroad, including staff exchanges, to ensure the free flow of ideas and access to the latest thinking to 'open up' India's traditionally insular bureaucracy. The IES would also oversee Quality India.

3.13 A New Pedagogy

To meet the skills of the twenty-first century, a radical transformation of pedagogy is required. We envisage a model whereby rote learning gives way to practical project orientation, in conjunction with industry and community, and where assessment is based far less on exams but rather on fulfilling national solutions obligations via the solutions/mission approach. One manifestation of this would be to provide degrees entirely based on projects. Project success would be based, in part, on feedback from stakeholders. In addition to the granting of degrees, micro-credentials would be granted at various points in the student journey, to reflect the gaining of competencies, thus reinforcing the importance of broader, generic competencies in a student's knowledge 'tool kit'.

The approach would explicitly incorporate curricula on emerging skills of communication, teamwork, and collaboration into instruction through a nationally mandated 'twenty-first-century skills programme'. Part of this would be changing the nature of instruction to emphasise debate, discussion and dialogue, joint discovery of knowledge between students and students and teachers. In this context, teachers would become more 'First among equals' and classrooms would become hubs of collaborative and creative activity (Ernst and Young, Federation of Indian Chambers of Commerce and Industry (FICCI) 2013). Of course, this would depend on a whole new approach to teacher training, new mindsets and new tools, which the new Teaching Academies would provide.

Over time, we would envisage pedagogy incorporating a more holistic approach encompassing values-based learning, self-discovery and community awareness.

3.14 Research Capability

Indian higher education needs to considerably enhance and strengthen its research capability. This could be done through provision of rigorous, high-quality research training methods to students by forming a cadre of 'roaming' leading researchers in

3.14 Research Capability

India, who could be exhorted (or paid) to provide instruction in best practice research methodologies. It would also mean a programme to attract leading edge researchers from abroad to undertake joint research in India (and abroad) and mentor 'up and coming' Indian researchers through an 'adopt a researcher' programme, with mentors sought from various sources, including especially India's vibrant research diaspora. This in turn would mean specific visa categories for science and technology and innovation professionals to migrate temporarily to India as part of opening up India to the world of ideas.

3.14.1 Funding Particulars

We argue that research funding from government should cover full costs of research, including infrastructure, research training and research activities themselves. Research funding should be provided separately from teaching and learning to ensure its priority, focus and scale, and avoid it being 'swallowed' up by other activities. A similar mode would apply to teaching separately. To give effect to this we propose the following and as flagged earlier:

- **Base funding** given to each cluster and distributed to constituent institutions, according to need, and for meeting various economic and social objectives linked to Solutions/Mission objectives
- Above base funding to clusters whose overall performance exceeds expectations and with bonuses distributed to stellar institutions within the Cluster. Performance would be measured by wider criteria in research beyond publications, to include community engagement, solving industry and community challenges and commercialisation of research. For teaching, employability of graduates, student experience, completion of project-based learning, and teacher capability, would be important, alongside traditional metrics of pass and fail rates. Conversely, performance that is below expectations would lead to reduced funding from the base.
- Competitive and Collaborative Cluster Funding: over and above the base (and performance-based funding) funds would be provided on a contestable basis to clusters to undertake additional projects which may, for example, be more 'blue sky' and may not attract funding through the base funding approach; and a collaborative fund to promote inter-cluster linkages and projects. In the case of teaching such funding would be directed at new pedagogy.
- In turn, from the competitive and collaborative funds, a cascading mechanism would be deployed for constituent institutions, i.e. intra-cluster competitive and intra cluster collaborative funding mechanisms.

Our approach would provide stability through guaranteed funding, while at the same time providing 'carrots and sticks' to facilitate greater performance and penalise weaker performance. In addition, through special funding, it would provide a delicate balance between collaboration and competition across the sector, providing for efficiencies while at the same time promoting knowledge synergies, and development of complementary capabilities.

3.15 Education, Training and Employment Brokers

Consistent with the notion of our Referral State would be the establishment of a series of education, training and employment brokers. These brokering arrangements would build on the Public Exchange System in India for job seekers, but would have far more of a remit to link education and training with employers. Brokers, who are experts in education and training, would provide ongoing education and career advice, mentoring and support to students, from an early age, through to university and college, and into employment. This would be part of a 'personalised-massification' model that we see eventually unfolding in India-providing mass education with a personalised touch, in which big data would be used to track student progress, including those at risk of drop out and discontinuation, and identify areas of personalised need. In this way, brokers would work with students individually and the school/university system, to provide an integrated approach to education and training, and eventually into employment. Such a mechanism would provide extra personalised support, including life coaching, for example, to complement the activities of a resource-stretched formal education system. Rather than relying on resource-constrained institutions to provide such support and which may not have the requisite expertise, our system would draw on external experts who would work in concert with universities.

There would be multiple entry and exit points for broker involvement. For example, students may choose to avail themselves of broker support in higher education rather than at school, and may choose to exit from the guidance of brokers at any stage.

One example of how this might work is as follows. Secondary students would use an identification card (or finger printed ID) to enter their details in an Education Kiosk (located in a post office, school, mall, library or other public space in both urban and rural India) or through their PC/Tablet/mobile phone. This would provide details on:

- Their academic record
- List of potential universities or institutions of higher learning, and their admission requirements
- Rankings of institutions, Indian ranked or Globally ranked
- Information on specialist capabilities of institutions (course offerings, research strengths)
- The cluster that institutions belong to and relationship with other institutions
- Quality Ratings of Institutions
- Details on facilities of institutions
- Teacher rating
- Solutions/Mission specific information.

More sophisticated applications of this approach could provide students with options for courses beyond the provision of the sort of basic information outlined above.

Armed with the information about course options and the like, students would then consult with education, training and employment brokers either in person or virtually, to guide and assist in choices, career paths and provide other support. It is envisaged that the brokers would be funded collectively by various tiers of government, and industry. Some user charges could be canvassed depending on socio-economic status of the student. The provision of initial information of the type canvassed would also serve as an important tool that enables students to objectively compare institutions, thus serving as another 'defacto' ratings mechanism.

3.16 An Internationalisation Plan for Higher Education

A key element of our programme is to promote internationalisation of higher education in India. As we have seen India's current approach to internationalisation is strongly driven towards outward student mobility rather than inward mobility.

What would be the elements of an integrated plan? We propose the following:

- Focus on students from all around the world, commencing possibly with greater inward mobility from the neighbouring countries as is happening now, but moving more globally over time
- Strategic use of the Indian diaspora as conduits to influence students to study in India, including offspring of diaspora, building on the Know India programme[20] (Government of India 2019b)
- Stronger emphasis on postgraduate students from abroad who are connected into global research networks, and who can assist in working on key projects at higher education institutions and in industry, as part of their study programme
- Financial inducements for overseas students through reduced fees if they can draw in other students to study in India, building on their student-based connections and networks
- Investment in leading edge facilities for overseas and local students including student infrastructure and amenities
- Greater provision of work opportunities following completion of studies in India through flexible study to work opportunities in priority projects
- Encouragement of Indian students to participate in high priority global scale projects including open source projects.
- Support, through international agreements (and possibly with some financial support) for the establishment of Indian institutions abroad to provide educational opportunities for Indians in overseas countries, and for local students there, as a means of further integrating India into teaching and research hubs abroad: at very

---

[20]The Know India program is for Indian diaspora youth to spend 3 weeks in India to raise their awareness of India, its progress and potential, and to share views and experiences.

least this arrangement would foster greater two-way international mobility and joint degrees.

3.17 The System in Its Entirety

The system in its entirety would need to be informed by a whole of higher education plans, encompassing 5, 15 year and annual dimensions (and aligned with the labour force plans canvassed earlier) overseen by the Indian Education Service and supported by cluster representatives as well as broader Councils of Advisers, comprising state and local government representatives, industry participants, educational experts, student representatives and community groups. Once again, this approach is not dissimilar to the approach followed in RUSA and the State Higher Education Councils (Government of India 2013b). The whole of higher education plans, would have at their core, the following key elements:

- A comprehensive view of industry trends, labour market and skills needs (including especially the twenty-first-century skills needs to be described earlier) over the medium (5 year) and long term (15 year), broken down where feasible into annual components
- Capacity enhancement and utilisation plans across the entire system to ensure that capacity is better utilised in institutions in the first instance, that investment programmes and priorities meet long-term needs and growth, and that capacity is better distributed across spatial areas to provide greater opportunity for students
- Making explicit the balance between physical and online delivery of education and training as part of capacity planning, including a wider remit for the 'non-institutional' players in education, such as the Khan Academy—thus these entities would be brought explicitly into the fold, with appropriate quality standards.
- Ensuring that any growing emphasis on international education does not 'crowd out' domestic student intake, but recognises the need to enhance international orientation of India's higher education sector
- That facilities, including research, gradually move to world best practice, and where possible draws on both collaborative provision and usage, and that infrastructure and capacity is explicitly targeted to foster critical mass and scale and more efficient and effective deployment of resources.
- Quality Standards as determined by Quality India.

There would be a continuous iterative process between these more aggregate plans and the plans of clusters and constituent institutions.

3.18 Road Map

Clearly, to implement what is proposed here would be a long haul. As such, it is envisaged that a comprehensive road map should be prepared which undertakes a transition to a new model. The road map would be aligned with the annual, 5 and 15 year time horizon of the plans. For illustrative and indicative purposes, we look at the nature of the needed reforms over a 5 and 10 year horizon.

The main tenets of the road map could be:

- As is occurring now, more autonomy for quality colleges as part of eventually removing the affiliation system
- Gradual incorporation in explicit fashion of the for-profit motive into the system, with important safeguards and probity requirements built in
- Progressive improvement in participation in global rankings, with a view to having said at least 1–2 universities in the top 200 within the next five years, and 5 Universities in the top 200 within the next fifteen years
- Improvement in quality standards progressively over time, with significantly more institutions accredited (e.g. 50%) in the next 5–10 years
- More integration of course offerings aligned to industry needs, with industry participation in the development and delivery of courses, as a basis for moving to fully fledged IFI's
- Greater focus on project orientation in the curriculum to move more easily into Solutions/Mission mode operation
- Consolidation of facilities and institutions with significant capacity under-utilisation as a basis for eventual further investment
- Progressive widening of the international student base from more countries, focussing on more developed of the developing world in the first instance
- Building a collaborative mindset among researchers through establishment of priority projects aligned with Solutions/missions including overseas collaboration.

In the long run, we consider that India can be an exemplar of a holistic, 'humanistic' approach to education, which would comprise a values-based education approach and notions of self and community discovery, drawing on India's rich traditions of philosophy and learning, as well as the more 'day to day' requirements. The solutions approach allows for both considerations, although the immediate priorities of employability and raising standards would take precedence. Nonetheless, in pedagogy and research, there is considerable scope for new values-based learning. For example, a solutions/mission focus around the environment would have as its focus scientific management of the environment alongside a values-driven approach emphasising sharing of public resources, less emphasis on material consumption and a stronger sense of how individual effort can contribute to the collective whole.

3.19 Conclusion

This chapter has pointed out the importance of education for economic and social prosperity, and civil society, and has taken a comprehensive look at India's performance in education, benchmarked against developed and developing nations. It has found that India's performance has not been strong in quality, research performance, innovation and diversity of subject and course offerings. Moreover, there are serious governance and structural flaws in a system which has involved massive institutional growth, including privatisation, rather than necessarily one that is driven by academic excellence or through any particularly well developed and articulated over-arching strategy. It appears that the state is in retreat at the very time when other countries are expanding their state roles to advance the knowledge economy. Nonetheless, we argue that the private sector does play an important role in the sector, in tandem with a robust government role.

Our analysis also shows that the Indian higher education sector is not especially well connected to industry, and is not particularly well equipped for the challenges of the future, especially in relation to emergent technologies and skills needs.

Our proposed radical overhaul, which nevertheless builds on initiatives underway by the government, aligns institutions and groupings (clusters) of institutions around **flexible** national solutions approaches to give the system more focus, scale and coordination and foster collaboration. It does away with the affiliation system. It allows for the cautious and explicit introduction of the pro-profit motive. Further, our system involves pathways, opportunities and choice within clusters and across clusters, and links higher education with vocational education in a seamless manner. Further, we would argue that our proposed approach would foster specialisation and diversity at the same time, with desperately needed capability in areas such as teaching and research. Beyond this, it explicitly builds a series of outward institutions as part of a comprehensive international plan.

References

Abraham V (2017) Stagnant employment growth: last three years may have been the worst. CPI (ML) Red Star. Accessed 6 Nov 2017

Agarwal P (2009) Indian higher education envisioning. The Future Sage Publications

Altbach P (2014) India's higher education challenges. Asia Pac Educ Rev 15:503–510

Asian Development Bank (ADB) (2015) Human capital development in the People's Republic of China and India: achievements, prospects and policy challenges

Badrinath V (2016) Further education and training, retraining: skilful India—a dream or reality. In: Pilz M (eds) India: preparation for the world of work. Springer VS, Wiesbaden

Bakshi H, Downing J, Oshorre M, Schneider P (2017) The future of skills: employment in 2030. Pearson and Nesta, London

Basu K (2019) India can hide unemployment data, but not the truth. The New York Times, 1 Feb 2019

References

Berger T, Frey C (2015) Future shocks and shifts: challenges for the global workforce and skills development, OECD education 2030. Research Paper Oxford Martin Program on Technology and Employment, Oxford Martin School

Bhat S, Siddharthan N (2013) Human capital, labour productivity and employment. In: Siddharthan N, Narayanan K (eds) Human capital and development, the Indian experience. Springer, India

Chowdry H (2009) Higher education funding presentation. Institute for Fiscal Studies. www.ifs.org.uk. Accessed 25 Oct 2017

Citi GPS (2016) Technology at Work 2.0. Oxford Martin School (University)

Cornell University, INSEAD, WIPO (2018) The global innovation index

Das G (2019) Jobonomics India's employment crisis and what the future holds. Hachette, India

Datta S (2017) A history of the Indian University system emerging from the shadows of the past. Palgrave MacMillan

Day N, Stigloe J (2009) Knowledge nomads why science needs migrants. Demos

Dreze J, Sen A (2013) An uncertain glory: India and its contradictions. Princeton University Press, Princeton, NJ

Ernst and Young, Federation of Indian Chambers of Commerce and Industry (FICCI) (2013) Higher education in India: vision 2030. FICCI Higher Education Summit 2013

Florida R (2003) Cities and the creative class. City and Community 2(1):3–19

Frey C, Osborne M (2015) Technology at work. The future of innovation and employment City GPS: global perspectives and solutions. Oxford Martin School

Frey C, Osborne M (2013) The future of employment how susceptible are jobs to computerisation. Oxford Martin Programme on Technology and Employment

GK Today (2018) Government launches study in India Program to attract foreign students, 19 Apr 2018. https://currentaffairs.gktoday.in/government-launches-study-india-programme-attract-foreign-students-2-04201854541.html

Government of India (1968) National policy on education

Government of India (1998) Department of Education, Ministry of Human Resource Development National Policy and Education 1986 as modified in 1992

Government of India (2010) Education in India 2007–2008. Participants and Expenditure, July 2007–June 2008. Ministry of Statistics and Programme Implementation, National Sample Survey Office (2010)

Government of India (2012a) All India survey of higher education 2011–2012. Ministry of Human Resource Development

Government of India (2012b) Intellectual property India. Annual Report 2011–2012. Ministry of Commerce and Industry, Department of Industrial Policy and Promotion, The Office of the Controller General of Patents, Designs, Trademarks and Geographical Indications

Government of India (2013a) Planning Commission twelfth five year plan

Government of India (2013b) Rashtriya Uchchatar Shiksha Abhiyan National Higher Education Mission (in association with Tata Institute of Social Sciences)

Government of India (2013c) All India survey of higher education 2012–2013. Ministry of Human Resource Development

Government of India (2014a) All India survey of higher education 2013–2014. Ministry of Human Resource Development

Government of India (2014b) Report on employment, unemployment survey 2013–2014, vol 1. Ministry of Labour and Employment

Government of India (2015a) All India survey of higher education 2014–2015. Ministry of Human Resource Development

Government of India (2015b) Economic survey 2014–2015. Ministry of Finance

Government of India (2016a) Report of the committee for evolution of the new education policy. Ministry of Human Resources, Development of National Policy and Education 2016

Government of India (2016b) Some inputs for draft national education policy 2016. Ministry of Human Resources, Development

Government of India (2016c) All India survey of higher education 2015–2016. Ministry of Human Resource Development
Government of India (2016d) National Sample Survey Office (2016). Education in India 71st round January–June 2014. Ministry of Statistics and Programme Implementation
Government of India (2016e) Annual report, 2015–2016. University Grant Commission
Government of India (2016f) Employment-unemployment survey, vol 1. Ministry of Labour and Employment
Government of India (2016g) Report on education, skill development and labour force, vol 111. Ministry of Labour and Employment
Government of India (2017a) All India survey of higher education 2016–2017. Ministry of Human Resource Development
Government of India (2017b) Intellectual property India. Annual report 2016–2017. Ministry of Commerce and Industry, Department of Industrial Policy and Promotion, The Office of the Controller General of Patents, Designs, Trademarks and Geographical Indications
Government of India (2018a) All India survey of higher education 2017–2018. Ministry of Human Resource Development
Government of India (2018b) Economic survey 2017–2018. Ministry of Finance
Government of India (2018c) Indian students studying in foreign countries Annexure-1 752725 students as on 18/7/2018. Ministry of External Affairs
Government of India (2018d) Ministry of Labour and Employment. National Career Service. www.ncs.gov.ai/pages/default.aspx. Accessed 31 Mar 2018
Government of India (2019a) Swayam https://swayam.gov.in/about. Accessed 27 Feb 2019
Government of India (2019b) Know India programme for young overseas Indians. https://kip.gov.in. Accessed 15 May 2019
Gupta A (2016) Grass roots innovation minds on the margin are not marginal minds. Penguin Random House, India
Gupta V, Raman C, Krisanthan B (2016) Secondary (9–10) and Higher Secondary (11–12) Education: preparation for the world of work: secondary and higher secondary education in India. In: Pilz M (ed) India: preparation for the world of work education systems and school to work transition. Springer
Hasan R (2017) Sustaining growth, ensuring inclusion 2017. In: Nayyar D, Hasan R (eds) Shaping India's future: essays in memory of Abid Hussain. Academic Foundation, New Delhi
ILO (2018) Employment by skills. https://www.ilo.org/ilostats. Accessed 18 July 2018
Institute of International Education (2017) Infographics and data. www.iie.org/en/research-and-insights. Accessed 21 Aug 2018
Jagannathan R (2018) The jobs crisis in India. MacMillan
Joshi K (2015) Higher education, social demand and social equity in India. In: Schwarzman S, Pinheiro R, Pillay (eds) Higher education in the BRIC countries investigating the pact between higher education and society higher education dynamics. Springer
Joshi V (2016) India's long road. The search for prosperity. Penguin Random House, India
Kapoor R (2017) Waiting for jobs: Indian council for research on international economic relationships. World paper no 348
Kapur D (2017) Liberalisation sans liberalism: the central Raj and the Perils of ideology and rents in higher education. In: Mohan R (ed) India transformed, 25 years of economic reforms. Penguin Viking
Kapur D, Mehta P (2017a) Navigating the Labyrinth. Perspectives on India's higher education. Orient Blackswan Private Limited, Hyderabad, India
Kapur D, Mehta P (2017b) Introduction. In: Kapur D, Mehta P (eds) Navigating the Labyrinth. Perspectives on India's higher education. Orient Blackswan Private Limited
Kathuria V, Raj S, Sen K (2013) Impact of human capital on manufacturing productivity growth in India. In: Siddharthan N, Narayanan K (eds) Human capital and development. The Indian experience. Springer, India

References

Khare M (2016) Higher Education/University: taking the skills march forward in India—transitioning to the world of work. In: Pilz M (ed) India: preparation for the world of work. Springer VS, Wiesbaden

Krishna V, Patra S (2016) Research and innovation in Universities in India. In: Varghese N, Malik G (eds) India higher education report 2015. Routledge

Kulkarni A (2018a) India's higher education sector: challenges and opportunities. Int Rev Bus Econ (IBRE) 2(1):2474–5146 (online), 2474–5138 (print)

Kulkarni A (2018b) Higher education blown by light winds of change. University World News, 1 June 2018. https://www.universityworldnews.com/post.php?story=201805301033246603. Accessed 5 June 2016

Kulkarni A (2019) Impact rankings highlight community role of universities, University World News, 18 May 2019. https://www.universityworldnews.com/post.php?story=2019051410375853. Accessed 20 May 2019

Kulkarni S (2012) Music of the spinning wheel Mahatma Gandhi's manifesto for the internet age. Amaryllis

Kumar P (2011) The ancient Nalanda Mahavira: the beginning of international education. J World Univ Forum 4(1)

Kumar S (2015) Building global India-how to unleash India's vast potential and transform its higher education system. ONS Group Fremont

Kumar K (2016) ITI's/ITC's: Industrial Training Institutes/Industrial Training Centres. In: Pilz M (eds) India: preparation for the world of work. Springer VS, Wiesbaden

Lanvin B, Evans P (Eds) (2018) The global talent competitiveness index: diversity for competitiveness. INSEAD, The ADECCO Group and TATA Communications

Lanvin B, Monteiro (Eds) (2019) The global talent competitiveness index entrepreneurial talent and global competitivenes. INSEAD, The ADECCO Group and TATA Communications

Leiden Institute (2018) CWTS Leiden ranking 2018. http://www.leidenranking.com/ranking/2018/list. Accessed 21 July 2018

Majumdar S (2016) Foreword: reflections on opportunities and challenges of skills development in India. In: Pilz M (ed) India: preparation for the world of work education systems and school to work transition. Springer

Mehrotra S (2016) The employability of tertiary-level graduates. In: Varghese N, Malik G (2016) India higher education report 2015, Routledge

Mehrotra S, Raman R, Kumara N, Kalaiyarasan, Rob D (2014) Vocational education and training reform in India. Business needs and lessons to be learned from Germany. Bartelsmann Stiftung

NITI Aayog (2017) India three year action agenda 2017–2018 to 2019–2020

NITI Aayog (2018) Strategy for New India@75

Pillay H, Ninan A (2014) India's vocational education capacity to support the anticipated economic growth. Contracted Research, BHP Billiton, Singapore

Pilz M (2016) Introduction: why India's focus on preparation for the world of work is highly relevant. In: Pilz M (eds) India: preparation for the world of work. Springer VS, Wiesbaden

QS (2018) Best student cities. https://www.topuniversities.com/city-rankings/2018

QS Intelligence Unit (2016) What matters to international students, focus on India

Ramaswami V (2016) Innovation by India for India. Siksha Publications, USA

Sahu S, Narayanan K (2013) Labour and energy intensity: a study of the pulp and paper industry in India. In: Siddharthan N, Narayanan K (eds) Human capital and development, the Indian experience. Springer, India

Schwab K (2016) The fourth industrial revolution: what it means, how to respond World Economic Forum, Jan 2016. www.weforumorg/agenda. Accessed 15 May 2019

Schwab K (2017) The fourth industrial revolution. Penguin Books

Schwartzman S (2015) Demands and policies for higher education. In: Schwartzman S, Pinheiro R, Pillay P (eds) Higher education in the BRICS countries, investigating the pact between higher education and society, higher education dynamics, vol 44. Springer

Scopus Research Papers. https://www.scopus.com/home.uri. Accessed 30 May 2018

Siddharthan N, Narayanan K (2013) Capital and development: introduction. In: Siddharthan N, Narayanan K (eds) Human capital and development, the indian experience. Springer, India

Tara S, Kumar N (2016) Primary and upper primary (1–8) Education: initiative for the world of work at the primary and upper primary education in India. In: Pilz M (eds) India: preparation for the world of work. Springer VS, Wiesbaden

Tharoor S (2016) An era of darkness. The British empire in India. Aleph Book Company, New Delhi, India

The Economic Intelligence Unit (2018) The automation readiness index: who is ready for the coming wave of automation? https://www.automationreadiness.eiu.com/. Accessed 30 Sept 2018

The Economist (2017a) India's Prime Minister is not as much of a reformer as he seems, June 24 2019. https://www.economist.com/leaders/2017/06/24/indias-prime-minister-is-not-as-much-of-a-reformer-as-he-seems. Accessed 2 Feb 2019

Times Higher Education (2018) University rankings 2019. https://www.timeshighereducation.com/world-university-rankings. Accessed 9 Oct 2019

Times Higher Education (2019a) University impact rankings. https://www.timeshighereducation.com/ranking/impact/2019. Accessed 5 May 2019

Times Higher Education (2019b) University subject rankings 2019. https://www.timeshighereducation.com/world-university-rankings/by-subject. Accessed 9 May 2019

Trilokekar R, Embleton S (2015) The complex web of policy choices: dilemmas facing Indian higher education reform. In: Schwarzman S, Pinheiro R, Pillay (eds) Higher education in the BRIC countries investigating the pact between higher education and society higher education dynamics. Springer

Trow M (2007) Reflections on the transition from Elite to Mass to universal access: forms and phases of higher education in modern societies since WWII. In: Forest J, Altbach P (eds) International handbook of higher education. Springer International Handbooks of Education, vol 18. Springer, Dordrecht

UN (2018) Human development indices and indicators. 2018 Statistical Update

UNESCO (2011) International standard classification of education

UNESCO (2017) Summary report of the 2015 UIS innovation data collection. Open Access

UNESCO (2018) https://data.uis.unesco.org. Accessed 20 July 2018

UNESCO (2019) https://data.uis.unesco.org. Accessed 15 Mar 2019

United States Patent and Trademark Office. https://www.uspto.gov/learnings-and-sources/statistics. Accessed 10 Oct 2017

Vyas M (2018) Employment stagnates in 2017–2018. Centre for Monitoring Indian Economy, 17 July 2018

Walsh T (2018) 2062. The world that AI made. La Trobe University Press, Melbourne, Australia

Williams R, Leahy A (2019) U21 ranking of national higher education systems 2019: a project sponsored by Universities 21

World Bank (2018a) Jobless growth? South Asia Economic Focus

World Bank (2018b) Data. https://data.worldbank.org/indicator. Accessed 26 July 2018

World Bank (2019) World development report 2019: the changing nature of work. World Bank, Washington

World Economic Forum (2015) New vision for education unlocks the potential for technology, prepared in collaboration with Boston Consulting Group Industry Agenda

World Economic Forum (2016) The future of jobs, employment, skills and workforce strategy for the fourth industrial revolution

World Economic Forum (2017) The global human capital report

World Economic Forum (in collaboration with AT Kearney) (2018) Readiness for the future of production report 2018

Chapter 4
Engagement

Abstract This chapter has a number of parts. It introduces the novel idea of a Knowledge Footprint designed to measure the extent and magnitude of a nation's embrace of a knowledge economy. It encompasses both domestic and international elements of knowledge flows. The chapter measures India's Knowledge Footprint against other countries, and finds that out of 15 countries India is ranked a disappointing fourteenth. The chapter then delves into key focus areas of exports to assess India's performance on this critical dimension of internationalisation. India is making some tentative inroads into becoming a knowledge intensive exporter. The chapter then turns to another 'E', that of entrepreneurship and finds that despite the optimism surrounding India's entrepreneurship, there are a number of missing elements in the overall ecosystem. The chapter also considers environment as an important element associated with the 'E' framework. A number of strategies are outlined in this chapter.

Keywords Engagement · Entrepreneurship · Knowledge footprint · Trade · Exports · Investment · Innovation fund

4.1 Parameters of Engagement

This chapter considers the third 'E' of the knowledge economy, engagement or the 'eyes and ears'. Engagement comes in many forms: the extent, nature and form of *integration* into the global economy in terms of flows of advanced goods and services, capital, technology, ideas, and know-how, people movements, connections between suppliers and globally demanding customers and enmeshing into complex global production or value chains. Engagement is not just about integration into the global economy. It is also about linkages within the domestic economy, encompassing the collaborative behaviours, joint knowledge discovery, transfers of know-how, and diffusion and deployment of knowledge within an economy. It is about the interaction at home and abroad between suppliers and customers, research bodies, education institutions and firms, and among firms themselves. There is a rich vein of literature, as we saw in Chap. 1, about linkages between actors in an economy, between suppliers, research bodies, education providers, and government. Moreover, the systems literature increasingly is about transcending national boundaries.

4.2 Approach to the Chapter

A centrepiece of this chapter, and indeed book, is the original and novel concept of the Knowledge Footprint.[1] A Knowledge Footprint captures the ability of a nation to participate in the creation, application, dissemination and diffusion of knowledge in its various dimensions, and, for its citizens to share in the benefits. It is the ultimate form of engagement. There are three forms of footprint which we develop: Domestic Knowledge Footprint; Global Knowledge Footprint; and Overall Knowledge Footprint. The Domestic Knowledge Footprint measures the resourcing, capability, diffusion and deployment of knowledge on a national scale, including the support for knowledge activities to flourish, while the Global Knowledge Footprint measures the ability of a nation to **project** its capabilities and approach to knowledge enhancement on a global scale, in effect the development and deployment of knowledge beyond a nations' boundaries to underscore its impact and influence globally. This is particularly important in the context of a world in which problems are often on a global scale. In measurement terms, the footprint represents input, output and outcome dimensions. The Domestic and Global Knowledge Footprints are combined into an Overall Knowledge Footprint.

4.2.1 Exports

Following consideration of the Footprint, we turn to a detailed discussion of India's performance in exports (and trade and global investment more generally). As we have seen, India's protectionist sentiment, emphasis on import substitution and self-reliance constrained its ability and willingness to produce for the world market. The export section looks at India's export performance over the last 20 years with a focus on knowledge intensive exports, to see what progress has been made, identify policy implications and propose a number of recommendations.

---

[1] The author was the lead in considering the Knowledge Footprint in the context of a University or educational institution (Kulkarni et al. 2015). This book takes the broad concept of a footprint and analyses it for countries in an extensive way.

4.2.2 Entrepreneurship

Entrepreneurship is an 'E' in its own right. It is the 'lifeblood' of a knowledge economy, as described in Chap. 1. It is closely aligned with engagement by serving as the connections between firms and leading-edge customers, as conduits to the market place and solving societal problems and commercial needs through innovation. Innovation and entrepreneurship are strongly aligned.

4.2.3 Environment

Finally, this book considers the natural environment, which is associated with the 'E' framework. We examine India's performance on a number of measures, and posit recommendations for improving performance.

4.3 Knowledge Footprint

As mentioned in Chap. 1, this book places a high premium on the global flows of ideas and know-how. Openness to ideas, influences and capabilities from abroad, are part and parcel of, and inextricably linked with a Domestic Knowledge Footprint. As such, many metrics around imports of advanced goods and services, patents by non-residents, and inward investments feature strongly in Domestic Knowledge Footprint. Access to ideas and know-how from abroad, from far and wide, mesh with one's own in complementary and synergistic fashion.

The Knowledge Footprint has more than 300 variables, comprising six sub-pillars in each of the domestic and global domains. Different data sets are used for the domestic and global footprints. As appropriate, metrics are scaled by size of economy and/or population, and by relative share of global economic size and global population. Only latest year data is used so the footprint is a snapshot in time. Moreover, on occasion, some metrics are repeated given that they can be deployed in many categories. Further, the choice of metrics and their categorisation is open to conjecture and debate and this is understood here. It is quite likely that others would classify metrics and variables under different headings. Their placement reflects the judgment of this author, and on occasion a paucity of suitable data is one of the determining factors. It should also be noted that because publicly available, more aggregate data is relied on, grass roots type innovations cannot be captured adequately here.

The footprint configuration and analysis should be seen as a trial and indicative. It is open to further development and refining. Its main purpose in this book is to exemplify how such a concept can be utilised and what tentative results show, thereby adding to the debate about the importance and impact of innovation. The footprint analysis is certainly not intended to be exhaustive but rather illustrative. As such, it is not accompanied by any sensitivity testing or modelling to determine causality among metrics. This is beyond the scope of the book, and could be picked up by others in ongoing research. The value lies in its comprehensive and novel conceptual framework. The Knowledge Footprint, especially in the global domain, should be seen more as a virtual footprint idea in the sense that it does not measure physical distance per se. Nevertheless, we do represent the results both in tabular form and diagrammatic fashion to give a sense of how it might look if applied on a spatial basis.

While there is some commonality of our approach with the Global Innovation Index (Cornell University, INSEAD, WIPO 2018), and to some extent the new Production Readiness Index (World Economic Forum 2018), and we readily recognise this, there are significant differences. First our index is divided into Domestic and Global knowledge sub-pillars, i.e. for Domestic and Global Knowledge Footprint to determine whether, and to what extent, innovative effort and impact is more domestically oriented or focussed on global integration, as a basis for understanding strategic priorities. Second, as we shall see shortly, our focus includes the importance of access and opportunity to engage in the knowledge economy, the extent to which people have the wherewithal to participate in the knowledge economy, and avail themselves of opportunities. Third, is the presence of many more indicators overall. Fourth, is the greater explicit weight given to the natural environment. Fifth, is the greater recognition given to innovative cities as representing 'magnets' of knowledge intensive activities and as drivers of wealth in the knowledge arena.

4.4 Footprint Methodology

The methodology is basic in that for each metric the leading country is given a score of 100, the next best a score as a proportion of 100 and so on. The scores for each metric are summed and divided by number of metrics to give a sub-pillar score for each sub-pillar. There are six sub-pillars as described shortly. The sub-pillar overall scores are then weighted to give pillar scores for Domestic Knowledge Footprint and Global Knowledge Footprint. Weights which are the same for the domestic and global cases are as follows: Knowledge Access and Opportunity (17%), Knowledge Support and Platforms (15%), Knowledge Capability (22%), Knowledge Resourcing (15%), Knowledge Relationships (12%), and Knowledge Translation and Transformation (19%). The Overall Knowledge Footprint, in turn, is derived by summing the pillar scores for Domestic Knowledge Footprint and Global Knowledge Footprint and then dividing by two. This methodological approach is consistent with aspects of the Global Innovation Index (Cornell University, INSEAD, WIPO 2018). As mentioned, and illustrated in Appendix 1, metrics are scaled by GDP and population, and as appropriate shares of global GDP, and population. Some metrics are given weightings, e.g. in education, postgraduate enrolment and outcomes are given higher weight than undergraduate. Appendix 1 provides a comprehensive list of metrics, data sources and approach taken.

The sub-pillars of the knowledge footprint are

- Knowledge Access and Opportunity
- Knowledge Supports and Platforms
- Knowledge Capability Development
- Knowledge Resourcing
- Knowledge Relationships
- Knowledge Translation and Transformation.

These same sub-pillars are at the domestic and global levels.

4.5 Domestic Knowledge Footprint

This section describes the sub-pillars in the overall Domestic Knowledge Footprint.

4.5.1 Domestic Knowledge Access and Opportunity Sub-pillar

A prime determinant of a Domestic Knowledge Footprint is access and opportunity. Without this, there is little prospect of citizens participating in the knowledge economy, either as contributors or beneficiaries. Access and Opportunity is a fundamental right of people to engage in the process and outcomes of knowledge deployment, and avail themselves of opportunities. As shown in Appendix 1, a variety of metrics are used in this sub-pillar including: enrolment in higher education, and vocational education, enrolment in knowledge intensive studies (proxy being STEM); enrolment by level of studies, with an increased weight given to postgraduates, as more likely to deepen the knowledge economy; enrolment in upper and lower secondary education as an access pipeline to higher education (also a significant departure from the Global Innovation Index); and broader parameters of access and opportunity, canvassing various dimensions of inequality, labour force participation and unemployment. Labour force participation, is in our view, important in understanding whether, and to what, extent citizens are alienated from the labour market as a key vehicle of the knowledge economy.

4.5.2 Domestic Knowledge Supports and Platforms Sub-pillar

Domestic Knowledge Supports and Platforms are foundational elements of the knowledge economy and have much to do with the enabling role of government discussed in Chap. 2. They are also linked to the fundamental attractiveness of the business environment and efficacy of associated institutions, as well as the support systems to facilitate a knowledge economy and society. There are a variety of metrics that have been used: *quality and competitiveness of the business environment*, essentially from the 2018 World Bank Doing Business Index (World Bank 2017) and its component indicators, and institutional parameters drawn from other sources including corruption, freedom, trust in institutions, and economic and social cohesion, as well as tolerance of minorities and immigrants and strength of labour–employer relationships; *support for underlying attributes of entrepreneurship* including willingness to embrace risk and change, the availability of risk capital and societal backing for entrepreneurship; and *platforms* for which we use a myriad of metrics related to access, availability and use of ICT in various ways, as key online instruments that enable knowledge to be developed, harnessed, and deployed.

Various studies and theories underpin the choice of metrics. For example, tolerance of minorities and immigrants, as derived from the Global Talent Competitiveness Index (Lanvin and Evans 2018), says much about a society's willingness to embrace insights, ideas and perspectives from all in society, and creating an environment in which, debate, dialogue and discussion and dissent are associated with knowledge creation and diffusion. These sentiments owe some to Richard Florida's work in highlighting the importance of tolerance and difference in shaping economic and social prosperity (Florida 2003).

4.5.3 Domestic Knowledge Capability Development Sub-pillar

Domestic Knowledge Capability Development is about those **core intellectual strengths** and assets that underpin a knowledge economy. They canvass the following: graduation rates at tertiary and secondary levels and tertiary education by level, i.e. undergraduate and postgraduate; graduates according to knowledge intensive disciplines (STEM), again as vital underpinnings of a knowledge economy; strength of higher education systems and institutions as reflected in university rankings and relevant components; academic papers produced as an important creation of new knowledge, and citations representing the quality of papers, and availability of researchers and scientists, as core drivers of capability. Also included here, where data is available, is Revealed Technology Advantage, which measures the extent to which a nation has an advantage in particular emerging and ubiquitous, enabling fields such as ICT, biotechnology and nanotechnology, drawn from the OECD (2017). Domestic Knowledge Capabilities also encompass capabilities associated with entrepreneurship, such as start-up skills, opportunity identification and human capital for entrepreneurship. This is distinct from the broader support system for entrepreneurship such as availability of risk capital, mentioned earlier.

4.5.4 Domestic Knowledge Resourcing Sub-pillar

Domestic Knowledge Resourcing captures a number of metrics. At one level it is the financial resources devoted to knowledge such as expenditure on research and development, and education, as well as investments in gross fixed capital formation, and financing via foreign direct investment (stocks and flows), and greenfield investments. Foreign Direct Investment is not only about financing and bringing in productive resources, but also embodies new and improved technology, management capability, and organisational/business models, important for a knowledge economy. Knowledge Resourcing also includes inward immigration (stock and scaled by working age) as embodying human resources that can be deployed for innovation and knowledge activities (including the different insights and ideas that they bring), and as consumer resources to stimulate economic activity, including as purchasers of innovative products and services. Inward immigration stock, as representing a broader labour resource for economy and society, is distinguished from other more specialised personnel such as scientists and researchers whom this author feels more closely aligns with knowledge capability building.

The Domestic Knowledge Resourcing sub-pillar also captures wider metrics around environmental management,[2] including renewable energy production and consumption, availability and management of scare natural assets such as water, various species, air quality, health impacts of the environment and emissions intensity. We view knowledge resourcing in a wider sense than purely expenditures on research and development and education, to encapsulate the capacity of a nation to manage its broader resources, including especially natural assets. Management of the environment is a critical function of a knowledge economy in the sense of utilising knowledge to conserve and manage effectively, efficiently and pro-actively scarce resources and natural assets. Further, in our view, the divide or distinction between the environment and the (knowledge) economy is in many senses an artificial one: they are highly interdependent and part and parcel of a unified, integrated approach to the overall allocation of resources, including natural resources, in an economy. In this context, we also include a separate section in this chapter on the environment, canvassing India's performance and prognosis and what can be done to improve its performance from a knowledge economy perspective.

4.5.5 Domestic Knowledge Relationships Sub-pillar

Domestic Knowledge Relationships are essential for exchanging ideas and information, collaborating to capitalise on specialist and complementary capabilities, jointly solve problems and challenges, engage in the process of collective knowledge discovery, to share costs and risks, and enhance productivity. These collaborative

---

[2] The Production Readiness Index, prepared by the World Economic Forum, captures environmental parameters.

relationships include between firms and suppliers, firms themselves, between firms and research providers, and with education institutions, for example. They enable the realisation of scale, productivity improvements, and development and diffusion of new and improved knowledge. This is particularly important in that problems and challenges are often too complex, risky and uncertain for individual firms and institutions acting alone. A range of metrics are used, including university-industry collaboration and state of cluster development from the Global Innovation Index drawn from the World Economic Forum, domestic collaborative papers and with industry, highly cited collaborative papers, industry income into higher education institutions, broader engagement between industry and higher education, and networking among businesses and individuals which encompass both professional/business and social networks. Also included here are metrics on urban agglomeration according to population, while we have also estimated city (urban) GDP, as a share of national GDP. Underpinning the latter is the idea that cities represent the coalescence and agglomerations of skills, know-how, ideas, capabilities and institutions (Cortright 2001), and are both the cause of, and solutions to, problems such as urban design, transport systems, carbon emissions, health and ageing and liveability.

4.5.6 Domestic Knowledge Translation and Transformation Sub-pillar

Finally, Domestic Knowledge Translation and Transformation is about domestic productive capacity, outputs and outcomes. It is much closer to the commercialisation of knowledge. As such, it comprises three types of metrics. The first centres on industrial development (value added, productivity, imports) in knowledge intensive manufactures and services and entrepreneurial performance (early stage entrepreneurship, new business density and established business activity). The second relates to employment in high and medium occupations (as distinct from the specialist researchers and scientists captured elsewhere) as the more general human resource capabilities utilised in knowledge intensive activities. The third type of metric is about patents, utilities, trademarks and industrial design, reflecting the translation of knowledge from ideas into the commercial arena.

4.6 Global Knowledge Footprint

In the case of the Global Knowledge Footprint, the same six sub-pillars remain. While there are some common metrics with the domestic footprint, there are many and significant differences. Consistent with the notion of *projecting* national capabilities onto the world stage, the focus on Global Knowledge Footprint is on export capabilities, shares of global activity (critical mass) and outward linkages.

4.6.1 Global Knowledge Access and Opportunity Sub-pillar

Global Knowledge Access and Opportunity focuses on inbound and outbound student mobility as providing opportunities for students and potential employees and researchers, eventually contributing to the global flow and stock of ideas through the circulation of ideas and know-how. This is consistent with the notion of 'brain circulation' as distinguished from traditional paradigms of 'brain drain versus brain gain', where 'brain circulation' is the circular and continuous movement of ideas and know-how around the world (OECD 2008). Also included is share of global value added in education services by country, and shares of world GDP, and GDP per capita levels. The latter two measures are deemed important in determining the basic capacity of countries to shape and influence the stock and flows of global knowledge. It is about the capacity to pay in many senses.

4.6.2 Global Knowledge Supports and Platforms Sub-pillar

Global Knowledge Supports and Platforms refers to the extent and manner in which nations can support and influence global efforts at innovation and knowledge development, including through its own values, beliefs and systems. While metrics are difficult to identify in this case, a number of proxies are possible. We include here foreign aid, enforcing export contracts (to assist with movement of goods and services abroad), export of government services, as a reflection of the influence of governance and public administration internationally, quality and strength of various types of infrastructure to facilitate trade and investment beyond national boundaries, and english language proficiency. The English Language Proficiency index as measured by Education First (2017) may raise some eyebrows. There is however considerable work to suggest that proficiency of english positively correlates with trade and technology flows, investment, economic growth, innovation (investment in R&D), and a variety of positive social indicators and 'soft power' influence. For example, societies in which adults have learned how to speak english tend for their people to be more internationally mobile, less hierarchical and more empowering of females (Education First 2017, 2018). In this context we do not apportion scores for the naturally english speaking countries in our benchmark set: U.K, Australia and U.S as this would provide an undue advantage. A further point of interest is that we use country scores from the Global Happy Planet Index (Jeffrey et al. 2016) and World Happiness Report (Helliwell et al. 2018), These indices give expression to the sort of core values and belief systems in countries which could foster strong global citizenship, contributing to the building of strong relationships abroad.

Global Knowledge platforms also includes international bandwidth measures as illustrative of communications and doing online business across national boundaries, and the use of virtual social and professional networks.

4.6.3 Global Knowledge Capability Development Sub-pillar

Global Knowledge capability measures share of world papers by country, citations of international papers, share of global value added in high and medium-high technology manufacturing and commercial service industries, international outlook of higher education institutions and outflows of scientists and emigration of the highly skilled. Emigration of highly qualified, knowledge intensive professions is an important demonstration of a nation's ability to shape global knowledge through the movement of highly skilled personnel. A vibrant diaspora is critical in the projection of a nation's capabilities onto the world stage. The share of global value added, and adjusted for by global GDP share, for various higher value sectors, is considered important in reflecting the critical mass of capabilities that a country can bring to bear on the international arena.

4.6.4 Global Knowledge Resourcing Sub-pillar

Global knowledge resourcing includes metrics similar to the domestic one with significant differences. Firstly, it includes measures relating to the global share of carbon emissions, adjusted for share of global GDP and global population. Also included here are overall emigration rates, as potential labour and consumer resources for other countries. In addition, we measure share of global Gross Expenditure on Research and Development and its components in business, higher education and government research to identify what contributions that countries can make to the collective global effort on research.

4.6.5 Global Knowledge Relationships Sub-pillar

Global Relationships capture the magnitude and extent of engagement in the knowledge sphere across national boundaries. As such, they include collaborative papers internationally, including in science and engineering, and citations associated with international collaborations. Also included are co-patenting across national boundaries, and participation by industries and enterprises in global value chains (backward and forward participation). Backward participation refers to extent of foreign value added in the gross exports of a nation and forward participation is domestic value added in the exports of other countries. Increasingly, global segmentation of production according to specialist capabilities and cost and other advantages is occurring, coordinated and linked through complex globally integrated value chains.

We also include cities as a fulcrum of relationships across national boundaries. Cities are global in nature serving not only as agglomerations of local activity, but also as magnets for international activity including investment, research and people flows. Cities are internationally renowned units of activity in their own right. As such, city-based metrics are included here in this global context. We use the consulting firm 2thinknow's classification of global cities according to different degrees of sophistication and innovation. The 2thinknow database covers cities according to their extent of innovation in 31 segments (industrial and community activities) across 162 metrics. The most innovative is nexus cities, followed by hub, node and upstart cities. For example, nexus has very visible and leading positions in innovation across many segments, while at the other end upstart has potential (2ThinkNow 2018).

4.6.6 Global Knowledge Translation and Transformation Sub-pillar

Global Knowledge Translation and Transformation, which as we explained previously, is more at the commercial end of the innovation and knowledge spectrum. It draws on exports of advanced manufacturing and services, and strength of patents, utilities, industrial design and trademarks lodged abroad. Also included are metrics around international outlook of entrepreneurs, and Revealed Comparative Advantage, for medium and high skill manufacturing, which measures the extent to which exports are disproportionately (or otherwise) weighted to these advanced sectors compared to a country's overall export profile.

4.7 Overall Findings of Footprint Analysis

The following tables indicate the performance of each country on the Overall Knowledge Footprint and Domestic and Global Knowledge Footprint pillars. Scores are indicated and Rank is included in the brackets.

As is to be expected and as seen in Table 4.1, the top positions in the overall footprint are taken up by the developed western world including the U.S, U.K, Germany and Australia in that order. The performance of the U.S and U.K reflects long term institutional strength, including in higher education, and strong business environments, exemplar research capability, and participation in trade and investment. Importantly, these top-ranked nations have been open also to inward migration and inward student mobility. These are important facets in their success and broader tolerance and openness to ideas. Australia is an interesting case. It is ranked fourth overall in spite of being better known as a natural resource economy, rather than as an innovator per se. However, the soundness of its institutions, freedoms, strengths in education, and openness to immigration places it in the upper reaches. Its weakness, reflecting its industrial structure, is in high value manufacturing.

Table 4.1 Knowledge Footprint Results

	Overall Knowledge Footprint	Domestic Knowledge Footprint	Global Knowledge Footprint
Australia	51.8 (4)	65.5 (3)	38.1 (7)
Bangladesh	23.5 (15)	27.9 (15)	19.0 (15)
Brazil	32.5 (13)	40.7 (11)	24.3 (14)
Chile	41.3 (9)	49.5 (9)	33.0 (9)
China	49.1 (6)	53.4 (7)	44.8 (4)
Germany	56.7 (3)	61.6 (4)	51.8 (3)
India	32.3 (14)	38.4 (13)	26.2 (13)
Japan	45.3 (8)	53.6 (6)	37.0 (8)
Korea	49.5 (5)	58.1 (5)	41.3 (6)
Malaysia	45.6 (7)	49.6 (8)	41.6 (5)
Russia	36.3 (11)	45.2 (10)	27.3 (12)
Sri Lanka	33.9 (12)	37.7 (14)	30.1 (11)
Thailand	36.6 (10)	40.7 (11)	32.5 (10)
U.K	59.5 (2)	66.7 (2)	52.1 (2)
U.S	63.4 (1)	68.4 (1)	58.4 (1)

Reflecting its growing desire to be an advanced economy, China is strongly placed in 6th place in the overall footprint. This is on the back of its growing investments in human capital, strength of its position at home and abroad in advanced manufacturing capabilities, a sound pro-growth business environment, and as a significant player in global value chains. However, its performance in the natural environment continues to be an area of concern, as with India.

India is a disappointing overall performer. Its overall footprint rank is 14th place, weakest of the BRIC economies, and against emerging Asian economies of Thailand and Malaysia, and only ahead of Bangladesh. India surprisingly and somewhat alarmingly lags Sri Lanka according to our findings.

4.7.1 Classifying Economies[3]

We classify economies according to the following scores for Overall Knowledge Footprint: Stellar countries (score 76–100); Leading economies (61–75); Established innovators (44–60); Emerging innovators (30–43); Nascent innovators (15–29); and Non-Innovators (0–14).

---

[3] The Global Innovation Index also has a classifying system, including denoting innovation leaders who perform 10% better than their GDP would suggest.

4.7 Overall Findings of Footprint Analysis

4.7.1.1 Leading Economies

According to this subjective categorisation, US is the only leading economy. A leading economy can be described as having strong capabilities in knowledge across the board in pillars and sub-pillars. The U.S occupies a top 3 position in more than 70% of the 12 sub-pillars.

There are **no** stellar knowledge economies in our view, having overall outstanding performances in absolutely all domains. U.S, for example, does not perform as strongly as other nations in emigration, and certainly not in the environmental domain. It overwhelmingly stands out in global knowledge cities, and leads in expenditure in research, and value added in medium and high technology industries and enterprise level performance. It also has a core strength in the quality and rankings of its higher education institutions, essential ingredients for a knowledge economy, a trait it clearly shares with other better performing nations.

4.7.1.2 Established Innovators

Seven countries are in the established innovator camp, characterised by the author as having solid performance in most elements, with one or more outstanding areas of capability. These countries are Australia, Germany, China, Japan, Korea, Malaysia and the U.K. As just one example, Korea has outstanding capability in Domestic Knowledge Relationships putting it in second place, suggesting depth and breadth in collaboration at home, and is third in Domestic Knowledge Translation and Transformation, indicating a strong ability to turn knowledge into commercially oriented outcomes. However, it lags in a number of other key areas, notably global relationships which transcend national boundaries. China has made it into the established category. It has core solid performers in almost all areas, being particularly prominent in its global scaleability to export products and services and likewise domestically, but again far weaker in global knowledge relationship building, much like Korea. The U.K just misses out on being a leading economy. It occupies top 3 positions in a number of sub-pillars, but does have some weaker areas, including Global Resourcing and Domestic Knowledge Translation and Transformation. Malaysia, perhaps surprisingly is another emerging country, which just makes it into established innovators camp. This is on the back of its strengths in Global Knowledge Relationships, Global Knowledge Supports and Platforms, Domestic Knowledge Translation and Transformation and Domestic Knowledge Resourcing. Malaysia is well placed in terms of its investments in information and communications technology-related activities, and is becoming a hub for international students.

4.7.1.3 Emerging Innovators

Then there is the emerging innovator group, which is principally occupied by the less developed world. There are six economies in this camp: Brazil, Chile, India, Russia, Sri Lanka and Thailand. This group, which includes India, is characterised by some strength areas and potential, but not enough all round capabilities when viewed against the totality of knowledge variables. There is a significant gap between the best and worst within and across the sub-pillars for these countries.

Finally, on its own is Bangladesh in the nascent category. It has one or two areas of capability, e.g. Global Knowledge Resourcing driven by a low emissions profile and it has some strengths in exports of government services interestingly. It should be noted encouragingly that there are no 'non-innovators' in our benchmark group.

There is a wide variety within the groupings it should be affirmed. For example, as mentioned, Malaysia just makes the established group with a very significant score gap to the UK and Germany, however who occupy leading positions in this group.

4.7.2 Key Further Analysis

Further analysis reveals some more interesting results. Firstly, the scores in the Domestic Knowledge Footprint are typically significantly higher than the Global Knowledge Footprint for all countries. While reflecting the choice of variables to some extent, it is also likely that this is because countries build their domestic knowledge base, capabilities and translation factors ahead of launching into global arenas. This appears to be the case regardless of a country's level of development, its size, and geography. Addressing local needs and challenges, and investing at home are clear priorities, as is building relationships among constituent actors at home, where clearly there is commonality of institutions, values and ways of doing things, thereby minimising risk and transaction costs. Moreover, it would take time to develop the capabilities required to be able to project these abroad. In many cases, this is also reflective of the models of development pursued in a number of countries based on the idea of developing the economy domestically before launching onto the world scene.

Interestingly, it does appear, with caveats, that the score differences between Domestic and Global Footprint among the less strongly performing countries is not as pronounced when compared to the more developed nations. Arguably, less advanced nations are striving for stronger performance in both domestic and global arenas, reflecting the growing internationalisation of their economies, and being beneficiaries of more open markets around the world. Of course, it could be that the scores in both domestic and global footprints are smaller, accounting for the less difference.

4.7 Overall Findings of Footprint Analysis

The rankings show consistency across Domestic and Global Knowledge Footprint arenas as is to be expected. For example, the U.S is the number one country in both Domestic and Global Footprints, while UK, Germany and Korea feature prominently and consistently across both. There is a sharper difference however for Australia, ranked 3rd in the Domestic Knowledge Footprint, but 7th in Global Knowledge Footprint. China's emphasis on an external orientation, is interestingly reflected in its stronger rank in the Global Knowledge Footprint (4th) compared to 7th in Domestic Knowledge Footprint.

4.7.2.1 Domestic Knowledge Footprint

This section considers the details and sub-pillars within the Domestic Knowledge Footprint (Table 4.2).

Table 4.2 Domestic Knowledge Footprint Sub-pillars (Where countries have the same score at the one decimal level, the author uses the data at the 2 decimal level to determine country and rank. This applies across all footprint parameters)

	Domestic Knowledge Access and Opportunity	Domestic Knowledge Capability Development	Domestic Knowledge Supports and Platforms	Domestic Knowledge Resourcing	Domestic Knowledge Relationships	Domestic Knowledge Translation and Transformation
Australia	81.5 (1)	70.7 (3)	79.4 (3)	54.6 (3)	72.6 (4)	37.8 (5)
Bangladesh	35.7 15)	22.3 (15)	40.1 (15)	23.7 (15)	31.4 (15): 31.39	18.4 (15)
Brazil	41.3 (13)	36.0 (13)	52.8 (13)	45.4 (6)	57.9 (8)	22.2 (13)
Chile	54.1 (8)	51.4 (8)	68.5 (7)	43.9 (7)	50.98 (10)	31.7 (10)
China	47.9 (11)	51.9 (7)	60.3 (10)	33.4 (12)	60.1 (7)	66.7 (1)
Germany	74.6 (2)	66.4 (4)	79.2 (4)	50.8 (4)	64.7 (6)	37.0 (7)
India	38.8 (14)	45.8 (9)	48.7 (12)	32.1 (13)	43.3 (12)	23.3 (11)
Japan	62.6 (4)	53.4 (6)	70.1 (6)	38.3 (9)	73.9 (3)	32.6 (9)
Korea	62.2 (7)	56.0 (5)	72.4 (5)	36.2 (10)	80.2 (2)	46.3 (3)
Malaysia	53.9 (9)	42.8 (10)	67.5 (8)	48.1 (5)	54.8 (9)	37.2 (6)
Russia	62.3 (5)	41.6 (12)	61.5 (9)	41.6 (8)	47.2 (11)	22.8 (12)
Sri Lanka	45.8 (12)	42.2 (11)	52.2 (14)	34.8 (11)	31.4 (14)	20.1 (14)
Thailand	53.3 (10)	30.6 (14)	56.6 (11)	31.1 (14)	41.8 (13)	35.4 (8)
U.K	72.9 (3)	77.5 (2)	83.7 (1)	57.4 (1)	72.5 (5)	38.4 (4)
U.S	62.3 (6)	82.7 (1)	81.7 (2)	55.7 (2)	84.2 (1)	46.4 (2)

On balance, and noting differences between countries, by and large, though the highest scores in Domestic Footprint are found in the Domestic Supports and Platforms category among the Domestic Knowledge Footprint sub-pillars. Countries have been active in investing in ICT capabilities as a key conduit for knowledge activities, while more generally, supports including business environment and institutional strength, feature prominently. Countries, for the most part, have been reasonably successful at providing the underpinnings for a knowledge economy.

It is also apparent that countries appear to prioritise the 'front end' of the knowledge spectrum, i.e. providing access and opportunity and promoting capability development domestically, in terms of higher education institutions, graduate outcomes, publication of research papers, and in nurturing and promoting key relationships and linkages through collaboration, for example between universities and industry. Yet, interestingly, this is not necessarily reflected in the scores for Domestic Knowledge Resourcing. Domestic Knowledge Resourcing scores are significantly less than for Domestic Knowledge Capability in a number of countries, which could impact on ongoing capability development and provision of access and opportunity. However, this could, in large measure, be dependent on the patchy performance in a number of countries on environmental/resource management.

In a similar vein, scores at the translation and transformation end are generally weaker than at the front end. Many countries still struggle in translating capabilities into clear commercial outcomes, and socially oriented, needs-based outcomes, potentially reflecting impediments and barriers to commercialising research, for example, in areas of intellectual property management, as well as labour market mobility impediments and the absence of effective technology transfer mechanisms.

4.7.2.2 Global Footprint

Turning to the sub-pillars in the Global Knowledge Footprint arena (Table 4.3), we see that country scores in each sub-pillar are by and large significantly lower than for counterpart pillars in the Domestic Footprint categorisation, reiterating the domestic focus compared to globalisation. India and China in some measure appear to buck this trend and the reasons for this will be canvassed shortly. As also mentioned, it is important to note that choice of metrics and variables plays a key role here.

4.7 Overall Findings of Footprint Analysis

Table 4.3 Global Knowledge Footprint Sub-pillars

	Global Knowledge Access and Opportunity	Global Knowledge Capability Development	Global Knowledge Supports and Platforms	Global Knowledge Resourcing	Global Knowledge Relationships	Global Knowledge Translation and Transformation
Australia	46.1 (2)	43.4 (5)	48.9 (6)	19.2 (13)	67.2 (3)	13.3 (10)
Bangladesh	17.3 (14)	25.8 (15)	33.9 14)	14 (14)	24 (15)	1.6 (15)
Brazil	21.1 (12)	32.3 (11)	36.2 (12)	Brazil 12.5 (15)	43.6 (11)	6.0 (14)
Chile	26.6 (8)	35.3 (10)	49.3 (5)	22.6 (10)	69.3 (2)	8.3 (13)
China	40.4 (5)	54.0 (3)	41.3 (10): 41.29	44.3 (2)	34.1 (13)	48.0 (2)
Germany	40.6 (4)	53.1 (4)	55.8 (3)	35.9 (5)	58.7 (6)	65.5 (1)
India	16.4 (15)	29.7 (13)	29.6 (15)	21.1 (11)	44.9 (10)	20.7 (9)
Japan	26.5 (9)	38.4 (7)	46.0 (7)	35.5 (6)	32.2 (14)	42.1 (5)
Korea	36.9 (6)	41.2 (6)	43.4 (8)	40.5 (4)	37.7 (12)	46.1 (3)
Malaysia	31.7 (7)	38.3 (8)	53.7 (4)	41.7 (3)	60.1 (4)	32.8 (8)
Russia	21.3 (11)	26.8 (14)	34.5 (13)	33.7 (8)	49.2 (8)	8.5 (12)
Sri Lanka	21.7 (10)	37.4 (9)	41.6 (9)	20.9 (12)	57.5 (7)	10.5 (11)
Thailand	17.3 (13)	32.1 (12)	41.3 (11): 41.25	24.4 (9)	49.2 (9)	35.0 (7)
U.K	43.4 (3)	63.6 (2)	61.6 (2)	34.8 (7)	72.4 (1)	40.3 (6)
U.S	57.4 (1)	66.5 (1)	66.4 (1)	54.4 (1)	59.2 (5)	45.9 (4)

The scores are generally the highest in Global Knowledge Relationships and Global Knowledge Supports and Platform sub-pillars. The former is in many senses to be expected since the mode of entering into the global innovation 'game' would often naturally be through relationships, and collaborative activity. It also reflects the growing integration of economies, including in the knowledge sphere, through value chain participation and personal connections. The strength of Global Supports and Platforms is reflected in the ubiquitous and virtual nature of ICT, the importance of infrastructure that crosses national jurisdictions (ports and air travel) and promulgation of support systems globally, via aid support, and projection of national values onto the global arena.

The weakest areas tend to be in the Global translation and Transformation, Global Knowledge Resourcing and Global Knowledge Access and Opportunity sub-pillars. In particular, the performance in Global Translation and Transformation reflects (with clear differences among countries), the relative weaknesses in export of high value goods and services, and the domestic focus of entrepreneurship and patenting (rather than patenting abroad).

Further, as with its domestic counterpart, Global Knowledge Resourcing reflects the lack of attention on a world scale to managing environmental issues, including especially the collective effort to reducing global emissions. Further, the performance in emigration is mixed, with as is to be expected, relatively stronger performance in this area by less developed economies. Global Knowledge Access and Opportunity is also at the weaker end. The capacity to support student inward mobility, as a key policy and strategic lever is constrained by facilities and attractiveness of institutions, for example, while the capacity of higher education institutions to internationalise more generally varies significantly by country. Also important in this category is the variation and weakness in a number of countries in global share of GDP and GDP per capita, constraining the ability to provide access and opportunity on a global scale.

4.7.2.3 Comparisons to Other Key Parameters

This section compares our Overall Knowledge Footprint index with the rankings of the Global Innovation Index and GDP per capita,[4] the latter as a measure of living standards and level of economic development (Table 4.4). Overall, there is significant consistency between our Footprint and the Global Innovation Index, in part reflecting

Table 4.4 Comparisons with other key indicators

Overall Knowledge Footprint Index	Global Innovation Index 2018	GDP per capita 2017 (PPP Constant 2011 International $)
US 1	UK 1	US 1
UK 2	US 2	Germany 2
Germany 3	Germany 3	Australia 3
Australia 4	Korea 4	UK 4
Korea 5	Japan 5	Japan 5
China 6	China 6	Korea 6
Malaysia 7	Australia 7	Malaysia 7
Japan 8	Malaysia 8	Russia 8
Chile 9	Thailand 9	Chile 9
Russia 11	Russia 10	Thailand 10
Thailand 10	Chile 11	China 11
Sri Lanka 12	India 12	Brazil 12
Brazil 13	Brazil 13	Sri Lanka 13
India 14	Sri Lanka 14	India 14
Bangladesh 15	Bangladesh 15	Bangladesh 15

Source Author, Global Innovation Index (2018), World Bank (2018a)

---

[4]The Global Innovation Index feature comparisons with GDP per capita.

4.7 Overall Findings of Footprint Analysis

some degree of commonality of metrics. Nonetheless, there are some differences. Firstly, in our estimation, the U.S is the highest ranked and U.S and U.K have swapped places when comparing our footprint with the 2018 Global Innovation Index. Care should be exercised in understanding these results. For example, while the U.K is ranked number one among the countries considered for the Global Innovation Index, it is not actually number one overall in the Global Innovation Index, that honour belonging to Switzerland. Other significant divergences can be noted. Japan's weaker performance in our Knowledge Footprint compared to the Global Innovation Index, in our view, relates at least in part, to the global dimensions of the footprint in which Japan does not fare anywhere near as well, e.g. Global Knowledge Relationships compared to Domestic Knowledge Relationships. Japan's approach to knowledge economy is more obviously and explicitly domestic oriented.

In our analysis, Australia is ranked higher at 4th place compared to 7th in the Global Innovation Index. It ranks better in our estimation than on the Global Innovation Index. This is in part due to a number of core strengths, accentuated in our schema, including widespread participation in education at the tertiary level, and lower and upper secondary (the strong pipeline levels), citation performance, acceptance of migrants, and strong scores on world happiness metrics.

When comparing our results on the overall Knowledge Footprint against GDP per capita, we find strong concordance generally, with some divergence. The sharpest difference is observed for China whose performance on our footprint suggests that it is 'punching above its weight' on knowledge and innovation compared to its overall level of development and living standards. This reflects strong and sustained investments in knowledge enhancing assets in China. It positions China well going forward as economies continue to rely more heavily on knowledge forms of competitiveness for advancement, while also recognising the challenges of ensuring that the benefits (and participation) of knowledge flows more equally across society, including in meeting critical societal needs through innovation. Japan, on the other hand, has a significantly current higher living standard than its position on Knowledge Footprint. This may raise crucial questions about long term sustainability of its current high living standards.

For India, its performance on our footprint is on a par with its level of economic development by rank, indicating that it is tracking as is to be expected. It performs slightly higher on the Global Innovation Index by rank than on our Footprint. We suspect that this is due in large measure to access and opportunity constraints in our framing, including especially in education and the labour market and obviously high degree of inequality, which we considered in previous chapters, and on environmental factors.

Figures 4.1 and 4.2 examine the Footprint for India with a spatial lens. Figure 4.1 shows how much of the country is 'covered' by knowledge activities and opportunities, i.e the Domestic Knowledge Footprint. If we the think of the country as scaled to 100 starting from its southern tip, then Fig. 4.1 shows how much India is replete with knowledge given its Domestic Footprint, compared to situations **if it had** the domestic footprints of China and the U.S. For example, if India, instead, had the Domestic Knowledge Footprint of the U.S, the coverage of knowledge in India would be greater. Analogously, Fig. 4.2 shows outward movement from India, i.e. its Global Knowledge Footprint. It shows that were India to have the Global

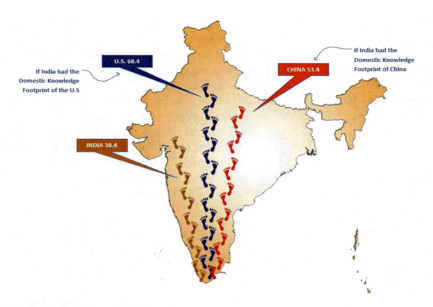

Fig. 4.1 Domestic Knowledge Footprint

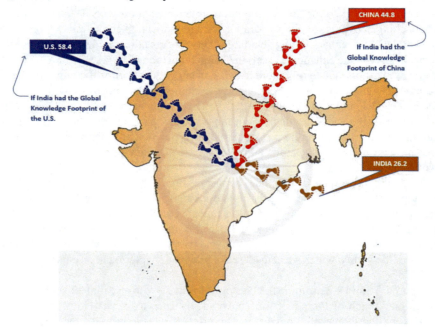

Fig. 4.2 Global Knowledge Footprint

4.7 Overall Findings of Footprint Analysis

Knowledge Footprint of China and the U.S, how much more of an impact it would have on knowledge diffusion beyond its national boundaries.

4.7.2.4 India's Performance in Greater Detail

The following sections discuss in more detail India's performance (Tables 4.1 and 4.2). At the outset, India's performance is disappointing. It is ranked 14th out of 15 countries on Overall Knowledge footprint, with slightly higher ranking for Domestic Knowledge Footprint (13th) and Global Knowledge Footprint (13th). By rank, India is no more relatively disposed to being more globally oriented in knowledge terms than domestically, a trait it shares with some countries, although a number of countries in fact have higher domestic ranks than global. Certainly, and as mentioned previously, all countries tend to have higher score on Domestic Knowledge Footprint than the Overall or Global Knowledge Footprints. In ranking terms, China is an interesting case in point. It has a Global Knowledge Footprint ranking of 4th which outperforms its domestic ranking of 7th, indicating the strength of its engagement with the global market, and weakness of other countries.

For India, its best-ranked sub-pillar domestically is Domestic Knowledge Capability, at 9th place, with a score of 45.8. This is in some measure because of its volume of papers relative to its research personnel, active journals per researcher, and Revealed Technology Advantage in niches such as ICT. Its next best-placed rank is 11th for Domestic Knowledge Translation and Transformation and 12th for both Domestic Knowledge Relationships and Domestic Support and Platforms, higher than its overall ranking of 14th, and higher than for Domestic Knowledge Footprint (13th). Its scores on Domestic Knowledge Relationships and Domestic Support and Platforms are 43.3 and 48.7 respectively. India does have the emergence of some semblance of a knowledge system and hence relationships, as reflected in reasonably strong performance on state of cluster development, and collaboration across organisations, while in Domestic Knowledge Supports and Platforms it does perform strongly on protection of minority investors and trust in institutions, despite widespread corruption, and to some extent on starting businesses. It should also be noted that in upcoming years, as India continues its climb up the World Bank Doing Business Indicators, its performance on that this part of the footprint may further improve. However, India underperforms relative to other nations on ICT use and access.

India's weakest area is in Domestic Knowledge Footprint is in Domestic Access and Opportunity, at 14th place, with a score of 38.8, weaker in rank than the Domestic Knowledge Footprint (13th) but on a par with overall Footprint (14th). It is simply the case that India is struggling to provide opportunity for its citizens in labour force participation, gross enrolment in higher education and lower tiers, despite improvements in recent years. India also suffers from various forms of inequality constraining access and opportunity. On education, capacity constraints and a myriad of regulatory and other issues, abound, as we saw in Chap. 3, while drop out's and discontinuations are significant for a variety of economic and social reasons.

India's ranking for Domestic Knowledge Resourcing is on a par with its Domestic Knowledge Footprint, 13th, (but ahead of Overall Knowledge Footprint ranking 14th). With a score of 32.1, India's 13th place on Domestic Knowledge Resourcing is associated with a solid performance on share of government expenditure on education accounted for by higher education, and somewhat surprisingly on immigration stock by age (productive age between 20 and 64), and greenfield investment, reflecting the growing attractiveness of India as a place to do business, especially in new projects. The performance on government expenditure on higher education gives rise to some conundrums. For example, a high share of government expenditure has come at the expense of expenditure on lower tiers of education or the pipeline. Further, the natural environment continues to be a major challenge and constraint.

On Domestic Knowledge Translation and Transformation, India is also ranked 11th with a score of 23.3, with reasonable performance in commercial services value added, and access to patents from abroad, although the latter is a "double edged sword". While indicating exposure to ideas from abroad, and this is encouraging, it can also infer limited domestic capability. India has very few other strength areas, in manufacturing, for example. It should be noted that generally, scores in this sub-pillar were much weaker across the board for countries.

4.7.2.5 Global Knowledge Footprint

Turning to Global Footprint analysis, we find that India is ranked 13th (Tables 4.1 and 4.3). It is relatively better than that on Global knowledge Translation and Transformation (9th), score 20.7, Global Knowledge Relationships (10th), score 44.9 and Global Knowledge Resourcing (11th), score 21.1.

In fact, India performs better ranking wise (not score terms) on Global Knowledge Translation and Transformation than it does domestically on the same pillar. While not having many strengths globally in this pillar it performs reasonably well on patents lodged abroad originating from India. Similar caution needs to be exercised here, as with the impact of patents from overseas. It is a fact that much of India's patenting abroad comes from foreign-owned multinationals located in India, rather than any real domestic, indigenous capability per se, while the positive externalities from overseas interests to local ones appear to be lacking.

India performs better than its overall Global Knowledge Footprint position on Global Knowledge Relationships by rank, driven in part by international co-patenting in health and environment, and strength of virtual social networks. Indeed, Global Knowledge Relationships is one of the rare cases where its score and rank exceeds its domestic counterpart. This suggests that when it comes to forging relationships India is relatively stronger in building and nurturing these relationships at a global level. One can surmise that India's large and influential diaspora, student mobility abroad and more generally growing awareness of opportunities beyond national boundaries, including a more outward orientation to policies, are keys.

In Global Resourcing, India's stand out area is in R&D performed by government, a legacy of the central planning era. This is a conundrum again-while undoubtedly a strength area, it can be argued that public research and development is conducted in isolation from business needs, and that spillover effects from public research into the private domain could be underdeveloped.

India's performance in Global Knowledge Capability Development is on a par with its ranking on Global Knowledge Footprint, but with a score and rank considerably lower than its domestic counterpart sub-pillar. It has only a few areas of reasonable performance, notably in citations from international science and engineering publications.

India's weakest ranks are in Global Knowledge Access and Opportunity and Global Knowledge Supports and Platforms, where both are **ranked last** of our benchmark group, and with considerably lower score in Global Knowledge Access and Opportunity compared to the domestic counterpart, and lower rank globally compared to domestically on this sub-pillar. India is particularly weak on inward international student mobility, a key criterion in the Global Knowledge Access and Opportunity category, recognising the resourcing constraints and lack of support facilities for international students. As we saw in the previous chapter, its base of international students is limited, coming mainly from geographically proximate areas, and it lacks support facilities for students. Nonetheless, the Indian Government is attempting to woo more students through its International Student Strategy. While outbound student mobility is considerably stronger, relative to India's global population share, it is weaker. India's global share of value added in education services is also weaker compared to many other countries, and its overall living standards on an international scale is also a constraint on its ability to shape access and opportunity globally.

As with its domestic counterpart, in relation to Global Knowledge Support and Platforms, India struggles despite it being a prominent provider of back office functions (and increasingly front office) and higher value services in ICT. The weakness of ICT is reflected in the international bandwidth, for example, compared to other countries, as is the case for a number of infrastructure domains involving trade and investment which transcends national boundaries. There seems to be a disconnect between ICT, the industry, and as a tool for the use by society for the betterment of their lives in India. On a more positive note, proficiency of english language is a strong area, as to be expected, while India fares reasonably on happy country indicators.

4.7.2.6 Distance to Frontier[5]

In this section (Table 4.5), we present India's performance relative to the frontier (best in class in the world), relative to the average of the BRIC nations as immediate competitors and comparators to India, and finally drawing on head to head comparisons with China.

---

[5]Distance to frontier is a common approach in these sorts of analyses, for example the World Bank Doing Business Index.

Table 4.5 Distance to frontier (Best in the World)

Domestic Access and Opportunity	42.7
Domestic Knowledge Capability Development	36.9
Domestic Knowledge Relationships	40.9
Domestic Knowledge Supports and Platforms	35
Domestic Knowledge Resourcing	25.3
Domestic Knowledge Translation and Transformation	43.3
Average gap domestic (measured by average of the domestic sub-pillar distances to frontier)	37.3
Global Knowledge Access and Opportunity	41
Global Knowledge Capability Development	36.8
Global Knowledge Relationships	27.5
Global Knowledge Supports and Platforms	36.8
Global Knowledge Resourcing	33.3
Global Knowledge Translation and Transformation	44.8
Average gap global (measured by average of the global sub-pillar distances to frontier)	36.7

When comparing India with the frontier or world's best, what is immediately apparent is that India's performance in score terms was significantly removed from world's best across all the sub-pillars. The average gap across the pillars is slightly more pronounced on the domestic parameters compared to the global ones.

While recognising that India is still not a leading economy in innovation and knowledge, the magnitude of the challenge is highlighted by these numbers. The most significant distance gap is in Global Knowledge Translation and Transformation, in which India's lack of an export orientation is very apparent. We will address this issue later in this chapter. Other critical areas of difference relate to Domestic Access and Opportunity, where as we have seen, India confronts enormous challenges of providing opportunities in education and economic life for its citizens. Interestingly, the gap between India and the best is not as pronounced for Domestic Knowledge Resourcing. This suggests that India's issues perhaps are less about resourcing and expenditure but rather about priorities and effectiveness of resource deployment and management. This is turn goes to the heart of its system of governance, accountability and transparency, issues addressed in the previous chapters. Investment in **capability building**, including the strength of its research and higher skills base, are still required.

4.7 Overall Findings of Footprint Analysis

Global Knowledge Relationships is India's smallest (yet significant) difference from the world's best. Arguably, as we have mentioned, Indians look outward when collaborating and when thinking of partnerships and engagement models, be it through research or people flows. Yet this is not reflected, as we have mentioned, necessarily to the same extent in terms of exports. The mode of international engagement is less through trade and investment, but through collaboration in papers, and co-patenting, and people flows, reliant on interpersonal or inter-institutional networks. By contrast, the gap is much more pronounced on Domestic Relationships, emphasising that India still has a way to go on building key linkages among its constituent actors at home. The gap is significant in both domestic and global domains for Supports and Platforms, meaning that India still has a way to go in some key foundational elements such as infrastructure and institutional parameters.

As can be seen in Table 4.6 India lags behind the *global average* across the board, but naturally the gaps are far less than the best in class. India is not above world average in any sub-pillar, which of course reflects the presence of a number of advanced economies in the benchmark set. The narrowest gaps in terms of average are in Global Knowledge Relationships, and the largest gap is in Domestic Knowledge Access and Opportunity, reinforcing earlier points.

Table 4.6 Distance to average global

Domestic Knowledge Access and Opportunity	17.8
Domestic Knowledge Capability Development	5.6
Domestic Knowledge Relationships	14.5
Domestic Knowledge Supports and Platforms	16.3
Domestic Knowledge Resourcing	9.7
Domestic Knowledge Translation and Transformation	11.1
Global Knowledge Access and Opportunity	14.6
Global Knowledge Capability Development	11.5
Global Knowledge Relationships	5.7
Global Knowledge Supports and Platforms	16
Global Knowledge Resourcing	9.3
Global Knowledge Translation and Transformation	7.6

4.7.2.7 Distance to BRICS

This section considers the divergence of India's performance from BRIC economies.

It should be noted that in considering the frontier of the BRIC nations, China is the standout with the leading score in 8 of the 12 sub-pillars (especially the global ones). Given that a specific and separate comparison between India and China is made shortly, we decided for this part of the analysis to use the average of the BRIC economies, to avoid repetition. It should also be noted for completeness that Russia is the leading economy of the BRICS for Domestic Knowledge Access and Opportunity, Domestic Knowledge Supports and Platforms and Global Knowledge Relationships. Brazil leads in one sub-pillar, Domestic Knowledge Resourcing. It is instructive that India does not lead BRIC nations in any sub-pillar.

India's gap to the average of the BRIC as shown in Table 4.7 naturally narrows considerably when compared to the global averages or the best in the world. We find that in two categories, Domestic Knowledge Capabilities and Global Knowledge Relationships, India in fact performs better than the average of BRIC nations. Thus, when compared to BRIC's average, India does possess a good core of capabilities in terms of graduates, papers produced, citations and scientific personnel. Nonetheless, even in BRIC contexts, India still lags the average in 10 out of the 12 sub-pillars.

Table 4.7 Distance to average BRIC

Domestic Knowledge Access and Opportunity	8.8
Domestic Knowledge Capability Development	2.0 (In India's favour)
Domestic Knowledge Relationships	8.8
Domestic Knowledge Supports and Platforms	7.1
Domestic Knowledge Resourcing	6.0
Domestic Knowledge Translation and Transformation	10.5
Global Knowledge Access and Opportunity	8.4
Global Knowledge Capability Development	6
Global Knowledge Relationships	1.9 (in India's favour)
Global Knowledge Supports and Platforms	5.8
Global Knowledge Resourcing	6.8
Global Knowledge Translation and Transformation	0.1

4.7 Overall Findings of Footprint Analysis

4.7.2.8 Distance to China

Finally, head to head comparisons with China are made in Table 4.8. By far the biggest gap in China's favour is in both Domestic and Global Knowledge Translation and Transformation. This reflects China's huge advantages in its ability to deploy, disseminate and diffuse knowledge through exports, patents, skilled employment and entrepreneurship. Developing, up-skilling and upgrading India's industrial base is a core challenge.

There is only one category in which India has an advantage over China, notably global connections and relationships, which is an area of relative strength for India as we have discussed. Domestic Knowledge Resourcing sees only a small increase for China over India with both countries constrained environmentally.

Broadly, inspite of its similar population size, China seems better able than India to provide opportunities in education and the labour market. This goes to the heart of its ability to keep people in the labour force, its investments in education and greater flexibility in the labour force, as well as advantage in governance of the economy. Some contend though that China (like other Asian countries) suffers from significant corruption, but that this has actually been directed at strategically important growth sectors of the economy (Crabtree 2018). In a nutshell, one of the key advantages China appears to have over India, as particularly reflected in its performance on global parameters, is scale, influence and critical mass in global terms, be it in global share of papers, value added in key industries, export orientation and scale

Table 4.8 India distance to China

Domestic Knowledge Access and Opportunity	9.1
Domestic Knowledge Capability Development	7.4
Domestic Knowledge Relationships	16.8
Domestic Knowledge Supports and Platforms	11.6
Domestic Knowledge Resourcing	1.3
Domestic Knowledge Translation and Transformation	34.3
Global Knowledge Access and Opportunity	24
Global Knowledge Capability Development	25.6
Global Knowledge Relationships	10.8 (In India's favour)
Global Knowledge Supports and Platforms	11.6
Global Knowledge Resourcing	23.8
Global Knowledge Translation and Transformation	32.1

of investments. A number of authors have commented on India's sub-scale industrial development for example, associated with inflexible labour and land laws, past policies of reservation and its import substitution model of development, which has constrained export development. The lack of globally recognised world-class ranked education institutions, and the absence of global brands, is also apparent (Das 2019; Jagannathan 2018; Joshi 2016; Puri 2017).

4.7.2.9 India's Performance by Metric

Finally, we consider India's relative performance by metric. These are then broken down into: Strong (either where India leads the 15 countries or is within 10 points of the leading economy); Solid (where India is between 11 and 20 points of the leading economy); Requires Improvement (where India is between 21 and 35 points of the leading economy); and Weakness (greater than 35 points away from the leader). It should be recognised that these are relative ratings compared to the world's best and thus, given its overall level of development, it would be a major stretch for India to bridge the gap any time soon. Nonetheless, if India aspires to be a leading-edge economic power, then these sorts of difficult thresholds and benchmarks are important to illuminate the magnitude of the challenges.

The following table provides an indication of Indian strength areas, solid performance and those areas requiring improvement. In summary, we find that of more than 300 metrics, that the strong metrics account for approximately 5% of metrics, solid 3% and 12% requiring improvement, with 80% or so weak (Table 4.9).

Although not shown in the above table, weaknesses abound in relation to: various elements of doing business (e.g. legal issues); ICT usage, access and skills, and broader infrastructure concerns; corruption indicators; Gross Expenditure on R&D; gross graduation rates; manufacturing strength, especially in higher value segments; a raft of environmental factors; access to education; and job creation in high value occupations (and more generally); ranked institutions of higher education; and various inequality measures.

India is characterised by very small, isolated pockets of either strength or solid performance. These are papers when scaled against researchers, greenfield investments, and some co-patenting activity, for example. Against this, is that as the number of researchers per 1000 FTE employed is very low (not necessarily in absolute terms), it inflates this ratio of papers to researchers. Moreover, it is hard to discern a *specific pattern to strength or reasonably performing areas for India compared to other nations*. China has built significant strength in manufacturing, increasingly moving up the value chain, and in exporting. Leading developed economies have built very strong institutions, including especially higher education, while other emerging and established Asian economies have built cohesive and strong clusters of economic activity in higher value-added segments. It is hard to see defining core strengths or 'brand' identity for Indian innovation and knowledge. The exceptions are for some isolated strengths in ICT, and to some extent in people flows across national boundaries, resulting in a vibrant diaspora. It should be noted that what strengths there are,

4.7 Overall Findings of Footprint Analysis

Table 4.9 Breakdown by metric

Strong	Solid	Requires improvement
Protecting minority investors	Income inequality	Gross enrolment lower secondary
Edelman trust index	Access to electricity	Students enrolled in knowledge intensive fields
Trust in business	Trust in Government	ICT use for B-B (Business to Business)
Papers per researcher (per 1000 FTE)	Trust in media	ICT use B-C (Business to Consumer)
Active journals per researcher (per 1000 FTE)	Revealed Technology Advantage in ICT	Starting businesses
Scientists staying in India	Collaboration across organisations	Ease of doing business
Product innovation	International co-inventions in patents overall	Access to credit (Doing Business)
Expenditure on tertiary education as a proportion of total government expenditure on education	Patents abroad/Researcher	Entrepreneurship as a good career choice
	Distribution of graduates when weighted by undergraduate and post graduate levels	Labour force participation
Immigrant stocks by age		Relevance of education system to economy
Share of global Greenfield investments inward		Paying taxes
English language proficiency		Ease of finding skilled employees
International co-patents in Health and environment		Freedom House Index
		3G coverage
Global share of government expenditure on research and development relative to share of global GDP		Govt success in ICT promotion
		ICT use and government efficiency
Share of emigration world stock		Impact of ICT on basic services
		Revealed Technology Advantage environment, health and biotechnology and nanotechnology
		Gross graduation from knowledge intensive disciplines
		Expenditure on education as a proportion of total govt expenditure
		University/Industry research collaboration
		State of cluster development
		General collaborative papers of Universities domestically
		Gross capital formation
		Medium skilled employment
		Citations from international science and engineering papers
		Citation impact of outflows of scientists
		Happy Planet Score
		ICT co-invention of patents
		Trademarks (Resident and non resident as a share of the world relative to its share of GDP)
		Renewable energy consumption
		Note ICT use B-B and B-C repeated

in ICT for example, in Revealed Technology Advantage (as measured by patenting), is obviated by the more general weakness in ICT access, utilisation and skills in the broader community, economy and society. The issue of the divide between 'have's and have nots' digitally is very significant. As we also saw, education in terms of access and opportunity, and quality are massive challenges. The magnitude of the challenge has been demonstrated in the previous chapter, and solutions suggested.

Many of the support structures for innovation are weak, or at least require improvement, such as tolerance of diversity, infrastructure, aspects of doing business (despite improvements), many other elements of the business environment,[6] and risk capital for entrepreneurship. We shall return to the latter in this chapter. Of interest though, is the strong performance on trust of the population in key institutions such as Government-this sits rather uneasily with India's weak performance on the Corruption Perception Index. Perhaps Indians respect the notion of foundational institutions, and associated hierarchy, structure and systems, rather than the actual performance of these institutions per se?

A cautionary point to note is that metrics used in the footprint analysis do not capture by necessity the jugaad or frugal type innovations, for which India is noted. Chapter 1 did indicate nonetheless the limitations of the jugaad type approach.

4.8 Trade

A key arm of internationalisation is exports (and trade and investment more generally). There are many studies which point to the importance of, and positive impact of exports on GDP per capita. Various studies confirm the impact and importance of exports and trade in realising economies of scale, productivity gains, fostering specialisation and knowledge capabilities, and in addressing balance of payments issues (Mehrara et al. 2014; Debnath et al. 2014; Kulkarni 2016). Others also contend specifically that quality, sophistication and innovativeness of exports contribute to growth, reinforcing that it is not only how much is exported but what and where, including new products and new markets, while quality improvements to existing products also matter. Further, higher foreign direct investment (FDI) tends to increase quality of exports in developing countries especially, and spurs domestic investment by lowering costs through adoption of new technologies (Anand et al. 2015).

---

[6]Figures for Business Environment are largely drawn from the World Bank Doing Business Index (2018), noting that India has continued to gain in the 2019 Index.

4.8.1 Exports[7]

This book considers India's export performance over the long run, to determine the extent to which India is becoming more knowledge intensive in its exports or the quality of exports is enhancing. Exposure to leading-edge customers abroad, and realising benefits from integration into complex global value chains which utilise skills, knowledge and capabilities, are keys to prosperity, and to realising secure, high wage paying jobs. While imports are also considered, our emphasis in the analysis is on exporting, since this has been a chronic weakness in India, and arguably of vital importance to generate wealth and prosperity, especially in knowledge economy contexts.

India's share of world exports of goods and services, while growing over the last two decades, has consistently been below that of its global share of GDP, suggesting a still domestic economy orientation. Moreover, India's share of global exports of goods and services has consistently lagged China's, even as China has been pursuing a domestic-led consumption model in recent years, and despite India's growing export share of GDP. In spite of a declining export/GDP ratio, China's sheer strength in size and economic growth has meant that its share of world exports has continued to rise (Wolf 2017).

India has been pursuing a greater export orientation in its economy over the last twenty years However, it is also the case that other nations have also expanding their exports. Arguably, India has been 'pulled through' by global demand and more open trade, rather than through necessarily a concerted, strategic and orchestrated export offensive. This is reflected in the fact that most of the countries in our benchmark set have also seen their global share of exports rising, except in some of the more developed countries.[8] There has also been a realignment in terms of the greater clout on world markets by other Asian and emerging economies, with China at the head of the queue. It is also the case that India has among the highest growth rates of exports overall in the last twenty years, but this has come from a low base.

There has been a post-liberalisation shift towards greater export orientation which is encouraging for India. Looking ahead, estimates are that for India to reach a world share of 5% of total merchandise exports by 2020 (on its 1.8% on 2015 levels) would require a compound annual growth rate of 27% over the five year period between 2016 and 2020 (Prasad 2017). This is a massive task.

---

[7]The section on trade builds on, modifies and enlarges a conference presentation by the author and subsequent journal article in the Indian Journal of Economics and Business (Kulkarni 2016). Permission has been granted by the editor of the journal, and Springer.

[8]The calculations by the author performed for exports, imports and foreign direct investment in this and the following sections are drawn from data from the United Nations Conference on Trade and Development (UNCTAD). Data is for 1996–2016. Trade data was accessed on 17/8/2017, and investment data on 12/4/2018.

4.8.1.1 Decomposition of India's Exports[9]

Drilling down, India's share of global exports has improved in all subcategories, as seen in Table 4.10. However, the global share of services exports has consistently exceeded India's share of global GDP.

Table 4.10 India's share of global exports by value (based on $m U.S. current dollars)

	1996	2006	2016	Compound annual growth rates India of exports 1996–2016 (%)	Compound annual growth rates world exports 1996–2016 (%)
All products	0.6	1.0	1.6	10.8	5.6
All manufacturing	0.5	0.8	1.4	11.0	5.5
Labour and resource intensive manufactures	1.9	2.1	2.9	7.4	4.3
Low skill manufactures	0.6	1.3	2.0	12.2	5.5
Medium skill manufactures	0.2	0.4	0.9	14.6	5.4
High skill manufactures	0.3	0.6	1.2	13.7	6.0
Services		2.3	3.3	8.8	5.0

Services data for 2006–2016 are used. There were some significant definitional and classification changes prior to this so for consistency we have used 2006–2016. In the data pertaining to India's total export breakdown by sector i.e. Table 4.11, for consistency only 2006–2016 is used
Source UNCTAD with author analysis

---

[9]Labour intensive and resource intensive manufactures comprise leather, textiles and clothing, glass, paper and wood industries.

Low skill and technology intensive manufactures include iron, steel, tubes, wire products, base metals, tools, motor cycles, trailers and semi-trailers, railway vehicles and equipment, ships/boats and office and stationery supplies.

Medium-skills and technology intensive manufactures cover household electronic equipment, apparatus for electrical circuits, rubber products, boilers and steam turbines, engines and motors, tractors, agricultural machinery, machinery for textiles, leather, paper, food processing, heating and cooling equipment, pumps, motor vehicles, prefabricated buildings, lighting fixtures.

High Skill and Technology Intensive Manufactures comprise office machines, automatic data processing machines, television and radio receivers, parts for machines, telecommunication equipment, chemicals and chemical products, medicinal and pharmaceutical products, aircraft and equipment, optical instruments and goods, measuring instruments, watches and clocks, musical instruments and art, photographic equipment, instruments an appliances and jewellery.

Source UNCTADSTAT Manufactured goods by degree of manufacturing.

4.8 Trade

Further, compound growth rates of Indian exports in all categories has been faster than the commensurate world compound growth rates, with the strongest growth noted for India in medium skills exports. However, it should be noted that medium skills export growth is from a low base, and India still only accounts for less than 1% of global exports in this category. Despite increasing its share of exports in India's overall export mix, medium skill manufactured exports lags other categories of manufactures, bar low skill, in the share of Indian exports in 2016 (Tables 4.11 and 4.12). We argue that medium skills exports could be important transitions to a more knowledge intensive-based economy, opportunities for which India could be missing out on. That this could be the case as seen in Table 4.13, which shows the changing composition of global manufacturing exports over the last twenty years.

Table 4.11 Share of Indian exports accounted for by industry by value (based on $m U.S Current Dollars)

	2006 (%)	2016 (%)
All products	63.6	61.7
Total manufacturing	36.2	38.3
Labour and resource intensive manufacturing	12.3	10.7
Low skill manufacturing	6.0	5.1
Medium skill manufacturing	6.5	8.7
High skill manufacturing	11.4	13.8
Services	36.4	38.3

Data for 2006–2016 is used to align with services data in the new classification
Source UNCTAD with author analysis

Table 4.12 Share of Indian manufacturing exports accounted for by category

	1996 (%)	2016 (%)
Labour and resource intensive manufacturing	54.6	27.9
Low skill manufacturing	10.7	13.2
Medium skill manufacturing	12.2	22.8
High skill manufacturing	22.5	36.1

Source UNCTAD with author analysis

Medium technology skills account for more than one-third of global manufacturing export by value (Table 4.13) currently (yet account for less than one-third of India's manufacturing exports Table 4.12). In terms of high skill exports, as an exemplar of cutting edge knowledge intensive manufacturing exports, India's share of global exports in this segment has grown (Table 4.10), is higher than for medium-skilled industries, and has increased in the mix of Indian manufactured exports rising from 22.5% in 1996 to 36.1% in 2016 (Table 4.12). These figures suggest, at face value, some shift in the direction of greater knowledge intensity in India's export profile.

Table 4.13 Composition of world manufacturing exports (shares)

	1996 (%)	2016 (%)
Labour and resource intensive manufacturing	17.1	13.8
Low skill manufacturing	9.3	9.3
Medium skill manufacturing	35.7	35.1
High skill manufacturing	37.9	41.8

Source UNCTAD with author analysis

Over the last twenty years, there has been a shift away from labour resource intensive industries, as a share of India's manufactured exports (Table 4.12) (and in the overall export profile in the last decade). When allied with the shift towards medium and high skill industries in composition of India's export profile, this is somewhat reflective of growing engagement in the knowledge economy. In terms of India's traditional employment in labour intensive and low skill areas, this could be a concern. In addition, while India's export mix may be shifting, this is not necessarily translating into major gains in terms of global market share. An even stronger export orientation as a share of GDP would be required, through a comprehensive, export-oriented strategy. The point is that India is not a manufacturing export powerhouse in raw terms.

Of interest also is that when looked at over the last twenty years, and despite China's shift towards a more domestic-led, consumption-driven model (China's export of goods and services to GDP has almost halved since 2006), India's proportion of Chinese exports **in all categories has fallen** (Table 4.14). The difference in the quantum of exports is revealing. In 2016, China's exports of high skill manufactures was 10 times that of India's, 14 times higher in medium-skilled manufactures, 9 times in low skill, and 11 times in labour intensive segments.

Table 4.14 India's proportion of China's exports

	1996 (%)	2016 (%)
Total all products	22	12.4
Manufactured exports	15.7	8
Labour intensive and natural resource exports	18.8	9.1
Low skill manufacturing	14.3	10.8
Medium skill manufacturing	9.5	7.1
High skill manufacturing	13.8	7.5

Source UNCTAD with author analysis

4.8 Trade

Of course, one can point to comparisons with China being flawed since India has pursued historically a different development model, focussing on import substitution and self-reliance, as opposed to China which has pursued an export-driven approach in the past. However, we contend that India's model of development has not enabled it to capitalise on the opportunities in global markets when trade has increased rapidly, missing out on opportunities to enhance wealth creation, job growth and scale and productivity, and that this needs to change going forward. China's ability to raise its per capita income strongly, and to move millions out of poverty is due in no small measure to the strength of its manufacturing and its trade policy, especially exports (Puri 2017). By contrast, there have been a myriad of issues relating to Indian manufacturing, and exports, many of which are policy related, including inflexible labour laws constraining firm size and critical mass, land use rigidities, costs of doing business, infrastructure access and efficiency issues (Puri 2017; Joshi 2016; Verghese 2018; Anand et al. 2015; Jagannathan 2018; Das 2019).

4.8.1.2 Export Products

Examining the top ten export products from India in 2016, drawing on the UNCTAD database, we find that they accounted for 42% of all product or merchandise exports. Just two products, pearls, precious and semi stones; and petroleum, both primary products, accounted for approximately 20% of merchandise exports. This highlights the narrowness of India's export product base, weighted towards primary products, and does not make an especially compelling case for India as a major global player in knowledge intensive goods, despite some movement towards becoming more knowledge intensive, which we saw previously. Of the top ten products, four are primary products, two are labour and resource intensive, two are medium skill and two are high skill exports. The backbone of India's exports in product terms is at the lower value end of the spectrum. Little has changed compositionally over the last twenty years in this regard. Separately, Francis (2015) contends that in recent periods of sharp decline in merchandise export growth in 2009–2010, and 2012–2013, manufactured export growth declined more sharply than the decrease in India's merchandise export growth and that 'This reflects the dismal performance of manufactured exports in the post crisis period' (Francis quoted in Kulkarni 2016, p. 46), and that India's manufacturing exports in the post-crisis years were not focussed on sectors that dominated global growth.

4.8.1.3 Revealed Comparative Advantage

A further clue as to any shifts towards knowledge intensity lies in Revealed Comparative Advantage (RCA). Revealed Comparative Advantage, pioneered by Belassa,[10] measures a country's export profile by industry or commodity relative to its overall share of exports, i.e. in effect it measures the extent to which a country's exports are disproportionately (or not) geared towards particular sectors or commodities. A score more than I means that a country has comparative advantage in a sector, whilst we suggest that a score between 0.7 and 0.1 could represent *potential* *c*omparative advantage. On this basis, overall India lacks comparative advantage in manufacturing, but scored 0.7 in 2016, which can be seen as a potential comparative advantage for manufacturing. This, however, is driven up by lower value segments. India has a clear comparative advantage in labour and resource intensive sectors, and to a lesser extent in low skills segments, at 1.4 and 0.99 respectively in 2016. Over the twenty year period to 2016, this has diminished in both these segments in the face of competition from other low-cost providers. It is also the case that despite improvements, India does not, and has not, possessed a comparative advantage in medium and high skill industry exports, its pattern of comparative advantage conforming to its traditional areas of relative strength in labour intensive and lower value sectors. As an aside, some interesting comparisons with other countries can be drawn. Both Bangladesh and Sri Lanka have, and have had, comparative advantage only in labour and resource intensive sectors reflecting a very narrow export advantage, while China has comparative advantage in all segments of manufacturing, which it has had for a number of years. It is also instructive that other emerging economies such as Malaysia and Thailand have comparative advantage in high skills in the latest data, and in medium skills for Thailand (but not Malaysia). Thus, these economies are moving in the direction of more sophisticated export orientation in their trade approaches and profile. More broadly, Mukherjee and Mukherjee (2012) find that the Revealed Comparative Advantage for Indian merchandise exports has always been less than 1, comparing it unfavourably with Brazil, China and South Africa.

4.8.1.4 Export Destinations

A further illustration of the narrowness of India's merchandise export base is reflected in the markets for India's manufactured exports. The top ten markets by destination for India's manufactured exports in 2016 reveal concentration: 63.3% of labour and resource intensive manufacturing exports were accounted for by the top ten destinations; 49.4% for low skill and technology; 47.1% for medium skills and technology; and 55.7% for high skills and technology. The top two market destinations, principally UAE and the U.S, accounted for 33%, 22%, 18% and 34% respectively. Thus,

---

[10]The Revealed Comparative Advantage is measured by country a's exports of good or industry b/world exports of good or industry b divided by total exports of country a/total world exports Mukherjee and Mukherjee (2012) for the formula based on Belassa's work.

4.8 Trade

India lacks breadth of market access, and is reliant on one or two markets for its destinations. Further, there has been no real evidence of any patterns of integration into regional production systems as such.

These findings expose India to vulnerability in the case of economic downturns of destination countries, exchange rate vagaries and rising protectionist sentiment (note the emerging stance in the U.S on trade policy). In addition, India is potentially missing out on the opportunities, including access to leading-edge customers that other, wider markets bring. Francis (2015) examined market destination trends and found that between 1999 and 2013, there was a decline in the share of developed countries in India's export mix, and an increasing share going to developing countries. In spite of liberalisation through Free Trade Agreements, India's exports have been unable to compete.

4.8.2 Services Exports

India's 'jewel in the crown' is perceived to be its services sector. Before considering exports, we look at some other data. India's share of global value added in services in 2016 was 2.2% rising from 1.2% in 2006, while its global share of knowledge intensive commercial services value added was 2.5%, compared to 1.3% in 2006. By contrast, China's global value-added share in services has risen over the same period from 3.4% to 11.9%, and is accentuated even further for knowledge intensive commercial services with share of global value added rising from 4.2% to 16.7%, second only globally to the U.S (National Science Foundation (NSF) 2018).[11,12] Thus, despite the perception of India's strength in services, including knowledge intensive services, this may be true more in the sense of services as a share of the Indian economy, not necessarily in global terms. China is more influential globally in services, as well as manufacturing, compared to India, including in knowledge intensive services.

Services exports is revealing as well. India's share of global services exports, drawing on UNCTAD data, has risen to 3.3% from 2.3% over the decade to 2016, while China's has increased from 3.1 to 4.3% over the decade. It is true that India's share of global services exports is significantly ahead of its global share of any manufacturing or merchandise category, reflecting clearly its sectoral orientation. However, there are some further contentious issues to consider. Just one sector, telecommunications, information and communication services, accounts for more than one-third of services sector exports alone, reflecting again somewhat the narrowness of India's services export base. Again, turning to Revealed Comparative Advantage (RCA) for services products we find that in 2016, India has had three sectors with comparative advantage i.e. greater than 1: Telecommunications, information and computer services; other business services; and personal services. In particular, telecommuni-

---

[11] Commercial Knowledge Intensive Services include business, financial and information services.
[12] Author calculations based on National Science Foundation (NSF) data.

cations, information and computer services stands out with RCA of 3.4. One other area, construction services can perhaps be regarded as having some potential with RCA of 0.7. A number of points are worth noting. First, that RCA for telecommunications, although strong, has declined since 2006 for India, while China's RCA in telecommunications although lower than India's currently, has been growing, posing a long term competitive threat to India. Further, China has a broader spread of services sector with comparative advantage compared to India, and has a clear comparative advantage in goods related services, which dovetails neatly with its manufacturing strengths, to form well developed integrated export-oriented clusters. The presence of such clusters is not anywhere near as apparent in India.

Data for service sector export markets by destination is sketchy. Some data for advanced economies suggests their services imports from India only account for a relatively small share of India's total services exports. Services originating from India and imported by the US, Euro area and UK together account for only one-fifth of services exports from India. Other data however suggests for some services, advanced economies are important trading partners (Hyvonen and Wang 2012). India may be missing out on opportunities in leading markets abroad.

4.8.2.1 Diversity, Quality, Sophistication and Complexity: Other Perspectives

Other studies find that the composition of India's merchandise exports has become more diversified over the approximately 20 year period from the early 1990s, although the share of medium and high technology exports in total goods exports is lower than the average of the emerging markets[13] and China. For most goods quality (based on average traded prices) is below emerging markets, while on sophistication measures (based on the extent to which a country's exports align to that of exports of high-income economies), India's services exports are sophisticated due to computer services (including higher value segments and not just business process outsourcing through call centres) and business services, and even more so than the average level of high-income countries, although this is not necessarily the case for goods exports (Anand et al. 2015).

Further, Indian services export share of GDP is higher than most advanced economies. Modern services[14] exports account for 70% of total commercial services (compared to 35% in emerging markets) resembling Ireland in composition. However, goods exports are the obverse and lower than comparative Asian economies, and well below China and Brazil (Anand et al. 2015).

---

[13] Emerging Market economies are defined as: Argentina; Brazil; Chile; China; Colombia; Hungary; Indonesia; Korea; Malaysia; Mexico; Peru; Philippines; Poland; Romania; Russia; South Africa; Thailand; Turkey and Ukraine.

[14] Modern services are defined as: finance; computer and information systems; royalties and licensing fees and other business; Traditional services comprise communications; insurance; transportation; travel; construction; personal, cultural and recreational services. The focus in the IMF paper is on commercial services exports, including Government services.

In relation to export complexity (which measures the diversity and ubiquity of exports where a higher index value is for countries which can produce a more diverse set of exports and which are less ubiquitous i.e. not produced by many countries), India is weaker than for peer emerging markets and China in merchandise exports, while services, although higher value and faring reasonably on ubiquity, tends to lack diversity in composition (Anand et al. 2015; Hyvonen and Wang 2012). Therefore, consistent with our findings is the need to both diversify and push in the direction of more sophisticated exports.

Indian services exports tend to be more labour intensive than manufacturing or mining exports stimulated by relatively cheap labour, a large tertiary educated workforce and familiarity with English language. Moreover, services exports have been driven by financial market deregulation, competition, tax concessions, special business zones, relaxation on foreign investment and foreign ownership (Hyvonen and Wang 2012).

Therefore, although important to the Indian economy, and being key drivers of the knowledge economy, services exports are not as significant compared to China, and are narrower in composition.

4.8.3 Imports

While the focus has been on exports in this chapter, of course, it goes without saying, that the import side of the equation needs to be considered.

Over the last twenty years, imports across all main categories of manufacturing, and services, have grown significantly in India, with the import share of GDP of goods and services rising from 11.7% in 1996 to 21% in 2016 (World Bank 2018b). Other data suggests that imports of goods and services have increased approximately eightfold in the decade from the early 2000s and that the process of liberalisation, including imports, has raised living standards (Panagariya 2018).

However, it is also the case that imports across the board have been significantly higher in China than India. Thus, China has been more integrated globally than India in trade in general, realising more the benefits of efficiency, scale, productivity and product diversity compared to India. Further, we found that in every category of manufacturing (with the odd exception of a year here or there), imports have exceeded exports for India. The only exception to this are labour and resource intensive manufactures, where exports have consistently been greater in value than imports. This reaffirms India's comparative advantage in labour and resource intensive manufacturing. While an open approach to imports is one that we favour, the imbalance between imports and exports in the higher value segments of manufacturing could imply that India is not especially internationally competitive in these areas, or has not taken advantage of export opportunities, leading to concerns about its trade deficit. The evidence for services is more mixed. India's exports have exceeded its imports in travel, telecommunications, finance and other business, but not other service industries. Overall, India's approach to services has not been as encumbered by the protectionist zeal which accompanied manufacturing policy, although some barriers are observed, including burdensome regulations (Verghese 2018).

Despite improvement over time post-liberalisation, India's overall trade openness[15] is found to be among the lowest in Asia, and while tariffs have reduced significantly over the last three decades, a protectionist sentiment continues to exist in policymaking (Verghese 2018). This is reflected in the reluctance to accept that access to imports lifts productivity and export performance, the fact that tariffs are still quite high by standards of many nations, including China, and many additional charges to business accompany the basic duty (and the gulf between bound or maximum tariff and actual tariff is significant allowing for flexibility to raise tariffs), while there continues to be an array of non-tariff barriers behind the border, and frequent changes to tariff and trade policies (Verghese 2018). The unease with liberalised trade regimes is also reflected in recent developments, including tariff increases announced in the 2018–2019 budget and the appointment of a task force to cut imports on items produced at home (Panagariya 2018). Protectionist orientation is never far away it appears.

Allied to this, is the overall weakness of India's trade policy stance. While India has signed a number of free trade and preferential arrangements with countries (and has taken a generally negative stance on global trade) including ASEAN, Korea, Japan and Malaysia, there has been a strong sense that these agreements have not worked to India's benefit, but rather have benefitted trading partners. These factors, aligned with India's core lack of competitiveness and innovation in many parts of manufacturing, has rather hindered the country (Puri 2017). The peculiarity of India's trade stance has resulted in an inverted duty structure which comprises high tariffs on raw materials and inputs, but low tariffs on finished products, constraining production of higher value, export-oriented goods. Francis (2015) also contends that despite a plethora of agreements with nations, India has been unable to compete effectively in exports.

4.8.4 Global Value Chain Linkages

Global value chain participation has become increasingly important, driven by companies which integrate and link production, marketing, research, sourcing and product development across the globe according to specialist capabilities and cost differentials. Gross exports that we have concentrated on to date may not give a totally accurate representation, due to the presence of imported intermediate inputs which are part and parcel of exports. These imported inputs benefit host nations in terms of promoting competition and productivity gains, providing access to specialist capabilities, facilitating knowledge transfers from abroad, and promoting integration into global value chains as mentioned (OECD 2013; Kulkarni 2016). Foreign value added

---

[15]India's trade openness i.e. exports+ imports/GDP has risen from 22% in 1996 to 40% in 2016. Author calculations from World Bank data https://data.worldbank.org/indicator accessed 11/3/2019.

or backward integration refers to imported inputs in the export of nations. On the other hand, is forward integration, which represents the extent of domestic value added in the exports of other nations, i.e. the value of inputs produced at home that are utilised in partner country exports (OECD 2017).

Data for backward and forward integration reveals important findings. First, India's foreign value-added share of gross exports, i.e. backwards integration, has increased significantly from 9.3% to 24.1% between 1995 and 2014 (OECD 2017). Without exception, all of our countries in the benchmark set have also experienced this, reinforcing their growing global integration in trade, certainly in terms of backward integration. The most globally (regionally) integrated in terms of backward integration in 2014 were Malaysia (40.8%), Korea (41%), Thailand (39.4%), and China (31.4%), with the latter somewhat static over the 20 year period. However, some have indicated that China's success as a factory of the world, and strength in higher value exports, is due at least in part as an assembler of sophisticated inputs made elsewhere (OECD 2013). Developed economies in our benchmark set have a stronger representation in forward integration compared to backward integration, reflecting their greater skills, innovative capabilities and global reputation, although all countries have enhanced forward integration compared to 1995 (OECD 2017). Interestingly, India's forward integration, as measured by its domestic value-added embodied in partner countries exports as a share of (India's) domestic gross exports, was, at 20.1%, higher in 2014 compared to China, 13.7%. However, in raw number values, India's forward integration is dwarfed by China's, reflecting the scale of China's global scale integration. Further, India's forward integration in raw terms is smaller than for a number of other countries in our benchmark set. Nonetheless, it is instructive that India's forward integration in percentage terms is higher than China's suggesting the gradual integration of India's domestic value-added as part of global production chains. It should be noted that like China and other developing economies, India's reliance on imported intermediates, i.e. backward integration, is higher and has continued to be higher, than forward integration in percentage terms (OECD 2017). India's growing forward integration, and some slight increase in its global share of high skill exports, does tentatively point to some movement towards a more knowledge intensive future.

4.9 Foreign Investment

Of course, trade is not the only dimension of global integration and engagement. We now turn to another mode of international engagement or integration, foreign direct investment. There are many reasons for foreign direct investment, both inward and outward, including seeking access to resources, skills, markets, technologies and marketing and distribution systems. It should be noted that in general, investment as a share of GDP is low in India compared to Asian countries, including China, Indonesia and the Republic of Korea, reflecting the fact that India's services-oriented economy require less capital intensive investment (Verghese 2018).

India has progressively dismantled barriers to foreign direct inward investment, including raising foreign equity limits, reforming the Foreign Exchange Regulations Act, streamlining approvals processes, implementing interest rate deregulation, capital market liberalisation and removals of restrictions on divestment and lock-in periods. In addition, are a range of national and state investment promotion efforts. However, there are still constraints in terms of the absence of projects with commercial appeal in the context of a still difficult business environment to operate in, unpredictable policymaking, lack of access for overseas investors in some sectors and various other screening practices, while the new approach to bilateral investment treaties weakens investor protection (Verghese 2018).

Inward Foreign investment data,[16] both inflow and stock terms, has shown strong compound annual growth. Between 1996 and 2016 compound annual growth rates of inward investment flows were 15.4% for India, but again from a low base, with its global share of foreign direct investment flows rising from just 0.6% in 1996 to 2.5% in 2016, roughly on a par with India's global export share. India's foreign inward stock consequently has grown by 20% (in compound annual terms) with its global share rising from 0.2 to 1.2%. India's growth in FDI inward flows exceeded that of the world over this period, and China's, but the latter's **global share of FDI inflows** exceeded India's significantly in both years, noting though, that between 1996 and 2016 China's share of global FDI inflows has fallen. As with trade, India has increasingly become a 'player' in investment globally, but with 'baby steps'. Moreover, the fact that in all our benchmark countries, inward FDI has grown, does suggest that India to some extent at least is being pulled on a global wave, and that investment is becoming more a mode of global integration, through complex value chains comprising trade and investment linkages. India is also becoming a participant, as an overseas outward investor, albeit in small measure, looking to access resources and markets among other things.

4.9.1 Greenfield Investments

What is important, and a pointer to the future, is that India is becoming a 'magnet' for greenfield investments, those entirely new ventures and projects, which should confer transfers of new know-how, management and other capabilities. The share of greenfield investment in India has risen from 2.3% of the world in 2003 to 7.6% in 2016, by contrast China has fallen from 17.7% in 2003 to 7.6% in 2016, to now be on a par with India. It would appear that at least as far as new projects are concerned, India is seen as the emerging 'hotspot', with potential. This may reflect a number of factors, including less reliance on these new project investments in China, as its economy transitions to a more consumption-led basis in a post-investment paradigm, and other emergent concerns more generally in the investment community regarding transparency and regulatory burdens in China, data security issues, and lack of term

---

[16] As mentioned previously, foreign investment author calculations are from UNCTAD data.

4.9 Foreign Investment

limits on political tenure in China (AT Kearney 2018). Correspondingly, and as its economy has matured, China's global share of outward greenfield investments has grown significantly between 2003 and 2016, compared to India's.

4.9.2 Favoured Destinations

Over the last few years, India has become a favoured destination for investment, as reflected in the A.T Kearney Annual Index of Global Investor Confidence. While 2018 saw India drop out of the top 10, it has been a consistently attractive place in the eyes of investors (Table 4.15).

In the 2017 investor report for the A.T Kearney confidence index (A.T Kearney 2017), the best and worst aspects of India were neatly summed up. Investors viewed India's diverse and growing market, talent, skills and technology as positives, while the negatives centred around India's business environment and institutions, including regulation, transparency and corruption, general security environment, quality of transportation and other infrastructure. 'Chaos' loomed as the single most negative. Further, about half of investors believed that China's investment environment was better than India's compared to 45% the other way. Thus, India continues to beguile for its diversity, paradoxes, unknowns and extremes—in investor eyes a modern, increasingly sophisticated economy, but parked uneasily alongside chaos and poor 'basics'—corruption, accountability and transparency. Bridging the gap between its best and worst continues to be a challenge.

Table 4.15 AT Kearney index investment confidence (Rank out of 25 countries)

	2015	2016	2017	2018
US	1	1	1	1
Germany	5	4	2	3
China	2	2	3	5
UK	3	5	4	4
Japan	7	6	6	6
India	11	9	8	11
Australia	10	7	9	8
Brazil	6	12	16	25
South Korea	16	17	18	18
Thailand	–	21	19	–

Source AT Kearney various issues with permission

4.10 Investment and Knowledge Intensive Industries

How attractive are knowledge intensive sectors to overseas investors?

What is also important is the contribution that FDI is making to India's knowledge intensive sectors. Drawing on very limited data that we have on equity flows by sector (Government of India 2018a), and classifying sectors by knowledge propensity,[17] we observe that overseas investment in knowledge intensive sectors was 61.2% of flows in 2016–2017, up from 52.2% in 2001–2002, and with a peak of 71.0% in 2006–2007, of the 3 years that we consider. This is consistent with the growing preference for India as a destination for newer investments, including especially in knowledge intensive sectors.

In the knowledge sphere three sectors stand out in in the latest year data, i.e. 2016–2017: business services (banking, finance and professional services); telecommunications; and computer software/hardware. This is consistent with India's export profile. These three accounted for $178,995 U.S million or 67.3% of overseas investment by equity in knowledge intensive sectors, and 41.2% of total foreign equity investment in 2016–2017. This again highlights the narrowness of India's economic profile, as with exporting. While specialisation is relevant and important, complementary specialisations, or clusters of capabilities are relatively absent in India, when considering both the trade and investment portfolios.

Drawing on various data sources, author calculations indicate that the overall growth in knowledge intensive foreign direct investment has exceeded growth in trade in knowledge intensive goods and services by a factor of two to one between 2006 and 2016 (although the trade quantum continues to be significantly higher).[18] Tentatively, this suggests that India's mode of internationalisation has been more inclined towards investment rather than trade, at least in growth terms.[19]

4.11 India's Engagement Policy

This section considers India's engagement policy stance in a number of dimensions. As a first step, we would argue for a Knowledge Footprint, along the lines suggested in this chapter, to be developed and monitored, as a basis for strategic priority setting. Beyond the Knowledge Footprint, we recommend various other things, outlined below.

---

[17] The author has classified the data into advanced manufacturing and advanced services, based on the sorts of industry classifications observed in UNCTAD and the National Science Foundation.

[18] Where knowledge intensive services are defined as commercial knowledge intensive services from NSF, and medium and high skill manufactures from UNCTAD, and knowledge intensive investments as defined above.

[19] Note that a fuller assessment would involve outward investment growth, however this is not available by industry.

4.11.1 India's Policy Stance

A core weakness of India's international economic policy stance, we argue, is the absence of a comprehensive, overarching strategy which would transform India into a much stronger internationally integrated nation, backed up by bold policies and a whole of internationalisation approach, linking trade, investment (both inward and outward), people flows and deep value chain integration in the knowledge sphere. Such an approach, would in our view, mean a more strongly global orientation, including improving currently underdeveloped trade relations. More of this will be considered later.

The Foreign Trade Policy (FTP) Statement 2015–2020 (Government of India 2015a) to our way of thinking, is more an administrative, process-oriented approach, ad hoc in bearing, yet replete with detail about import duties and concessions, trade dispute provisions, and streamlining of procedures and processes. Although these things are important, they would be of more benefit if accompanied by a larger and more strategic view. The mid-point review (Government of India 2017) builds on the FTP with further incentives for the labour intensive and services, support for Micro, Small, Medium Enterprise MSME) export sector, credits for exporters for GST, single window for exporters and importers, removal of logistics bottlenecks, and self-assessment of duty free imports for export purposes. In fairness, though the Towns of Excellence (IBEF 2019), which promotes exports from towns as dynamic industrial clusters, is promising in knowledge economy terms.

It is true that India has facilitated a better environment for business, including making approvals processes more transparent, reducing tariffs on imported inputs (with caveats expressed earlier), greater use of electronic means for accessing government services (e-biz portal for example), special enterprise zones and development of various free trade agreements, although these have produced mixed results, as we have seen. What we argue though is that liberalisation type measures are 'one side of the coin', and that internationalisation is complex and multifaceted, requiring not only **liberalisation** but **integration** through long term, deliberative strategies enabling India to obtain greater overseas market share, building connections into leading-edge customers abroad and becoming part of complex global value chains. This is associated with participating in, and obtaining the benefits of the global deployment of knowledge. Our focus is less on rules and terms of access to markets, especially for exports, but much more about developing, nurturing and building on *capabilities* for success.

Our model for a modern, globally oriented and integrated ideas and knowledge economy for India, is predicated on a much greater openness in trade and investment. To be sure, this could be phased in an orderly transition, depending on circumstances, local conditions and structural impact (industries, communities, regions) and be informed by benefit-cost analysis regarding timing and speed of reduction of import restrictions. Nonetheless, this is the key thrust of what we propose couched firmly in the knowledge economy, including facilitating the movement of ideas to and from abroad. No one country has a mortgage on ideas and know-how.

4.11.1.1 Towards a New Approach

The centrepiece of what we propose would be to position, develop and promote India as being the 'ideas road', (analogous to, but distinct from the Chinese 'one belt, one road'), focused on the innovation and knowledge sphere, initially perhaps centred on the Asian Region, including especially South Asia, but over time expanded globally. What exactly is meant by this? In our view, this means that India would position itself as a regional and eventual global problem solver, **providing solutions** to complex challenges in areas of urban development, health, demographics, environmental management and social development.

Under this approach, researchers, technologists, community groups, and including village level innovators, both from India and abroad, would be deployed in large scale, collaborative projects to solve key challenges—a series of mass open source projects if you like. This would be augmented by India becoming a 'trial and experimental' hub for such projects, including prototyping, testing and initial small-scale commercialisation of manufacturing and services outputs, which are then progressively scaled up and exported to the world. To support this, we recommend the development of a major international collaborations exercise driven by Collaborate India to (a) identify key projects of international and local importance (b) identify and facilitate key problem-solving groups in India and around the world (c) refer, and coordinate specific matters around intellectual property (IP) management to other agencies and experts.

This approach would, in turn, be supported by a number of measures: an experimental fund to promote 'blue sky' thinking; special innovators visas to make travel into India easy for participants in such programmes and projects; differentiated, nuanced and multifaceted intellectual property regimes that provide incentives for those who transfer proprietary know-how to other Indian project participants, and in other instances 'fast track' IP regimes to enhance the rapid diffusion of know-how, balanced against the need to support originators of knowledge; support for rapid trialling, prototyping and early commercialisation of products and services, through a National Enterpreneurship and Innovation fund (NEIF), emanating from the solutions projects; automatic approvals for projects involving foreign and local investments which meet 'solutions' criteria; and market piloting to identify and utilise differentiated markets, initially in India, where project outcomes can be tested, drawing on India's diverse and increasingly sophisticated consumer base, as a springboard for large scale export of products and services abroad, emanating from these projects; and liberal royalty regimes that allow overseas participants in projects to share in their benefits. Thus, rather than the natural predilection for government's to intervene on a whole industry level for a lengthy period of time, we propose that interventions could be undertaken on a project by project basis with support withdrawn as projects reach maturity.

The value of this approach lies in meshing India's knowledge with that from the world to create practical tangible solutions, drawing on knowledge synergies and complementary capabilities. It also allows for linkage between various types of innovation, including grass roots oriented innovation, with more formal scientific endeavours. India has the diversity in terms of its innovative capabilities and potential and should aim to bring together the various insights, perspectives, knowledge and experience to make this happen. The role of government would be consistent with the approach we have outlined throughout this book-to refer, facilitate and bring together participants.

A variant on this could be the establishment of an ideas zone,[20] internationally focussed, initially either on regional lines or a BRIC basis (and then extending in reach over time) to promote the interchange of ideas, know-how, shared knowledge infrastructure and mobility of people between institutions and the corporate sector. This could be on a **stand-alone** basis or carved out as part of broader Free Trade Agreements (FTA's) seeking to remove barriers to cooperation in knowledge flows, and/or removing impediments to mobility of innovators and researchers. In a BRIC context, the BRIC Bank could be mobilised for more funding for shared infrastructure, directed at knowledge economy precepts.

Beyond measures already indicated and extending beyond purely solutions mode, a variety of other policies are advocated by the author:

- *An integrated whole of internationalisation approach 'Make from India'* which provides priority for export linked foreign investment, support in certain cases for outward investment which can pull through exports from India, and a comprehensive value chain integration programme. The latter would involve identifying which global value chains India can realistically be part of as suppliers of advanced know-how, skilled manufactured products and services, with appropriate support, including market intelligence, capability upgrades and agreements on access with other countries.
- *Export transitions* to move India towards a more high-skilled, knowledge-exporting nation—this would involve the complete 'cradle-grave-cradle' of exports, i.e. support and nurturing of export development, maintenance, growth and restructuring at all stages of an export journey. We recognise that at least early on, India will need to provide support for exports in the lower skilled, labour intensive areas to provide greater employment opportunity. Nonetheless, over time, to position India as a knowledge player, and create higher value, higher paid and more sustainable jobs, a concerted effort to promote exports of more skill intensive products and services is required. Part of this challenge will also be to widen and deepen India's product/service base to avoid reliance on narrow pockets of products and services and narrowly based export markets: this could mean for example developing and expanding India's exports in underserved markets such as Latin America.
- *Export linkage* programmes to promote clusters of exports. These clusters would have three main and differing components (a) exports of integrated manufacturing and services to export whole systems—one possible candidate could be to develop India as an exporter of 'green' knowledge, encompassing both environmental

---

[20]A somewhat similar notion is that of an Asian area Research Zone put forward by the Australian Chief Scientist Australian Government: Chief Scientist Science, Technology, Engineering and Mathematics, Australia's Future (2014).

management products, and associated services (b) clusters of large enterprise and MSME exports with the larger firms using 'market pull' to bring smaller enterprises along with them in the export journey through mentoring support, supply chain initiatives oriented to exports and technology and knowledge transfers across the value chain (c) spatial linkages which would see firms in rural areas working with enterprises in urban centres, to develop integrated spatially driven supply chains, the products and services of which could be exported. It could also be important for India to give priority, and appropriate incentives for foreign direct investment to be located in rural areas, to support industrial development in India's regions, and to promote exports from rural areas.
- *Alumni India strategy* to tap into India's diverse, large and vibrant diaspora, to facilitate market and commercial connections. This could be facilitated by the Indian Government further reaching out and connecting with the Indian diaspora through (a) specific awards for Indian diaspora who facilitate export and trade connections in the knowledge arena for Indian enterprises, building on the Pravasi Bharatiya Divas awards held bi-annually[21] (b) facilitation of 'commerce clubs' via Indian Embassies, between Indian entrepreneurs and diaspora entrepreneurs to build trade, investment and cultural clubs (c) drawing on Indian students and academics abroad as conduits to attracting overseas students to study in India, and through academic and researcher links (d) actively utilising the diaspora as part of the 'Ideas road' initiative outlined earlier, in terms of drawing on knowledge, experience, insights and track record, and including further targeted NRI/diaspora incentives to promote investment in knowledge intensive activities, such as diaspora knowledge bonds.

4.11.2 The Importance of Entrepreneurship

Entrepreneurship is an important element of the 'E' framework and is a key conduit for innovation, knowledge, growth and productivity. Chapter 1 articulated the importance of entrepreneurship, its links to innovation and its various meanings. According to the Global Entrepreneurship Development Institute, 'It is entrepreneurs operating in a supportive institutional environment that provide the transmission mechanism from knowledge to economic growth by raising productivity' (Acs et al. 2017, p. 23) and that there is a positive correlation between entrepreneurship and productivity, and entrepreneurship and innovation globally, higher in the latter case. Further, the authors from the Institute point out that, '…It is hard to imagine entrepreneurship in the 21st century without the power of technology-driven inventions' (p. 26) and that 'new things or new ways of doing things' are vital to economic development, jobs and prosperity (p. 27).

---

[21] Award to Indian Diaspora on the day of the birth of India's most famous expatriate Mahatma Gandhi.

4.11.3 Entrepreneurial Issues

A number of issues have been raised regarding the state of, and support for, entrepreneurship in India. Various inhibitors have been identified, including lack of access to finance, especially at the early stage, an education system which is in many senses inimical to entrepreneurship, incubation facilities operating in silos and their need to become more 'real world', absence of networking, mentoring and cultural support, and lack of tolerance of failure. These factors have been associated with the difficulties of exiting, and the need to promote greater collaboration and coordination, including among Government Ministries (NITI Aayog 2015). Surveys of entrepreneurs in manufacturing found that most believe that access to knowledge about markets and technology could be enhanced, and skill levels to conduct business raised, including marketing, branding, as well as having better access to overseas markets (NITI Aayog 2015).

4.11.3.1 Government Policies

To be sure, the Government has placed a great deal of emphasis on entrepreneurship in recent years, addressing various of these issues, including taking a much more ecosystems view, most notably through the Startup India program (Government of India 2016a). This has the main features of: further removing impediments to doing business, through, for example, self-certification compliance against various labour and environmental laws; establishment of the Startup India hub as a single point of contact from an ecosystem viewpoint, through a coordinated effort linking institutions, incubation, mentorship and financial support; fast track patent application processes, including working through specialist facilitators; relaxation of public procurement guidelines to promote greater participation by Micro-, Small-, Medium-Sized Enterprises (MSMEs); enhancing faster exits for start-ups; greater funding support through a Fund of Funds, credit guarantees for start-ups, tax exemptions on capital gains and other taxation support (e.g. income tax exemptions for 3 years); strengthening and consolidating incubation and pre-incubation training; implementation of innovation challenges; establishment of new research parks and innovation centres of national institutions; and innovation focussed programmes for students. There is also an array of state government policies.

These Startup India policies are supported by an array of other measures, conducted, for example by the Ministry of Micro-, Small-, and Medium-, Enterprises (Government of India 2018b), such as: support for technology sectors, including practical training, promotion of digital payments, credit linked capital subsidies, microloans, rural industry measures; ASPIRE (a scheme for the promotion of Innovation, Rural Industry and Entrepreneurship) to create jobs; promotion of an entrepreneurship culture and grass roots economic development through various mechanisms, including accelerators and support for micro clusters; online registration of MSME's; schemes for the regeneration of traditional industries through

(Pm India 2015) skills and capacity building, market development and branding and loans for the microenterprise sector via the Pradhan Mantri Mudra Yojana Program (Government of India 2015b).

Standup India is based on loans of between 10 crore and 1 lakh for Scheduled Caste, Scheduled Tribe and Women entrepreneurs, in the manufacturing, services and trade sector, operated by commercial banks (Government of India 2019).

These measures, in varying degrees, allied with the latent entrepreneurial talent of Indians from many walks of life, broader economic growth, and the opening up of India to the rest of the world, including in venture capital markets, has led to change in India. According to the optimistic Nasscom-Zinnov report, India has the third largest ecosystem in the world, with start-up growth in the last five years of the order of 12–15%, well above growth rates of previous periods. India has 18 unicorns (start-ups which currently have a valuation more than 1 billion U.S dollars), with 8 added in 2018 alone, (India now has the third highest number of unicorns in the world but well short of the USA and China). Start-ups are dominated by four sectors: software; fintech; health care; and market place, e.g. retail, and have cross border orientation (both inward and outward) and are fuelled by technologies such as the internet of things, block chain, data analytics, artificial intelligence, drones and 3D printing (to a lesser extent), and supported by an array of incubators and accelerators (Nasscom Zinnov 2018).

Others are also positive and optimistic about the growth in start-ups and unicorns, both actual and potential, and the strong regional presence of start-ups in Bengaluru, Mumbai and the Delhi National Capital Region (NCR), driven by the energy of their founders and competitive engineering costs, among other things (INC 42 2018). According to the Startup Genome report 2017, which measures aspects such as market reach, talent, funding, growth and performance, and takes a lifecycle and ecosystems approach, Bangalore is ranked 20th in the top 20 ecosystems in the world. While this is undoubtedly a laudable performance in terms of concentration of start-ups with high value fuelled by energetic founders, the report does point to challenges in respect of human resource access and quality among engineers (although low cost and young), an inability to access global customers, although linkages with other ecosystems is sound, and below global average levels for female founders (Startup Genome 2017). Further, despite the optimism, even Inc 42 (2018) has concerns about gaps in start-up ecosystem funding, including fewer start-ups assisted at the seed stage, and limited investors coming in, which could have adverse impacts down the track.

Concerns have been expressed also about tardiness in implementation regarding the credit guarantee fund under Startup India as well as smaller than envisaged amounts under the Fund of Funds, on top of criticism regarding the severity of taxes on angel investments (Usmani 2019).

4.11.3.2 Queries

Yet for all this, the author has some misgivings. The new start-up 'craze' is narrowly framed, limited to a few sectors and a few areas in India, although noting the emergence of start-ups in smaller towns. The dynamism, optimism and flair of some entrepreneurs is masking the large numbers of businesses that lack skills, knowledge, capabilities and access to support (Rosling 2017). Further, the emphasis on start-ups, including in policy, while obviously important as a launching pad, does not necessarily canvass the whole of lifecycle, including especially growth, scaling up, becoming more sophisticated, internationalising, and meeting and addressing the challenges of renewal and structural change. Microloans, for example, while laudable as an instrument of social change among other things, keeps firms small. Comparisons of the size of 35-year-old firms with start-up size in India, U.S and Mexico, reveals that the size of firms in India declined by about one quarter, Mexican firms doubled in size and US firms grew in size ten-fold (Nageswaran and Natarajan 2016). These authors indicated that 40–60% of difference in total factor productivity (TFP) has been due to misallocation of resources and capital among millions of micro/small businesses, when the intention should be to grow, and more broadly, there is evidence to suggest that countries with a large informal economy have more frequent growth crises, as in India, with growth spurts punctuated by sudden stops. The large numbers of unorganised, informal enterprises is a major factor behind these results. Other analysis contends that in the U.S, a typical forty-year-old plant is eight times the size of a new one, compared to 1.5 times in India, reflecting the twin concerns of limited growth of existing firms, and that vast numbers of firms are not productive but which continue to exist (Subramanian 2018). In essence, the dynamism of 'churn' is absent. Yet another insight is that small family-owned businesses, which abound in India, are characterised by a lack of delegation to, and absence of trust in, non-family members (Das 2019).

There is some evidence of failure rates, which in itself could be a sign of dynamism, but is also problematic if the new entries and growing firms are continually outweighed by the departures. Further, the policy approach is in many senses 'institution heavy' with an orientation towards parks, accelerators and incubators. Support capabilities such as mentors, training programmes and toolkits are not necessarily present (Nasscom and Zinnov 2018). Other policy imperatives include moving from start-up hubs to sector specialist hubs, a global market orientation, patent filing support, and testing and certification capabilities. *A broader, holistic view of businesses to move through transitions is required in our view.* Moreover, the multitude of unregistered, informal businesses which make up the 'heartbeat' of Indian entrepreneurship, is not well catered for in policy and support.

4.11.4 The Missings

A key focus in this book, illuminating many of the points above, is what we describe as a series of 'missing elements' in India when assessed against a range of business types, innovation and employment, and by gender, leading to some policy and strategy prescriptions.

4.11.4.1 Missing Opportunities?

The first 'missing' is the absence of productive entrepreneurs per se. India has one of the lowest rates of business density per 1000 population (World Bank 2018c).[22] Improving this would add considerably to GDP. Our 'back of the envelope' approximate calculations show that hypothetically, if India were to adopt the new business density rate of other nations based on World Bank data, the impact on GDP would be extremely significant, ranging from $2.6 U.Sb if the Japanese business density were achieved, to almost 300 billion if the 'stretch' of the Russian business density were achieved, as shown in Fig. 4.3. However, it should be noted that these calculations

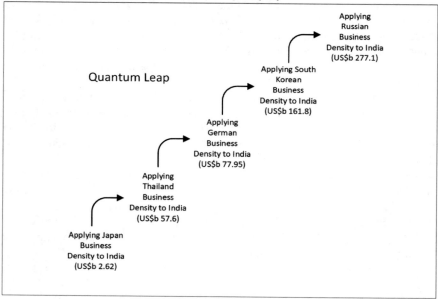

Fig. 4.3 Entrepreneurship in India. *Source* Author estimates based on World Bank data for 2016 or latest available.

---

[22]Data refer to 2016.

4.11 India's Engagement Policy

are based on limited liability company data. One must exercise caution as India's entrepreneurial database is comprised in large measure of own account businesses and informal enterprises.

The Global Entrepreneurship Monitor 2017–2018 (Global Entrepreneurship Monitor Consortium 2018), confirms many of the issues relating to India's 'missings'. Firstly, Total Early Stage Entrepreneurial (TEA) activity, which measures the extent of entrepreneurial activity in either nascent (the percentage of 18–64 year olds who have committed resources to starting a business but have not paid salaries and wages for more than 3 months) or new businesses (the percentage of 18–64 who have moved beyond the nascent stage and have paid wages and salaries for more than 3 months but less than 42 months), demonstrated that in 2017–2018, India had just over 9%, of such businesses, among the weakest of our comparator countries, with the exception of Germany, Japan, U.K and Russia.

When we add the established business rate, of 6.2% (% of adult population 18–64 who are currently owner managers of an established business i.e. earning owning and managing a running business that has paid salaries, wages or any other payment to the owners for more than 42 months), also at the weaker end, to early stage entrepreneurs, then total entrepreneurial activity is of the order of just over 15% of the 18–64-year-old population, placing India at the bottom end of our 15 economy comparator set.

Of course, it is the **type** of entrepreneurship and its economic impact that matters. Merely owning a business, particularly if it is based on not being able to obtain a job, i.e. necessity or defensive entrepreneurship, is not particularly a pathway to the knowledge economy.

In 2017–2018, India had a slightly higher proportion of those total early stage entrepreneurs in opportunity driven entrepreneurship (39.1%) i.e. those who are aspirational, growth oriented and seeking new horizons, than in necessity entrepreneurship but well short of comparator countries, and significantly below the previous year. For example, some 66% of TEA in China currently are opportunity based, Brazil has 59.4%, Malaysia and Thailand almost 90%. India's rate of opportunity entrepreneurship is well below the Asian and Oceanic average of 74.4% (Global Entrepreneurship Monitor Consortium 2017, 2018).

Similarly, of concern, is the missing 'pipeline': only 10.3% of latent entrepreneurs in the age 18–64 range intend to start a business in the next three years, down from 14.9% in 2016–2017.[23] (Global Entrepreneurship Monitor Consortium 2017, 2018)

Yet clearly these things take time, and increasingly in India, public perception and image of entrepreneurship are changing for the better. For example, 56.2% (up from 46.7% in 2016–2017) claim that there is 'high status' accorded to entrepreneurship, and 53% (up from 44.4% in 2016–2017), believe that entrepreneurship is a good career choice (Global Entrepreneurship Monitor Consortium 2017, 2018).

---

[23] Excluding individuals who are involved in any stage of entrepreneurial activity.

Thus, the groundwork of public opinion is there, albeit not necessarily as strong as other countries. Cautiously, India is moving into having greater public support for, and realisation of, the importance and impact of entrepreneurship, although a significant minority still do not exhibit such beliefs. This might, at least in part, be attributed to the 'family effect'—a preference for stable, secure, paid employment.

4.11.4.2 The Missing Middle

A second 'missing' relates to the relative absence of medium-sized enterprises. Using the data pertaining to the micro-, small- and medium-sized enterprise category (MSME), we observe that medium-sized enterprises account for just 0.01% of business in the MSME category, while small enterprises in fact only account for 0.5%. Overwhelmingly, the Indian MSME sector is dominated by micro firms (Government of India 2018b). While these enterprises, often informal, unregistered, own account businesses provide some means of income, they lack scale, employment capacity and growth orientation, bringing into sharp question their viability, let alone being significant knowledge economy players.

When we consider growth rates, as proxied by the filing of entrepreneurs' memorandum, which is registration to start production, and representing the formal registered business, we find that between 2007–2008 and 2014–2015, the share of medium-sized enterprises registered increased from 0.3% to 1.9%. Over the same period, small businesses grew from 9.7% to 16.7% and microenterprises lost some ground from 88.7% to 81.4%, although are still the most dominant (Government of India 2015c). In examining the change since September 2015 when India moved to online registration, the growth has been extremely pronounced. Since September 2015 to September 2018, Indian online registrations have grown by 5135039, well in excess of the period between 2007–2015 (2196902). While the online registration system has elicited easier conditions for doing business it has not yet seen any clear shift to medium scale production. For example, since September 2015, the medium-sized enterprise share of the **growth** in registrations has only been 0.4% (Government of India 2018c). While it is self-evident that entrepreneurs starting production formally would do so at small scale, the relative absence of medium-sized enterprises is concerning. Other data confirms that the MSME sector does not contribute significantly to India's overall production, employment or capital investment (Nageswaran and Natarajan 2016).

Why do we focus on medium-sized enterprises? Arguably, medium sized enterprises provide both the relative size, scale and critical mass important for productivity gain, resourcing and employment generation, compared to smaller sized categories, while at the same time, maintaining the nimbleness, agility and flexibility, so essential for innovation, that large enterprises may be lacking.

Indian medium sized manufacturing companies tend to be more innovative than other size categories. According to UNESCO data (UNESCO 2017), 38.3% of medium-sized manufacturing businesses in India are innovative, compared to 22.8% of large firms and 22.9% of small firms.[24] Thus, from a knowledge economy perspective *India's most innovative companies are precisely in the size range in which India is totally under-represented in*.

However, this needs to be put in perspective: the data also suggests that the majority of manufacturing companies are not innovation oriented. Indeed, only 35.6% of manufacturing firms in India are innovation-active.[25] Overall, manufacturing in India lacks the essential cutting edge innovation thrust found in other countries (UNESCO 2017).

Other data[26] confirms that of microfirms in manufacturing, 11.5% are product innovators, compared to 15.4% for small firms, 15.8% for large firms and 20% for medium-sized firms. Some 29.8% of medium-sized enterprises are process innovators, compared to 19.3% of large firms, and 15.9% of small firms and 11.4% of micro firms (UNESCO 2018).

4.11.4.3 Missing Knowledge and Innovation

Following on, how innovative are Indian entrepreneurs and can this be a missing element? As defined in the Global Entrepreneurship Monitor (Global Entrepreneurship Monitor Consortium 2018) innovation is a product that is new to all or some customers and few/no businesses offer the same product. On this score, India ranks mid Table (28 out of 54) for early stage entrepreneurship. This is consistent with its overall performance, for example, on the Global Innovation Index, which has India 57th out of 126 countries (Cornell University, INSEAD, WIPO 2018). On the raw figures, some 25.6% or a quarter of businesses in the GEM survey are innovative—

---

[24] According to UNESCO (2017), innovative firms are those that have implemented product or process innovations, while innovative active firms are those that implemented or abandoned or are undertaking innovative activities for product or process innovations regardless of organisation or marketing innovations. Non-innovative are those that did not implement, nor have abandoned nor undertaking ongoing activities for product or process regardless of organisational or marketing innovation. Unless otherwise specified, innovative activities cover product or process innovations.

[25] There is not necessarily concordance between the definitions of firm size employed by UNESCO and the Indian Government Ministry of Micro-, Small- and Medium-Sized Enterprises. The UNESCO definition is based on employment while the Ministry is based on investment. In the UNESCO database, micro are 0–99 employees, small 100–499 employees, medium 500–999 and large greater than 1000 employees. According to the Ministry, micro manufacturing is investments not exceeding twenty five lakh rupees, small is between 25 lakh and 5 crore, medium is greater than 5 crore but less than 10 crore, while for services micro service businesses are those that do not exceed ten lakh, small are between ten lakh and 2 crore and medium are more than 2 crore but not exceeding 5 crore. An Indian Lakh is 100,000 rupees and a crore is 10 million rupees. It should also be noted that the UNESCO survey is based on manufacturing alone, while the MSME is both manufacturing and services, and India is not a strong performer in manufacturing.

[26] This data refers to 2009.

not an especially strong result in terms of advancing in the knowledge economy. However, India is on par with a number of our comparator countries.

Returning to the UNESCO data (UNESCO 2017), close to 75% of manufacturing innovators undertake organisation and marketing innovation, compared to a much smaller share for product and process innovation, arguably the real value added is formed in the latter. This innovation orientation in India is at odds with most of our comparator countries, including both the developed and emerging ones. The nature of innovation activities is interesting. India's innovation activities are dominated by acquisition of machinery (as it is for other high-income countries) rather than in-house or contracted R&D or training, for example. Other countries in our benchmark set have a broader dispersion of innovation activities. Further, the market introduction of innovations in India is lowest among the benchmark countries for which data exists.

Some 77% of venture capitalists surveyed indicated that India suffers from an absence of pioneering innovation, driven by new technologies or unique business models. Imitation for the domestic market is the most usually employed approach, which constrains the ability to expand internationally. Key factors for the situation are lack of employees with correct skills, funding constraints and crucially, the lack of interaction between start-ups and established firms, vital for access to markets, capital and skills, and the exchange of ideas. Poor business ethics and inexperienced leadership are also constraints according to the survey (IBM Institute IBM 2016). Closed down start ups are because of attempts to reprise and mimic Western business models. Context and local circumstances can matter for entrepreneurship. India also lacks a presence on the Forbes global innovative company lists (D'Cunha 2017).

The focus in India has also been on firms in service-based start-ups rather than product based ones due to weaknesses in R&D, high risk in products compared to services, including because of longer payback for funders, lack of product management skills, broader human resource constraints as well as the need to harness ecosystems capability (Silicon India 2019).

Some further insights into the innovation performance of the Indian corporate sector tell an important story. Using data for registrations (filings) i.e. the formal enterprises, and classifying sectors according to perceived knowledge orientation,[27] as seen in Table 4.16, the share of knowledge-centric MSME's in India was 21.9% in 2014–2015, from 16.4% in 2007–2008. Put alternately, around one-fifth of India's MSME sector is in what we would call knowledge sectors.

---

[27] Author classifications consistent with UNCTAD and other definitions. Author calculations.

4.11 India's Engagement Policy

Table 4.16 Filing by Knowledge Number of Registrations (share in brackets)

	2007–2008	2014–2015
Manufacturing machinery/equipment nec	8055 (4.7)	16189 (3.8)
Manufacturing office/accounting/computing machinery	253 (0.1)	1444 (0.3)
Manufacturing electrical machinery/apparatus nec	3539 (2.0)	7005 (1.6)
Radio, TV and communications equipment	1026 (0.6)	2103 (0.5)
Manufacture of medical precision, optical instruments, watches, clocks	900 (0.5)	3694 (0.9)
Manufacture of chemicals, chemical products	6692 (3.9)	9451 (2.2)
Manufacture of motor vehicles, trailers and semi trailers, other transport equipment	598 (0.3)	2251 (0.5)
Post and telecommunications	676 (0.4)	918 (0.2)
Financial intermediation except insurance and pension funding	9 (0.005)	1434 (0.3)
Activities auxiliary to financial intermediation	82 (0.5)	281 (0.07)
Insurance and pension funding except compulsory social security	3 (0.002)	59 (0.01)
Computer and related activities	2715 (1.6)	13998 (3.3)
Research and development	112 (0.06)	250 (0.06)
Other business activities	2685 (1.6)	29261 (6.9)
Education	65 (0.04)	1573 (0.4)
Health/Social work	94 (0.05)	1997 (0.5)
Total Knowledge Intensive Sectors	28286 (16.4)	93565 (21.9)
Total (all sectors)	172,703	425,358

Source Government of India (2015c) and author calculations

The dominant sectors are few: machinery and equipment, chemicals, chemical products and computer and related activities, highlighting the narrowness of India's economic and entrepreneurial base, and the reliance on too few firms and too few industries. Opportunities in newer sectors and markets could be passing India by.

4.11.4.4 Other Relevant Data on Innovation and Knowledge

The Global Entrepreneurship Monitor data (Global Entrepreneurship Monitor Consortium 2018) shows that India's Total Early Stage entrepreneurs are overwhelmingly located in just one sector, retail. While we recognise that advances in retail technology, especially online sales, are important, the dependence on one sector reinforces the message of narrow or shallow pockets. India's much vaunted ICT sector only accounts for 0.4% of early stage entrepreneurial activity, and professional services, finance and education and health, as key knowledge intensive services, account for less than 20% of businesses. Manufacturing as a potentially powerful engine of growth and innovation only accounts for around 5% of businesses. Thus, in India's

Table 4.17 Deloitte Asia Pacific Fast 500

	2013	2017
India		
Number	78	53
Top place	2nd	68th
Number in top 50	10	nil
Number in top 10	3	nil
China		
Number	128	119
Top place	12	1st
Number in top 50	10	25
Number in top 10	0	5

Source Deloitte and author calculations

emerging new entrepreneurial class, i.e. the early stage entrepreneurs, the focus is not necessarily on knowledge creating businesses and activities.

Further insights into the innovativeness of Indian entrepreneurs are observed when considering the Deloitte annual 500 Fast Technology firm dataset. Every year Deloitte ranks the top firms in the Asia Pacific Region in various technology sectors, according to firm growth (Deloitte 2013, 2017) (Table 4.17).

What is clear is that India has far less companies in the top 500 now than it did in 2013 (China declined by a smaller account). More tellingly, India's top ranking company is ranked 68th compared to second just four years ago. By contrast, China is strongly represented in the upper echelons including taking hold of the number one spot.

The narrowness of India's industrial base is exemplified by the fact that in both years, software firms have dominated the rankings, with more than 70% of firms being in this one sector. Currently, there are a small number of firms in the media, and hardware sectors but none in life sciences and clean technology, areas of emerging growth and opportunity. To the extent that there is any cluster evident in India, it only is associated with the ICT industry. India lacks a broad base of high performing, high growth, knowledge intensive sectors.

4.11.4.5 India's Missing 'Stayers'

Part of the issue around business growth and sustainability is the relative lack of 'staying power' of Indian early stage entrepreneurs. Of our benchmark set, for which data is available, India has the highest rate of discontinuation i.e. percentage of the population between 18 and 64 who are either a nascent entrepreneur or owner-manager of a new business, that have discontinued a business in the past 12 months, either by selling, shutting down, or discontinuing an owner/manager relationship with the business (Global Entrepreneurship Monitor Consortium 2017).

While discontinuation is not necessarily a negative since it can be indicative of dynamism, structural change and healthy churn of economic activity in the Schumpeterian tradition, the very high discontinuation rate among early stage entrepreneurs[28] and the fact that growth in businesses is exceeded by discontinuations, suggest some areas of concern, as do the reasons for discontinuation.

Key reasons for discontinuing a business include 'selling the business', 'lack of profitability' and 'problems in accessing finance'.[29] Various reports have highlighted concerns about the lack of finance including especially from the formal finance sector (Rosling 2017; KPMG and IMC 2017; NITI Aayog 2015). According to the Sixth Economic Census (Government of India 2016b), 78.2% of non-agricultural establishments (slightly higher in urban areas), are reliant on self-financing, basically their own savings or those of their families, followed by donations and transfers from agencies, including Government, with borrowing from financial institution a laggard 2%. Even more starkly, almost 92% of MSME's had no finance, with only 5% having access to institutional finance and 3% from non-institutional sources. Constraints pertain to lack of collateral in the micro sector and gaps in working capital in the small and medium sectors (KPMG and IMC 2017). We will have more to say about financing later in the chapter.

4.11.4.6 Innovative Versus Innovation Active Firms

Further insights are observed when considering the difference between innovative firms and innovation active firms. The former refers to firms that have implemented product or process innovations, while the latter consists of firms that have implemented innovations, or have abandoned them, or are continuing them.

From our benchmark set of countries, it is interesting to note that India has the largest gap between innovation active and innovative firms, as a percentage of manufacturing firms, i.e. the percentage of innovation active firms outweighed considerably the innovative firms (UNESCO 2017). This could suggest considerable abandonment of innovation activities among firms, or that Indian firms are not translating activities into actual implemented outcomes to a large extent. If so, then it points to difficulties that Indian firms may have in continuing to sustain innovation, be it about financing, skills, external supports and long term commitment.

---

[28] In 2017–2018, GEM used discontinuity rates of all businesses, including early stage and established business. The discontinuity rate was significantly lower in 2017–2018 compared to 2016–2017. We use the 2016–2017 data to highlight the issues concerning early stage possibly more vulnerable enterprises.

[29] The lack of finance was even stronger as a reason for discontinuation in 2017–2018 as is unprofitability.

4.11.4.7 Missing Employment

The problem with Indian entrepreneurship, and consistent with our notion of the 'missings' is that of employment creation. Indian entrepreneurs are not necessarily significant job creators, nor *intend* to create jobs. This is particularly problematic at a time when India needs to create large scale jobs to meet the needs and aspirations of its 'demographic dividend'. While the MSME sector contributes around 110 million in employment (Government of India 2018b), some sources say that India is adding more than 1 million of working age population per month (World Bank 2018d), highlighting the magnitude of the challenge in employment terms. Other data suggests that the share of employment accounted for by the MSME sector is well below a number of comparable countries (KPMG and Confederation of Industry 2015). Thus, the role of fast-growing entrepreneurs as engines of employment growth is not especially the case in India. Other data points also to the nature of the problem. Some 95.5% of India's total establishments had 1–5 workers, with only around 3% of establishments employing 6–9 workers, and 1.37% of firms employing 10 or more workers. Some 71% of businesses are own account establishments without any hired workers (Government of India 2016b).

Thus, the one-person operation, the street corner business trying to make ends meet, account for the bulk of the employment. Many, many businesses will need to be created and maintained to grow jobs, an unlikely event in our view, especially given the issues of sustainability of businesses, and high discontinuations, all of which, in any case says little about innovation and knowledge.

That Indian businesses do not create jobs is in large measure is related to inflexible labour laws, which inhibit larger firms from employing, as we have discussed in the previous chapter, restrictive trade practices, and the protection of small-scale firms. It also speaks to the significance of necessity type entrepreneurship i.e. people becoming entrepreneurs due to adverse labour market conditions. In turn, these entrepreneurs do not create jobs, thus contributing to a negative (or only very slightly positive) vicious lack of job cycle.

The worrying employment numbers is also to be seen in the data from the Global Entrepreneurship Monitor (GEM) around *employment intentions*. For India, in 2017–2018 (Global Entrepreneurship Monitor Consortium 2018), some 63.5% of Total Early Stage employers expect to create zero jobs in the next 5 years, 27% say 1–5 jobs, and only 9.5% say 6+ jobs. Among all the countries that we consider, India has the highest proportion (bar Brazil) that expect to create zero jobs in the next five years and with the exception of Brazil, India has weakest performance in relation to creating 6+ jobs.

4.11.4.8 Missing Linkages

A vibrant ecosystem for entrepreneurship is founded on key linkages between firms and financiers, suppliers, customers, institutions and regulatory agencies. In recent

4.11 India's Engagement Policy

times Indian policymakers have placed greater emphasis on incubators and accelerators to nurture and provide specialist support for firms to establish and grow.

Yet it appears that Indian innovation active firms have somewhat underdeveloped relationships. While unfortunately data is not available on whom entrepreneurs cooperate with, some clue is provided by where manufacturing firms obtain their information from. For Indian manufacturing firms the most important source of information are from clients/customers, followed closely by 'within enterprise' sources and their suppliers (UNESCO 2017). Thus in a positive vein, Indian firms are connected into their supply chain counterparts, but the data shows that Indian firms are far less likely to draw on information from research bodies, both public and private, and higher education, a trait it must be noted it shares with various nations. In this sense, India can be viewed as a having a limited or quasi ecosystem for entrepreneurship, rather than a much broader, well rounded one. This goes to the heart of traditional disconnects in India between the goals, aspirations and imprimatur of research and higher education bodies compared to the market orientation of enterprises, a feature that we have noted in the previous chapter.

Related to this are the 'hampering factors' for innovation active firms. Principally, these centre on lack of funds (and high costs of innovation) within the enterprise group and from externally, reinforcing the lack of linkage to financial markets (UNESCO 2017). Interestingly, lack of qualified personnel emerged as a very significant hampering factor, again suggesting a disconnect between entrepreneurship and the education system, which we spoke of in Chap. 2. For non-innovative firms similar barriers emerge.

The importance of the foundational aspects and strength of ecosystem is also underscored by the Global Entrepreneurial Development Institute's Global Entrepreneurship Index (Acs et al. 2017). It covers 14 main variables (elements of the ecosystem) at both the individual level and institutional level.[30]

India is ranked in the middle of the world, some 68th out of 137, in the Global Entrepreneurship Index (Acs et al. 2017), which is broadly comparable to its midranking in the Global Innovation Index. We note though that, for the developed countries, in our comparator set, and even more broadly among the developed world, it is the institutional scores that score more highly than the individual level, suggesting that the support systems, the 'architecture' or institutional arrangements and the overall business environment, are core strengths and the basis of success. The observe is the case for most developing countries in our comparator set and beyond, in which institutional parameters lag individual ones, by some considerable margin. This suggests that the support systems are not on a par with innate talents, creativity and inherent capabilities of individuals. For India, the score in the institutional parameters is less than the individual ones (although not by much), which does suggest that India needs to improve on both to elevate it out of its 'middling' overall performance.

---

[30]The 14 broad variables are: opportunity perception; start up skills; risk acceptance; networks; cultural support; opportunity start up (motivation by opportunity rather than necessity) technology absorption; human capital; competition; product innovation; process innovation; high growth; internationalisation; and access to risk capital.

Further, it also suggests that the improvements in institutional performance in India have been positive, reflecting some of the recent policy reforms.

Digging further for India, the weaker areas (i.e. scores less than overall score) in combined individual and institutional parameters, are in networking, cultural support, technology absorption, risk capital and high growth orientation, with strengths (scores higher than overall score) in risk acceptance, product and process innovation, internationalisation and competition (creation of unique products and ability to enter markets). By far the weakest area is in technology absorption, which is the ability to rapidly absorb new technologies, keeping abreast of new technologies, and forge technology partnerships (Acs et al. 2017).

These findings are, in our view, consistent with India's insular, innovation and entrepreneurial ecosystem to the extent that there is one: closed in large measure to ideas and know-how from abroad, a legacy of import substitution; limited interaction and engagement between industry and researchers, e.g. public research disconnected from industry; lack of labour market flexibility and mobility between sectors; and broader issues such as effectiveness of intellectual property management. An ideas and innovation-driven economy needs to be open to, and adapt and mesh ideas from all around the world, and be connected locally.

The relative strength in product innovation in the Global Entrepreneurship Index is puzzling in the light of our earlier discussion. However, the measure for product innovation is based on potential for new products and the ability to imitate or adopt existing products. The imitative factor may be significant in this context bringing to bear some of the earlier discussion.

From a broader systems context, the venture capital industry, and early stage capital is still relatively immature compared to the U.S and Europe, with smaller deal size and limited exits. Funding support from venture capitalists tends to be limited to a few sectors, such as e-commerce or the 'tried and true' services, and focuses on incremental rather than breakthrough innovations, due to lack of knowledge, expertise and experience among venture capitalists about other sectors, including more risky manufacturing sectors. In addition, there is a tendency more generally for venture capitalists to not work closely enough with founders and managers of firms or add value to businesses, because of lack of expertise and absence of sensitivity to business needs and aspirations (Rosling 2017).

4.11.4.9 Missing Areas

A further area for consideration is the spatial imbalance of entrepreneurship in India. Using MSME data, it is observed that the top 10 states account close to three-quarters of total MSME enterprises with just two states, Uttar Pradesh and West Bengal accounting for 28% of total enterprises (Government of India 2018b).

Our calculations, based on the growth in filings (Udyog Aadhaar Memorandum) or registrations shows an even further concentration by state. Close to 90% of the formal enterprise sector growth in terms of registrations since September 2015 has been driven by 10 states (Government of India 2018c). Two states Bihar and Maharashtra account for 28%. There is a reasonably strong concordance between growth and share, suggesting further concentration by state in years to come.

What this is telling us is that potentially there is unbalanced industrial and enterprise development in India. The majority of states do not appear to participate in the entrepreneurial development of the country. This may be linked to state-based weaknesses of finance institutions, regulatory arrangements and difficulties of doing business, which impede entrepreneurship on a local basis in the absence of a seamless national market. Weaknesses in education and training institutions, and even possibly lack of aspiration, are all potentially at play.

A comprehensive approach to entrepreneurship, which includes spatial development and sustainability of new businesses is required, including coordinated policy support across the nation. While competition between states in terms of attracting and retaining entrepreneurs has merit in promoting efficiency, and ensuring that each state puts 'its best foot forward', competition can also be wasteful particularly where it involves 'bidding wars' to attract and retain businesses.

4.11.4.10 Missing Gender

A comprehensive report by the Global Entrepreneurship Monitor (2016–2017) on gender (Kelley et al. 2017) found that there is a significant difference between intention, performance and outcomes in India, between females and males, in favour of the latter.

Indian women were less likely to be early stage entrepreneurs, intend to become entrepreneurs or have established businesses compared to men. In fact, bar a few countries in our benchmark set, India has one of the largest gaps between female and male early stage entrepreneurship (Kelley et al. 2017). Other data confirms that of the proprietary MSME enterprises, males owned close to 80% of businesses, with even higher shares found for males in small businesses (95%) and medium-size classes (97%). It is only in the micro sector that females have a degree of higher ownership (20%) which reflects the impact and importance of microloans in supporting female entrepreneurship and the growth of home-based businesses (Government of India 2018b). However, this can be limiting for women wishing to break out of the very small end of the entrepreneurial landscape. Moreover, the spatial breakdown imbalance of Indian female ownership is a cause for consideration. Just one state, West Bengal, accounts for almost a quarter of female ownership of MSME's, 23.4% (Government of India 2018b).

The divergences extend beyond the formation of businesses. Indian females are less likely to be innovative than males (however Terjeson and Lloyd (2015) claim that innovation among Indian women is a strength), less prone to employ labour, but were on a par with males on opportunity-based entrepreneurship, and less involved in necessity entrepreneurship (Kelley et al. 2017). However, later data produced by the Global Entrepreneurship Monitor (Global Entrepreneurship Monitor Consortium 2018) suggests that male opportunity-based entrepreneurship was much more likely than female, and the opposite for necessity-based entrepreneurship. Indian Census data confirms that women entrepreneurs are overwhelmingly own account enterprises, without hired workers (more than 80%), and are strongly centred in agricultural activities (more than one-third). Overall, only 14% of businesses are run by females (Government of India 2016b). Manufacturing accounts for approximately one-third of female business activity, but the data will not allow us to discern the breakdown to establish whether these are in knowledge intensive activities. One would suspect that this is not the case, especially given negligible female activity in knowledge intensive services activities for which data is available.

Access to finance continues to be an issue. Close to 80% of female-owned businesses rely on self-finance, 15% from donations and transfers (Government of India 2016b), with less than 1% of funding derived from borrowings from financial institutions. Despite the prevalence of self-help groups in India, loans from this category account for only 1% of finances (Government of India 2016b). Self-help groups may lack the access to funds, the expertise and experience in deployment of funds, or their priorities lie elsewhere.

Other key differences between male and females are telling. Indian female entrepreneurs are less likely to be strong in opportunity perception according to 2016–2017 GEM (Kelley et al. 2017) which could at least in part point to less opportunity and connection in relation to key market information, capability perception, knowing an entrepreneur (which points to the absence of strong networks), while females were less likely to be investors. However, interestingly, Indian women are less likely than males to discontinue businesses than males, and less likely to do so because of lack of finance (but more likely to do so because of unprofitably). Discontinuation is of course a doubled edge sword since it can be a sign of dynamism in the entrepreneurial sector. Nonetheless the less likelihood of discontinuation arguably could be linked to women having less job opportunities than males (which is also reflected in the higher necessity-based entrepreneurship rates among Indian females) in the latest GEM 2017–2018 (Global Entrepreneurship Monitor Consortium 2018). Interestingly, Indian females are more comfortable with risk than males (Kelley et al. 2017), suggesting, in our view that the experiences in life hold women in good stead in this regard, and that the issue is more about **support for taking risks**.

However, Indian females had a clear edge in the propensity to export (Kelley et al 2017). This would relate to females participating disproportionately in industries, e.g. textiles and garments, which align with India's broader comparative advantage on world markets. However, one could not discount the possibility that the Indian female diaspora abroad provides markets and market access for counterparts in India. Perhaps, even discriminatory purchasing patterns at home may persuade Indian women to enter overseas markets.

4.11.5 What Is to Be Done?

The foregoing sections have revealed some important challenges confronting the Indian entrepreneurial sector. To be sure, in recent times the Indian Government has implemented a number of initiatives aimed at stimulating the sector, as we have seen before.

However, we suggest a different approach.

4.11.5.1 Business Typology in India

A key to our approach is the development of a **comprehensive yet tailored strategy**. As a first step, we argue that a much more differentiated, nuanced approach is necessary, given that India is a land of diversity, home to many and different types of businesses, which require different levels, types and forms of nurturing and support. We use **competitiveness characteristics** and drivers of **competitive advantage** to identify business types, their needs and appropriate policy support. Typology based on firm size categories do not, in our view, capture fully the *defining differences* in firm attributes, capabilities and needs and hence policy/strategies, although firm size is useful as a basis for benchmarking against other nations in the foregoing analysis. Moreover, data obviously is constructed largely along firm size lines.

Ten types of businesses have been identified. To be sure there are likely to be considerable overlaps between these categories. It is possible that a business could belong to more than more category.

Nonetheless, we find a segmentation of business types to be a useful way to proceed to enable a more focussed, nuanced, tailored approach to policy and strategy.

The business types range from the smaller enterprises through to the diversified global conglomerates. The focus here is on Indian owned enterprises, recognising through the importance of foreign-owned corporations in India. One of our examples, Driptech is an overseas company. Ownership patterns are not the key determinant of our approach. The businesses here are also focussed on knowledge and innovation, but couched in the broadest of terms, including product, process and organisational innovations.

The following table highlights our typology (Table 4.18).

Table 4.18 Typology of businesses in India

Type of business	Drivers of competitiveness/bases of competitive advantage	Examples	Future opportunities	Possible constraints and challenges	Policy thrust areas based on needs
Niche segmenters	Identifying and exploiting specific defined segments according to socio-economic criteria, gender, age, religion, income, cultural characteristics	Firms serving Bottom of the Pyramid e.g. Drip Tech	• Continuing to identify and exploit new segments, as more people enter middle class, and as others below middle class emerge (new Bottom of the Pyramid)	• Lack of income among consumers • Very narrowly segments being exhausted	• growth phase programs • Assisting in continual innovation to find new niches
Social purpose vehicles	Socially oriented businesses seeking large scale, low cost delivery with quality	Arvind eye care, Jaipur foot	• Exporting business models outside India • Seeking to build add on offerings beyond basic "no frills" models	• Containing costs through any expansions • Research and innovation challenges associated with new offerings • Governance challenges as businesses become more professional	• Assistance with exporting • Support for value added offerings

(continued)

4.11 India's Engagement Policy

Table 4.18 (continued)

Type of business	Drivers of competitiveness/bases of competitive advantage	Examples	Future opportunities	Possible constraints and challenges	Policy thrust areas based on needs
Community enhancement enterprises, often NGO's	Business that seek to address locally based issues	Ensyde-e waste initiative, Grass roots enterprises	• Expansion to other localities • Building scale	• Access to finance and management capabilities • Attraction and retention of skilled staff • Incompatibility of local contexts with other local and national contexts and requirements • Community acceptance of aims and objectives	• Assistance with finance • Diffusion of capabilities to broader audiences • Training and skills development • Linkage with other community enterprises, including in other jurisdictions
Technopreneurs	Development and deployment and diffusion of new technologies and applications. Agility, technological nimbleness are key characteristics	Gridbots India	• Continual development and application of new technology e.g. internet of things businesses, AI and Robotics	• Attempting to stay ahead of the game technologically or at least keep up with fast pace competition • Regulatory challenges e.g. technology ahead of regulations	• New fast track regulations • Support for market intelligence, market development • Risk support

(continued)

Table 4.18 (continued)

Type of business	Drivers of competitiveness/bases of competitive advantage	Examples	Future opportunities	Possible constraints and challenges	Policy thrust areas based on needs
Integrative businesses	Companies that are integrated in and benefit from complex global value chains, as suppliers, and outsource vehicles. Drivers of advantage linked to specialist capabilities in research, product development, inputs, and cost and scale advantage. Technology transfer by lead companies in the chain also important	Wheels India	• Moving into multiple global value chains • Technological upgrading to move into higher value segments	• Potential value chain disruptions from: shifting purchasing patterns of leading companies; new technologies; new competitors in value chains; and emerging protectionist sentiment	• Negotiating trade and investment and market access agreements • Support for technological upgrading • Support for new value chain opportunity • Support for new market development • Supporting foreign investment regimes, and strength of business environment
Diasporic businesses	Business run by Indian Diaspora that exploit commercial linkages and connections between home and host country	Attra Info Tech (Dhanji, Rangan)	• Potential expansion of such businesses as Indian Diaspora grows in number and geographic dispersion	• Meshing home and host country ways of doing business • Continued commitment of owners to both countries	• Supporting NRI investment and technology transfer regimes • Supportive complementary foreign investment regimes

(continued)

4.11 India's Engagement Policy

Table 4.18 (continued)

Type of business	Drivers of competitiveness/bases of competitive advantage	Examples	Future opportunities	Possible constraints and challenges	Policy thrust areas based on needs
Institutional break out (spin offs)	Firms that spin out and spinoff from research institutions and centres of excellence commercialising new knowhow, access to and utilisation of cutting edge Intellectual Property	Vyomme	• Unlocking the know how and latent technology in institutions	• Institutions not doing market relevant, commercially required research • Rigidities in mobility of personnel between public research institutes and private enterprise • Barriers to start up including lack of access to finance, skills, management experience • IP management and ownership barriers	• Incubator support • Removal of Regulatory barriers around IP ownership and management • Commercialisation skills development and enhancement
Government business enterprises	Provision of essential services at national and state level	Oil and Natural Gas Corporation of India, state owned electricity companies	• Development of new efficient, effective models of delivery • Partnerships with private sector • Export of know how	• Balancing commercial requirements with social need • Promoting greater accountability, transparency and Bureaucratic/Ministerial interference	• Strong corporate governance and regulatory oversight mechanisms • Sound finances

(continued)

Table 4.18 (continued)

Type of business	Drivers of competitiveness/bases of competitive advantage	Examples	Future opportunities	Possible constraints and challenges	Policy thrust areas based on needs
Diversified conglomerates	Economies of scope and scale associated with large/deep pockets	Tata	• Outward investment	• Over stretch in extent and magnitude of diversification	• Strong business environment • Ensuring regulation and red tape is not overly cumbersome but maintaining social and environmental imperatives
Constraint based innovators	Businesses which derive advantage from innovating around resource constraints for example	Mitti Cool and jugaad businesses	• Build scale • Develop export capability	• Continuing to refine quality • Not losing the character and culture of businesses	• Assisting in placing business on a more commercial, professional footing through finance, marketing, training, business development

Niche Segmenters are those businesses that aim to identify and exploit particular niches in the Indian economy, be they niches based on socio-economic status of households, demographic groups, cultural factors and so on. We would argue that certain elements of 'Bottom of the Pyramid' [31] segments, i.e. those lower socio-economic groups, could fit into this camp as target customers. Our focus in the niche segmenter group is on commercial aspects rather than social or merit goods, which are captured elsewhere. Drip tech (2019) is a company specialising in irrigation systems for small-scale farmers while Hindustan Lever, which makes small scale soap for the less well-off, who can only afford small quantities, are cases in point.

Related are the *Social Purpose Vehicles*, whose primary aim is to provide social benefit on a large scale, low-cost basis with high quality. The chain of Arvind Eye Care hospitals, is an example, which performs mass eye surgery at low cost, charging wealthier people high premiums, thus subsidising the less well-off who are provided eye surgery free (or close to) of charge (Karmali 2010; Aravind Eye Care System 2019; Govel Trust 2015).

Then there are the very specific *Community Enhancing Enterprises* which are focused on particular local areas, attempting to fill a need, provide solutions and address challenges at a small scale, local level. This could subsequently form the basis of expanding to other communities. An example of this is Ensyde, a small-scale NGO operation in a local area in Bangalore, which aims to reduce electronic waste by facilitating a central deposit and collection point for waste, among other things (Ensyde 2019).

Changing tack, here are those dynamic 'edgy' *technopreneurs*, knowledge-based businesses, whose main drivers are the rapid development, deployment, and diffusion of new and improved technology products and services. A number of Indian software businesses fit the bill. One example is Gridbots, a robotics systems and technology company (Gridbots 2019).

Then there are what we describe as *integrative businesses* whose key drivers centre on being integral elements of complex global and domestic production chains, as suppliers of specialist capabilities, products and services, or as outsourced vehicles, based on competitive advantage, be they in cost, product development, research or access to raw materials. An example of this is 'Wheels India' producing and supplying wheels globally as part of global automotive value chains (Wheels India 2019). While not immediately apparent as yet, this category could also include Indian firms being lead enterprises in value chains.

---

[31] Bottom of the pyramid firms is the term coined famously by Prahlad (2005) to indicate lowest income segments and how firms can exploit these markets by developing products and services specifically for them.

Continuing the more international flavour are *'diasporic' businesses*. These are enterprises owned and run by members of the Indian Diaspora, with a "foot in both (or multiple) camps". They link their roots and ties back in India with their new homelands, developing successful businesses that span home and host country, building on their connections, cultural and other ties. An example of this is Attra Infotech, a solutions-based diasporic software company which has interlinked operations in Australia and India (Dhanji and Rangan 2018).

Also are what we describe *as constraint innovators*. These are firms, which have much in common with jugaad firms and are those which specifically innovate around constraints, be they natural resource, environmental or social constraints. One example of this is Mitti Cool, which is an evaporative cooling refrigerator based on innovating around lack of availability of electricity on a regular, reliable basis (Radjou et al. 2012).

Then there are the *institutional breakout businesses* that emerge around cutting edge intellectual property, in the form of spin off's from research in institutions, be they private research institutes, government laboratories or higher education institutions. The key to these businesses is to create commercial (and/or wider social) value and benefit from leveraging and unlocking research in institutions. Vyome is a successful dermatology-based company which has come out of the CSIR public research institution stable, specialising in commercial treatments for skin disorder (Singh 2012; Government of India 2013; Vyome 2015).

Two more distinct business types can be identified: Government Business Enterprises which have the role of delivering essential activities in an efficient and productive as possible manner, having due regard for social need. Various state-owned power companies in India are examples. Of course, there is the ongoing debate about whether these businesses should remain in public hands, a debate beyond the scope of this book.

Finally are the large scale, diversified conglomerates, which exploit scale and scope at home and abroad, utilising their 'deep pockets' and market reach, producing multiple product and service lines, and increasingly engage in outward investment. The Tata Group in India is a good example of this (Tata 2019). While some of these larger enterprises such as diversified conglomerates and Government Business Enterprises are not typical of the usual notion of entrepreneurship, which is generally the smaller end of the spectrum, we do mention them to round off the corporate structure and classification in India. Our proposed policies would not particularly apply to these two categories of companies.

To be sure, there are likely to be considerable overlaps between these categories. It is possible, and indeed likely at times, likely that a business could belong to more than one category. For example, diasporic businesses could well be overlapping with value chain integrators, while community enhancers could have significant common elements with constraint innovators.

4.11.5.2 Towards a Comprehensive Entrepreneurship Policy

The purpose of the typology has been to develop a nuanced and segmented view of entrepreneurship in India. Our policy approach has three interdependent core dimensions: targeted and hands-on support based on *type of firm and their characteristics*, as outlined in the firm typology above, through careful understanding and guidance around needs, competitive drivers, circumstances and opportunities; targeted support around lifecycle-pre-start-up, start-up, expansion and growth (including export), renewal (as technologies and market conditions potentially change), and restructuring/exit; and linking strategies with a solutions focus.

4.11.5.3 National Entrepreneurship and Innovation Fund (NEIF)

At the outset, we propose the introduction of a National Entrepreneurship and Innovation Fund (NEIF) which is a 'Fund of Funds' (Fig. 4.4).[32] A fund of funds can be justified on the grounds of generating scale, focus, and coordinating and linking various sources and types of funds.

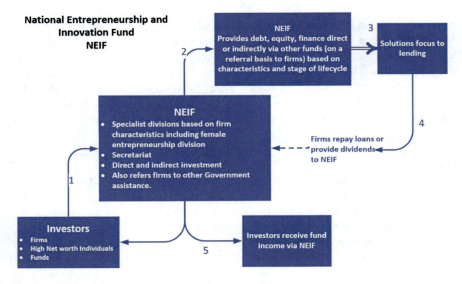

Fig. 4.4 National entrepreneurship and innovation fund (NEIF)

---

[32] Startup India also has a fund of funds approach, different in size and scope from ours.

The NEIF would be a consolidated pool of funds designed to provide loans, equity and venture debt on favourable terms, to firms of all sorts, based on their *competitive characteristics*. Investors in the fund buy equity in the fund. It would have some government funding (initially 50–50) both as leverage to attract private funding and to underwrite the system. As the fund grows and stabilises the government component would decline and be taken up more by institutional investors and individuals. The fund would be open to foreign investors as well. Other key hallmarks of our system would be:

- Investors in the fund would receive tax breaks on their income share from the fund, e.g. dividends, loan repayments
- There would no contributions tax into the fund and contributions above a certain amount would receive preferential dividend status
- The fund itself would pay considerably less tax on its overall income compared to the corporate tax rate
- Flexible exit rules from the fund: This would also involve exemption from capital gains tax on equity provided that the equity is held for more than 5 years: for holdings of less than 5 years capital gains tax would apply on a sliding scale
- The fund can invest directly into firms, as well as indirectly through other finance vehicles, also acting as a referral or vouchsafe for other fund types.

A distinguishing feature of the fund is that we introduce the concept of the flexible market system of taxation benefits for investors in NEIF. By this, we mean that the investors can choose to receive their tax breaks in the form that best suits their corporate circumstance such as limited tax holidays, tax rate reductions or tax deductions against other forms of investment. Thus, the form of tax break is chosen by the recipient themselves. While we do not doubt the administrative complexity of this exercise, nonetheless it is a demonstration of a more flexible approach, one that meets the needs of particular businesses. However, given its likely complexity, this flexible approach can be introduced over time. Until such time, a standard tax break could be implemented.

The NEIF would have specialist divisions supported by a strong staff secretariat. The specialist divisions would be broken down by firm type, and includes a female entrepreneurship division. The fund would be more than just a vehicle for deploying funds, but encompass advisory, facilitation, nurturing and networking dimensions.

Funding support, be it in the form of either equity or loans would be structured according to a firm's life cycle with the emphasis on *transitional finance* to support firms moving from one *stage of their life to another*. This transitional element is largely absent in India in our view, with its focus and orientation towards the micro end of the spectrum or start-ups. For example, one key priority would be to target finance for those moving from the micro and small firm sector to medium enterprises, a key weakness as we have seen. Thus, the funding support would be flexible in type and size, but based on the whole of life cycle support.

4.11 India's Engagement Policy

The system would be 'energised' by the presence of entrepreneur and innovation brokers, in this way more firmly linking innovation with entrepreneurship in the development of new and improved products and services. Brokers could be successful retired entrepreneurs, including diaspora members (to open Indian up to innovators to collaboration opportunities abroad), industry association members or consultants who would work with 'would be' entrepreneurs and innovators to get them 'pre-entrepreneurship' ready. There would be hands-on support to ensure that entrepreneurs could be developing business plans and assist with opportunity spotting as well as to promote awareness of the potential of entrepreneurship. The entrepreneurial broker would then refer the entrepreneur/innovator to one of the specialist divisions of NEIF described above. The specialist divisions would then work through the lifecycle progression of firms, at each stage setting key performance indicators for the entrepreneurs to meet to either (a) receive further funding (or not) and (b) move from stages, e.g. early stage to expansion, etc. A key to loan and equity support would be to fill gaps in the market place for funds.

This system is consistent with our notion of the facilitative or Enabling State in which there is a key emphasis on brokerage, information provision, networking, accountability and transparency and networking.

The NEIF serves as a demonstration effort with ongoing momentum. Thus, entrepreneurs availing themselves of the NEIF would have their progress documented and rated on a star scale according to meeting performance benchmarks, as well as having an associated risk rating. These convey signals for other funding that the entrepreneurs might seek, and would serve as a de-facto screening to customers and suppliers and other partners, about entrepreneurial performance.

Beyond this, the specialists in the NEIF would refer entrepreneurs to other forms of government support and/or other sources of funding, as appropriate, for example, if crowdfunding is more relevant. Depending on the value of the required support, need as well as again meeting certain performance benchmarks, entrepreneurs would be able to available themselves of 'entrepreneurial vouchers' [33] which would enable firms to 'buy' specialist packages of assistance be it market intelligence support, export development assistance, technological upgradation, etc. Again, in the name of user choice and flexibility this would mean that entrepreneurs could purchase support via a one-stop shop assistance (available electronically) rather than rely on traditional bureaucratic means of applying for grants from agency to agency. The vouchers would enable integrated packages to be 'purchased' to a certain value, combining incentives according to specific need. These vouchers could be sold, if not used, creating a secondary market for assistance. This would also mean that firms would be incentivised to use vouchers in an efficient manner.

---

[33] Other jurisdictions use vouchers.

In addition, there are cross-specialisation arrangements within NEIF to promote collaboration across, and between enterprise types, e.g. for example to link technology-based enterprises with community enhancement businesses to exploit knowledge synergies, promote learnings, and address complex problems in a complementary way, drawing on relative capabilities and expertise. The NEIF would work closely with Collaborate India in this respect. Their roles are complementary. Collaborate India is the overarching collaborative, partnership-oriented body, across many domains, and NEIF is at the specific funding level.

The NEIF would also have as a priority, value chain linkages to promote linkages between smaller rural enterprises, and leading larger urban enterprises. Such an arrangement would work on the basis of the smaller rural enterprises serving and becoming part of the value chains driven by larger enterprises. It would have multiple benefits including stimulating enterprises in areas where for example MSME's are lacking, noting that there are significant spatial distributional anomalies in enterprises across states and locations, while providing access to the market entrée, technology support and the management know-how of larger enterprises. In turn, as appropriate, larger enterprises could be supported with incentives to provide training and technological upgrading support to smaller enterprises. FDI and other capital flows could be promoted in rural areas and enterprises as an entrée into urban India, serving as a springboard ultimately into export markets.

To ensure scale, focus and efficiency of resource allocation, priority would be given to entrepreneurs who can potentially or actually add value in solving complex challenges, both 'mainstream' and social entrepreneurs. These challenges centre on natural resource and environmental management, urbanisation, health and social services, inclusivity and addressing inequality, among others. However, while these are priority solutions areas or missions, it is not to suggest that resources from NEIF are exclusively directed at these challenges. The solutions or missions are broad based enough to encapsulate a variety of sectoral, spatial, technological, project and skills contexts and domains. Targeted intervention in the traditional sense of selecting narrow sectors and sub-sectors and supporting them for lengthy periods and with favourable regulations, or protective anti-competitive elements, is not the method envisaged. Interventions through NEIF are much more about *broader based capabilities*, subject to rigorous performance accountabilities, and sunset clauses for intervention, but with flexibility about the nature, type and extent of intervention.

4.11.5.4 Introducing Ideabank

A further important policy initiative that we propose is 'Ideabank' (Fig. 4.5). This is in many ways the opposite of traditional banking. In a more traditional banking sense, ideas chase funds, here almost funds chase ideas. Ideabank has more relevance to social purpose, smaller grass roots innovations, reinforcing our solutions/ missions approach. IdeaBank would be organised along the lines of a fully fledged bank, and as such have analogous roles, functions and powers.

An idea of a citizen (or groups of citizens), say for example, for a recycling project, is deposited into Ideabank, and innovation/entrepreneur brokers will work with the

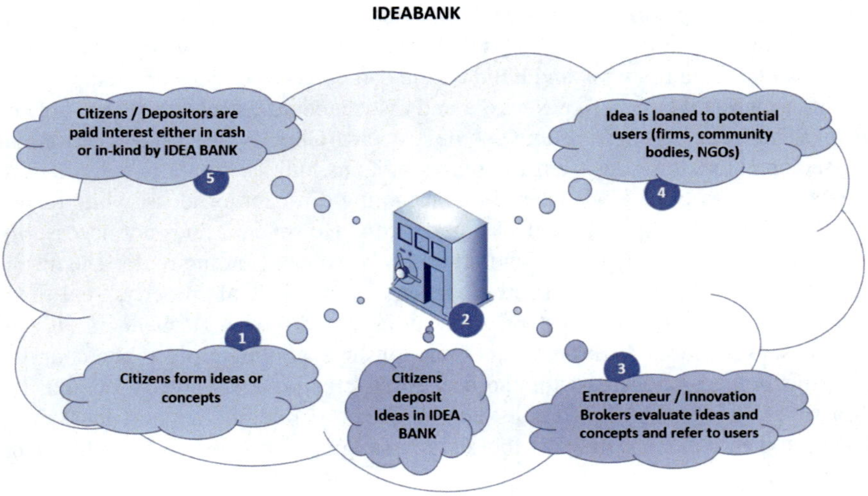

4.11 India's Engagement Policy

IDEABANK

- Citizens form ideas or concepts (1)
- Citizens deposit Ideas in IDEA BANK (2)
- Entrepreneur / Innovation Brokers evaluate ideas and concepts and refer to users (3)
- Idea is loaned to potential users (firms, community bodies, NGOs) (4)
- Citizens / Depositors are paid interest either in cash or in-kind by IDEA BANK (5)

Fig. 4.5 Idea bank

originators and refer the ideas to potential users be they firms, community groups, NGO's and the like. If the idea is accepted in principle, interest payments would be made to the originator while the idea is being developed and progressed to use stage-either for commercial exploitation or societal need. In the process, original proponents of the ideas would work closely with potential users in concert with the entrepreneur/innovation brokers. Thus, Ideabank loans out the idea to users and charges interest payments to them. The difference between the interest charged to users, and interest payments to originators, constitutes the operating margin for the Idea Bank to cover costs. IdeaBank would be run on a not for profit basis, backed up by a representative Board, and with initial funding from government agencies.

We envisage two types of interest payments to originators: a lower premium when the idea is at the early, more unformed state; and at a higher rate as the idea becomes at a more operational stage. Payments could be 'in-kind' fashion such as priority access to educational opportunities, if the project is an education based one.

When the idea becomes fully operational, the interest payments to originators stops, and originators have a stake in the returns (e.g. part ownership in the venture) from their idea. Originators could also choose to sell their stake at which point ownership of the project and activity transfers to the users.

Entrepreneurship and innovation brokers have a key role to play in coordination and facilitation, consistent with our notion of creating the Referral State. Even more explicitly, the brokers can refer the project to the Divisions of NEIF, as stated above, at any point for further specialist funding and assistance. The brokers could be the same individuals and entities as in NEIF. IdeaBank is integrated with, but has a separate existence from, NEIF. It is more directed at individuals and households, citizen groups and smaller scale, grass roots businesses. It deals with ideas at a very raw stage, often from the marginalised individuals and groups in society, rather than more established entities whose ideas and operations are more developed.

Ideabank would draw on, and build on the database, experience and expertise of the very successful Honey Bee Network and associated infrastructure,[34] thus obviating the need for an expensive, cumbersome structure (Gupta 2016). Like Honey Bee it is based on unlocking ideas from all around India, including especially marginalised groups. The Idea Bank is also based on promoting diffusion of ideas, while recognising the intellectual property of idea generators. However, it does not necessarily involve the traditional, expensive and often cumbersome patenting route. The mechanism here is designed for a collective approach to intellectual property, 'real-time' support for all parts of the system, and pay as you discover mechanisms. It also embodies, as mentioned, the building of relationships, pooling projects and connecting project/idea proponents with end users, thus creating knowledge value chains. Over time, the system could be developed to incorporate and support ideas from abroad, and adding value in India, thus creating a 'grass roots' led global value chain movement.

IdeaBank also allows a constant stream of payments to those originators of ideas, thus enhancing individual and community living standards. Further, there is flexibility: idea proponents may choose to receive their payments in non-monetary ways but rather through in-kind access to essential services or public goods.

4.11.5.5 Intellectual Property

The approach taken in this book has been to encourage the free flow of ideas domestically and to and from abroad. As such, it takes a more open approach to allow access to intellectual property and know-how, a view supported by others (Martin 1995; Agarwal 2018; Basheer and Agarwal 2017). Nonetheless, it does need to be recognised that originators of knowledge should be allowed to appropriate its returns, but in a non-exploitative manner. As such, some balance is required between allowing access versus protection of intellectual property. To this end, we propose that IP should generally be made available widely, or that the length of time for protection of IP be reduced, both subject to public interest testing, where public interest pertains to India and globally. The approval to grant wider access to knowledge (or for it to be restricted for a specified time period), would depend on the 'degree of public interest', with various thresholds set. The public interest test would include criteria of (a) public benefit subject to full benefit/cost with all costs included (b) the extent to which the innovation can generate further innovations, i.e. a 'momentum effect'. In addition, sharing of returns to originators, including especially for grass roots and newer innovators, as part of the IdeaBank brokers who work with users

---

[34] The IdeaBank does have elements in common with the Honeybee network, but also key differences in that we envisage IdeaBank to be constituted as a formal bank, offering interest payments and loans, and deposit facilities, and being linked to the NEIF to provide a seamless and integrated whole.

and innovators, would be part of the policy and framework. In turn, patent review would be regularly instituted to ensure non-exploitative behaviour.

The Indian Government IP policy of 2016 (Government of India 2016c) focussed on administrative reforms and capacity building, linkage between users and innovators, strengthening IP protection and enforcement and raising awareness of IP. However, the approach has been criticised on the grounds of not considering the ecosystem and broader capabilities in which intellectual endeavour is situated (e.g. financing, education, culture), not paying enough attention to exploitative behaviour on the part of patent holders, and that many innovations occur 'off patent' in any case, while patents have been known to block further innovation efforts (Agarwal 2018; Basheer and Agarwal 2017).

4.12 The Environment

Mahatma Gandhi: 'One must care about the world one will not see' (India's Intended Nationally Determined Contribution to the UNFCCC: Working towards Climate Justice undated p. 3), and 'We should act as "trustees" and use natural resources wisely as it is the moral responsibility to ensure that we bequeath to the future generations a healthy planet' (p. 1).

In this section we briefly consider India's natural environment in its own right, while cognisant of the interdependence between the environment and engagement: the engagement between humans and nature; between the interdependent elements of the ecosystem; between economy and the environment; between nations in the management of collective global resources; and between businesses and consumers in the market place through new and improved products and services.

4.12.1 India's Situation

Of course, it must be remembered that despite all its gains, India is still a developing country in many ways, with limited access to basic services for many people, grinding poverty and lack of jobs and job security. With all these contending and competing priorities, it would be understandable in some measure if the environment took a 'back seat'. However, there is another way: to link environment and economic development through innovation and knowledge, to create new products and services, apply new technologies and to develop innovative new management approaches to improving the environment.

Yet, by any measure, India's natural environment is in a parlous state. Our knowledge footprint work considered some of these metrics to understand India's environmental constraints, and revealed that India was behind many comparator economies. Any casual visitor to India would immediately notice the choking and congested cities, the deleterious impacts on health of diminished air quality, untreated waste, threatened species, and poor water quality and management. According to one estimate, India has 14 out of the world's 15 most polluted cities (Times of India 2018).

The Environmental Performance Index (EPI) prepared regularly by Yale University, monitors the environmental performance of 180 countries. It does not make for pretty reading. It is a sad fact that India is ranked 177th out of 180 on the latest EPI Index (Yale 2018), a deterioration on its rank in 2016 and 2014, inspite of growing awareness and policies towards the environment. Of our benchmark countries, India performs by far the worst in the EPI Index, and when digging deeper, is 'rock bottom' on environment health (180th) which comprises air quality (178th), water and sanitation (145th) and heavy metals discharge (175th). A slightly better performance is observed on ecosystem vitality (140th out of 180), with only one category, forestry and fisheries management under 100th place. In almost all of the subcategories India is the weakest or close to weakest performer of our benchmark set (and indeed globally), including those countries that India has a higher level of economic development than. The poor result highlights the important linkages across the entire environmental space, the need to take an integrated, comprehensive approach, which captures the interdependencies, and possible trade-offs. It also points to haphazard development in India, absence of strong regulatory and enforcement mechanisms, the 'not in my backyard syndrome', and old and outmoded production techniques. However, citizen activist groups and NGO's are making a difference in at least raising awareness of the perils facing India and the planet.

The cost to the Indian economy of environment degradation has been modelled, with the annual cost of environmental damage ranging from 2.6% to close to 9% of GDP (World Bank 2013). Moreover the burden of environmental damage is borne disproportionately among the poor and females, lacking access to sanitation and adequate water quality, among other concerns. As one further example, the estimated health impact of urban air pollution is estimated to be a mind-boggling 1,989,773 disability-adjusted life years (World Bank 2013).

We argue that Knowledge and innovation are vital 'circuit breakers' for the environment. Development, application and diffusion of knowledge to meet specific environmental challenges and contexts is key.

As an initial tentative conceptual framework, we contend that in terms of policymaking goals, the Environmental Footprint and our Knowledge Footprint should be seen as mirror images. From a policy point of view, the intention should be **to reduce** Environmental Footprint over time, while **increasing** the Knowledge Footprint (subject to constraints around financing, skills and capabilities). The import of this is that Environmental Footprint operates in the physical space which has natural limitations, while the Knowledge Footprint operates in the context of having multiple uses, and increasing returns of knowledge. Over time, the gap between Environmental Footprint and Knowledge Footprint, should be narrowed and eventually the Knowledge Footprint is highly developed and widespread enough to address environmental challenges.

4.12.1.1 Environmental Management and Knowledge Management

To give expression to these sort of ideas, we construct the following figure (Fig. 4.6), which shows **changes** in the EPI index (Yale 2014, 2018), as a de-facto or proxy representation of an Environmental Footprint, compared to **changes** in the Global Innovation Index (as a de-facto measure of the Knowledge Footprint since our own Knowledge Footprint is only one year), between 2014 and 2018 (Cornell University, INSEAD, WIPO 2014, 2018). This provides an indication of the extent to which countries are improving their environmental performance compared to whether they are improving their knowledge and innovation capabilities.

Quadrant one is where countries are *improving* both their environmental and knowledge performance or put alternatively, reducing their Environmental Footprint and improving their Knowledge Footprint. The strategic implication of this is to continue to build the capabilities in both arenas, and forge stronger relationships between knowledge development and environmental management.

Quadrant three is where environmental performance is improving but knowledge performance is declining. One possible implication of this is that over time there is, and will be less innovative capability to address environmental problems, and that the environmental performance improvement may not be sustained, at least in insofar as knowledge antidotes pertain to the environment. It could also mean that there is a disconnected system in the sense that resources devoted to environmental management are coming at the expense of knowledge capability building in an 'either-or' manner, rather than viewing them as interdependent elements of complete systems. Another possible interpretation is that learnings associated with better environmental management have not been effective in influencing, shaping and assisting in knowledge development and diffusion more generally.

Quadrant four is where both environmental performance and knowledge performance are declining. This means diminished capabilities on both fronts, and that

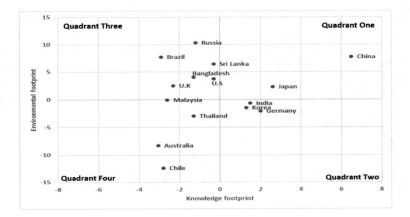

Fig. 4.6 Comparing Environmental footprint with Knowledge footprint

investments and policy priorities are seemingly aimed at other unrelated parts of the economy, potentially leading to downward spirals in competitiveness, and a growing inability of knowledge and innovation to address environmental concerns. Reprioritisation of, and increased investment in, policies and strategies towards environmental management and innovation capabilities are of importance, and urgently required.

Quadrant two is where the environmental performance is declining but knowledge footprint is improving suggesting that knowledge enhancing activities are not prioritising the environment, or that diffusion and dissemination of knowledge is not effective in addressing environmental issues, or that the activities/products of knowledge creation itself are harmful to the environment. Greater synergy, building of 'knowledge-enviro systems', and prioritisation of the environment in knowledge capability building is called for.

Applying this framework to our benchmark countries shows that the majority of countries (6) fall in quadrant three, i.e. with better environmental management, but weaker performance in knowledge or innovation performance. Overall, it seems that there is no pattern to the quadrant location by development levels: there are mixes of countries of various development levels in the quadrants. These countries are Russia, Sri Lanka, U.S, Bangladesh, U.K and Brazil.

Only two countries, China and Japan, are in quadrant one where knowledge and innovation performance and environmental management are improving. Certainly in the case of China, its sustained investment in education, research, and knowledge capability building and diffusion, allied with its growing prioritisation, for example, in renewable energy, is important.

Four countries—Australia, Chile, Malaysia and Thailand are in the camp of diminished capability and performance on both fronts, i.e. quadrant four. This is most pronounced for Chile.

Germany, India and Korea belong to that camp where environment performance is diminishing, but innovation and knowledge is improving, i.e. quadrant two suggesting, as we mentioned above, some systems weaknesses, and lack of linkage between environmental concerns and burgeoning knowledge capability.

Of course, this cursory analysis needs to be viewed with some caution, and too much should not necessarily be made of the results. It is reflective of **changes** in score in both over a four year period only as a guide to the **directions** in knowledge and environmental performance. Further, it does not measure actual absolute scores in time, rather it is about directional change in score. Nonetheless, this framework does give an indication of shifts in emphasis and priorities among policymakers and other actors.

As is to be expected though, more developed countries consistently score higher in **absolute** terms in both indices. This is to be expected given the greater capacity to pay for environment and knowledge, stronger foundational capabilities in research, skills, and more advanced overall institutional support structures.

4.12.2 Policy Suggestions for India

It should be recognised that India has, and is in the process of implementing a number of initiatives through various missions, e.g. solar energy and sustainable agriculture; some market-based measures including energy saving certificates, via Perform, Achieve and Trade (PAT) arrangements relating to energy efficiency; energy efficiency standards; National Action Plan on Climate Change; waste to compost programme; coal cess; and a National Forest Policy which considers both economic development, sustainable management of forest resources and use of technology to monitor and measure resources, as well as community engagement (Climate Action Tracker 2019; International Energy Agency 2019; Indian Institute of Forest Management 2016; Government of India 2008; India's Intended Nationally Determined Contribution to UNFCCC).

In addition, India has goals of reducing emissions intensity of GDP by 20–25% over 2005 levels, by 2020, and by 30–35% by 2030, as per its UN commitments (Climate Action Tracker 2019). It is true also that the share of renewable energy is expected to increase from 19% in 2016 to 39% in 2030, and there is an emerging sector in hydroelectricity, alongside solar and wind energy and in the case of the latter, India is the fourth largest producer in the world (Verghese 2018). India also has a target around renewable energy usage (175 GW by 2022) and to reduce imports of oil and gas by 10% by 2022–2023 (Niti Aayog 2018; Verghese 2018). However, given the huge current and expected demand for energy, it is also the case that India continues to be reliant on coal and oil (more than 77% of the energy mix), including imports.

In spite of achievements, more must be done and urgently. There needs to be much greater emphasis on a coordinated, comprehensive and integrated approach to environmental management, with an emphasis on knowledge and innovation. This would mean development of a medium-longer term knowledge-enviro plan which identifies, outlines and links environmental challenges in energy and resource management, and climate change, with innovative solutions drawn from input from stakeholders, representing all segments of society, and linking the various types of innovation (high level research and community based, grass roots solutions) in solutions or mission mode.

The focus in this book is on responses to climate change, rather than the full gamut of environmental concerns in India, although recognising the interdependencies.

4.12.2.1 Pricing and Institutional Arrangements

At the outset we argue for a much stronger market-oriented approach to pricing of natural resources, to better reflect costs of usage, including environmental costs, and better align demand and supply of resources. As mentioned in Chap. 2, one such approach could be environmental footprint pricing, which prices (natural) resources, on a comprehensive basis, according to the expected environmental footprint of households and businesses, and its impact, supported by appropriate measurement and monitoring capabilities, including development of sensor technologies. Usage of resources (and impact on the environment) above the expected environmental footprint would mean higher prices and vice versa for below. Alternatively, this could be structured along the lines of providing opportunities for those who use resources below the expected baseline to sell credits, analogous to a cap and trade-based approach. Further, would be the gradual removal of subsidies for energy use for favoured interests, and moving to single seamless national energy market.

There should also be enhanced coordination and consistency in the management of the environment, climate, energy and waste through an overarching body, Conservation India, overseeing all these dimensions, and capturing interdependencies and working closely with state instrumentalities. The Commission for Government could have ultimate oversight of Conservation India.

4.12.2.2 Mitigation: Energy and Climate Change

It is proposed that a comprehensive energy transition plan, which articulates, with clear objectives, targets and time frames, the orderly and eventual phasing out of fossil fuel energy towards renewable forms, building on emergent strengths in solar and wind, should be undertaken to drive emissions reductions. A clear focus would be on the need for both enhanced access to energy across the whole of India and security of supply. Thus, the plan would recognise that, given India's large and growing energy needs, at least for time being, coal and fossil fuel energy will still be an important source. The energy transition plan would be based on comprehensive benefit-cost analysis, including social benefit and costs, regarding the optimal timing, nature and extent of phasedown of coal and upscaling of renewables.[35] Such a plan would reflect full cost (and benefits of course) of a major shift towards renewables, including any subsidies, impacts on employment, spatial economies and stranded fossil fuel assets. In so doing, the tradeoff's can clearly be identified (based on community engagement), measured and publicly communicated as part of 'Right to Knowledge'. Benefits/Costs, as far as practical, would be couched in terms of Indian and global impacts.

Among the other key elements associated with the mitigation, energy and climate change plan are:

- Stimulating and fast tracking the research, development and diffusion of support capabilities such as battery storage for solar power, for example. Other opportunities abound, drawing on rapid development and deployment of knowledge in areas such as solar thermal at scale, carbon capture, cleaner coal and pumped hydro-electric power (Verghese 2018)
- Rapid renewable energy switching capabilities among renewable sources, and hybridisation (between fossil fuel power, and various forms of renewable energy),

---

[35] Subramanian (2018) articulates similar propositions regarding relative mix of renewables and coal, in calling for consideration of broader costs in making policy, including stranded assets and impacts on spatial development.

4.12 The Environment

and the establishment of renewable energy clusters linked to industrial hubs and rural areas
- Flexible land use policies to allow (parts of) farms (individually and collectively) to be converted to renewable energy parks, as part of distributed energy hubs (to lessen the pressure on the national grid) and enabling farmers to be part or full owners in these establishments. This would also be a means of diversifying farmer income by selling energy into the grid
- Solar panel proliferation on a 'wherever possible and practical basis', building on initiatives such as solar panels over canals and waterways, on rail and other transport, and on buildings (India's Intended Nationally Determined Contribution to the UNFCCC 2018; The Straits Times 2019)
- Establishing environmental issues, including energy management and climate change, as a key plank of India as the 'Ideas road' concept, noted earlier in this chapter, to solve complex problems
- Zero net emissions regimes across entire supply chains, including waste, canvassing financial and other supports for production processes that work towards this target-this would also include leading firms serving as mentors for other firms in the production chain (and vice versa as appropriate)
- Establishment of climate change ratings for firms, based along the lines of energy efficiency standards for appliances, but linked to emissions, e.g. lower emissions garner a higher rating. Exemplar firms could be selected as 'Best practice' demonstrators to showcase their activities and provide learning experiences for other firms. An important and welcome initiative in India is the establishment of a spatially based climate vulnerability index as a basis for more concerted, and focussed effort (Koshy 2019)
- Promotion of advanced metering and sensor technologies to enable households, industry and energy authorities to monitor usage patterns, and price accordingly, having due regard for the distributional implications
- Traffic light warning signals associated with initial approval of major projects (and ongoing projects with review mechanism) based on 'red', 'amber' and 'green' signals, with green signals being given automatic environmental approvals or continuation, amber representing modifications to initial project specifications or while in progress, and red either initial rejection or halting down the track. This would be part of continuous project monitoring through the life of a project from an environmental perspective, not just at the initial stages.

4.12.2.3 Adaptation

In parallel, we would advocate a comprehensive climate change **adaptation** plan to accompany mitigation measures. Although mitigation should be the primary focus to reduce emissions, at least in the interim, India could develop leading capability in adapting to climate change and for export purposes, such as climate resilient infrastructure and buildings, and various other industrial application of adaptation technologies. This would be linked to Knowledge Advantage Plans as described in Chap. 2.

4.12.2.4 Capability Development

More broadly, and building on the foregoing analysis, is that there is a great deal of opportunity in developing, promoting and exporting the 'R' concept of development, linked to innovation and knowledge. These are Recycling (use inputs and components again); Repairing (promoting enterprises which repair goods, and move away from the 'throwaway' culture); Renting (shifting the emphasis from ownership to leasing of goods and services akin to the 'uberisation' of environmental goods and services); Re-creating (using the by-products from industrial process and waste to create new industries); Re-designing (using the sustainable design methodology, and associated production techniques to create new products) and Retrofitting (support for existing buildings and establishments to be more efficient and environmentally friendly in resource management). These 'R' capabilities would be supported by IdeaBank, NEIF and drawing on the services of entrepreneurial and innovation brokers, as outlined earlier.

4.13 Conclusion

This chapter introduced the concept of the Knowledge Footprint and observed that India is a disappointing 14th out of 15 countries, in part reflecting its lack of export orientation, absence of broad-based high-quality educational institutions, and weakness in supporting infrastructure and institutions among a myriad of other things. Nonetheless, India is becoming more open to the world, and its diaspora is among the world's most vibrant.

We then examined India's trade performance in more detail, with a focus on exports. India is taking some tentative steps towards more knowledge intensive exports, but it remains a small player in world terms. India however is becoming an important destination for foreign investment, including greenfield investments, although noting that foreign investors regard India as 'chaotic'. There is a sense that India's pattern of internationalisation has been driven in growth terms by investment rather than trade. India is making some inroads into outward foreign investment. A series of policy recommendations to hasten India's internationalisation, especially exports, is proposed.

This chapter then examined entrepreneurship in detail and finds that despite the apparently impressive growth in start-ups there are some concerns as reflected in a series of 'missings' i.e. missing medium-sized sector, the relative weakness in innovation, spatial imbalance in entrepreneurship, gender-based constraints, and absence of employment generation. Indian entrepreneurship tends to manifest itself when labour market conditions are tough.

We advocate a segmented approach to entrepreneurship development in India, focussing on the type of firms by competitive characteristics and drivers. Two main policy thrusts that we advocate are the establishment of a Fund of Funds, the National Entrepreneurship and Innovation Fund (NEIF), and an approach to capture and diffuse more grass roots type innovations, through establishment of IdeaBank, which would have genuine **bank functions and powers**.

Finally, we considered the environment. India's natural environment is in a parlous state and the costs to its economy and society prohibitive. We advocate a comprehensive approach to environmental management, with a focus on knowledge, and integrated mitigation and adaptation measures, with primacy for appropriate pricing of natural resources.

Appendix 1: Knowledge Footprint Methodology, Metrics and Sources

Keynote: For all metrics, either in raw value or calculated ratios by the author or in scores obtained from other indices, e.g. Global Talent Competitiveness Index, author has recalibrated to give 100 score for best performing country in comparator set, with all other countries scaled accordingly. Any other weightings or adjustments for metrics are included in specific notes below. To obtain the score for each of the sub-pillars, e.g. Domestic Knowledge and Opportunity, scores for each metric within the sub-pillar are aggregated and divided by the number of metrics to obtain a raw score for each sub-pillar. Where countries do not have data, a score for that metric is not assigned. The raw scores for each sub-pillar derived then have weights applied to them, and the weighted sum gives the pillar score (s) for Domestic Knowledge Footprint and Global Knowledge Footprint. Weights, which are the same in both the domestic and global case, are as follows: Domestic Knowledge Access and Opportunity (17%), Domestic Knowledge Support and Platforms (15%), Domestic Knowledge Capability (22%), Domestic Knowledge Resourcing (15%), Domestic Knowledge Relationships (12%), and Domestic Knowledge Translation and Transformation (19%). The Domestic and Global Knowledge Footprint scores are then summed and divided by 2 to obtain an Overall Knowledge Footprint. This author has scored countries higher the more open they are in trade, investment and intellectual property. On some other metrics such as unemployment and inequality, naturally the lower the value the higher is the score.

Knowledge Footprint	Metrics	Sources and notes
Domestic Knowledge Access and Opportunity	Gross enrolment ratios for lower secondary, upper secondary and tertiary Distribution of tertiary enrolment ISCED 6 (Bachelor Equivalent) ISCED 7 (Masters Equivalent), ISCED 8 (Ph.D. equivalent), with weightings of 20% in score for ISCED 6 and 40% each for ISCED 7 and ISCED 8 % of students enrolled in tertiary in knowledge intensive fields	Data for Gross Enrolment is for 2016 or latest year. UNESCO data.uis.unesco.org accessed 16/7/2018. For tertiary education from UNESCO, knowledge intensive fields defined as natural sciences, maths/statistics, ICT, engineering, manufacturing and construction, agriculture, forestry and fisheries, health and welfare and services. Author scoring for 100 for best performing country then adjusted accordingly for other countries.

(continued)

(continued)

Knowledge Footprint	Metrics	Sources and notes
	Vocational enrolment Education	Vocational enrolment from data/scores derived from Global Talent Competitiveness Index (2018) by Lanvin and Evans (editors) (2018) The Global Competitiveness Index: Diversity for Competitiveness, INSEAD, The ARECCO Group and TATA Communications. Based on total number of students enrolled in vocational program of a given level of education as a percentage of total number of students enrolled in all programs. Author scoring for 100 for best performing country then adjusted accordingly for other countries.
	Inequality, income inequality, life expectancy inequality and overall human development inequality	Inequality measures % from UN Human Development Report 2016 (data is for 2015 www.hdr.undp.org) accessed 6/5/2018. Author scoring for 100 for best performing country then adjusted accordingly for other countries.
	GDP per capita	GDP per capita 2017 $ppp constant 2011 international dollars World Bank Data https://data.worldbank.org/indicator accessed 24/7/2018 Author scoring for 100 for best performing country then adjusted accordingly for other countries.
	Labour Force Participation	Labour Force participation (% of total population 15 years and above) 2017 World Bank Data https://data.worldbank.org/indicator accessed 17/7/2018. Author scoring for 100 for best performing country then adjusted accordingly for other countries.
	Unemployment	Unemployment (% of labour force 2017) World Bank Data https://data.worldbank.org/indicator accessed 17/7/2018. Author scoring 100 for best performing country and then adjusted accordingly for other countries.
Domestic Knowledge Supports and Platforms	Imports of government goods and services/GDP	Imports of government goods and services from World Trade Organisation for year 2016. http://stat.wto.org/Home/WSDBHome.aspx accessed 18/7/2018. Author calculation as a share of GDP ($U.Sm) World Bank Data https://data.worldbank.org/indicator accessed 17/7/2018. Then Author scoring for 100 for best performing country then adjusted accordingly for other countries.

(continued)

Appendix 1: Knowledge Footprint Methodology, Metrics and Sources

(continued)

Knowledge Footprint	Metrics	Sources and notes
	Tolerance of minorities, tolerance of migrants, labour-employment co-operation, business government relations, ease of finding skilled employees, relevance of education system to economy	Tolerance of minorities (parameters of discrimination, powerlessness, communal, ethnic, sectarian and religious violence based on Fragile States Index). Tolerance of migrants (based on Social Progress Index), Labour-Employment Co-operation, Business Government Relations, Ease of Finding Skilled Employees, Relevance of Education System to Economy are all survey scores from the Global Talent Competitiveness Index (2018) (Lanvin and Evans (editors) (2018). The Global Competitiveness Index: Diversity for Competitiveness, INSEAD, The ARECCO Group and TATA Communications), where surveys of business leaders are conducted by Global Talent Competitiveness Index. Scoring is 1–7 where 1 is the weakest and 7 is the best. This Author has then recalibrated to give the best performing of our benchmark countries a score of 100 and other countries adjusted relative to the best country.
	Ease of doing business, starting a business, construction permits, getting electricity, property registration, getting credit, protection of minority investors, paying taxes, enforcing contracts, resolving insolvency	Ease of doing business overall, starting a business, construction permits, getting electricity, property registration, getting credit, protection of minority investors, paying taxes, enforcing contracts, resolving insolvency scores all from World Bank Doing Business Index (2018). World Bank uses official data and surveys and provides scores based on a distance to frontier (best performing) concept. Scores recalibrated by author to give the best performing of our benchmark countries a score of 100 and other countries adjusted relative to the best country. Source World Bank Doing Business Index (2018).
	Corruption perception index scores	Corruption Perception Index (CPI) scores from Transparency International 2018 Corruption Perception Index and recalibrated by author to give 100 for the best country and then others adjusted accordingly. https://www.transparency.org/cpi accessed 20/7/2018 2018 The CPI draws upon 13 data sources which capture the assessment of experts and business executives on a number of corrupt behaviours in the public sector, including: • Bribery • Diversion of public funds • Use of public office for private gain • Nepotism in the civil service • State capture
	Edelman trust barometer 2018 overall scores and scores for trust in government, trust in media and trust in business	Edelman Trust Barometer 2018 based on online survey to questions of trust, with overall score/index an average of trust in Government, Media, Business, NGO's. Then Author re-calibration and scoring for 100 for best performing country and adjusted accordingly for other countries https://www.edelman.com/research/2018-edelman-trust-baraometer accessed 20/7/2018.

(continued)

(continued)

Knowledge Footprint	Metrics	Sources and notes
	Freedom house index score 2018	Freedom House Index 2018 overall scores based on expert views, desk research, on the ground research, for Political Rights (electoral process, political pluralism, political participation, effective functioning of Government), Civil Liberties (freedom of expression and belief, association and organisation rights, rule of law, personal autonomy, individual rights). Then Author re-calibration and scoring for 100 for best performing country and adjusted accordingly for other countries. https://freedomhouse.org/report/freedom-world/freedom-world-2018 accessed 20/7/2018.
	Fixed Telephone subscriptions per 100 people 2016, Mobile cellular subscriptions per 100 people 2016 Fixed broadband subscriptions per 100 people 2016, secure internet servers per million people 2017	Fixed Telephone subscriptions per 100 people 2016, Mobile cellular subscriptions per 100 people 2016, Fixed broadband subscriptions per 100 people 2016, secure internet servers per million people 2017. Then Author scoring for 100 for best performing country and adjusted accordingly for other countries. These data are from World Bank https://data.worldbank.org.indicator accessed 18/7/2018.
	3G coverage (% of population) 2016, Mobile cellular prices 2016 (% of GNI), Fixed Broadband prices 2016 (% of GNI), Mobile Broadband Prices (% of GNI 1 GB) 2016, Mobile Broadband prices (% of GNI) 2016 500mb	3G coverage (% of population) 2016, Mobile cellular prices 2016 (% of GNI), Fixed Broadband prices 2016 (% of GNI), Mobile Broadband Prices (% of GNI 1 GB) 2016, Mobile Broadband prices (% of GNI) 2016 500mb. Then Author scoring for 100 for best performing country and adjusted accordingly for other countries. These data are from International Telecommunications Union The Information Society Report Volume 2 2017 Country data pertains to 2016.

(continued)

Appendix 1: Knowledge Footprint Methodology, Metrics and Sources

(continued)

Knowledge Footprint	Metrics	Sources and notes
	Percentage of individuals using internet 2016, percentage of households with internet at home 2016 percentage of households with PC 2016, Government online service index scores 2016, Govt success in ICT promotion 2016, Impact of ICT on new services and products 2016, Internet access in schools 2016, ICT use and Government efficiency 2016, E-Participation (usefulness of Government websites, ICT use for business to business, ICT use for business-consumer	Percentage of individuals using internet 2016, percentage of households with internet at home 2016, percentage of households with PC 2016, Government online service index scores 2016, Government success in ICT promotion 2016, Impact of ICT on new services and products 2016, Internet access in schools 2016, ICT use and Government efficiency 2016, E-Participation (usefulness of Government websites), ICT use for business to business, ICT use for business-consumer. Source for these figures is based on surveys, including of executives, conducted by World Economic Forum and based on scoring of 1–7 where 1 is the weakest and 7 is the best. Source World Economic Forum (WEF) Information Technology Report 2016 Network Readiness Index reports. weforum.org/global-information-technology-report-2016/network.readiness accessed July 25 2018. Government online service index scores 2016, Government success in ICT promotion 2016, Impact of ICT on new services and products 2016, Internet access in schools 2016, ICT use and Government ethics 2016, E-Participation (usefulness of Government websites), 2016, ICT use for business to business, ICT use for business-consumer. These measures based on survey by WEF where score of 7 is best and 1 is weakest. Then Author scoring for 100 for best performing country and adjusted accordingly for other countries. Information Technology Report 2016 Network Readiness Index reports.weforum.org/global-information-technology-report-2016/network.readinesss accessed July 25 2018.
	ICT IDI Index (2017)	IDI ICT Index (2017) combines ICT access, use, skills into a single index Source International Telecommunications Union (ITU Measuring the Information Society Volume 1. Then Author re-calibration and scoring for 100 for best performing country and adjusted accordingly for other countries.
	Competition, Risk Capital, Cultural Support 2018	Competition (level of product or market uniqueness of start up's, extent of market power by established businesses, and effect of competition regulation) Risk capital (informal investment in start up's and measure of capital market depth) and Cultural Support (how positively county population views entrepreneurship as a career choice) scores. Scores/percentage from Global Entrepreneurship Development Index reflect individual and institutional variables based on official data and surveys from Global Entrepreneurship Monitor. Source Acs et al. (2017), Global Entrepreneurial Index (2018). Author scoring for 100 for best performing country and adjusted accordingly for other countries.

(continued)

(continued)

Knowledge Footprint	Metrics	Sources and notes
	Entrepreneurship as a good career choice, high status to entrepreneurship, media attention to entrepreneurship	Entrepreneurship as a good career choice, high status to entrepreneurship, media attention to entrepreneurship, scores from Global Entrepreneurship Consortium Entrepreneurship Monitor 2017/18. Data is for percentage of adult population 18–64 who believe that entrepreneurship is a good career choice, percentage of adult population 18–64 who believe that high status is afforded to successful entrepreneurs, percentage of adult population 18–64 who believe that there is a lot of positive media attention for entrepreneurship in the country. Author scoring for 100 for best performing country and adjusted accordingly for other countries.
Domestic Knowledge Capability Development	Papers, citations per document (all documents) Researchers per FTE 1000 papers per researcher FTE 1000	Papers for 2017 and citations per document (average citations to documents published during 2016) from Scimago Journal and Country Rank 2017. https://www.scimagojr.com accessed 15/7/2018 Author scoring for 100 for best performing country and adjusted accordingly for other countries. Researchers per 1000 FTE 2016 or nearest date UNESCO data.uis.unesco.org accessed 16/7/2018, Author scoring for 100 for best performing country and adjusted accordingly for other countries. Papers per researcher FTE 1000 author calculation of ratio and scoring. Author scoring for 100 for best performing country and adjusted accordingly for other countries.
	Science and Engineering Articles in all fields. Active journals per researcher	Science and Engineering Articles in all fields National Science Foundation, Science and Engineering Indicators 2018 (data pertains to 2016) https://www.nsf.gov/statistics/2018/nsb2018/data/tables accessed 15/7/2018. Author scoring for 100 for best performing country and adjusted accordingly for other countries. Active journals per researcher FTE 1000 calculated by author based on number of journals from OECD Compendium of Bibliometric Science Indicators 2016 (data for 2014) and Researchers from UNESCO. Then author scoring for 100 for best performing country and adjusted accordingly for other countries.

(continued)

Appendix 1: Knowledge Footprint Methodology, Metrics and Sources

(continued)

Knowledge Footprint	Metrics	Sources and notes
	Average Relative Citations all papers. Share of science and engineering publications in top 1% most cited papers	Average relative citations 2014 (the average relative citations measures average of a given area of geography or sector for each publication. The relative citation divides each publication citations count by the average citation count of all the same type of publications in that sub-field and year) National Science Foundation, Science and National Science Board https://www.nsf.gov/statistics/2018/nsb2018/data/tables accessed 15/7/2018 author scoring for 100 for best performing country and adjusted accordingly for other countries. Also from National Science Foundation, Science and Engineering Indicators are share of science and engineering publications in the top 1% most cited (2014 data). Author scoring for 100 for best performing country and adjusted accordingly for other countries.
	Percentage of publications among 10% most cited, Percentage of papers in top 10% most cited for Biochemistry, genetics, molecular biology, computer science, materials science, neuroscience	Percentage of publications among top 10% most cited and Percentage of papers in top 10% most cited for biochemistry, genetics and molecular biology, computer science, material science and neuroscience from OECD Science, Technology and Industry Scoreboard 2017 data pertains to 2015. Author scoring for 100 for best performing country and adjusted accordingly for other countries.
	Revealed Technology Advantage (RTA) for ICT, Environmental Science, Health, Biotechnology and Nanotechnology	Revealed Technology Advantage by technology area is the share of patents of an economy in a particular technology area relative to the share of total patents belonging to the economy. Data from OECD Science, Technology and Industry Scoreboard 2017 data pertains to 2015. RTA for Biotechnology and Nanotechnology relates to 2007–2009. Data is from OECD Compendium of Bibliometric Statistics 2016. Author scoring for 100 for best performing country and adjusted accordingly for other countries.
	Average overall score Top ten institutions in Times Higher Education Ranking. Average score for Teaching top ten Institutions in Times Higher Education. Number of Institutions in top 200 Times Higher Education. Number of Total Ranked Institutions Times Higher Education. Number of Ranked Institutions/enrolment, Average Score for top 10 in Academic Reputation QS Rankings	Institutional rankings from Times Higher Education 2018 Rankings https://www.timeshighereducation.com/world-university-rankings accessed 24/7/2018 author calculations based on average score of top ten institutions. For number of ranked institutions/enrolment, author calculations where enrolment is for 2016 or nearest available year from UNESCO data.uis.unesco.org accessed 24/7/2018. QS Rankings 2018 for academic reputation with author calculations for average top ten institutions on academic reputation score https://www.topuniversities.com/university-rankings accessed 8/8/2018. In all cases author scoring for 100 for best performing country and adjusted accordingly for other countries.

(continued)

(continued)

Knowledge Footprint	Metrics	Sources and notes
	Quality of Management Schools	Quality of Management Schools scores based on survey of business leaders by Global Talent Competitiveness Index (2018) (Lanvin and Evans (editors) (2018) The Global Competitiveness Index: Diversity for Competitiveness, INSEAD, The ARECCO Group and TATA Communications) Author scoring for 100 for best performing country and adjusted accordingly for other countries.
	Gross Graduation Ratio lower secondary, Upper Secondary, Tertiary. Gross Graduation. Distribution of graduates by Knowledge Intensive Fields. Distribution of graduates by ISCED 6, 7, 8	Gross Graduation ratios 2016 or nearest year from Lower Secondary, Upper Secondary, Tertiary first degree programs (ISCED 6, 7), UNESCO data.uis.unesco.org accessed 16/7/2018 Distribution of graduates knowledge intensive fields (same classification as for enrolment) for 2016 or nearest year UNESCO data.uis.unesco.org accessed 28/4/2018. Distribution of graduates by ISCED with author weightings of 20% for ISCED 6, 40% for ISCED 7, 40% for ISCED 8. UNESCO data.uis.unesco.org accessed 20/7/2018 Author scoring for 100 for best performing country and adjusted accordingly for other countries.
	Education attainment of population (Bachelor's or above)	Educational attainment of population (non-cumulative), Bachelor's both sexes 2015 UN Development Report 2016 Author scoring for 100 for best performing country and adjusted accordingly for other countries.
	Inflows of Scientific Authors, Returnees, Stayers	Inflows of scientists, returnees and stayers based on international mobility of scientific authors for 2016, as a percentage of total scientific authors. Mobility is referenced by comparing an author's affiliation to an institution in an economy for the last publication compared to closest available publication previously OECD Science, Technology and Industry Scoreboard 2017 Author scoring for 100 for best performing country and adjusted accordingly for other countries.

(continued)

Appendix 1: Knowledge Footprint Methodology, Metrics and Sources

(continued)

Knowledge Footprint	Metrics	Sources and notes
	Opportunity perception, Start-up skills, Risk acceptance, Opportunity start up capabilities, Human capital for entrepreneurship, Product Innovation, Process innovation	Opportunity perception (entrepreneurial opportunity perception potential of population weighted against freedom of country and property rights), Start-up skills (perception of start-up skills of the population weighted with quality of education), Risk acceptance (inhibiting effect of fear of failure of the population on entrepreneurial action combined with country risk) Opportunity start up (propensity of individuals to pursue potentially better quality opportunities weighted by taxation and quality of Government services), Human capital for entrepreneurship (% of start-up's founded by those with higher than secondary education with qualitative measures of firms training staff, and labour market freedom), Product Innovation (tendency of firms to create new products weighted by technology transfer capacity of country), process innovation (use of new technology by start up's combined with GERD and potential of country to conduct applied research), scores from (Acs et al. 2017) Global Entrepreneurship Development Institute, Global Entrepreneurship Index (2018). Data from Global Entrepreneurship Index, presented as scores/percentages, drawn originally from Global Entrepreneurship Monitor surveys and official data. Then Author scoring for 100 for best performing country and adjusted accordingly for other countries.
Domestic Knowledge Relationships	Collaboration across organisations, use of virtual social networks, use of virtual professional networks	Collaboration across organisations, use of virtual social networks, use of virtual professional networks are scores based on business leader surveys with scores from 1 to 7 with 1 as weakest, 7 as strongest. Scores from Global Talent Competitiveness Index (2018) by (Lanvin and Evans (editors) (2018) The Global Competitiveness Index: Diversity for Competitiveness, INSEAD, The ARECCO Group and TATA Communications), then Author scoring for 100 for best performing country and adjusted accordingly for other countries.
	University/Industry Research and collaboration, State of cluster development	University/Industry Research Collaboration and State of cluster development scores from Global Innovation Index (2018) (Cornell University, INSEAD, WIPO 2018). State of cluster development (geographic concentration of firms, suppliers, producers of related products and services, and specialised institutions) with scores of 1 = weakest and 7 = best. Author scoring for 100 for best performing country and adjusted accordingly for other countries.
	Average Industry Income for top ten Times Higher Education Ranked Institutions	Average Industry Income (score) for top ten Times Higher Education Ranked Institutions from Times Higher Education Rankings 2018 Rankings, with author calculations for average of top ten ranked institutions and scoring for 100 for best performing country and adjusted accordingly for other countries https://www.timeshighereducation.com/world-university-rankings accessed 24/7/2018.

(continued)

(continued)

Knowledge Foot-print	Metrics	Sources and notes
	Average share of collaborative papers of top ten Universities, average share of industry collaborations of top ten universities, and average share of overall domestic collaborations of top ten universities	Collaborative paper data from Leiden Institute rankings www.leidenrankings.com/rankings accessed 21/7/2018 for years 2013–2016, all fields and for collaboration on a full count basis. Author calculations and scoring for 100 for best performing country and adjusted accordingly for other countries. Share of collaborative papers in total papers for top ten Universities (average), Share of industry collaboration papers in total papers for top ten universities (average), and Share of domestic collaborations in total papers for top ten universities (average). Author calculations based on Leiden database pertaining to 2013–2016, and scoring for 100 for best performing country and adjusted accordingly for other countries. Where some countries do not have ten institutions the score is discounted by proportion. Note overall domestic collaborations estimated by author.
	Enterprise Networking	Enterprise Networking, based on surveys and other data, including official data (potential and actual entrepreneurial ability to access/mobilise opportunities and resources, and ease of access to reach others ie knowing entrepreneurs and agglomerations: urbanisation and infrastructure access) score from Acs et al. (2017) Global Entrepreneurship Index Global Development Institute 2018. Author scoring for 100 for best performing country and adjusted accordingly for other countries.
	Domestic collaboration % of all documents. Top 10% most cited documents with domestic collaboration	Domestic collaboration % of all documents for 2003–2012 from OECD Compendium of Bibliometric Scientific Indicators 2016. Top 10% most cited documents led by domestic collaboration with no international collaboration from OECD (% of all papers) Science, Technology and Industry Scorecard (2017) year pertaining is 2015. Author scoring for 100 for best performing country and adjusted accordingly for other countries.
	QS Employer reputation score average top 10 Institutions	QS https://www.topuniversities.com/university-rankings accessed 8/8/2018 Author calculations and then scoring for 100 for best performing country and adjusted accordingly for other countries. 2018 data.
	Percentage of total population in urban areas. Percentage of total population in urban agglomerations of more than 1 million	Population figures for total and urban for 2017. World Bank https://data.worldbank.org/indicator accessed 27/7/2018. Author scoring for 100 for best performing country and adjusted accordingly for other countries.

(continued)

Appendix 1: Knowledge Footprint Methodology, Metrics and Sources

(continued)

Knowledge Footprint	Metrics	Sources and notes
	Urban GDP/Capita	Urban GDP per capita for 2017 estimated by author, recognising limitations of approach, based on removing agricultural value added from total GDP on assumption that agricultural value added is in rural areas. 2017 GDP based on constant 2011 prices, international dollars Source World Bank https://data.worldbank.org/indicator accessed 15/7/2018 Population data from World Bank as in previous section. Author calculations and scoring for 100 for best performing country and adjusted accordingly for other countries.
Domestic Knowledge Resourcing	GERD/GDP, GERD per researcher, GERD distribution by BERD, HERD and GOVERD	GERD/GDP 2016 or latest year, GERD per researcher 2016 or latest year, GERD distribution by BERD, HERD and GOVERD for 2016 or latest year sources UNESCO data.uis.unesco.org accessed 16/7/2018. GERD weighted by BERD (40%), HERD (40%) and GOVERD (20%) Author calculations and scoring for 100 for best performing country and adjusted accordingly for other countries.
	Government expenditure on education/GDP	Government expenditure on education/GDP 2016 or latest year. Sources UNESCO data.uis.unesco.org accessed 16/7/2018. Author calculations and scoring for 100 for best performing country and adjusted accordingly for other countries.
	Education expenditure/Government Expenditure Government expenditure on tertiary education/total Government expenditure on education	Education Expenditure/Government Expenditure 2016 or latest year. Government expenditure on tertiary education/total Government expenditure on education 2016 or latest year. UNESCO data data.uis.unesco.org accessed 16/7/2018. Author scoring for 100 for best performing country and adjusted accordingly for other countries for these metrics.
	Initial Government funding per student lower secondary, upper secondary and tertiary	Initial Government funding per student lower secondary, upper secondary and tertiary 2016 or latest year: Sources UNESCO data.uis.unesco.org accessed 16/7/2018. Author scoring for 100 for best performing country and adjusted accordingly for other countries.
	Water stress (freshwater withdrawal/available water)	Water stress (freshwater withdrawal/available water) 2015 or latest year. World Bank Data https://data.worldbank.org/indicator accessed 20/7/2018. Author scoring for 100 for best performing country and adjusted accordingly for other countries.
	Water productivity (GDP per cubic meter of total freshwater withdrawal constant 2010 US Dollars)	Water productivity (GDP per cubic meter of total freshwater withdrawal constant 2010 US Dollars) 2016 or latest available year. World Bank Data https://data.worldbank.org/indicator accessed 20/7/2018. Author scoring for 100 for best performing country and adjusted accordingly for other countries.

(continued)

(continued)

Knowledge Footprint	Metrics	Sources and notes
	Renewable freshwater resources per capita Annual freshwater withdrawal % of internal resources	Renewable freshwater resources per capita 2014 or latest. Annual freshwater withdrawal % of internal resources 2014 or latest available year. Sources for water data here and above. World Bank https://data.worldbank.org/indicator accessed 20/7/2018. Author scoring for 100 for best performing country and adjusted accordingly for other countries.
	Environmental Health Water Resources and waste treatment	Environmental Health. Water Resources and waste treatment. Sources: Yale Environmental Protection Index scores 2018 Environmental Performance Index https://epi.envirocenter.yale.edu accessed 20/7/2018 (best country score = 100) Author scoring for 100 for best performing country and adjusted accordingly for other countries. EPI Yale uses a range of data from academic research, industry reports, remote sensing data, official statistics, survey and questionnaire with their scoring system based on the situation of each country relative to best and worst corresponding to targets in range of 0–100 where best is close to 100 and worst closest to 0. Targets are based on either international agreements or expert judgement. Then Author scoring for 100 for best performing country and adjusted accordingly for other countries.
	Terrestrial protected areas (% of land area)	Terrestrial protected areas (% of land area) 2016 or latest year. World Bank https://data.worldbank.org/indicator accessed 20/7/2018 Author scoring for 100 for best performing country and adjusted accordingly for other countries.
	Marine protected areas (% of territorial water)	Marine protected areas (% of territorial water) 2016 or latest year Source World Bank https://data.worldbank.org/indicator accessed 20/7/2018. Author scoring for 100 for best performing country and adjusted accordingly for other countries.
	Species protection index	Species protection index Source: EPI Yale Environmental Index scores 2018 https://epi.envirocenter.yale.edu accessed 20/7/2018 (re-calibrated by author for 15 countries best country score = 100) Accessed 20/7/2018 Author scoring for 100 for best performing country and adjusted accordingly for other countries. Renewable electricity output (% of total electricity output) 2015 or latest year.
	Renewable electricity output (% of total electricity output) Renewable energy consumption (% of final energy consumption)	Renewable energy consumption (% of final energy consumption) 2015 or latest year World Bank https://data.worldbank.org/indicator accessed 20/7/2018 Author scoring for 100 for best performing country and adjusted accordingly for other countries.

(continued)

Appendix 1: Knowledge Footprint Methodology, Metrics and Sources

(continued)

Knowledge Footprint	Metrics	Sources and notes
	Air Quality 2018 (environmental health)	Air Quality 2018 (environmental health). Author scoring 100 for best country and others adjusted accordingly. Source EPI Yale Environmental Index scores 2018.
	Water and sanitation 2018 (environmental health)	Water and sanitation 2018 (environmental health). Author scoring 100 for best country and others adjusted accordingly. Source EPI Yale Environmental Index Scores 2018.
	Air pollution 2018 (climate and energy)	Air pollution 2018 (climate and energy) Source: EPI Yale Environmental Index scores 2018 https://epi.envirocenter.yale.edu. accessed 20/7/2018. Then Author scoring for 100 for best performing country and adjusted accordingly for other countries.
	CO_2 emissions per capita CO_2 emissions kg per 2011 $ppp of GDP	CO_2 emissions per capita 2014 or latest year CO_2 emissions kg per 2011 $ppp of GDP 2014 2014 or latest year Sources: World Bank https://data.worldbank.org/indicator accessed 17/7/2018. Author scoring for 100 for best performing country and adjusted accordingly for other countries.
	International inward migration stock/population Share of world immigration stock Share of immigrant world stock/share of world population Share of immigrant stock by age	Immigration data for 2017 and by age (20–64 years of age) from United Nations Department of Economic and Social Affairs, Population Division Trends in International Migration Stock 2017 https://www.un.org/endevelopment/desa/population/migration/index revision accessed 20/7/2018. Population data for 2017 (medium variant) from United Nations Department of Economic and Social Affairs Population Division 2017 World Population Prospects https:/www.un.org/en/development/desa/population/publications/database accessed 20/7/2018. Author calculations and then scoring for 100 for best performing country and adjusted accordingly for other countries.
	Gross capital formation/GDP 2017	Gross Capital Formation % of GDP 2017 World Bank www.indicator.org accessed 18/8/2018. Author scoring for 100 for best performing country and adjusted accordingly for other countries.
	Inward investment flows/GDP 2016	Inward investment flows/GDP 2016 Inward investment from https://unctadstat.unctad.org/wds/reportfolders/reportfolders.aspx accessed 12/4/2018, GDP from World bank Indicator www.worldbank.indicator.org accessed 17/7/2018. Author calculations and then 100 score for best country and others adjusted accordingly.
	Inward investment flows/Global flows 2016	Inward investment flows/Global flows 2016 Source is https://unctadstat.unctad.org/wds/reportfolders/reportfolders.aspx accessed 12/4/2018, Author calculation and then 100 score for best country and others adjusted accordingly.

(continued)

(continued)

Knowledge Footprint	Metrics	Sources and notes
	Inward investment flows global share/global GDP share 2016	Inward investment flows global share/global GDP share 2016: Source for inward investment https://unctadstat.unctad.org/wds/reportfolders/reportfolders.aspx accessed 12/4/2018, GDP from World Bank Indicators www.worldbank.indicator.org accessed 17/7/2018. GDP in current $U.S millions 2016. Author calculations and then scoring for 100 for best performing country and adjusted accordingly for other countries.
	Inward investment stock/world stock	Inward investment stock/world stock. Source: https://unctadstat.unctad.org/wds/reportfolders/reportfolders.aspx accessed 12/4/2018, Author calculation and then 100 score for best country and other countries adjusted accordingly.
	Inward investment stock world share/global GDP share	Inward investment stock world share/global GDP share. Source https://unctadstat.unctad.org/wds/reportfolders/reportfolders.aspx accessed 12/4/2018, GDP from World bank Indicator www.worldbank.indicator.org accessed 17/7/2018. Author calculation and then 100 score for best country and others adjusted accordingly.
	Inward Greenfield investment/GDP	Inward Greenfield investment/GDP 2016. Source Destination Greenfield investment data from UNCTAD World Investment Report 2018 Annex Tables as of June 2018 Year relates to 2016. GDP from World bank Indicator www.worldbank.indicator.org accessed 17/7/2018. Author calculation and then 100 score for best country and other countries adjusted accordingly.
	Inward Greenfield investment/World Greenfield	Inward Greenfield investment/World Greenfield 2016. Source Destination Greenfield investment data from UNCTAD World Investment Report 2018 Annex Tables as of June 2018 Year relates to 2016. Author calculation and then 100 score for best country and other countries adjusted accordingly.
	Inward greenfield flows world share/global GDP share	Inward greenfield flows world share/global GDP share. Greenfield destination investment data from UNCTAD World Investment Report 2018 Annex Tables as of June 2018. Year relates to 2016, GDP 2016 from World Bank Indicators www.worldbank.indicator.org accessed 17/7/2018. GDP in current $U.S millions. Author calculations and then scoring for 100 for best performing country and adjusted accordingly for other countries.

(continued)

Appendix 1: Knowledge Footprint Methodology, Metrics and Sources 267

(continued)

Knowledge Footprint	Metrics	Sources and notes
Domestic Knowledge Translation and Transformation	Value added/employment for high technology manufacturing, Medium-high technology manufacturing and for commercial services 2016	Value added for high technology manufacturing, Medium-High technology manufacturing and commercial services: Source National Science Board, Science and Engineering Indicators for value added https://www.nsf.gov/statistics/2018/nsb2018/data/appendix accessed 17/7/2018. Employment data accessed from International Labour Organisation for high and medium skills https://www.ilo.org/ilostat accessed 19/7/2018, author estimations for ratio and then scoring for 100 for best performing country and adjusted accordingly for other countries.
	Value added medium-high technology manufacturing/GDP 2016 Value added High Technology Manufacturing/GDP 2016 Value added Commercial services/GDP 2016	Value added medium-high technology manufacturing, high technology manufacturing, commercial services 2016 data from Source National Science Board, Science and Engineering Indicators for value added for https://www.nsf.gov/statistics/2018/nsb20181/data/appendix accessed 17/7/2018. GDP data for 2016 from World Bank https://data.worldbank.org/indicator accessed 17/7/2018 Author calculations for ratio and then scoring for 100 for best performing country and adjusted accordingly for other countries.
	Import services/GDP Import services/world import services. import services world share/GDP world share 2016 Import medium skill manufacturing/GDP, import medium skill manufacturing/world imports, import medium skill world share/GDP world share Import high skill manufacturing/GDP, import high skill manufacturing/world imports, import high skill world share/GDP world share	Import data for 216 for services, high and medium skills manufacturing from UNCTAD database for trade by manufacturing and services https://unctadstat.unctad.org/wds/reportfolders/reportfolders.aspx accessed 17/8/2018, GDP from World Bank accessed https://data.worldbank.org/indicator accessed 17/7/2018. Author calculations for shares then scoring for 100 for best performing country and adjusted accordingly for other countries.
	High skill occupational share of total employment, and medium-high skill occupational share of total employment	International Labour Organisation ILO https://www.ilo.org/ilostat accessed 19/7/2018 accessed 19/7/2018. Data is for 2017. Author scoring for 100 for best performing country and adjusted accordingly for other countries.
	Total early stage entrepreneurship (TEA)	Percentage of 18–64 year olds with early stage businesses. Source Global Entrepreneurship Monitor Consortium (2018) Global Entrepreneurship Monitor Global Report 2017/18. Author scoring for 100 for best performing country and adjusted accordingly for other countries.
	Total established businesses	Percentage of 18–64 year olds with established businesses. Source Global Entrepreneurship Monitor Consortium (2018) Global Entrepreneurship Monitor Global Report 2017/18 Author scoring for 100 for best performing country and adjusted accordingly for other countries.

(continued)

(continued)

Knowledge Footprint	Metrics	Sources and notes
	Opportunity driven early stage entrepreneurship as a percentage of total early stage entrepreneurship	Percentage of TEA who are opportunity driven. Source Global Entrepreneurship Monitor Consortium (2018) Global Entrepreneurship Monitor Global Report 2017/18 Author scoring for 100 for best performing country and adjusted accordingly for other countries.
	Percentage of entrepreneurs expecting to create six or more jobs in the next 5 years	Percentage of TEA. Source Global Entrepreneurship Monitor Consortium (2018) Global Entrepreneurship Monitor Global Report 2017/18. Author scoring for 100 for best performing country and adjusted accordingly for other countries.
	Innovation in businesses products in new to all or some customers and few/no businesses offering same products	Percentage of TEA. who say that product innovation is new to some or all customers and few/no businesses offer the same products. Source Global Entrepreneurship Monitor Consortium (2018) Global Entrepreneurship Monitor Global Report 2017/18. Author scoring for 100 for best performing country and adjusted accordingly for other countries.
	GEDI technology absorption	Scores for Technology Intensity of Country' Start up activity with country capacity for firm level technology absorption, based on survey (from GEM) and official data. Source: Acs et al. (2017) Global Entrepreneurship Development Index (2018) Global Entrepreneurship Development Institute. Author scoring for 100 for best performing country and adjusted accordingly for other countries.
	GEDI high growth	Scores for High Growth (percentage of high growth businesses that intend to employ at least ten people and plan to grow more than 50% in five years ie gazelles, also availability of venture capital and business strategy sophistication) based on survey (from GEM) and official data. Source: Acs et al. (2017), Global Entrepreneurship Development Index (2018) Global Entrepreneurship Development Institute. Author scoring for 100 for best performing country and adjusted accordingly for other countries.

(continued)

Appendix 1: Knowledge Footprint Methodology, Metrics and Sources 269

(continued)

Knowledge Footprint	Metrics	Sources and notes
	Resident + non-resident patent applications in country/world patent applications, resident + non-resident patent applications world share by country/world GDP share, resident patent applications/GDP, non resident patent applications in country/GDP, resident patent applications/researcher Resident + non-resident Trademark applications in country/world Trademark applications, resident + non-resident Trademark applications world share by country/world GDP share, resident Trademark applications/GDP, non resident Trademark applications in country/GDP, resident Trademark applications/researcher Resident + non-resident Industrial Design applications in country/world Industrial Design applications, resident + non-resident Industrial Design applications world share by country/world GDP share, resident Industrial Design applications/GDP, non-resident Industrial Design applications in country/GDP, resident Industrial Design applications/researcher Resident + non-resident utility patent applications in country/world utility payment applications, resident + non-resident utility patent applications world share by country/world GDP share, resident utility patent applications/GDP, non-resident utility patent applications in country/GDP, resident utility payment applications/researcher	All data refers to 2016. Patent, utility, Industrial Design and Trademark data for residents from World Intellectual Property Organisation (WIPO) WIPO IP Statistics Data Center https://www3.wipo.int/IPstats accessed 4/8/2018 Number of researchers (FTE) from UNESCO data.uis.unesco.org accessed 16/7/2018. Author calculation of ratios and then scoring for 100 for best performing country and adjusted accordingly for other countries.
Global Knowledge Capability Development	Global share of Value Added Medium-High Technology manufacturing. Global share of medium-high technology value added as a share of global GDP	Value Added Figures for 2016 from National Science Foundation, Science and Engineering Indicators https://www.nsf.gov/statistics/2018/nsb2018/data/tables accessed 15/7/2018. Author calculations and scoring 100 for best country and others adjusted accordingly.

(continued)

(continued)

Knowledge Footprint	Metrics	Sources and notes
	Value Added High Technology Global Share, Global share of High technology value added as a share of global GDP. Value Added Global Share of Commercial Knowledge Intensive services, Global share of Knowledge Intensive Commercial Services value added as a share of global GDP	GDP for 2016 (US$ millions current prices) for 2016 from World Bank Indicators World Bank Data https://data.worldbank.org/indicator accessed 15/7/2018. Author calculations and then scoring with best country at 100 and others adjusted accordingly.
	Percentage of world papers. Percentage of world papers/percentage of world population	Papers for 2017 from SciMago (Scimago Journal and Country) https://www.scimagojr.com accessed 15/7/2018, and adjusted for population, population data for 2017 from UN Population data for 2017 (medium variant) from United Nations Department of Economic and Social Affairs Population Division 2017 World Population Prospects https://www.un.org/en/development/desa/population/publications/database accessed 20/7/2018. Author calculations and then scoring for 100 for best performing country and adjusted accordingly for other countries.
	Citations from International Science and Engineering Publications	Citations from International Science and Engineering Publications % National Science Foundation: Science and Engineering Indicators 2018 data relates to 2014 www.nsf.gov/statistics accessed 15/7/2018. Author scoring for 100 for best performing country and adjusted accordingly for other countries.
	International outlook average scores of top ten institutions	International outlook average scores of top ten institution https://www.timeshighereducation.com/world-university-rankings 20/7/2018 Author calculations and scoring for 100 for best performing country and adjusted accordingly for other countries.
	Outflows of scientists	Outflows of scientists 2016 (% of authors by last main recorded affiliation). A mobility episode is when an author who is affiliated to an institution in a given economy in his/her last publication in 2016 was previously affiliated to an institution in a different economy. OECD Science, Technology and Industry Indicators (2017). Author scoring for 100 for best performing country and adjusted accordingly for other countries.
	Expected citation impacts of scientist outflow	Expected citation impacts, an experimental measure, based on citations associated with mobility experience, relative to average citations and also based on journal rank and score. OECD Science, Technology and Industry Scoreboard 2017 data relates to 2016 Author scoring for 100 for best performing country and adjusted accordingly for other countries.

(continued)

Appendix 1: Knowledge Footprint Methodology, Metrics and Sources

(continued)

Knowledge Footprint	Metrics	Sources and notes
	Share of world journals	Share of world journals: OECD compendium of bibliometric scientific indicators 2016 data is for 2014 Author scoring for 100 for best performing country and adjusted accordingly for other countries.
	Percentage of open access document output	Percentage of open access document output: https://www.scimagojr.com accessed 15/7/2018. Author scoring for 100 for best performing country and adjusted accordingly for other countries.
	Emigration of the highly educated	OECD Connecting with Emigrants 2015: OECD and selected non OECD destinations. Highly educated is those with ISCED 5 and above. Author scoring for 100 for best performing country and adjusted accordingly for other countries.
Global Knowledge Access and Opportunity	Inbound tertiary mobility rates Outbound tertiary mobility rates Inward tertiary students as a share of world tertiary inbound students Inward tertiary students as a share of world inbound tertiary students/share of global population outbound tertiary students as a share of world tertiary outbound students outbound tertiary students as a share of world outbound tertiary students/share of global population	Data relates to 2016. Inbound and outbound tertiary mobility rates from UNESCO data.uis.unesco.org accessed 16/7/2018. World Population data from World Bank www.Worldbank.indicator.org accessed 10/8/2018 for 2016 data. Author calculations for other parameters and scores. Raw data for inbound and outbound tertiary mobility from UNESCO UNESCO data.uis.unesco.org accessed 16/7/2018. Population data from World Bank https://data.worldbank.org/indicator accessed 16/7/2018. Author calculation and scoring for 100 for best performing country and adjusted accordingly for other countries.
	Value Added Education Services/GDP, Global Share of Value added education services, Value added education services global share/global GDP share	Value Added data for 2016 from National Science Board: National Science and Engineering Indicators https://www.nsf.gov.statistics/2018/nsb2018/data/tables accessed 13/5/2018. GDP data from World Bank https://data.worldbank.org/indicator accessed 13/5/2018. Author calculation and scoring for 100 for best performing country and adjusted accordingly for other countries.
	Share of World GDP	Share of World GDP GDP 2016, constant 2011 ppp international dollars GDP data from World Bank indicators www.Worldbank.indicator.org accessed 13/5/2018. Author calculation and scoring for 100 for best performing country and adjusted accordingly for other countries.
	GDP per capita	GDP per capita 2017 constant 2011 ppp international dollars GDP https://data.worldbank.org/indicator accessed 24/7/2018 Author scoring for 100 for best performing country and adjusted accordingly for other countries.
Global Knowledge Supports and Platforms	Trading across borders	Trading across Borders score from World Bank Doing Business Index (2018) Author scoring for 100 for best performing country and adjusted accordingly for other countries.

(continued)

(continued)

Knowledge Footprint	Metrics	Sources and notes
	Exports of Government goods and services/GDP, Exports of Government goods and services/world exports Exports of Government Goods and Services world share/ global GDP share	Data pertains to 2016. Exports of Government Goods and Services from WTO accessed 17/7/2108, GDP data https://data.worldbank.org/indicator accessed 24/7/2018. Author calculations and scoring where 100 is the best country and others adjusted accordingly.
	Air transport/local population Air transport/share of world Air Transport share of world/share of world population	Air Transport registered carriers departing worldwide (domestic takeoff's and takeoff's abroad of air carriers registered in the country) 2017 World Bank https://data.worldbank.org/indicator accessed 24/7/2018. World Population Data for 2017 from World Bank accessed 10/8/2018. Author calculations for ratio and scoring where 100 is the best country and others adjusted accordingly.
	Port Traffic Container share of world traffic, Port Traffic Container traffic share of GDP, Port Traffic Share of World/Share of world GDP	Port Traffic (measures flow of containers from land to sea transport modes, and vice-aversa) in twenty foot equivalent containers: incorporates coastal as well as international journeys) data for 2017 from World Bank https://data.worldbank.org/indicator accessed 17/7/2018. Share of Global GDP 2017 (GDP in $US millions), GDP for 2017 www.data.worldbank.org/indicator accessed 17/7/2018. Author calculations for ratio and scoring where 100 is the best country and others adjusted accordingly.
	Happy Planet Index 2016	The Happy Planet Index is an overall score based on data for well-being (how satisfied people are with life overall from a poll); Life expectancy; Inequality of outcomes (in terms of length of life, how satisfied they are), Ecological Footprint (the average impact of a person in a country on the environment). Latest Year data Jeffrey et al. (2016) The Happy Planet Index: 2016. A global index of sustainable well-being. London: New Economics Foundation Author re-calibration and then scoring 100 for best country and others adjusted accordingly.
	Well-being score from Happy Planet Index	Based on Well-being score then Author re-calibration and scoring where 100 is the best country and others adjusted accordingly.

(continued)

Appendix 1: Knowledge Footprint Methodology, Metrics and Sources

(continued)

Knowledge Footprint	Metrics	Sources and notes
	World Happiness Report 2018	The World Happiness Report encompasses GDP per capita is in terms of Purchasing, healthy life expectancy, Social support (question about being able to count on relatives or friends if in trouble), Freedom to make life choices (poll question), Generosity (question about donating money to a charity in the past month), corruption perception (question about whether corruption is widespread in Government or Business). Each of these variables is calculated to contribute to an overall score, relative to that in a hypothetical country Dystopia (denoted because it has values equal to the world's lowest national averages). Source: Helliwell et al. (2018). World Happiness Report 2018, New York: Sustainable Development Solutions Network UN. Data for 2015–2017. Author scoring where 100 is the best country and others adjusted accordingly.
	ICT Use for B-B and ICT Use for B-C	These measures based on survey by World Economic Forum where score of 7 is best and 1 is weakest. Then Author scoring for 100 for best performing country and adjusted accordingly for other countries. Source World Economic Forum (WEF) Information Technology Report 2016 Network Readiness Index accessed July 25 2018. Author scoring 100 for best country and others adjusted accordingly.
	English Language Proficiency Index	The English Proficiency Index is based on scores from online testing of English language proficiency scores Source English First 2017. Education First EPI English Proficiency Index (2017) (EPI) https://www.ef-australia.com.au/epi/ accessed 24/7/2018. Author scoring where 100 is the best country and others adjusted accordingly. Note that Australia, U.K and U.S have been excluded as this would have provided undue advantage.
	International Internet Bandwidth	International Internet Bandwidth 2016 Kb/s per internet user Source: World Economic Forum (WEF). Information Technology Report 2016 Network Readiness Index reports.weforum.org/global-information-technology-report-2016/network.readiness accessed July 25 2018 accessed July 25 2018. Author scoring where 100 is the best country and others adjusted accordingly.
	QS Best Student Cities 2018	QS Best Student Cities as determined by number of cities in top 100, then Author scoring where 100 is the best country and others adjusted QS https://www.topuniversities.com/city-rankings/2018 accessed 8/8/2018.

(continued)

(continued)

Knowledge Footprint	Metrics	Sources and notes
	Foreign Aid/GDP	Aid data from OECD Development Co-operation Report 2018 **joining forces to leave no-one behind**. GDP from World Bank for relevant year GDP from World Bank https://data.worldbank.org/indicator accessed 9/9/2018. Author calculations and scoring where 100 is the best country and others adjusted accordingly.
Global Knowledge Relationships	International collaborative papers	International collaborative papers as a share of total papers Sci Mago Scimago Journal and Country Rank https://www.scimagojr.com accessed 15/7/2018 author calculations, and scoring where 100 is the best country and others adjusted accordingly.
	International Collaborative papers of Universities	Share of international collaborative papers of Universities in all papers, average of top ten universities for 2013–2016 from Leiden database. Source Leiden Institute rankings www.leidenrankings.com/rankings accessed 21/7/2018, author calculations and scoring where 100 is the best country and others adjusted accordingly.
	International co-inventors in all patents, international co-inventors for patents in ICT, Health, Environment	International co-inventors as a percentage of economies IP 5 patent families where IP5 patent families are patents within the 5 IP offices (European patent office, Japan, Korea, China and U.S). International co-inventors are IP5 families featuring at least one foreign co-inventor. Data for 2012-Source OECD Science, Technology and Industry Scoreboard 2017. Author scoring where 100 is the best country and others adjusted accordingly.
	Foreign Value Added in Gross Exports (%) and Domestic Value Added of country embodied in partner country exports as a share of domestic gross exports of original country	OECD Science, Technology and Industry Scoreboard 2017, data pertains to 2014. Author scoring where 100 is the best country and others adjusted accordingly.
	Foreign leading authors in international collaboration Domestic leading authors in international collaboration	Foreign leading authors in international collaboration and Domestic leading authors in international collaboration, both in percentage of international collaboration, 2015 fractional count basis. Author re-calibration: Sources OECD Science, Technology and Industry Scoreboard 2017 Author scoring where 100 is the best country and others adjusted accordingly.
	Top 10% of most cited documents led by domestic author as part of international collaboration (%) Top 10% most cited documents led by foreign author as part of international collaboration	Top 10% of most cited documents led by domestic author as part of international collaboration (%) and Top 10% most cited documents led by foreign author as part of international collaboration: Sources OECD Science, Technology and Industry Scoreboard 2017 with author recalibration, data is for 2015 Author scoring where 100 is the best country and others adjusted accordingly.

(continued)

Appendix 1: Knowledge Footprint Methodology, Metrics and Sources

(continued)

Knowledge Footprint	Metrics	Sources and notes
	Global Innovative Cities	Global Innovative Cities based on 2thinknow consulting classification of nexus, hub, node and upstart cities for 2018. Nexus, hubs, node and upstart cities are most innovative in that order. Author has counted number of cities in each classification and applied weights (40% for nexus, 30% for hub, 20% for node and 10% for upstart). Source 2ThinkNow 2018 Publishing the world's most innovative cities ranking https://2thinknow.com accessed 20/8/. Author scoring where 100 is the best country and others adjusted accordingly.
	Virtual Professional Networks Virtual Social Networks	Virtual Professional Networks and Virtual Social Networks: scores from Lanvin B and Evans P (editors) 2018 The Global Talent Competitiveness Index: Diversity for Competitiveness, INSEAD, The ARECCO Group and TATA Communications) Global Entrepreneurship Talent Competitiveness Index 2018, Author re-calibration and scoring where 100 is the best country and others adjusted accordingly.
Global Knowledge Resourcing	World share by country of Global Expenditure on Research and Development (GERD). GERD world share/share of Global GDP Business Expenditure on R&D as a share of Global GERD. Business share of global GERD/share of global GDP Higher Education Expenditure on R&D as a share of Global GERD. Higher Expenditure share of global GERD/share of global GDP Government Expenditure on R&D as a share of Global GERD. Government Expenditure share of global GERD/share of global GDP	Expenditure on research and development from UNESCO data.uis.unesco.org accessed 28/7/2018. Data is for 2016 or latest available year. Author calculations of ratios. Ppp $ constant price 2005, GDP from World Bank https://data.worldbank.org/indicator accessed 28/7/2018. Author calculations and scoring where 100 is the best country and others adjusted accordingly.
	World Share of CO_2 emissions World Share of CO_2/share of world GDP	Data pertains to 2014. Co2 emissions from World Bank www.World Bank.Indicator.org accessed 17/7/2018, GDP 2014 constant 2011 ppp international dollars https://data.worldbank.org/indicator accessed 17/7/2018. Author calculations and scoring where 100 is the best country and others adjusted accordingly.
	Outward Foreign Investment Flow/World Outward Investment flow Outwards Foreign Investment Flow/GDP Outward Foreign Investment flow world Share/World GDP share Outward FDI stock/World FDI outward Stock Outward FDI stock/Global Share of GDP	Investment data for outward flow and stock 2016 source ($m) https://unctadsta.unctad.org/wds/reportfolders/reportfolders.aspx accessed 12/4/2018, GDP data for 2016 in $m from World Bank https://data.worldbank.org/indicator accessed 17/7/2018, Author calculations and scoring where 100 is the best country and others adjusted accordingly.

(continued)

(continued)

Knowledge Footprint	Metrics	Sources and notes
	Greenfield investment source/GDP Greenfield investment source/World Greenfield source Greenfield source world share/Global GDP share	Greenfield investment data from UNCTAD World Investment Report 2018 Annex Tables as of June 2018. Year relates to 2016, author calculations. GDP from World Bank https://data.worldbank.org/indicator accessed 17/7/2018. Author calculations and scoring where 100 is the best country and others adjusted accordingly.
	Emigrant stock/population Share of emigrant stock/share of world population	Emigrant data for 2017 from UN https://www.un.org/endevelopment/desa/population/migration/index. accessed 18/7/2018, Population data from World Bank https://data.worldbank.org/indicator accessed 17/7/2018, author calculations and scoring where 100 is the best country and others adjusted accordingly.
Global Knowledge Translation and Transformation	Entrepreneurship Internationalisation	The degree to which a country's entrepreneurs are internationalised as measured by businesses' exporting potential weighted by the level of complexity of the country. Acs et al. (2017) Global Entrepreneurship Index Global Entrepreneurship Development Institute 2018. Author scoring where 100 is the best country and others adjusted accordingly.
	Services exports/world services exports Services exports/GDP Share of world services exports/share of global GDP Medium skills exports/world medium skills exports Medium skills exports/GDP Share of world Medium Skills exports/share of global GDP High skills exports/world High skills exports High skills exports/GDP Share of world High Skills exports/share of global GDP Revealed Comparative Advantage for Medium Skills Exports	Export data for 2016 and GDP for 2016 from UNCTAD https://unctadsta.unctad.org/wds/reportfolders/reportfolders.aspx accessed 17/8/2017, GDP from World Bank www.World Bank.Indicator.org accessed 20/7/2018. Author calculations and scoring where 100 is the best country and others adjusted accordingly.
	Revealed Comparative Advantage for High Skills Exports Patents Abroad/Researcher Patents Abroad/GDP Trademarks Abroad/Researcher Trademarks Abroad/GDP Industrial Design Abroad/Researcher Industrial Design Abroad/GDP Utility Patents Abroad/Researcher Utility Patents Abroad/GDP	Revealed Comparative Advantage 2016 author calculation and scoring where 100 is best country and others adjusted accordingly. Calculation method in Chap. 4 of this book. Intellectual property data for 2016 from WIPO IP Statistics Data Center https://www.wipo.int/IPstats accessed 4/8/2018. Number of researchers (FTE) for 2016 or latest year from UNESCO data.uis.unesco.org accessed 16/7/2018, GDP Data for 2016 from World Bank https://data.worldbank.org/indicator accessed 18/7/2018. Author calculations and scoring where 100 is best country and others adjusted accordingly.

References

2ThinkNow (2018) Publishing the world's most innovative cities ranking. https://2thinknow.com. Accessed 20 Aug 2018

Acs Z, Szerb L, Lloyd A (2017) The global entrepreneurship index 2018. The Global Entrepreneurship and Development Institute, Washington, D.C., USA

Agarwal P (2018) India's IP policy: a brave act?. Decoding Indian Intellectual Property Law, Spicy IP

Anand R, Kochher K, Mishra S (2015) Make in India: which export can drive the next wave of growth? IMF working paper WP/15/119

Aravind Eye Care System. www.aravind.org. Accessed 13 Apr 2019

AT Kearney (2017) The 2017 foreign direct investment confidence index glass half full (by Laudicina P, Petersen E)

AT Kearney (2018) The 2018 A.T Kearney foreign direct investment confidence index investing in a localised world (by Laudicina P, Petersen E, McCaffrey R)

Australian Government (2014) Chief Scientist science, technology, engineering and mathematics Australia's Future

Basheer S, Agarwal P (2017) India's new IP policy: a bare act. Indian J Law Technol 13:1–26. Accessed 13 Apr 2019

Climate Action Tracker (2019) India www.climateactiontracker.org. Accessed 12 Apr 2019

Crabtree J (2018) The Billionaire Raj a journey through India's new gilded age. Oneworld Publications Ltd

Cornell University, INSEAD, and WIPO (2018) The global innovation index

Cornell University, INSEAD, and WIPO (2014) The global innovation index

Cortright J (2001) New growth theory, technology and learning: a practitioner's guide. Rev Econ Dev. Literature and Practice: no 4. Impressa Inc

D'Cunha S (2017) 90% of Indian start up's will fail because of lack on innovation study says. Forbes, 18 May 2017. https://www.forbes.com/sites/suparnadutt/2017/05/18/startups-in-india-fail-due-lack-of-innovation-according-to-a-new-ibm-study/#702e8220657b

Das G (2019) Jobonomics India's employment crisis and what the future holds. Hachette, India

Debnath A, Laskar A, Bhattacharjee N, Mazmuder N (2014) Is India's GDP really led by export? A further examination. J Transnatl Manag 19(4):247–260

Deloitte Technology (2013) Fast 500 Asia Pacific 2013

Deloitte Technology (2017) Fast 500 Asia Pacific 2017

Development Commissioner, Micro, Small and Medium Enterprises. Ministry of Micro, Small and Medium Enterprises

Dhanji S, Rangan H (2018) Leveraging Australia's Indian diaspora for deeper bilateral trade and investment relating with India. Australia India Institute

Drip Tech: A Jain Irrigation Company (2019). http://www.driptech.com/. Accessed 6 Mar 2019

Education First EPI EF English Proficiency Index (2018) (EPI). https://www.ef-australia.com.au/epi/. Accessed 25 Apr 2019

Education First EPI English Proficiency Index (2017) (EPI) https://www.ef-australia.com.au/epi/. Accessed 17 July 2018

Environmental Synergies In Development (ENSYDE) (2019). http://www.ensydeindia.org/. Accessed 9 Feb 2019

Florida R (2003) The rise of the creative class. Basic Books

Francis S (2015) India's manufacturing sector exports: a focus on missing domestic inter-sectoral linkages. Institute for Studies in Industrial Development New Delhi Working Paper 182

Global Entrepreneurship Monitor Consortium (2017) Global entrepreneurship monitor global report 2016/17

Global Entrepreneurship Monitor Consortium (2018) Global entrepreneurship monitor global report 2017/18

Govel Trust (2015) Aravind Eye Care System. https://www.aravind.org/. Accessed 1 Mar 2019

Government of India (2008) National action plan on climate change. https://pmindia.nic.ainpg01-52.pdf. Accessed 15 May 2018

Government of India (2013) Press information. Bureau Government of India, Ministry of Science and Technology, Vyome Therapeutics Inc., 29 Aug 2013

Government of India (2015a) Foreign trade policy, 1 Apr 2015–31 Mar 2020

Government of India (2015b) Pradhan Mantri Mudra Yojana Program. www.pmindia.gov.in/newsPM

Government of India (2015c) Entrepreneurs memorandum (Part-11). Data on MSME sector. http://www.dcmsme.gov.in/publications/emii-2014-1. Accessed 15 June 2018

Government of India (2016a) Action plan start up India

Government of India (2016b) All India report of sixth economic census. Ministry of Statistics and Programme Implementation, Central Statistics Office

Government of India (2016c) National intellectual property right policy. Ministry of Commerce and Industry, Department of Industry Policy and Promotion

Government of India (2018a) Foreign investment data equity flows. www.data.gov.in/catalog/foreign-direct.investment. Accessed 16 Apr 2018

Government of India (2018b) Annual report 2017–2018. Ministry of Micro, Small and Medium Enterprises

Government of India (2018c) Udyogaadhaar. Ministry of Micro, Small and Medium Enterprise. https://udyogaadhaar.gov.in/UA/UAM_Registration.aspx. Accessed 5 Sept 2018

Government of India (2017) 2017 Foreign trade policy statement. 2017 mid-term review. Ministry of Commerce and Industry

Government of India (2019) Stand up. https://www.pmindia.gov.in/en/news_updates/pm-launches-pradhan-mantri-mudra-yojana/. Accessed 15 May 2019

Gridbots (2019) https://www.gridbots.com/. Accessed 6 Feb 2019

Gupta A (2016) Grassroots innovation, minds on the margin are not marginal minds. Penguin Random House India, Haryana, India

Helliwell J, Layard R, Sachs J (2018) World happiness report 2018. Sustainable Development Solutions Network, New York

Hyvonen M, Wang H (2012) India's services exports. RBA Bulletin, Reserve Bank of Australia

IBM Institute for Business Value (2016) Entrepreneurial India. How start ups redefine India's economic growth

INC 42 (2018) State of the Indian start up eco-system

India Brand Equity Foundation (IBEF) Foreign trade policy of India update April 2019 (Relates to Towns of Export Excellence) www.ibef.org. Accessed 29 Apr 2019

India Institute of Forest Management (2016) (Draft) National forest policy 2016: empowered communities. healthy ecosystems, happy nation

India's Intended Nationally Determined Contributions (Works Towns Climate Justice) to United Nations Frameworks Convention on Climate Change. www.nmhs.org.in/pdf/India%20INDC%20To%20UNFCCC.pdf. Accessed 20 May 2018

International Energy Agency, Perform, Achieve, Trade (PAT) Scheme India. www.iea.org/policiesandmeasures/pams/in. Accessed 12 Apr 2019

Jagannathan R (2018) The jobs crisis in India. MacMillan

Jeffrey K, Wheatley H, Abdallah S (2016) The happy planet index: 2016. A global index of sustainable well-being. New Economics Foundation, London

Joshi V (2016) India's long road. Penguin Allen Lane, Haryana, India

Karmali N (2010) Aravind Eye Care's Vision for India. Forbes, 5 Mar 2010. https://www.forbes.com/global/2010/0315/companies-india-madurai-blindness-nam-familys-vision.html#5c664be5c7eb. Accessed 10 Dec 2018

Kelley D, Baumer B, Brush C, Greene P, Mahdavi M, Majbouri M, Cole M, Dean M, Heavlow R (2017) Global entrepreneurship monitor women's entrepreneurship report 2016–2017

References

Koshy J (2019) A climate vulnerability index for India. The Hindu, 14 Mar 2019. https://www.thehindu.com/sci-tech/energy-and-environment/a-climate-vulnerability-index-for-india/article26537153.ece. Accessed 20 Mar 2019

KPMG and Confederation of Industry (2015) The new wave Indian SME

KPMG and IMC, Chamber of Commerce and Industry (2017) Catalysing MSME entrepreneurship in Indian capital, technology and public policy

Kulkarni A, Calderon A, Douglas A (2015) Towards a knowledge footprint framework: initial baby steps. In: Webber K, Calderon A (eds) Institutional research and planning in higher education global contexts and themes. Routledge

Kulkarni A (2016) Indian export competitiveness and performances: a comprehensive analysis. Indian J Econ Bus 15(1):39–73

Lanvin B, Evans P (eds) (2018) The global talent competitiveness index: diversity for competitiveness. INSEAD, The ARECCO Group and TATA Communications

Martin B (1995) Against intellectual property philosophy and social action. 21(3):7–22 (July–September 1992)

Mehrara M, Haghnejad A, Dehnavi J, Meghbodi F (2014) Dynamic causal relationships among GDP, exports and foreign direct investment (FDI) in the developing countries. Int Lett Soc Hum Sci 14:1–19

Mukherjee S, Mukherjee S (2012) Overview of India's export performance: trends and drivers. Indian Institute of Management Bangalore, Working paper no 363

Nageswaran VA, Natarajan G (2016) Can India grow? Carnegie India

NASSCOM Zinnov (2018) India start-up eco system. Approaching escape velocity

National Science Foundation (NSF) (2018) Science and engineering indicators. https://www.nsf.gov/statistics/2018/nsb20181/assets/nsb20181.pdf. Accessed 20 Oct 2018

NITI Aayog (2015) Report of the expert committee on innovation and entrepreneurship

NITI Aayog (2018) Strategy for New India @ 75

OECD (2008) The global competition for talent. Mobility of the highly skilled

OECD (2013) Interconnected Economics benefitting from global value chains

OECD (2017) Science, technology and industry scoreboard

Panagariya A (2018) India's trade policy folly: current turn to import substitution will take economy down from Turnpike to direct road. The Times of India, 25 July 2018. https://timesofindia.indiatimes.com/blogs/toi-edit-page/indias-trade-policy-folly-current-turn-to-import-substitution-will-take-economy-down-from-turnpike-to-dirt-road/

Prahlad C (2005) The fortune at the bottom of the Pyramid. Eradicating poverty through profits. Wharton School Publishing

Prasad H (2017) Reviving and accelerating India's export: policy issues and suggestions. Government of India, Ministry of Finance, Department of Economic Affairs, Economic Division (Accessed by Sathish R, Kumar S, Singh S and Sharma R)

Prime Minister launches Pradhan Mantri Mudra Yojanna, 8 Apr 2015. Accessed 10 Sept 2018

Puri H (2017) India's trade policy dilemma and the role of domestic reform. Carnegie India, Washington, USA

Radjou N, Prabhu J, Ahuja S (2012) Jugaad innovation, a frugal and flexible approach to innovation for the 21st centrury. Random House Group Limited, London, UK

Rosling A (2017) Boom country? The New Wave on Indian Enterprise. Hachette, India

Silicon India (2019) Why India lacks product-based start up's. www.siliconindia.com/shownews/why_india_lacks_productionbased_startups. Accessed 13 Apr 2019

Singh S (2012) Curing common skin disorders. Forbes. http://www.forbesindia.com/article/scientist-entrepreneurs/curing-common-skin-disorders/33755/1. Accessed 5 Jan 2019

Start Up Genome (2017) Global start up ecosystem report 2017 in partnership with GEN, Cruchbase and Orb

Subramanian A (2018) Of counsel. The challenges of the Modi-Jaitley economy. Penguin Viking

Tata Group Home Page. https://www.tata.com. Accessed 24 May 2019

Terjesen S, Lloyd A (2015) The 2015 female entrepreneurship index. Global entrepreneurship development index
The Straits Times (2019) Bright future for floating solar panels in S-E Asia, 9 Feb 2019. https://www.straitstimes.com/business/bright-future-for-floating-solar-panels-in-s-e-asia. Accessed 13 Mar 2019
The Times of India (2018) 14 of the world's most polluted cities in India, 2 May 2018. https://timesofindia.indiatimes.com/city/delhi/14-of-worlds-15-most-polluted-cities-in-india/articleshow/63993356.cms
UNCTAD Trade Statistics. https://unctadstat.unctadstat.org/wds/reportfolders/reportfolders.aspx. Accessed 17 Aug 2017
UNCTAD Investment Statistics. https://unctadstat.unctadstat.org/wds/reportfolders/reportfolders.aspx. Accessed 12 Apr 2018
UNCTADSTAT Manufactured Goods by Degree of Manufacturing. https://unctadstat.unctad.org/EN/Classifications/DimSitcRev3Products_Tdr_Hierarchy.pdf. Accessed 28 July 2018
UNESCO (2017) summary report of the 2015 uis innovation data collection. Information Paper N37, Mar 2017
UNESCO (2018) Innovation statistics (relating to 2009) https://data.uis.unesco.org. Accessed 15 Aug 2018
Usmani A (2019) Startup street: three years on, Modi's startup funding plan fails to take off. https://qrius.com/startup-street-three-years-on-modis-startup-funding-plan-fails-to-take-off/
Verghese P (2018) An Indian economic strategy to 2035: navigating from potential to delivery. A report to the Australian Government
Vyome (2015). https://www.vyometx.com/. Accessed 20 Apr 2019
Wheels India Limited (2013). https://www.wheelsindia.com. Accessed 26 Mar 2019
Wolf M (2017) Entry into the global economy. In: Mohan R (ed) India transformed 25 years of economic reform. Penguin Viking
World Bank (2013) Indian diagnostic assessment of select environmental challenges and analysis of physical and monetary loss of environmental health and natural resources, vol 1
World Bank (2017) World bank doing business index 2018
World Bank (2018a). GDP per capita, https://data.worldbank.org/indicator. Accessed 17 Aug 2018
World Bank (2018b). Trade Data, https://data.worldbank.org/indicator. Accessed 18 Dec 2018
World Bank (2018c) Business density. https://data.worldbank.org/indicator. Accessed 2 Apr 2018
World Bank (2018d) Jobless growth? South Asia economic focus spring 2018
World Economic Forum (2018) Readiness for the future of production report 2018 (in collaboration with A.T Kearney)
Yale Center for Environmental Law and Policy (2014) Environmental performance index. https://epi.envirocenter.yale.edu/about-epi. Accessed 25 July 2018
Yale Center for Environmental Law and Policy (2018) Environmental performance index. https://epi.envirocenter.yale.edu/about-epi. Accessed 25 July 2018

Chapter 5
Empowerment

Abstract Empowerment is fundamental to allowing all in society to participate in, and share in the benefits of a knowledge economy. The focus in this chapter is on female empowerment. A comprehensive literature search is undertaken around a number of dimensions of female entrepreneurship pertaining to labour force participation, social factors, access to finance and entrepreneurship among others. A Gender Knowledge Footprint is developed and presented, comparing Indian females with males and across BRIC countries. The analysis finds that females do not have anywhere near the opportunity to embrace the knowledge economy compared to males. A number of strategies to enhance female empowerment are presented.

Keywords Empowerment · Gender footprint · Self-help groups · Labour force participation · Financial inclusion

5.1 Introduction

Empowerment is critical to the process and outcomes of innovation. It is the 'heart and soul' of innovation and the knowledge economy. The freedom, wherewithal and ability to generate ideas, with recognition and respect, and the capacity to share in the fruits of innovation, is a core component of a knowledge-based economy.

The focus of this chapter is on female empowerment in India. The hidden or largely absent face of Indian women in innovation and empowerment, except confined to certain domains, due to complex traditions, social mores and customs, has prevented females from participating in the economic process more generally but innovative process more specifically. At its most stark and boiling down to the narrowest construct, is that by advancing female equality through employment India could realise an increase of 18% in GDP over 'business as usual', amounting to $770U.S billion in 2025 (McKinsey and Company 2018). This is the largest potential gain in the Asia Pacific Region. Other data suggests that the country would be 27% richer if as many women worked as men, while yet more analysis shows that husbands and sons engaging in an extra hour of household tasks could increase the female workforce by five percentage points (The Economist 2018a).

However, this is only part of the story. A most alarming representation of the parlous situation is found in a survey of experts conducted by Thompson Reuters (Thompson Reuters Foundation 2018) about the world's most dangerous country for women. India unfortunately came out in number one position, including being the worst for sexual violence, human trafficking, cultural traditions (including mutilations and abuse of various kinds, female infanticide, child and forced marriage), 3rd worst in non-sexual violence and discrimination (jobs and ability to make a living, access to nutrition and education and discrimination in land and property), and 4th weakest in healthcare (access to medical professionals). This damning result, even when allowing for India's level of development, points to a complex interplay of economic, social, traditional and institutional factors. Fostering a more collaborative society, learning through practical problem-solving initiatives, better targeted welfare and other initiatives in employment and education, institutional reforms and attitudinal shifts are needed. The sorts of policies that we advocate in this chapter, hopefully in some way, move in a positive direction, recognising the various measures that have been put in place in India.

5.2 Literature Review

While the following brief literature review does not necessarily focus on the knowledge economy, it is considered appropriate to canvass a wider realm of issues since female disempowerment and disadvantage is complex, multifaceted and comprising many interconnected elements.

This literature review comprises seven core domains

- Institutional studies
- Social Norms
- Labour market Participation
- Entrepreneurship and industrial Sphere;
- Health and emotional well-being
- Knowledge-based approaches
- Financial studies.

5.2.1 Institutional Studies

Self-Help Groups (SHG's) abound in India. These are fundamentally collectives run by women for women, with varying degrees of public policy support, aimed at raising female awareness of rights, identity, access to services and institutions, and income-generating opportunities.

The benefits of SHG's have been variously identified in studies as improved outcomes for women in the following areas: health and nutrition; education for girls;

5.2 Literature Review

family planning support; increased respect in the household; increase in mobility, independence and positive impacts on confidence, self-worth and self-esteem; greater insight into rights, and exposure to institutions, government agencies and support services; and enhanced collective identity for women (Husain et al. 2014).

However, some question the efficacy of Self-Help Groups in meeting the needs of the truly disempowered. Self-selection can play a role, i.e. those women in the public domain or better off economically join such groups. One study which compared newer members of an SHG to older members, to measure the programme impact of SHG's in 6 municipalities in West Bengal, found that the SHG provided significant positive benefits for new members in only two parameters, albeit important, out of five (improved status within the family and reduced tolerance of domestic violence), but negligible results in three other parameters comprising household decision making, financial autonomy associated with income from the SHG, and greater aspiration for girl child, including more desire for education (Husain et al. 2014).[1] The same study did find significant evidence of the self-selection effect, and also that the SHG had not introduced new economic impact, but rather enabled economic activity previously undertaken to be undertaken with greater labour and capital on a more systematic basis. This in turn supplemented family income, and was thus more acceptable to men.

Other studies which examined the impact of the Mahila Samakhya (MS) Program (Education for Women), based on a self-help group notion in rural Northern India, finds positive impacts for participating women in terms of employment, ability to go out without permission of males, political engagement, and that there were similar flow on benefits even for women who did not participate in the program (Kandpal et al. 2013). The case study in Appendix 1 highlights the strengths and weaknesses of the MS program. Yet another study of the Self-Employed Women's Agency (SEWA) in Rajasthan found that women who lived in villages with SEWA programs or who were members of the SEWA's village level SHGs, benefitted from greater participation in group programs, achieved enhanced empowerment domestically, in terms of greater household decision making, realised greater awareness of public services, and an ability to take action to access these rights and receive better services. However, benefits did not particularly extend in large measure to the economic realm for those participating in the program, save for some gains (Desai and Joshi 2013).

5.2.1.1 Political Participation

Studies have dealt with political participation in local panchayat elections, noting that it is mandatory to have at least 30% female representation in local Panchayat

---

[1] If the programme impact prevails, newly inducted members would not be empowered or have lower levels of empowerment than older members who would be empowered. If self-selection was present, meaning that women tended to be engaged in SGH who were in the public arena or better off economically, then empowerment levels of the two groups would be broadly similar.

bodies via reservation policies.[2] Various studies find positive impacts of female political participation in panchayat leadership roles in terms of provision of public goods, improved perception of women's abilities and less likelihood of female leaders taking bribes compared to males, and that bribes paid were up to 3% lower for villages with a female leader (World Bank 2012). Another study finds that teenage girls exposed repeatedly to women leaders are more likely to confront traditional norms, express a wish to marry later, have fewer children and obtain more skilled jobs (World Bank 2012). On the question of perception, the World Bank suggests that having female leadership did not change village preferences for male leaders but it did diminish stereotypes about gender roles, and removed males' adverse views about the effectiveness of female leadership (World Bank 2012). Yet another comprehensive study found that despite reservations, many women still experienced discrimination and deep-seated attitudes including lack of real, tangible voice in panchayat bodies. Males accompanying females to meetings, and acting as the defacto elected representative, are just a few manifestations of a lack of independence and identity for females (Kalaramadam 2016).

One particular study found that political reservations increased village level female entrepreneurship, concentrated however in household-based entrepreneurship, rather than independent facilities, while finding that the surge in entrepreneurship was not linked to government contracts or access to finance, but rather through the 'exhortation impact'. However, the same study found no evidence of increased employment in manufacturing after reservations, in either the unorganised or organised sectors (Ghani et al. 2013a, b).

5.2.1.2 Legal Considerations

Some work concentrates on the impact of inheritance law reform on empowerment. Using the reform to the Hindu Succession Act (where women have equal rights to inheritance as men), and impacts on first and second generations, a study finds positive impacts on second generations for girls education, female child labour, educational spending and attainment and health, with even larger impacts than for the first generation. For example, having a mother who capitalised on the reforms, raises the amount of time spent studying by girls twofold compared to brothers (Deininger et al. 2014). The study also observed that first generation positive impacts were also found for assets that women bring into marriage, increased leisure time, sanitation, access to financial accounts and reduction in fertility. It also found that the survival rates of daughters has increased due to inheritance reform benefits for females, however there is also the concern that the share of daughters born to those who benefitted from the reforms has declined, possibly associated with sex-selection abortions. 'Missing' girls continues to be a problem (World Bank 2012).

---

[2]The 1992 amendment to the 73rd Constitution provided for at least one-third of total seats of the rural tiers of Government (village, block, district) should be reserved for women.

However, questions have been raised as to the effectiveness of implementation of land laws, since tradition and diehard attitudes have often meant weak enforcement (World Bank 2012). Various studies point to women's asset ownership in India and other places, including land, being associated with lower domestic violence, while reforms to inheritance laws have produced benefits such as marriage delays, increased education levels (by an average of 11–25% in years of schooling), and resulted in lower dowry payment (World Bank 2012). In a negative sense, the lack of land titles for females has adversely impacted female access to institutional credit, and that in many instances in practice, the presence of males is required for females to access loans. Analysis in Karnataka, a state in India, has shown that more land holding male-headed households received visits from agricultural extension services compared to women, pointing to systemic institutional weaknesses pertaining to gender. In Kerala, another Indian State, female ownership of property diminishes the likelihood of violence (World Bank 2012).

5.2.2 Social Norms

Other studies and empirical observations look at social norms, culture and ingrained attitudes.

A survey found that 52% of women and 42% of men consider wife beating is justified on a number of grounds, and that as recently as 2016, 22% of women reported spousal physical or sexual violence in the last 12 months (McKinsey and Company 2018). Other work contended that women believe that spousal violence is acceptable for 'disobedience' and intended such transgressions but seldom for reasons relating to staying within the 'rules' (World Bank 2013). Other studies focus on dowry. One, which examined the link between dowry and the National Rural Employment Guarantee Scheme, observed a decrease in dowry deaths due to the husband's family having less requirement to obtain payments from the bride's family, but the obverse is the case for other types of violence, including kidnappings, sexual harassment and domestic violence (Amaral et al. 2015). Others contend that dowry has the potential to increase the risk of spousal violence. On the contrary, a study in Tamil Nadu finds that dowry has a 'protective value' in the sense of increasing economic resources of households, enhancing the social status of the husband and his family, and enabling women to have some measure of authority over finances (World Bank 2013), but overall the evidence is mixed.

Some point to the historical legacy of the design, development and application of laws inherited from colonial times where colonial legislation largely governed public spaces, and indigenous laws presided over private spaces, as being pertinent to gender equity, inclusion and empowerment. As is claimed 'This perception of women as victims or subjects-rather than individuals with the right to their own identity, sexuality and other forms of self-expression-has circumscribed the social and legal provisions for women's safety. Only girls and women who fulfil their roles and duties in the private space of the household have the right to protection from violence in the public space' (World Bank 2013, p. 7).

Much attention has been paid to life cycle violence and deprivation, including excess female child mortality (often associated with abortion), and later in the life cycle linked to lack of support and attention in health care, education and other facilities, and the prevalence of child marriage (World Bank 2012, 2013).

Various work considers the intergenerational effects of violence: children of poorly educated mothers are at greater risk of child abuse in India, and that women who have suffered spousal abuse are likely to abuse their children (and also engage in female child mortality); interestingly that women who saw their mother being abused are at greater risk of spousal violence, but this could also be associated with greater reporting (World Bank 2013). Various studies, which focus on the male experience, concluded that men who experience or witness gender inequities are likely to prefer sons which are often a catalyst for excess female child mortality (World Bank 2013).

Some contend, across the South Asian region, that maternal education reduces the risk of neglect or mortality of daughters, while others find somewhat surprisingly, that higher levels of maternal education are associated with greater neglect and death of daughters (World Bank 2013).

Research (World Bank 2013) shows that post-primary school education for women in India is significantly associated with diminished risk of, and greater disclosure of, intimate partner violence due to the greater ability to voice concerns, more respect from other household members, and when employed, greater financial independence, although the evidence relating to employment is not incontrovertible. The violence generated against women can decrease with women's earnings, with womens' assets being a protective factor.

Various studies (World Bank 2013) consider the education of men. Post-primary education for men provides some protection against physical violence while secondary and higher education is strongly connected with less defined notions of 'masculinity' among Indian men; however some studies do find that men's higher education is associated with greater risk of spousal violence because such educated men may demand a higher dowry, which is often associated with higher violence risks; many studies contend that there is a significant association between household poverty and risks of intimate partner violence due to stress of poverty and male angst of not being able to provide for the family.

Another important study (Biswas 2017) highlights the theoretical and empirical understandings of spousal violence in India. In theoretical terms, there is the status inconsistency theory (family as a power system with men controlling the resources including earnings from members and any threat to this established order incites violence); backlash theory (anti-feminist denial of womens' aspirations, achievements and demands for equality); exchange theory (males utilise financial control and violence for overall control). Using national family health survey data in India, a total of 124,385 women and 74,369 men were surveyed and the following was observed:

- Spousal violence is noticeably higher among employed women compared to unemployed women
- Women in lower level jobs, e.g. labouring jobs, experience more spousal violence than those in middle order jobs, such as clerical work, compared to those in higher level work such as professionals, technical and managerial work
- Curiously, women in higher level jobs are more likely to face violence than those in middle-level jobs due to 'encroachment' into male-dominated areas
- Agricultural workers face all the many types of violence among employed women (emotional, sexual, verbal, physical)
- Types of violence differ by job category, e.g. agricultural workers face the highest of all types of violence among employed women, clerical women face more verbal and emotional violence than women in professional jobs, and women in professional jobs face more physical and sexual violence than clerical.

The study, and the others that we have canvassed, point to the ingrained nature of violence against women, associated with male dominance in society, economy, and in the family. In relation to the latter, family reputation hinges on intolerance of females speaking out.

5.2.3 Labour Force Participation

There has been extensive research on female labour force participation and its determinants and impact in India. Labour force participation has been particularly low by international standards for females in India and declining, especially in rural areas, while worker population ratios for females are considerably lower than for males. Although participation in education to some extent accounts for the decline in labour force participation, it by no means accounts for the entirety of the decline.

Some contend that economic development, education and labour force participation in Asian economies show a 'U' shaped pattern. That is, at lower levels of economic development, in an agricultural economy, women's work is more pronounced (even unpaid) as participants in the labour force through working on family farms or enterprises. This is also associated with lower education levels, higher fertility rates, and lower family income. As the economy transitions to manufacturing and there is less role for agriculture, then this lowers female participation in the labour market (ADB 2015; Das et al. 2015). As Lahoti and Swaminathan (2019) indicate, agriculture and related activities are easier to combine with other household duties that are dominated by females, while jobs in the early stage of industrialisation especially are often not attractive to, or encouraged for women, because of the stigma against participation in blue-collar activity. Further, as the income levels of families rise, womens' employment is perceived to be less necessary due to social dictates, e.g. marriage. As the economy further grows and develops, education levels improve, fertility rates drop and the rise of services theoretically opens up growth opportunities for females.

However, while there is a hint of a 'U' shaped curve in India (ADB 2015; McKinsey and Company 2018; Sorsa et al. 2015; World Bank 2012), a number of other studies found no real evidence of a U shaped curve linking labour force participation with growth, income and economic development, save for a few states (Lahoti and Swaminathan 2019; Bhalla and Kaur 2019). The U shaped though curve is much stronger in relation to education and labour force participation (Das et al. 2015; Chatterjee et al. 2018).[3]

Studies which look at women's labour force participation vis-à-vis males find that education levels of the male spouse has a more pronounced negative effect on females labour force participation (each extra year of a male education means a drop in female participation of 1 percentage point), compared to the positive effect of female education. This is also associated with the 'status' view, where female labour force participation is linked to male employment and livelihood, income and associated status (Das et al. 2015).

Other literature (Sorsa et al. 2015) finds that there are a number of constraints to female labour force participation in India: religious factors and social stigma; presence of young children has a negative impact on participation for urban women (having a child less than 6 years old whereas children of ages 6–14 is insignificant in urban and rural areas); negative effects of marriage on labour force participation of females (marriage decreases the probability of female labour force participation by 7.8% in rural areas, more than twice urban areas); negative impacts on female labour force participation associated with parents in law in rural areas; availability of, and access to, banking services increases the probability of female labour force participation; improved infrastructure is important for female participation, including through time savings, as females engage in obtaining energy sources for cooking; The National Rural Employment Guarantee has had a positive impact on female labour force activity; and some labour regulations which restrict female working hours, for example, constrain participation.

One study points to increases in education levels in rural India among females leading to decline in labour force participation because of greater perceived returns to home-based work compared to market work (Afridi et al. 2018).

Others however are more inclined to the view that declines in female labour force participation (between 2005 and 2012) have been because there has been a scarcity of suitable jobs for women. In a traditional society, women's work is more acceptable if it takes place in locations regarded as safe and secure, providing flexibility to simultaneously perform household duties and chores which agriculture fits, and in a protected area (Chatterjee et al. 2015). However, the number of farm jobs has dropped off dramatically, with no real replacement jobs, associated with mechanisation, among other things (McKinsey and Company 2018; Das 2019; Jagannathan 2018). The demise in agricultural jobs has disproportionately disadvantaged women, while growth in industry and service jobs have been nabbed by men (90% and 80% of these jobs respectively). The industries that have generated jobs on mass for females

---

[3] Chatterjee et al. (2018) find also that other family income explains only part of the U shaped curve with lack of employment opportunities explaining the rest.

in other emerging economies such as clothing and footwear, associated with labour market rigidities, are not present (The Economist 2018b). Lahoti and Swaminathan (undated) contend that women have not possessed the skills for many service sector jobs.

Others similarly contend that between 2005 and 2012, farm jobs collapsed in villages, and even more particularly the scarcity of suitable jobs for women has become particularly marked in the expanding areas that are considered to be neither truly rural nor fully urban, with no real replacement (Chatterjee et al. 2017). A recent McKinsey study commented on the constraints for female employment in urban areas, due to childcare costs, less flexible and more regulated type of work. One can see growth in construction jobs in urban areas not being particularly conducive to female engagement (McKinsey and Company 2018).

In a similar vein the stagnation in urban labour force participation has been associated with job opportunities for females confined to a few traditional 'female sectors' (e.g. garments, software/call centres). Widening the sphere of industries in which Indian females can seek employment to overcome the current narrow segments is key (McKinsey and Company 2018).

A focus of work has also been inequality *within* the female labour market (Ara 2015). In the context of declining overall female work participation in urban areas, the share of the most educated, high caste and richest, as well as other minorities, has risen. Job losses have been most pronounced for the unskilled, illiterate, poorest and lowest castes. In terms of the structure of employment, female employment in the regular/salaried sector has increased (but declined for self-employed and casuals), even so, females are concentrated in lower paying, stereotypical jobs. There are significant inequalities within the salaried employment classifications, with those in the richer classes occupying the more formal sector jobs which are more stable, secure and offer social security benefits. More generally, women in the poorest segments of society are locked into the most vulnerable types of jobs.

5.2.4 *Entrepreneurship and Industrial Sphere*

The Global Entrepreneurship Monitor produces comprehensive data for more than 100 countries including gender breakdown of key statistics. Chapter 4 provided some insight into female entrepreneurship in the context of a series of 'missings'. This section reiterates those contentions. According to the 2017–2018 Global Entrepreneurship Monitor (Global Entrepreneurship Monitor Consortium 2018), females in India are under-represented in early stage entrepreneurial activity compared to men, are more likely to pursue 'necessity' entrepreneurship (i.e. undertaking entrepreneurship because job paying employment prospects are dim) and less likely to pursue opportunity-based entrepreneurship than males (more long term aspirational, career-oriented growth type entrepreneurship). Other key factors found in the 2016–2017 Women's Entrepreneurship Report (Kelley et al. 2017) are that females are less likely to have entrepreneurial intentions; are less inclined to discontinue than males (and when it does happen it is more because of lack of profitability); less inclined to hire staff and to be innovative, However, females are more likely to be exported oriented than males, owing to being active in sectors which are more female specialised and aligned with the nation's comparative advantage, e.g. garments, and interestingly, are less likely to be deterred by fear of failure. However, on key criteria of knowing an entrepreneur, spotting and capitalising on opportunities, and investing in business, females are less well placed than males. The strength of familial and friend ties in supporting and financing business is more pronounced for females, re-iterating the crucial nexus of 'inner circle' support for females rather than institutional support.

Other studies of entrepreneurship contend that differences in female and males productivity are more explained by differences in access to productive resources, and inputs (where these are a function of business size and type of sector) rather than being gender innate (World Bank 2012).

According to the Global Female Entrepreneurship Index prepared by the Global Entrepreneurship Development Institute (Terjesen and Lloyd 2015), drawing on individual and institutional variables, reasonable strength areas for Indian females are in the following: capacity for, motivation and action in identifying opportunities; increasing income; freedom to operate; new product development, technology usage (potentially at odds with other studies around mobile internet usage to be discussed later); and market monopoly niches. Constraints are observed in the extent of female entrepreneurship vis-à-vis males, in access to finance, knowing other entrepreneurs and associated networks, reinforcing the findings of the Global Entrepreneurship Monitor.

Kumbhar (2013) points to a number of attitudinal and societal barriers to rural female entrepreneurship in India, including neglect by financial institutions, absence of financial freedom, family priorities, self-confidence and esteem barriers, mobility constraints, and lack of professional education.

Another study on the determinants of entrepreneurship (Daymard 2015) found that for entrepreneurs with workers, education and labour force participation are the strongest drivers of entrepreneurship. A ten percent increase in the average years of education enhanced the number of female entrepreneurs with workers by close to 20%. However, education is not significant for entrepreneurs without workers. This could be linked with the nature and type of businesses, e.g. businesses with no employees could be in informal, own account, home-based ventures. There are clear benefits of education, including enhanced confidence, ability, risk taking (educated entrepreneurs can take more risks and hire workers because education improves prospects of obtaining jobs if business ventures are not successful), and reductions in social stereotyping. Interestingly, access to bank credit and income per capita, were neutral in respect of female entrepreneurship, in terms of neither facilitating nor being barriers to any type of entrepreneurship. However, it should be noted that the study focussed on formal rather than informal types of credit, and did not have the benefit of using microdata. Further, female entrepreneurs with workers, have tended to have less dependent children than those without workers, allowing more time to devote to business among other things, while female political representation at

5.2 Literature Review

the State level bears no relationship overall to female entrepreneurship. An increase in population density is associated with greater female entrepreneurship with and without workers due to market size and scale effects, however it is not necessarily a strong relationship: a 10% increase in population density is associated with increases in the rate of female entrepreneurship with workers by 3%.

5.2.5 Value Chains

Other work (Ghani et al. 2013a, b) points to the relationship between gender entrepreneurship and value chains in unorganised/informal manufacturing in India, in the tradition of agglomeration economies. A key finding is that female-owned input businesses play an important role in creating other female-owned enterprises (and that male businesses play a similar role for male counterparts), but male owned input businesses do not have an impact on female businesses and vice-a-versa. Similar effects are, but to a lesser extent, found for the labour market as per input businesses. However, for final output businesses there is only a weak positive connection between local female (and male-owned) owned businesses and further female business development, but the effect of both on male business development is stronger. The upshot of this is the importance of stimulating female input businesses as a basis for further female business development, in the manner of gender cluster policies.

5.2.6 Health

While gains have been made in some health domains, including maternal mortality rates, eradication of certain diseases, family planning initiatives and infrastructure improvements (e.g. Clean India) which positively affects health), the parlous nature of health and health care, including especially for females, is known. Another 'battleground' is opening up significantly around mental health. A recent comprehensive study by the National Institute of Mental Health and Neuro Sciences (NIMHANS) (2016) encompassing 12 States, found that while 'any' mental morbidity, either currently or lifetime, was more pronounced for males compared to females (especially current substance use disorder, current alcohol use disorder, prevalence of schizophrenia and other psychotic disorders) mood disorders (current and lifetime), depression, neurotic and stress disorders, anxiety (current) and suicidal risk over the last month, in both the moderate and high risk categories, were higher for females. Thus, while females and males are both affected by mental illness, in some categories, it is more clearly more the case for females. The NIMHANS work points generally to large economic impacts of such conditions, in both urban and rural contexts, and that low levels of education and work status are key factors which disproportionately affect women.

The report calls for a comprehensive approach to better integrate physical and mental health, stronger capability in addressing mental health, greater use of technology, providing reskilling and employment opportunities for those employed, and better planning of the health system as a whole.

Recent work (Roy et al. 2016) has focussed on the social–emotional health of adolescent girls and young women in Jharkhand in Northern India in terms of the impact on education and employment aspirations. This work examined self-efficacy (self-belief in the ability to cope with difficult demands and achieve objectives) depression/mental health (patients were questioned on how often people are bothered by certain problems over the last two weeks) and hope (questions about expecting good things to happen and being excited about the future). It found that self-efficacy and mental health are key determinants of aspiration among adolescent girls in education and employment. Key correlates of self-efficacy in turn included age, previous training, and an enabling environment, such as whether girls have family/social support, feel connected to, and have empowered parents, and other successful role models to look up to. The implication of this work is that policy intervention could be targeted at socio-emotional capital, as a basis for stimulating education and labour market participation.

5.2.7 Knowledge Economy

There are a number of studies in what we might loosely call in the knowledge economy sphere.

A detailed study (Amin and Islam 2015) of females in management in developing countries, relevant to India, found that the likelihood of female top manager is strongly and positively related to education enrolments in primary, secondary and tertiary levels relative to men, and that the likelihood of female managers is higher for smaller firms, for firms that have one or more female owner, in firms with more women than men among staff, and among younger firms. Older, larger firms are less predisposed to hiring female managers. However, macro factors such as overall economic development, culture, and women's presence in parliament were only weakly associated with top female managers, highlighting the importance of micro factors specific to firm type and their characteristics. The study (Amin and Islam 2015) draws attention to broader assessments in the literature, including the Similarity-Attraction Theory or the Attraction-Selection-Attrition theory which centres on attraction and retention of senior personnel. Male-dominated settings reinforce male domination in enterprises.

Further, informal mentorship, which may be male-dominated, leads to greater male progression, and women find access to networks difficult, due to various organisational, interpersonal and other barriers, including information deficiencies, and stereotypical views.

Recent work by McKinsey and Company (2018) points to considerable bottlenecks in the career pipeline in a number of countries, including India, in which there are diminishing shares of women as the pipeline advances from tertiary graduates to entry level professionals, to senior management and then Board positions. Compared to a number of countries, India's starting base is lower in terms of the female share of tertiary graduates and senior ranks in the workplace, with the exception of Board members, where there are mandated rules about female participation. India is among the countries with the sharpest fall off between college graduates and entry level employment. A range of barriers generally are put forward (across Asia Pacific economies), also pertinent to India, including: the requirement to work anywhere, anytime; balancing work and domestic responsibilities; absence of female role models; lack of female friendly policies; and a range of other constraints such as less effort and aspiration by women in career promotion activities (McKinsey and Company 2018).

Even more fundamentally, in India, is a prevailing view that university is more important for males and that female engagement in the labour force is at the expense of childrens' welfare. This finding was much more pronounced in India than in other Asia Pacific Economies, including less developed ones than India (McKinsey and Company 2018). Research showed that 84% of Indians agreed that when jobs are scarce, men should have more right to a job than women, and more than 40% of young Indians believe that it is preferable for women not to work (The Economist 2018a, b).

The World Bank (2012) also indicates that males have larger job ladders (promotion pathways that connect lower and higher level positions) and rungs, while female jobs are closer together so promotion yields less advancement for women than males. The World Bank also points to weaker business networks among females compared to males, and issues around lack of confidence in the workplace reinforced by social norms.

5.2.7.1 Researcher Performance and Opportunity

Analysis of publications in Life Sciences in India by gender, found that there were significant gaps for females relative to males in number of researchers, levels of publication outputs, impact of research (citations), and in international collaboration (but females were more represented in domestic collaboration), and in international journals, and that females were more likely to publish in lower impact factor journals (Garg and Kumar 2014). In another study, male patenting performance considerably outweighed female patenting, across a number of countries not just India (Martinez et al. 2016).

Recent work by the Economist Intelligence Unit (The Economist Intelligence Unit 2015) on female researchers in South Asia (Afghanistan, Bangladesh, India, Nepal, Pakistan and Sri Lanka), found that only 20% of authors were female, the percentage of women in research and science and engineering roles was just 15%, and that females were under-represented in senior positions in academia. Women's participation dropped off considerably after the undergraduate level. Male-dominated boards and professional networks, privileged positions in research funding, compounded by lack of transparency around promotions, mobility constraints for women, gender insensitive organisational practices (and harassment), and lack of enthusiasm among women to pursue a research career (linked to reasons advanced above), family reasons, and the absence of awareness of the links between publishing and visibility, important for advancement, were all constraining factors for females.

The Association of Academies and Societies of Sciences in Asia (AASSA 2015) drew attention to the mismatch between those with Ph.D's and in faculty positions, with a further drop off at more senior levels in academia, academies and in Government laboratories, as well as mismatches between studying science and undertaking scientific research as a career. Further, the share of women faculty and students in science and engineering in India diminished with the perceived high status of institutions. The study also finds that the proportion of women scientists who have never married is higher than for males, and that for women scientists being married to male scientists is more than double the reverse case. These findings, in our view, got to the heart of the lack of identity and independence for females, and that to forge a career implies either not being in committed relationships or marrying within the profession, a barrier not encountered by men. The study did also however draw attention to a variety of reforms, including scholarships for women researchers, internships, grants, establishment of the Indian Association for Women, mentorship programmes, a biotechnology park for women, and encouragement for women to return to work through 'stop the clock' facilities when on maternity leave, and transfers of both spouses if engaged in the same service.

There are also significant cultural and attitudinal barriers. Some 59% of women in STEM roles observed a 'testosterone laced culture' compared to 25% in the U.S, and 57% indicated a 'late-night geek culture', compared to 31% in the U.S (McKinsey and Company 2018).

Other work looks at empowerment in more technology intensive settings. Analysis of a program which connected communities with recruiters for higher value telephone work found that these communities were more likely to have lower expectations of dowry, and that it was more reasonable for women to live alone prior to marriage, and to work before and after marriage and childbirth (World Bank 2012). Recruitment services that provided information and advice to families about job prospects for women increased the chances of girls aged 5–15 to be in school by 3–5% points but had no effect on boys. Further, 10% of women are more likely to be involved in wage work as a result of this recruitment service activity. There are further beneficial health impacts for girls (World Bank 2012).

Access to, and ability to use ICT, is increasingly vital for conducting business, obtaining access to job information, developing and maintaining business and social networks, for awareness raising, including of rights, mentoring and other forms of support, and for advocacy. On this score, according to various measures, India is lagging. We are using considerable part of this data for the Gender Footprint to follow.

An authoritative study (Rowntree GSMA 2018), found considerable gaps among Indian females relative to males in mobile phone ownership, services used by mobile owners and mobile internet usage. These gaps are exacerbated in rural areas. Among a range of barriers to mobile ownership and use of Internet, which are more prevalent for women, are cost, handsets not being in a preferred language, reading and writing difficulties, safety and security concerns, not knowing how to use a mobile phone, and having no access to an internet enabled phone. It should be noted that a number of these constraints also pertain to men in India to a lesser extent (except for access to Internet-enabled phone), and for the most part, Indian women face gaps relative to other international counterparts. Critical are some attitudinal and perception issues, more pronounced for females, such as the 'internet is not relevant', 'lack of family approval' and the 'lack of awareness of the mobile internet' (Rowntree GSMA 2018).

An earlier study (Intel and Dalberg 2013) also pointed to Indian females (one in five) believing that the 'internet is not for them', and identified issues around lack of interest, disapproval by family, including possibility of 'viewing things inappropriate', lack of access, including safety concerns regarding visits to cyber cafes, and fear of 'something going wrong' if handling computers, often a view that is perpetrated by family members. A range of other data confirms the attitudinal and other constraints (McKinsey and Company 2018): 49% of women did not see the value of the internet; 60% of men indicated that they are to have priority over women in accessing the internet; fines have been imposed on girls using a mobile outside the home in a rural part of India; 79% of women indicated that society would judge them negatively for using the internet, more than 30% higher than for the average in Asia Pacific, while some 19% indicated that they would use the internet more if they were not subjected to surveillance and criticism. To be fair, there are a range of initiatives that are underway including 'bicycle based' outreach teaching services, various activities by Self-Help Groups, online talent platforms and international NGO activity (McKinsey and Company 2018).

5.2.8 *Financial Inclusion Studies*

Financial inclusion is another important domain for empowerment, providing the wherewithal to engage in the economy, promote independence from male exploitation, and to instil confidence and self-esteem. According to the World Bank Financial Inclusion Index (Demirgüç-Kunt et al. 2017), although there has been an improvement in females having bank accounts, women struggled to raise money in emergencies compared to men, were less likely to use mobile money accounts, and more inclined to rely on family and friends and savings clubs for money. This suggests that there is a lack of institutional support in this domain.

The Indian Government has made significant progress on financial inclusion through the Pradhan Mantri Jan Dhan Yojana (PMJDY) instituted in 2014, a comprehensive plan to provide bank services to all households, including through technology-enabled means, and also the provision of add on services such as overdraft facilities, debit card and insurance cover (Singh and Naik 2018).

In a survey/case study in Karnataka state, encompassing both farmers and non-farmers through a gender lens, Singh, Naik find that a higher percentage of females opened general accounts and specific PMJDY accounts than males, among farmers and non-farmers. Females though prefer to open PMJDY accounts using financial intermediaries compared to males, rather than to directly open accounts. This is associated with distance barriers facing females. Further, using accounts was a constraint for females compared to males, for both farmers and non-farmers. Lack of formal education is not a constraint for female farmers to open accounts, but for non-farming females, results were mixed. It should be noted that female awareness, of and assistance from, government established customer service centres (advisory and assistance kiosk style centres) is encouraging. In addition, for females, visits to the home by banks and SHG's to assist with financial literacy is important (Singh and Naik 2018). Encouragingly, there has been some shift in terms of awareness and access, but many barriers remain.

Apart from PMJDY other important initiatives have been put in place, including more micro entrepreneurship loans through the Pradhan Mantri Mudra Yojana, of which 47.5% has gone to female entrepreneurs, and various other measures prevail, for example, having females designated as heads of households for financial accounts (McKinsey and Company 2018). However, old habits die hard as only 18% of these women went to the bank without being accompanied by males, and 86% of households indicated male dominance in financial decision making (McKinsey and Company 2018). The World Bank similarly found that 20% of participants in a study indicated that husbands have total control over wives' earnings (World Bank 2012).

A study examines the impact of microcredit on women's empowerment, as reflected in the value of work time, drawing on field work in rural Andhra Pradesh (Garikipati 2012). The study finds that rather than access to credit per se, it is the *use* of credit that is vital to women's empowerment. Access to credit alone will not particularly improve the value of women's work time: this is because women's loans are mainly used to improve households productive assets which are typically controlled by men, thus allowing men to spend more time in self-employment, and less in wage work. When women however, use loans to develop and improve businesses that they operate, thus enhancing their ownership of productive assets, then they are seen to be spending considerably more time in self-employment (Garikipati 2012). Thus, policies could be targeted towards not just access to microcredit but use and control of assets.

There is limited work overall, it has to be said, relating to Indian females and the Knowledge Economy. Much of the literature focuses on the broader parameters concerning empowerment, and we have included key aspects to illuminate the complex and multifaceted interplay of factors impinging on empowerment and the more general disadvantage facing females. These boil down to lack of facilitatory networks and institutional supports, extreme disadvantage in the labour market, economic structural change militating against females, and a variety of deep-seated social mores, conventions and attitudinal barriers.

5.3 Gender Knowledge Footprint

This section focuses on developing a Gender Knowledge Footprint, to examine the extent of female participation in the knowledge economy. It is constructed in the light of the literature review just undertaken, and attempts to fill a void in the knowledge economy space through an empirical lens.

As with the overall Knowledge Footprint in Chap. 4, this footprint measures the extent and magnitude of knowledge creation and development, diffusion and opportunity.

The categories are the same as the Overall Knowledge Footprint, focussing on the many dimensions of the knowledge system, incorporating: Knowledge Access and Opportunity; Knowledge Support and Platforms; Knowledge Capabilities; Knowledge Resourcing; Knowledge Relationships; and Knowledge Translation and Transformation.

In the gender footprint, however, we do not make a distinction between domestic and global footprint unlike the knowledge footprints of Chap. 4. This is because opportunities and capacities tend to be focussed and considered in more local contexts, encompassing tradition, cultural, religious and political specificities. However, it is the case that where appropriate and in some areas, international data is used to demonstrate the engagement of gender internationally. From a practical viewpoint, there are also many data limitations with a more widespread use of such metrics. In some cases, the metrics used in the Gender Knowledge Footprint and their placement among sub-pillars may be different from the placement of these metrics in the sub-pillars in the overall Knowledge Footprint of Chap. 4. Moreover, weights attached to the sub-pillars differ from those attached to the overall Footprint of Chap. 4.

5.3.1 Three Variations on the Footprint

We present three variations of the Gender Knowledge Footprint. The first relates to comparisons between females and males in India, across the various pillars described above. The second is a comparison of males and females in each of the BRIC nations. The third compares females with females, and males with males, for BRIC nations, i.e. females in India compared to females in Brazil, China and Russia, and likewise for males. These various dimensions provide a complete picture of the relative performance of Indian females. It was not considered appropriate to use the 15 countries that were used in the previous chapter due to data limitations, and the vastly differing levels of economic and social development. The data elements described below pertain to the comparison of males and females in India. They are modified, to reflect comparative BRIC data in the other two footprint cases.

There is significant overlap between the metrics used in the gender and overall footprints of Chap. 4, however noting that there are significant differences as well. For example, metrics such as investment are not included.

Some features of the labour market such as vulnerable employment are included, as are literacy rates. In addition, we introduce a particular spatial dimension within India, for available metrics, broken down into urban and regional components, where available. We also identify the 'best' and 'worst' individual states of India for males and females to obtain comparisons and insights as to the distribution of performance spatially. The best and worse State for males and females allows us to see to what extent the best performing state for males differs from the best performing state for females and similarly for the weakest states.

5.3.1.1 Gender Knowledge Footprint Sub-pillars

This section examines the various metrics in the knowledge footprint parameters. It describes the rationale for selection and the range and extent of metrics.

5.3.1.2 Knowledge Access and Opportunity Sub-pillar

Knowledge Access and Opportunity comprises enrolment patterns in lower and upper secondary education, and tertiary enrolment, and in knowledge intensive arenas, which basically align with STEM fields. This pillar also includes labour force participation, unemployment and underemployment, vulnerable employment, and access to social security provision (in India). This provides a rounded view regarding access to, opportunity and participation in education and the labour market. Labour force dimensions represent the extent to which the respective genders participate in the economy, including the knowledge economy, and its process of ideas generation and exploitation. An innovation and ideas economy, for example, must have as one its core aims the creation of high value, sustainable jobs.

5.3.1.3 Knowledge Supports and Platforms Sub-pillar

Knowledge Supports and Platforms owe much to the inherent institutional features and enablers of activity in an economy. As such, we include core factors such as life expectancy, health indicators, time spent in unpaid and paid work, access to financial markets and land titles, and political representation by gender, as well as attitudes to freedom of choice and safety perceptions. By intent, the metrics in the gender footprint are more strongly oriented towards social factors compared to the Overall Footprint of Chap. 4. In addition, we draw on extensive data on relative awareness, access and usage of ICT across gender through various surveys and research in the public domain. The divide between 'haves and have not's' in the digital age, is, in our view, a key determinant of the extent of gender participation and the development and diffusion of new ideas. In short, Knowledge Supports and Platforms are the critical foundational elements which allow for gender participation in the process and outcomes of knowledge.

5.3.1.4 Knowledge Capability Development Sub-pillar

Knowledge Capability refers to the strength of core capabilities, differentiated by gender, canvassing graduation rates, graduates from STEM, researchers and publications and entrepreneurial capability (e.g. ability to spot opportunities), seniority in academia and in government agencies, by gender. The premises of this sub-pillar are the underlying core strengths in the knowledge economy that would shape, for example, downstream commercial activities by enterprise, the strength of the education system in churning out graduates who would work in the knowledge intensive sector and, research capability to develop new and improved products and services and technology, and address societal challenges.

5.3.1.5 Knowledge Resourcing Sub-pillar

Knowledge resourcing refers to the relative financial resources that either gender is afforded in the development and deployment of knowledge. While more difficult to obtain precise data on this, the author draws on gender GNI per capita produced by the United Nations, gender Gross National Income (GNI), and GNI (and Government expenditure) per male and female student in lower secondary, upper secondary and tertiary levels, as well as gender-based estimates of the amount of financial resources available to researchers. In the sense that we use it, GNI is measured not only as the total productive output and wealth of an economy but also the resources that can be deployed to fund key knowledge intensive activities. Thus, the gender breakdown represents the 'claim' on the nation's resources by both genders. As with the overall footprint, immigration is included here as a non-financial metric pertaining to augmentation of human capital resources.

5.3.1.6 Knowledge Relationships Sub-pillar

Knowledge Relationships are about the extent of collaborative activity and relationships that are gender related. These include the capacity to access and be connected to ideas and know-how. Data is drawn from a variety of sources. The metrics here include knowing entrepreneurs, female and male respective investments in business, collaborative research papers by females and males, and inbound and outbound tertiary mobility by gender, with a focus on postgraduate students as more sophisticated bastions of knowledge, and the emigration of the highly educated. The latter two are justified on the basis of the important transfers of ideas and know-how and synergies in knowledge discovery and deployment that can reside with international students and highly educated migrants. We also include the relative performance of Indian born males and females in the U.S in terms of employment in knowledge intensive occupations, and as owners of businesses by number and value. The U.S is used as it represents a very significant and influential diaspora for Indians, which has shaped Indian economic development in many ways through technology, research, commercial connections and investment and trade. The respective contributions of gender in the U.S are proxies for the potential influence of the diaspora back home, in a number of domains including culture, commerce and academia.

5.3.1.7 Knowledge Translation and Transformation Sub-pillar

Knowledge Translation and Transformation represent the more 'downstream' dimensions of the knowledge chain in the sense of being closer to commercial application, job and wealth creation and directly and explicitly addressing societal challenges and objectives. Included here are gender-based data on patents, impact factors of papers, employment in **knowledge intensive occupations and industries**, entrepreneurial activity, exporting, wage levels and purchasing power by gender, and the extent of wage and salary earners by gender as distinct from casual, more informal[4] work, recognising that wage and salary earning is the more stable and secure employment, likely associated with the knowledge economy. Wage and Salary earners are also broken down into urban and rural segments to obtain a sense of any spatial gender bias to higher paying, more value-added jobs.

5.4 Scores and Discussion for India: Males Versus Females

Individual metrics are scaled to 100 for females and males as comparators (with best gender given a score of 100 and the other gender adjusted accordingly), aggregated and divided by number of metrics to provide sub-pillar scores. These sub-pillars are then weighted and aggregated to develop an overall Gender Knowledge Footprint Score. The weights are: Knowledge Opportunity and Access 20%; Knowledge Supports and Plathorms 18%; Knowledge Capability Development 18%; Knowledge Resourcing 15%; Knowledge Relationships 12%; Knowledge Translation and Transformation 17%. The weights are different to those in the Footprint Analysis of Chap. 4.

The scores are provided for the pillars as follows[5]: (Table 5.1)

---

[4]While labour market participation, unemployment and underemployment could also reside in knowledge translation and transformation, we argue that these indicators are more representative of female opportunity in the sense of having some connection to the labour market, as an important foothold or precursor to **high value jobs** which are represented in knowledge translation and transformation.

[5]Scores are derived by the following: For each metric in the sub-pillar, a best performing gender is given a score of 100, and the other gender is given a score relative to this. Scores for each metric are added up for each gender and divided by the number of metrics to obtain a sub-pillar score. To obtain an overall gender footprint score weights are attached to the relevant sub-pillar: opportunity and access pillar is worth 20%, Knowledge Capability 18%, Knowledge Translation and Technology 17%, Knowledge Support and platforms 18%, Knowledge Relationships 12%, Knowledge Resourcing 15%.

5.4 Scores and Discussion for India: Males Versus Females

Table 5.1 Gender Knowledge Footprint One: Males and Females India

	Males	Females	Difference male and female
Knowledge Access and Opportunity	95.0	71.9	23.1
Knowledge Supports and Platforms	97.9	67.7	30.2
Knowledge Capability Development	97.7	55.1	42.6
Knowledge Resourcing	97.1	63.8	33.3
Knowledge Relationships	93.3	61.6	37.7
Knowledge Translation and Transformation	86.5	77.6	8.9
Overall Gender Knowledge Footprint	94.7	66.7	27.8

The higher the score the better the gender performance on that pillar, with the optimal being 100. The purpose of this exercise is to give broad orders of magnitude of difference rather than precise outcomes.

Some key observations can be made. Firstly, that in all sub-pillars of the footprint, and the Overall Gender Knowledge Footprint, males in India considerably exceed females by score. *Overall, it can be surmised that Indian females approximately have two thirds the engagement of males in the knowledge economy of India (scores of 66.7 and 94.7 in the Overall Gender Knowledge Footprint respectively).*

The largest gaps can be found in the Knowledge Capability Development, Knowledge Relationships and Knowledge Resourcing.

Applying a spatial lens (Fig. 5.1) shows that Indian males have access to, and participate in knowledge in all its dimensions, nearly across the entire country and considerably more so than for females.

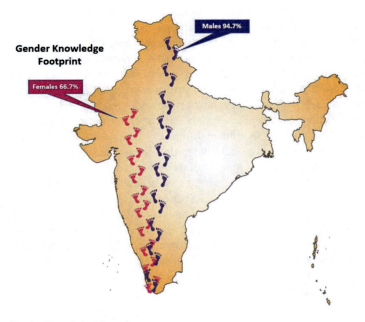

Fig. 5.1 Gender Knowledge footprint

5.4.1 Detailed Discussion

India females perform less well on Knowledge Capability Development, which goes to the heart of the numbers of researchers and scholars across all segments of research (government laboratories, higher education and business), graduates in STEM-related fields, and seniority in academia among other things. Due to various types of 'glass ceilings', Indian females are not as well represented as males in the higher echelons of academia, nor in academies and government agencies. Moreover, as a nation, Indian females have far less population with at least some secondary education compared to males, which in turn is linked to Knowledge Access and Opportunity.

Entrepreneurial capability, as a core or knowledge capability provides some interesting insights. As displayed through the Global Entrepreneurship Monitor data, Indian females perform less strongly than males in spotting of opportunity and perceptions of capabilities, but perform better in not being hamstrung by fear of failure. Thus, Indian females are bold, confident and not scared of risk when provided with the opportunity. However, Indian females perform much weaker on preference for self-employment and entrepreneurial intentions, which may point to constraints operating at the societal level.

Indian females are *under-resourced* in the knowledge economy sphere when compared to males, as represented by the various gender dimensions of GNI. This in turn could be a key driver of the relative weakness in gender capability metrics.

On Knowledge Relationships, again Indian female performance lags relative to males. Thus, the deep, dense 'old boys' networks, which drive finance, business and sharing of ideas, important for a knowledge economy, appear to be not as accessible for females nor are there necessarily strong female centric networks. This bears out the literature that we considered in the previous section. In addition, the influencing role of Indian males in the U.S in terms of number and value of firms is relatively higher than for females. We would suggest that this means the capacity of the male diaspora to shape economic and other activity in India is higher than for females.

We also draw attention to the weaker performance of females in India on Knowledge Supports and Platforms. Indian females are under-represented in key institutions such as in parliament, boards of enterprises, land titles and have less access to finance. In particular, there are very significant differences in access to ICT, in terms of ownership of mobile phone (particularly in regional areas), usage of internet and social media. Of concern is lack of awareness of these new technologies, thus exacerbating the digital divide in India. It is the case, however, that for health indicators such as life expectancy, that Indian females have better outcomes.

The smallest gap between males and females is in Knowledge Translation and Transformation. Indian females can, and do, succeed in key activities such as entrepreneurial activity and relative employment in knowledge intensive sectors, and to a slightly lesser extent in skill intensive occupations. *It suggests that the bigger concerns are upstream in terms of providing the opportunity, support and wherewithal to succeed in the knowledge economy.*

5.4.2 More Detailed Score Breakdowns

Table 5.2 highlights the magnitudes of the differences in sub-pillar scores for India. We use the data in an illustrative sense here rather than exhaustive, to capture the main indicators. The following table is divided into three components: where the score difference between females and males is less than 10 points in favour of males or where females score higher—this we describe as 'broad parity' and where females obtain higher score this is noted in the text; where scores for males is higher by 11–25 points we describe as 'warranting attention'; and where males score more than 26 points higher than females is described as 'urgent imperative'.

Table 5.2 Gender Knowledge Footprint Score Breakdowns: India

	1–10 difference in score in favour of males (or where females lead): broad parity	11–25 difference in favour of males (warranting attention)	26 and above in favour of males: urgent imperative
Knowledge Access and Opportunity	Enrolment share by gender in lower secondary and higher overall enrolment share for females in ISCED 7 (Masters)	Enrolment share by gender in upper secondary and tertiary (ISCED 6), enrolment in knowledge intensive spheres, security of employment and underemployment	Labour force participation, including spatial breakdown, unemployment, Ph.D. enrolments
Knowledge Supports and Platforms	Life expectancy (in favour of females), having financial accounts, disability adjusted life years (in favour of females), freedom of choice	Access to emergency funds, mobile phone ownership	Land titles, unpaid work, female share of boards and parliamentary seats, borrowing to start or expand a firm, making and receiving digital payments, having a mobile money account, social media usage, mobile phone ownership, mobile internet usage and awareness of mobile internet

(continued)

Table 5.2 (continued)

	1–10 difference in score in favour of males (or where females lead): broad parity	11–25 difference in favour of males (warranting attention)	26 and above in favour of males: urgent imperative
Knowledge Capability Development	Share of graduates by gender in ISCED 6 and ISCED 7 (ahead for females in both) Undeterred by fear of failure (females ahead)	Share of graduates in knowledge intensive arenas by gender (STEM) and in Ph.D. graduates, opportunity perception for females in entrepreneurship, preference for self-employment	Researchers, academics in senior roles, entrepreneurial intentions, capability perceptions, research output, population with at least some secondary education, Scientists in Academies and Government Research Agencies
Knowledge Resourcing	Share of government expenditure on lower secondary	Share of government expenditure in tertiary and upper secondary	GNI per capita and GNI levels, GNI per student in lower, upper secondary and tertiary levels
Knowledge Relationships	Emigration rates of the highly educated (in favour of females)	Shares of inbound international students in knowledge intensive arenas (as a share of female and male international students respectively)	Knowing entrepreneurs, collaborative research papers, investments in business by family, receiving and sending domestic remittances, contribution of diaspora to U.S economy, overall inbound international student mobility
Knowledge Translation and Transformation	Medium skill occupations (% female, % male), entrepreneurial exports (in favour of females, % female, % male), knowledge industry employment in favour of females (% of female employment compared to % of male employment)	Early stage entrepreneurial activity (% male, % female), wage and salary earners (% of males, % of females), high skill occupations (% male, % female)	Inventors (patents), established business activity, opportunity entrepreneurship, employment to population ratio, non-teaching senior roles, gender purchasing power and income, job creation of entrepreneurship

5.4 Scores and Discussion for India: Males Versus Females

As can be seen in Table 5.2, males dominate by individual metrics in India. Some key factors stand out:

- The strong bias in favour of males in labour market outcomes, many of which are in the urgent imperative category, including labour force participation, employment rates and unemployment levels.
- The severe weaknesses in female outcomes in areas critical to the knowledge economy in researchers, senior academics, research outputs and patents, and the need to improve performance in knowledge intensive enrolment and graduates, noting especially the weaker performance in Ph.D. for females but relatively better performance in undergraduate and Master's level. This suggests a 'degree based glass ceiling' whereby females are constrained or discouraged from pursuing the highest levels of education.
- The need to lift urgently overall wealth, opportunity and resourcing for females as measured by GNI (and associated parameters) for females.
- The particularly weak performance in a number of the different support domains, including ICT usage and access, various financial parameters such as borrowing to start a business, and to a lesser extent access to emergency funding.
- Weaker performance requiring attention in entrepreneurship parameters, if not at urgent levels.
- There are some areas of promise where the gap between males and females is not as significant (broad parity) or where females are ahead, including export performance, enrolments in undergraduate and Masters degrees, some health outcomes and the growing ownership of financial accounts by females. It should also be noted that in some cases where females are ahead, this is relative to the female population, e.g. enrolment data, rather than in total numbers per se.

5.4.3 Gender Knowledge Footprint in BRIC Countries

This section compares India to the other BRIC countries, as comparators with broadly similar aspirations, trading and investment potential, and to a certain extent economic size and level of development. Two types of analysis are considered here as mentioned previously: the first is footprint comparing females with males in each of the BRIC countries; and the second is to compare the relative footprint size by gender across BRIC nations, e.g. female footprint in India compared to female footprint in other countries and male versus male across BRIC countries.

While the analysis comparing Indian females to males is somewhat replicated here, the results are different. This is because the number of variables is considerably reduced when undertaking the BRIC analysis (compared to just India), due to lack of comparative inter-country data. For example, spatial distribution of access in education by gender is not available at the BRIC level, although it is in the India specific case.

5.4.4 Results: Males Versus Females for BRIC Nations

The key points to note when considering males versus females for BRIC nations (Table 5.3) are that:

- In each of the BRIC countries, the overall male footprint is higher than for females suggesting that gender disadvantage is pervasive across all the BRIC countries.
- However, the disadvantage for females is particularly accentuated in India which has the largest overall gap between males and females in score, in fact double the gap compared to other BRIC nations. Russia has the smallest gap reflecting in part its higher level of economic development.
- When disaggregating by sub-pillar we find that with the exception of Knowledge Access and Opportunity in Russia, males lead females in all the sub-pillars of the knowledge footprint: this suggests that the nature of female disadvantage is broad-based across all parameters, rather than being confined to particular aspects or sub-pillar segments.
- Once again, in each of the pillars, the gap between females and males is sharpest in India although Brazil does have considerable inequity in a variety of pillars.
- The biggest gaps in India are in Relationships, Support Systems and Resourcing but interestingly not in Capability unlike the 'pure Indian case' outlined earlier: This is because that footprint analysis had data on researchers, seniority in academia, gender publications, and female participation in national academies, in which the

Table 5.3 Gender Knowledge Footprint for BRIC Nations: Comparing male to female in individual BRIC countries

	India		Brazil		China		Russia	
	Female	Male	Female	Male	Female	Male	Female	Male
Knowledge Access and Opportunity	76.7	91.9	84	86.1	84.4	86.95	87.9	87.6
Knowledge Supports and Platforms	70.6	95.4	75.7	91.7	84	95.5	84.95	91.3
Knowledge Capability Development	83.3	95.2	86.95	90.9	86.3	93.5	81.3	88.1
Knowledge Resourcing	61.3	100	74.8	96.7	67.9	100	83.5	98.3
Knowledge Relationships	58.7	94.5	82.3	93.9	80.9	89	90.3	91.98
Knowledge Translation and Transformation	70.7	89.7	65.2	87.1	85.95	94.9	75.9	92.1
Overall BRIC Gender Knowledge Footprint	71.2	94.2	78.3	90.7	82	93.2	83.7	91.2

gap is extremely high between females and males, and which do not appear for the BRIC comparisons due to data limitations.
- Knowledge resourcing is a significant issue in Brazil and China suggesting that spending patterns, resource allocation and investment priorities, are skewed heavily in favour of males, more so than in other sub-pillars.
- Generally, the gaps between females and males is less pronounced in Russia, compared to other BRIC countries, suggesting a greater opportunity and capacity for Russian females to participate in the knowledge economy. For example, interestingly, females in Russia are more strongly represented in knowledge intensive sectors and in high skill occupations than males (as shares of female and male population respectively).
- With the exception of India, the disadvantage faced by females is smallish in the case of access and opportunity (measured by enrolments, human development index, labour force participation), for BRIC countries, yet the gap is more significant in the other more "foundational elements" such as supports and resourcing. Thus a more comprehensive approach to empowerment is required in these countries.

5.4.5 BRIC Intra-gender Comparison

Whereas the previous analysis focussed on comparing females and males on various parameters in BRIC countries, this analysis uses the same data to compare footprints within gender, i.e. females versus females and males versus males, in BRIC countries (Table 5.4).

Table 5.4 Intra-Gender Knowledge Footprint Comparisons in BRIC countries

	Females				Males			
	India	Brazil	China	Russia	India	Brazil	China	Russia
Knowledge Access and Opportunity	67.7	74.6	75.9	85.1	76.7	71.7	77.1	82.7
Knowledge Supports and Platforms	57.8	68.5	86.7	77.8	71.1	75.4	89.4	78.3
Knowledge Capability Development	72.6	81.4	76.96	56.4	77.4	80.3	79.8	61.6
Knowledge Resourcing	35.4	40.7	52.8	84.7	46.6	42.5	57.3	83.6
Knowledge Relationships	49.3	42.8	78.2	74.3	70.1	51.8	75.2	77
Knowledge Translation and Transformation	46.9	55.8	76.7	67.4	59.9	63.9	76.4	75.99
Overall BRIC Gender Knowledge Footprint	56.2	62.6	75	74.3	67.6	65.9	76.5	76.3

The following key points are observed:

- The overall Gender Knowledge Footprint for females in India is lower than for females in all other BRIC countries suggesting that the relative disadvantage for females is higher in India when compared to females in other BRIC countries. China has the highest footprint for females. Overall scores for males is higher than for females, and this is replicated in the pillars.
- For males, India's footprint is higher than Brazil but weaker than for males in other nations suggesting that disadvantage is pervasive for both genders in India compared to BRIC countries. There are therefore contextual factors that shape the performance of both females and males in India, associated with overall economic development levels, ability to fund knowledge intensive investments and general quality of institutions and human capital as possible factors.
- It should also be noted that even though Indian males perform better than females in India as shown previously, they are still less well off in knowledge economy terms with counterparts in other countries.
- For India's females, the weakest scores relative to their gender counterparts is in Knowledge Resourcing, Knowledge Translation and Transformation and Knowledge Relationships (except compared to Brazil). Indian females suffer from lack of resources, funding and investing in their knowledge economy requirements, compared to other countries, while its females are less able to participate in knowledge economy activities downstream such as patents, high skill employment, and employment outcomes more generally, and knowledge intensive entrepreneurship. Nor are Indian females as well connected into knowledge economy networks compared to other females.
- A similar pattern, but not to the same extent as above, is found for Indian males. Generally, as we have seen however, Indian males perform better than their Brazilian counterparts.
- For Indian females, the strongest score is in Knowledge Capability Development (but still weaker than females in other nations except surprisingly Russia), suggesting some core strengths in terms of knowledge economy graduates, entrepreneurial innovation, where Indian females are rated the highest, being undaunted by fear of failure. These are important traits to build on:
- With the exception of Knowledge Relationships, for Brazil, and Capability Development for Russia, there is no sub-pillar for which Indian females outperform other females in BRIC countries, and there are significant gaps in key areas, e.g. supports, compared to China. This finding is to some extent true but less apparent for males where, for example, Indian males lead their Brazilian counterparts in various pillars.

5.5 Policies

Based on our foregoing analysis, and the literature review, this section posits some recommendation for India to enhance female empowerment.

5.5.1 Gender Knowledge Footprint

We propose that a Gender Knowledge Footprint along the lines canvassed in this chapter, be made mandatory for agencies in government to measure and monitor performance against. Thus, increasing the female footprint needs to be a fundamental task for public agencies, where civil servants are assessed against improvement. Performance enhancement incentives should be granted for positive footprint improvement, and penalties for footprint shrinkage. Footprint can be assessed on a national or regional scale.

Closely aligned with this would be the implementation of 'opportunity parity' audits, initially on a voluntary basis in the private sector. These would measure the gaps in gender on the full suite of 'opportunity criteria' including (a) access to senior management and senior stakeholders, and represent responsibilities of females and males in employment (b) participation in, and access to mentoring and networks (c) access to training (d) promotional opportunities (e) pay and conditions, and savings/retirement benefits.

These opportunity parity audits could be publicised and companies are given ratings by an independent body as a basis for data-driven objective action by firms to address gender gaps. It would signal to the market place the desirability of a firm as a place to do business with, and to work in. It could also, over time, be part of reporting obligations and disclosure to corporate regulators, and be linked to any assistance and support from Government. Even in the initial voluntary stage, the implied pressure of non-participation could be an important catalyst for change.

5.5.2 Institutional Change

This section considers a range of institutional mechanisms and reforms that could be undertaken.

5.5.2.1 Female Ombudsperson

One major institutional change that we propose is the establishment of a National Female Ombudsperson Office, with counterpart chapters in states and regions. Accountable directly to the national parliament (and with chapters at lower tiers) such a mechanism would have wide-ranging powers and enforcement mechanisms. Its functions would include (a) Initiating and commissioning inquiries into the status and issues around female empowerment (b) acting as a complaint 'aggregator' to scale up and coordinate grievances to give greater voice and expression to complaints (c) seeking program linkage across agencies to promote critical mass and scale and provide consistency of action (d) driving advocacy on empowerment, including information dissemination and awareness campaigns (e) serving as a fast track referral mechanism to refer issues to specialised agencies, including the formal legal system and quasi-courts such as the Nari Adalat[6] (f) employing a cadre of individuals at local levels (and possibly even on a voluntary basis) to serve as change agents in the community, working in concert with relevant agencies (g) while working with and through agencies to capture synergies, the ombudsperson office would have 'over-ride' powers to supersede the actions of individual agencies.

5.5.2.2 Land Access

Overcoming challenges of land ownership is a hugely difficult one, in spite of legislative reforms. As mentioned, this is one of the key supports to the knowledge economy that is lagging considerably for females. To overcome disadvantage in land and title ownership is to attempt to address centuries-old community prejudices, norms and barriers. While legislation is in place to safeguard the rights of female ownership, this is not always necessarily translated into practice (World Bank 2012). As such, we make a number of recommendations.

- Large scale projects, requiring government approval, of both public and private nature and on private and public land, must consider gender impacts and implications before proceeding
- That government purchasing of produce from agricultural land could be conditional at least on joint ownership of land[7]
- Encouragement be given to women's self-help groups, e.g. favourable loan terms, for self-help groups purchasing land on behalf of female entrepreneurs, and for community housing and the like, with titles in female hands
- That government release of new lands for projects and public auctions give some priority to females in the bidding process, e.g. some margin of allowable price differential.

---

[6]Quasi-courts which often deal with various issues such as domestic violence through mediation and negotiation.

[7]A not dissimilar aspect is mentioned in World Bank (2012).

5.5.2.3 Education Institutions

The proposed education model canvassed in chapter three called for specialist academies in teaching for example, and in promoting state capability in public administration and public services. These would also need to be established through a specialist gender lens aimed at overcoming institutional impediments, such as gender participation in law and enforcement agencies. More broadly, issues have been raised as to lack of females in police and other key legal institutions, and lack of gender sensitivity in these institutions (World Bank 2012).

5.5.3 Women in Knowledge Program (WIK)

We advocate a comprehensive approach to facilitating female access to, participation and engagement in the knowledge economy. This has a number of key dimensions. While female ownership of financial accounts has grown, as we saw in the literature review, access to finance to start a business remains a concern.

As such, a scheme from 'micro to macro' finance could be instituted to address financial needs for all stages of the female entrepreneurship journey pertaining to the knowledge economy. Support would be provided at all stage of the entrepreneurial journey, including social enterprise, through specialist advisers and collective online support networks of entrepreneurs (drawing from either retired entrepreneurs and existing mentors). From micro to macro-finance would commence with initial small-scale offerings from microcredit, and move through the successive growth and enhancement stages of enterprises, based on meeting clear criteria around (1) project viability (2) meeting a commercial need or community problem-solving challenge (3) to facilitate access to credit at a later stage. It would be funded and facilitated by NEIF, as discussed in Chap. 4. The key is that each stage leverages further funding, subject to performance measurement.

The second component of WIK is to implement procurement ready programmes to enable female owned and managed small to medium-sized enterprises obtain training in bid preparation, navigating government agencies and establishing business cases as a pre-finance requisite, for example. The intent of this programme is to provide female firms with a more level playing field in accessing government contracts.

Another initiative could be to tweak the Mahatma Gandhi National Rural Employment Guarantee Act (MGNREGA) (at least 100 days of guaranteed paid work in rural India for unskilled work) scheme to assist female participation in the paid labour force. The scheme has had mixed reviews. Some literature (Dreze and Sen 2013) highlight its positives. Data indicates that under the scheme, the demand for work rose by 10% in 2018–2019 compared to the previous year, and representing the highest level of work from the scheme since 2010–2011. A great deal of this work has, however, been attributed to climate-related factors, but other contend that it reflects high unemployment. It has also been suggested that there is insufficient funding for the scheme (The Wire 2019), while there is also a sense that people have been quitting factory jobs (often more dangerous) to take advantage of the scheme and return home to rural areas, thus leading to more mechanisation in factories (Karnik 2017).

Three proposals can be put forward here: a female-targeted MGNREGA; a knowledge-based MGNREGA targeted at more knowledge intensive sectors and occupations; and that MGNREGA be widened to move beyond rural areas to include urban centres (Gupta 2016; Das 2019).

The next component of the Women in Knowledge Program is to stimulate greater participation in research by women. First, would be the establishment of a Female Academy of Science (linking up and aggregating any such similar bodies), to advocate, promote and publicise (through large scale information programs) female scientific and research achievements. The Academy would provide structured research training in concert with, but also supplementing institutional training, drawing on best practice methodology, and building networking support for female researchers. Networking support would involve the establishment of research mentoring systems for established female researchers to 'buddy up' with emerging researchers, and serve as ongoing guides. These mentorships, which may not necessarily be provided by females, would draw on prominent diaspora abroad and utilise visiting researcher programmes. The Academy would also serve as a matching service linking researchers (both female and male) drawing on repository of researchers, their areas of expertise and interest, and details of their outputs and achievements. An initial focus at least could be on addressing gender specific research and challenges.

In addition, more broadly, we would argue for the establishment of BRIC clubs to promote information sharing, engage in collaborative projects and facilitate inter-BRIC mobility of researchers on shorter and longer term projects.

Beyond this and building on the work of the Association of Academies and Societies of Sciences in Asia (AASSA 2015) is to mandate the development and implementation of female-oriented facilities in university and government laboratory capital plans, including creches, campus housing, and more flexible hours. A number of initiatives have been put in place more broadly by government and NGO's in areas such as education and training, online support, platforms and networks, financial inclusion, digital literacy and health care support (McKinsey and Company 2018).

5.5.4 Work–Life Balance

One of the critical challenges facing Indian women (and indeed women more generally) is the issue of work–life balance. This could be addressed through the establishment of a *National Telecommuting Mission*, which would make it mandatory for companies, government agencies and other bodies, depending on type of work and sector, to offer telecommuting facilities for females. Telecommuting could be done at home, or in nearby facilities including public facilities such as libraries and cultural centres and even in shopping precincts. These facilities would be allied with creche and other supports including elderly care. While initially targeted at females, this policy approach would, over time, be widened to include males. It is not the intention to provide succour for those seeking to consolidate gender stereotyping. The overwhelming aim is to raise female participation in the labour market.

In addition, and perhaps more contentiously, would be the concept of 'working from another person's home'. This would involve employees working in, for example, an elderly neighbours home to both undertake their paid work but also 'keep an eye' out for those in need, in turn developing and building neighbourhood social capital. This could address in part, at least the emerging issue of ageing in India, which does not appear to receive much attention in the public debate and discourse. Of course, we recognise the difficulties with such a program, including trust issues on the part of employers, logistics, and access to appropriate ICT facilities in other homes.

To support the National Telecommuting Mission specifically, but also more broadly, would be a massive exercise in training in ICT access and usage, in its various forms, including through mobile, tablets and personal computers. This would be accompanied by an IT awareness and training guarantee, funded by the government, to address specifically gender gaps as determined by annual national IT audits, where national IT audits would determine infrastructure, usage and skill gaps. One approach to promote the diffusion of devices, if that is deemed to be a gap, could be through bulk public procurement of say tablets, leased back at subsidised rates, including purchasing of older generation models cheaply and from abroad (thus providing environmental benefits through reduction of e-waste: incidentally we would envisage the National Telecommuting Mission could provide further benefit in terms of addressing traffic congestion for example).

The National Telecommuting Mission would link up training initiatives underway, expand outreach programmes and the use of roving trainers, and provide free educational content not charged on bills (Intel and Dahlberg 2013) as well as extending the remit of the Common Service Centres beyond the financial domain to include specific IT training. One further possibility is to support IT training on a 'learn it yourself' basis through IT TV, television programs in local language spelling out how to use ICT applications. Further, the Mission would be backed up by free or heavily subsidised WIFi accounts in female accounts (the magnitude and extent of the WiFi need would be determined by the ICT audit), facilitated by WiFI capacity expansions open to developers.

5.5.5 Attitudinal Changes

Fundamental changes in attitude, beliefs and actions around the role of women in economy and society, are required. This was underscored by the literature and other key data which shows that systemic biases and prejudices are well and truly ingrained and entrenched. While recognising that these social mores take time to alter, and recognising the vast work done by womens' collectives, government and non-government agencies, there are some small reforms that we suggest. First, would be to widen the remit of Self-Help Groups to encourage, where feasible, more men to participate, interact and support these groups, to enable them to garner broader insights into gender issues. This could have the exhortative impact of men becoming change agents themselves. Second, is to implement compulsory gender studies at all levels of education from primary through to tertiary level to build awareness, sensitivity and understanding of gender issues from an early age.

One interesting variation on our latter proposal is a project in Haryana which has examined the provision of classes on gender-stereotyping in 150 schools compared to schools without classes. Males who participated in classes were less likely to believe that boys should be favoured in education compared to girls, and less predisposed to believing that males should have the final word about household decisions. Further, the study found that participating boys were less likely to consider that women should tolerate violence in the name of keeping families together, or that womens' most important role is being a homemaker. Similar results were observed for girls participating in the classes. To a lesser extent boys who received the classes were more likely to have helped out in the house (The Economist 2019).

We would also advocate the creation of Empowerment Challenge Projects at the local level. Funded by local bodies, these projects would involve collaborative teams of males and females (not necessarily from the same family), chosen and funded on a contestable basis, to develop and provide practical, tangible insight and solutions to such things as (a) shared household responsibilities, (b) addressing domestic violence, (c) financial independence and management, (d) innovative access to government services (e) female entrepreneurship.

Challenge projects would be funded on the basis of their practicality, capacity for wider adoption and applicability, and to serve as demonstration exemplars. Ongoing monitoring and evaluation of these projects would be required. Projects could be auspiced via Self-Help Groups. In addition, we would argue that similar collaborative male–female activities be undertaken at schools in the form of 'mock' projects requiring solutions, as a mandated part of the curriculum.

5.5.6 Employment and Security

This section puts forward a raft of suggestions particularly pertinent to employment and labour force participation.

5.5.6.1 Employment

The earlier section advocated an enhanced and expanded MGNREGA as an approach to stimulating paid employment for females, given the parlous situation of females in the labour market. In addition, previous chapters focussed on stimulating economic growth and entrepreneurship in solutions areas, a revamped education and training system aligned to employer and economic need, and a targeted UBI to enhance job skills. In our view, these measures, in addition to ones provided here, could go a fair way to enhancing female empowerment in the labour market arena. Our approach of transitions to a knowledge economy can hopefully result in the development of more secure, stable and high paying jobs.

Data has confirmed the high incidence of unpaid work in India, particularly among females (OECD 2019[8]). One further proposal is to provide 'imputed time' wage, whereby an income is provided to females for the imputed value of unpaid work. This imputed value, paid into female bank accounts (thereby strengthening the impetus for female bank accounts) could be either in the form of income via cash or provision of vouchers to be used in the purchase of education and health, and it could be supplementary to the UBI mechanism outlined in Chap. 2. However, it is important to note that such a mechanism should be seen as a temporary one, otherwise running the risk of 'locking in' females to traditional roles.

Further, as part of the Enabling State, it is also advocated here that labour market brokers be established to identify, promote and facilitate job opportunities for females including in rural areas. Focussing on females, the aim would be to enhance the transition from non-work to work, and from informal work to participation in the formal sector, with an eventual emphasis on knowledge sectors. These brokers could be linked to the National Career Service as an adjunct service. To fund the proposal, upon receiving employment, a small retrospective fee would be charged to females.

5.5.6.2 Security

Promoting greater security and support for those in paid employment is necessary, given the extent of vulnerable and informal employment, including especially of females in the unorganised sector.

We propose a number of elements. First is a mandated set of consistent minimum work, pay and other conditions and standards pertaining to both the organised and unorganised sectors. Second, is the establishment of a National Entitlements Office whose function would to oversee the 'organisation' of the unorganised sectors. In addition, would be the establishment of Indocare, a commercial vehicle, with public and private ownership, supported by an expert board. Tax benefits would be provided to firms who invest in Indocare. Indocare would have the function of purchasing bulk entitlements from specialist social security providers, e.g. health and other forms of insurance and retirement finance products, where purchasing is made on a competitive basis. These purchases would in turn be re-sold to firms, with firms notionally in the unorganised sector receiving government funding support. Firms would purchase entitlements based on the negotiated needs of employees, giving employees the right to trade off, for example, more health insurance compared to life insurance, more take-home pay compared to retirement income, etc. Employees would be required to contribute to the entitlement bundles, the extent of contribution depending on their capacity to pay. The Government has made recent attempts (Gomes 2018), it should be recognised, in bringing greater welfare and other supports for the unorganised sector, although whether these are far-reaching reforms, is questionable.

---

[8] Data sourced in 2019 from OECD Gender Portal but data relates to latest year available.

The system we believe has a number of advantages: a competitive model to promote efficiency and innovation in offerings; bulk purchases giving rise to scale benefits and potentially lower costs; addressing distributional outcomes through blanket coverage of some form; and flexibility based on individual choice and need. Of course, there are likely to be costs associated with data gathering and collection, and implementation more broadly. This system could be trialled first for females but is clearly much more encompassing of gender. There would also need to be mechanisms to provide personalised support for information, awareness raising and assistance in usage, consistent with our notion of the Enabling State.

5.5.7 Financing and Funding

We emphasise that the policies presented here should be thought of as *options*. For example, with respect to the social security and employment generation schemes, careful identification of any linkages to a UBI would need to be made to ensure capacity to pay on the part of governments and employers, administrative capability in implementation, avoidance of duplication and waste, and underpinned by robust benefit and cost analysis. We are presenting a **menu of possibilities**.

5.6 Conclusion

This chapter has examined the contemporary literature relating to female empowerment, covering institutional parameters, labour force participation, health matters, engagement in entrepreneurship and industry development, participation in research, access to ICT and mobile phones, and financial inclusion. By and large, the literature finds considerable disempowerment, and disadvantage facing females in India, often associated with deep-seated social mores.

This chapter then developed a Gender Footprint and examined it in three domains, within India and by way of comparisons with BRIC nations, for females against males, and on an intra-gender basis. In all cases, the disadvantage facing Indian females is pronounced, especially in the key areas of Access and Opportunity, Supports and Relationships.

A series of policy recommendations are made including better use of data to promote awareness, greater access to productive resources, strengthened institutional support, including the establishment of a Female Ombudsman, a Women in Knowledge programme, and firmer employment security. In addition, and above all, this chapter calls for education of men, and problem-solving challenges for both females and males jointly. We consider that these integrated measures would go some way to addressing weak female labour force participation, and lack of empowerment more broadly. Above all, fundamental changes to the way society view the role of females is called for.

Appendix 1: Case Study on Mahila Samakhya

This appendix presents a case study of Mahila Samakhya (MS). MS (meaning Girls Education) is a national program, with state and district chapters, which exemplifies the catalytic, facilitative nature of the state, that we argue is central feature of a knowledge economy and society, which seeks to fundamentally empower women, unlock and leverage ideas, know-how and innate talents. The MS program which began in a few states, focussed initially on scheduled caste and tribe members, and was supported in its early days in part by NGO funds from abroad. It has its origin in the New Education Policy of 1986. This policy, revised in 1992, recognised explicitly the need to redress traditional gender imbalances in educational access and attainment, while recognising that enhancing infrastructure alone would not address the problem, and that 'the empowerment of women is possibly the most critical pre-condition for the participation of girls and women in the educational process' (Government of India 2019a, p. 1).

While notionally an education program, the MS has not had as its focus traditional precepts of education, embodying literacy and numeracy. Rather, it is concerned with self-discovery, empowerment, participation, creating a learning environment, promoting critical thinking and fostering awareness of rights. The program is a 'bottom's up' one with women driving its scope, pace and nature with a focus on learning in its broadest senses to enable skills acquisition, thereby assisting in decision making (Indian Institute of Management 2014).

The program is less about tangible measurement based on key performance indicators (although it does contain such metrics) but its imprimatur and value lie in intangibles such as facilitation, discussion, awareness raising, self and group discovery and the building of esteem that comes from involvement. The sanghas or village level collectives of females, work on identifying challenges and obstacles and developing collective solutions at the local level. The sanghas are the focal points of the system, where women meet, reflect and discuss without fear or favour, canvassing broad areas such as domestic violence, health issues, harassment, access to finance, legal rights, access to government services, assistance with education, and support for family members (girls). Sanghas are supported by sahayagoni or facilitators, chosen collectively, to facilitate activities (Indian Institute of Management 2014; Government of India 2019a). MS has been successful in enhancing mobility of females, obtaining greater voice in the household, stronger participation in education, including for girl family members, raised awareness of rights, and questioning of discriminatory arrangements, and participation in village level meetings.

Thus, the working model has been based on a blend of collective decision making at the sangha level and coordination between state and national governments in a facilitative, consultative manner. The programme has been implemented through a registered society under the broad guidance of the Education Minister and Education Secretary of the concerned state. The advantage of a registered society is that it provides flexibility and a degree of autonomy. MS is neither a purely government nor non-government structure and therefore adopt the best elements of both. The apparatus combines the checks and balances of government with the flexibility and openness of non-government agencies (Government of India 2019a).

Over time, sanghas have been encouraged to, and have become, more aggregated autonomous federations, disentangling from the MS structure and processes, as they mature.

The architecture of the programme is as follows (Government of India 2019b):

- The scheme has been under the broad guidance of the Education Minister and Secretary in the State Concerned
- There is a state MS Society Executive Committee (with representatives from the Government of India, state governments and program personnel) for broad oversight
- District Implementation Unit (District Program Coordinator, and Resource Personnel for every 100 villages)
- State Program Office (State Program Director, Resource Persons, Consultants and Support Staff)
- National Project Office (National Project Director, Consultants and Support Staff)
- District, State and National Resource Group (trainers, NGO and gender and development experts for policy advice and Implementation)
- MS Block Resources Unit (under the supervision of the District Implementation Unit) where a block is a collective of districts or villages.

While the sangha or village level collective for women is the focus of this programmes in this disaggregated, empowered model, it is supported by a number of these oversight, advisory, information provision and training mechanisms cascading from national to local levels.

Sanghas work on the basis of voluntary contributions (mostly time) by members, facilitated by sahayagonis and supported by the MS architecture. According to one assessment, about a quarter of the time is contributed towards health issues (23%), children's education (15%), women's literacy (13%) and social and gender issues (14%). The sanghas have to show a good track record before they receive official MS program funding (Indian Institute of Management 2014).

The sanghas work on the basis of collective decision making, consultation and consensus, but use voting if necessary. The other key attribute of MS is the innovative use of learning techniques for awareness raising and advocacy. For example, this is achieved through songs, plays, dramas and camps (Indian Institute of Management 2014).

While sanghas are focussed on the issues, constraints and challenges facing individual members, there are many broader, and significant benefits beyond this. These include: participation of sangha members in village level decision making apparatus (local panchayat or village elections, gram sabha discussions (i.e. meeting of all adults in the village which typically have the final say); greater demands for, and success in obtaining local public goods (water, electricity, lighting); and broader advocacy in areas such as anti-alcohol campaigns. Another critical domain is the involvement of sangha members to assist the victims of domestic violence of non-members, thus highlighting the growing confidence, assistance and reach of sanghas (Indian Institute of Management 2014; Government of India 2019c).

According to a review despite their intentions, 'collective process can often be exclusionary by privileging those who are able to participate in the process and ignoring others who are voluntarily or involuntarily excluded' (Indian Institute of Management 2014, p. X). The success or otherwise of MS needs to be judged by its capacity of its members to bring community-wide change beyond its membership by challenging norms (Indian Institute of Management 2014).

On this score, the program has been successful. In addition to the broader benefits noted earlier, other key positives include working with non-members to address issues of education, health, agriculture and law, e.g. running night classes open to all, obtaining election cards and identity cards, opening up bank accounts, undertaking school enrolment campaigns, facilitating vaccination and medicine distribution programmes, and support for domestic violence campaigns directed at non-members (Indian Institute of Management 2014). Another analysis confirms benefits intergenerationally through bringing about vaccination for young people in the community, and more broadly in the community fostering greater trust, education awareness and creation of relationships and social capital outside of traditional caste and kinship boundaries, and developing community projects (Jha and Menon 2016).

Sangha members have also been active in ensuring that girls from marginalised groups become part of mainstream schooling (by visiting homes, counselling parents, motivating students, and organising for support for parents to allow schooling); negotiating safe transport routes; supporting parents to fill out scholarship forms; and ensuring that students have access to books and sanitation facilities (Indian Institute of Management 2014).

Two other features of the MS are worth indicating. The first is the provision of MS sponsored schools themselves (kendras) for students unable to attend mainstream schools. This involves the provision of schooling to year ten, preparation for state board examinations, and integrating into mainstream schools. MSK residential kendras are for girls who have dropped out of school or whose education has been neglected by parents. The second is the establishment of the nari adalats, which are quasi women's law courts, a grass roots initiative of the sangha women of MS providing a 'gender sensitive, cost-effective and quick response' to problems that are in the family domain (Indian Institute of Management 2014, p. 74). The focus of the quasi-courts is to work out compromise, and via negotiation try to change perceptions through peer support, allied with fear of embarrassment and social censure of the guilty. The nari adalats have formed links with mainstream courts, local village elected representatives, NGO's and police and activists. Nari adalats do not take on criminal cases such as murders, and are mostly concerned with domestic violence and marital conflict. Cases not settled in nari adalats go to courts (only 1 in 5 go to the courts). Unsettled cases are usually about maintenance cases or property disputes (Indian Institute of Management 2014).

Yet a number of issues and challenges have, and continue to confront MSK (Indian Institute of Management 2014; Jha and Menon 2016):

- With its focus on the social domain, MS has been less successful in the economic domains. Vocational training for example has not led to business development creation, and employment, as envisaged, due to the lack of links to other parts of the economy (e.g. production techniques, access to raw materials, market connections). Economic empowerment of sangha members looms as a key challenge.
- Another key challenge for MS specifically (and India generally) is the need to embrace ICT, and its benefits in terms of networking, empowerment, dissolving of boundaries, providing community support, and accessing key services.
- Moving to autonomous federation status has proved to be challenging in terms of having less funding and administrative support from MS.
- Sanghas (and Federations in varying degrees) have tended to lack the capacity for organised business planning, processes and systems, financial planning and the ability to obtain extra funding. This is likely to be a more significant problem as the sanghas seek to become autonomous Federations. More broadly, capability building at the sangha level is a key issue.
- MS kendras have not been overly successful necessarily in integrating with the broader curriculum of educational agencies in mainstream education, or influencing and advocating pedagogy. Moreover, MS kendra suffered from having a dearth of experienced staff, to teach specialised subjects and often have lacked suitable infrastructure.
- A pressing challenge is to track MS alumni to identify success stories, and identify gaps in learning and employment among alumni.
- MS has at times struggled to establish a distinct identity because of the need to both work within government structures, while at the same time challenging powerful interests in government. Moreover, MS also has suffered from a lack of visibility in the sense of being a small program.
- MS is much stronger at 'negative freedom' (obtaining freedom from external interference, e.g. addressing harassment) compared to 'positive freedoms' which is about pro-actively influencing political and legal institutions that it engages with
- Finally, there are concerns that bureaucratic reshuffling of the program could mean diminished commitment to MS, especially in recent times.

Appendix 2: Gender Knowledge Footprint Methodology

Individual metrics are scaled to 100 for females and males as comparators (with best gender given 100 and other gender adjusted accordingly), and aggregated, and divided by the number of metrics, to provide sub-pillar scores. These sub-pillars are then weighted and aggregated to develop an overall Gender Footprint Score. The weights are: Knowledge Opportunity and Access 20%; Knowledge Supports and Platforms 18%; Knowledge Capability Development 18%; Knowledge Resourcing 15%; Knowledge Relationships 12%; Knowledge Translation and Transformation 17%. The weights are different to those in the Footprint Analysis of Chap. 4.

Naturally, for some metrics such as unemployment, under-employment, and social indicators like suicide rates, the lower the value, the higher the score. In these cases, the gender which has the lower value is the best performed and receives a score of 100, with the adjustment made accordingly for the other gender.

Gender Knowledge Footprint

Knowledge Footprint	Metrics	Sources and notes
Knowledge Access and Opportunity	Overall enrolment share female and male for lower secondary, upper secondary and tertiary	Enrolment data for 2016 from UNESCO data.uis.unesco.org accessed 16/10/2018. Author scoring 100 for best gender and adjusted for the other gender.
	Gross enrolment ratios	Gross enrolment ratios lower secondary, upper secondary and tertiary 2016, males and females data from UNESCO data.uis.unesco.org accessed 16/10/2018. Author scoring 100 for best gender and adjusted for the other gender.
	Enrolment ISCED 6, 7 and 8 % female, % male, and overall female share, overall male share	ISCED 6, 7, and 8 for 2016 % female, % male, and overall female share, overall male share for 2016. In both types of analysis weights are applied ISCED 6 (20%), ISCED 7 (40%), ISCED 8 (40%). Enrolment data for 2016 from UNESCO data.uis.unesco.org accessed 16/10/2018. Author calculation and scoring 100 for best gender and adjusted for the other gender.
	Enrolment knowledge intensive fields	Enrolment in knowledge intensive fields (STEM) 2016 %female, % male, and female share and male share of overall Enrolment data for 2016. Data from UNESCO data.uis.unesco.org accessed 16/10/2018. Author calculation and scoring 100 for best gender and adjusted for the other gender.
	Labour force	Labour force, female and male share of total labour force, labour force % of female population (15–64) and labour force % of of male population 15–64 data for 2017 World Bank https://data.worldbank.org/indicator accessed 16/10/2018. Author scoring 100 for best gender and adjusted for the other gender.
	Literacy	% of females older than 15, % of males older than 15 data for 2017 World Bank https://data.worldbank.org/indicator accessed 16/10/2018. Author scoring 100 for best gender and adjusted for the other gender.

(continued)

(continued)

Knowledge Footprint	Metrics	Sources and notes
	Unemployment	Unemployment % of female labour force, % of male labour force data for 2017 World Bank https://data.worldbank.org/indicator accessed 16/10/2018. Author scoring 100 for best gender and adjusted for the other gender.
	Youth unemployment	Youth unemployment 2017 % of female labour force and % of male labour force ages 15–24 https://data.worldbank.org/indicator accessed 16/10/2018. Author scoring 100 for best gender and adjusted for the other gender.
	Vulnerable employment	Vulnerable employment (own account and contributing family workers) 2017 % of female employment, % of male employment https://data.worldbank.org/indicator accessed 16/10/2018. Author scoring 100 for best gender and adjusted for the other gender.
	Human development index	2017 Scores for males and females. Source UN (2018) Human Development Indices and Indicators Statistical Update. Author scoring 100 for best gender and adjusted for the other gender.
	Labour force spatial breakdown by state	Labour force best urban female, and best urban male, labour force best rural male and best rural female, labour force best urban and rural male and female. Labour force worst urban female, and worst urban male, labour force worst rural male and worst rural female, labour force worst urban and rural male and female. Source: Government of India Ministry of Labour and Employment: Employment-Unemployment Survey Volume 1 2015–2016. Author scoring 100 for best gender and adjusted for the other gender.
	Unemployment by spatial breakdown	Unemployment best urban female, and best urban male, unemployment best rural male and best rural female, unemployment best urban and rural male and female. Unemployment Worst Urban Female, and Worst Urban Male, unemployment Worst Rural Male and Worst Rural Female, unemployment Worst Urban and Rural Male and Female. Source: Government of India Ministry of Labour and Employment: Employment-Unemployment Survey Volume 1 2015–2016. Author scoring 100 for best gender and adjusted for the other gender.
	Under-employment	Worked less than 12 months (available 12 months) for Regional and urban female and male, urban female and urban male, rural male and rural female. Source: Government of India Ministry of Labour and Employment: Employment-Unemployment Survey Volume 1 2015–2016. Author scoring 100 for best gender and adjusted for the other gender.
	Paid leave	% paid leave Urban Male and Urban Female, Rural Male and Female, and Urban and Rural Female and Male. Source: Government of India Ministry of Labour and Employment: Employment-Unemployment Survey Volume 1 2015–2016. Author scoring 100 for best gender and adjusted for the other gender.

(continued)

Appendix 2: Gender Knowledge Footprint Methodology 323

(continued)

Knowledge Footprint	Metrics	Sources and notes
	Social security access	% of access to social security Urban Male and Female, Rural Male and Female, Urban and Rural Male and Female. Source: Government of India Ministry of Labour and Employment: Employment-Unemployment Survey Volume 1 2015–2016. Author scoring 100 for best gender and adjusted for the other gender.
	Contract	% of working on some contract Urban Male and Female, Rural Male and Female, Urban and Rural Male and Female. Source: Government of India Ministry of Labour and Employment: Employment-Unemployment Survey Volume 1 2015–2016. Author scoring 100 for best gender and adjusted for the other gender.
	Non availability of jobs	For undergraduates, non-availability of jobs matching education, skills and experience for Males and Females. Source: Government of India Ministry of Labour and Employment: Employment-Unemployment Survey Volume 1 2015–2016. Author scoring 100 for best gender and adjusted for the other gender.
Knowledge Supports and Platforms	Life expectancy at birth	For females and males Life expectancy at birth (2017) Source UN (2018) Human Development Indices and Indicators Statistical Update. Author scoring 100 for best gender and adjusted for the other gender.
	Mean years of schooling	Mean years of schooling (2017) Source UN (2018) Human Development Indices and Indicators Statistical Update. Author scoring 100 for best gender and adjusted for the other gender.
	Mortality rates	Mortality rates 2016 (adults per 1000 people), Suicide rates per 100,000 people 2015, Justification for wife beating Sources for these data UN (2018) Human Development Indices Staistical Update. Author scoring 100 for best gender and adjusted for the other gender.
	Suicide rates Freedom of choice Feeling safe Justification for wife beating	(2010–2016), freedom of choice and feeling safe 2012–2017: Source UN (2018) Human Development Indices and Indicators Statistical Update. Author scoring 100 for best gender and adjusted for the other gender.
	Land title ownership Time spent in unpaid work Time spent in paid work Share of board positions	Land title ownership, agriculture 2014, Time spent in unpaid work latest year, Time spent in paid work, latest year, Share of Board positions (largest publicly listed companies) 2016. Sources OECD Gender Portal https://www.oecd.org/gender accessed 17/10/2018. Author scoring 100 for best gender and adjusted for the other gender.
	Share of seats in parliament	Share of seats in parliament 2017 data Source: Source UN (2018) Human Development Indices and Indicators Statistical Update. Author scoring 100 for best gender and adjusted for the other gender.

(continued)

(continued)

Knowledge Footprint	Metrics	Sources and notes
	Disability adjusted life years	World Health Organisation Estimated DALY's by all causes https://who.int/gho/publications/world-health-statistics/en accessed 6/4/2019. Author scoring 100 for best gender and adjusted for the other gender.
	Having financial account, borrowed money in the last year, borrowed for education or school fees, borrowed for health or medical, borrowed from financial institution, borrowed from savings club, coming up with emergency funds possible and not possible, making digital payment, received digital payment, having a mobile money account, used mobile phone or internet to access financial institution in the last year	Data for females and males for 2017 or latest year Having Financial account, borrowed money in the last year, borrowed for education or school fees, borrowed for health or medical, borrowed from financial institution, borrowed from savings club, coming up with emergency funds possible and not possible, making digital payment, received digital payment, having a mobile money account, used mobile phone or internet to access financial institute in the last year: Source for these data World Bank Financial Inclusion Database Global Findex Database.xlsx Demirgüç-Kunt, A, Klapper L, Singer D, Ansar S, Hess J accessed 24/10/2018. Author scoring 100 for best gender and adjusted for the other gender.
	Social network usage	% of adults (% F, % M) who use social network sites (facebook, twitter), males and females Source: Pew Research Center "Social Media use continues to rise in developing countries but plateaus across developed countries June 19 2018" https://www.pewresaerch.org. Author scoring 100 for best gender and adjusted for the other gender.
	Facebook and Instagram users	Overall share of facebook and instagram use by female and male share Source: We are social Global Digital Report 2018 https://digitalreport.wearesocial.com accessed 25/10/2018. Author scoring 100 for best gender and adjusted for the other gender.
	Linkedin	Overall share of males and females using Linkedin Snapshot of Digital India July 2018 Ethinos Digital Marketing www.slideshare.net/ethinos accessed 27/10/2018. Author scoring 100 for best gender and adjusted for the other gender.
	Digital inclusion index	McKinsey and Company Digital Inclusion Index (2018) For males and females in McKinsey 2018 The Power of Parity: Advancing Women's Equality in Asia Pacific. Focus India. Author scoring 100 for best gender and adjusted for the other gender.

(continued)

Appendix 2: Gender Knowledge Footprint Methodology

(continued)

Knowledge Footprint	Metrics	Sources and notes
	Make receive calls on mobile, send/receive SMS, use mobile internet, use instant messaging, use social media, browse internet, download/use apps, Make/receive video calls, mobile ownership, mobile internet usage, gender gap in mobile ownership (Urban and Rural), gender gap in mobile internet usage (urban and rural), awareness of mobile internet among men and women	% Make receive calls on mobile, send/receive SMS, use mobile internet, use instant messaging, use social media, browse internet, download/use apps, Make/receive video calls, mobile ownership, mobile internet usage, gender gap in mobile usage (urban and rural), awareness of mobile internet among men and women: Source for these data Rowntree O (GMSA) 2018 Connected Women The Mobile Gender Gap Report data pertains to 2017. Author scoring 100 for best gender and adjusted for the other gender.
	Female and male share of total distance enrolment, female and male share of post graduate distance enrolment (% female, % male), overall female and male share of total post graduate distance enrolment Access to training to start a business (% male, % female)	Female and male share of total distance enrolment, female and male share of post graduate distance enrolment (% female, % male), overall female and male share of total post graduate distance enrolment: Source for this data Government of India Ministry of Human Resource Development All India Survey Higher Education (AISHE) 2017–2018. Author scoring 100 for best gender and adjusted for the other gender 2013 data Sources OECD Gender Portal https://www.oecd.org/gender. OECD Gender portal accessed 17/10/2018. Author scoring 100 for best gender and adjusted for the other gender.
Knowledge Capability Development	Researcher by gender, researcher by gender in business, higher education and government, private not for profit	Researcher by gender (overall share), Researcher by gender in business (overall share), Researcher by gender in higher education (overall share) and Researcher in government (overall share). Data pertains to 2016. Source for these data UNESCO data.uis.unesco.org accessed 16/10/2018. Author scoring 100 for best gender and adjusted for the other gender.
	Total R and D personnel by gender, total technicians by gender	Total R and D Personnel by gender (overall share), Total Technicians by gender (overall share). Data pertains to 2016. Source UNESCO data.uis.unesco.org accessed 16/10/2018. Author scoring 100 for best gender and adjusted for the other gender.
	Gross graduation ratios: lower secondary, upper secondary and tertiary (ISCED 6 and 7)	Gross Graduate ratios: Lower Secondary, Upper Secondary and Tertiary UNESCO data 2017 or latest year data.uis.unesco.org accessed 17/10/2018. Author scoring 100 for best gender and adjusted for the other gender.
	Graduates ISCED 6, 7, 8	Percentage of overall ISCED 6, 7 and 8 graduates by gender 2016 or latest year with weightings for 20% ISCED 6, 40% ISCED 7 and 40% ISCED 8 UNESCO uis.unesco.org accessed 17/10/2018 latest year. Author calculation and scoring 100 for best gender and adjusted for the other gender.
	Graduates in knowledge intensive fields	Percentage of overall graduates in knowledge intensive fields by gender, and percentage of knowledge intensive field graduates (% female, % male) 2016 or latest year. UNESCO uis.unesco.org accessed 17/10/2018 accessed 17/10/2018. Author calculation and scoring 100 for best gender and adjusted for the other gender.

(continued)

(continued)

Knowledge Footprint	Metrics	Sources and notes
	Preference for self-employment, feasibility of self-employment, attitudes to entrepreneurial risk	Preference for self-employment 2012 (% f, % m), feasibility of self-employment (% f, % m) 2012, Attitudes to entrepreneurial risk (% f, % m) 2013: Source for these data Sources OECD Gender Portal https://www.oecd.org/gender. Accessed 17/10/2018. Author scoring 100 for best gender and adjusted for the other gender.
	Gender entrepreneurial intentions	Gender Entrepreneurial intentions (% of m, % f aged 18–64 who intend to start a business within 3 years) Source Global Entrepreneurship Monitor Women's Entrepreneurship Report 2016-2017. Author scoring 100 for best gender and adjusted for the other gender.
	Gender innovators	Gender Innovators (%m, % f of Early Stage Entrepreneurs who offer a product which is new to all or some customers and few/no businesses offer the same product). Source Global Entrepreneurship Monitor Women's Entrepreneurship Report 2016-2017. Author scoring 100 for best gender and adjusted for other gender.
	Gender capability perception	Gender capability perception (% m, % f aged 18–64 who believe they have the required skills and knowledge to start a business) Source Global Entrepreneurship Monitor Women's Entrepreneurship Report 2016-2017. Author scoring 100 for best gender and adjusted for the other gender.
	Gender opportunity perception	Gender opportunity perception (%m, % f aged 18–64 who see a good opportunity to start a business in the area where they live). Source Global Entrepreneurship Monitor Women's Entrepreneurship Report 2016-2017. Author scoring 100 for best gender and adjusted for the other gender.
	Undeterred by fear of failure	Undeterred by fear of failure: Source for data by gender (% female, % male population 18–64): Kelley et al. (2017) Global Entrepreneurship Monitor Women's Entrepreneurship Report 2016–2017. Author scoring 100 for best gender and adjusted for the other gender.
	Gender share of teaching staff in Higher Education Gender share of total teaching staff (Professor, Associate Professor)	Female and male share of total teaching staff, female and male professors as a share of total teaching staff, female and Male Associate Professor share of total teaching staff, female professor share of total female teachers, male professor share of total male teachers, female associate professor share of total female teachers, male associate professor share of total male teachers, female and male professors as a share of total professors, female and male share of total Associate Professors Source: Government of India Ministry of Human Resource and Development AISHE 2017–2018. Author calculation and scoring 100 for best gender and adjusted for the other gender.
	Gender distribution of Fellows in Indian National Science Academy, Indian Government Scientific Organisations	The Association of Academies and Societies of Sciences in Asia (AASSA) Women in Science and Technology 2015. Author scoring 100 for best gender and adjusted for the other gender.

(continued)

Appendix 2: Gender Knowledge Footprint Methodology

(continued)

Knowledge Footprint	Metrics	Sources and notes
	Share of publication outputs in life scientists by gender	Female and male share of total publications (2008–2009). Source: Garg and Kumar (2014) Scientometric Profile of Indian scientific output in life sciences with a focus on the contributions of women scientists, Scientometrics 98 1771–1783. Author scoring 100 for best gender and adjusted for the other gender.
	Population with at least some secondary education	% of females and % males aged 25 and above for 2010–2017 Source UN (2018) Human Development Indices and Indicators Statistical Update. Author scoring 100 for best gender and adjusted for the other gender.
Knowledge Resourcing	GNI per capita (2011 ppp) 2017 Female and Male, GNI Female and Male	GNI per capita data pertains to 2017. Source UN (2018) Human Development Indices and Indicators Statistical Update. Author scoring 100 for best gender and adjusted for the other gender.
	GNI per researcher Male and Female	Author calculations and scoring 100 for best gender and adjusted for the other gender. Based on GNI figures and researcher figures for 2016 or latest years. GNI figures from UN (2018) Human Development Indices and Indicators Statistical Update. Researcher figures from UNESCO data.uis.unesco.org accessed 16/10/2018.
	Female and Male GERD, Female and Male GERD per researcher	Female and male GERD 2016 author calculations based on share of researchers and GERD data (2005 000 ppp) UNESCO data.uis.unesco.org accessed 16/10/2018 accessed 16/10/2018, Female and Male GERD per researcher author calculation based on these data sources for 2016. Author scoring 100 for best gender and adjusted for the other gender.
	Government expenditure on females and males for lower secondary, upper secondary and tertiary	Author estimates and scoring 100 for best gender and adjusted for the other gender of share of Government expenditure (constant ppp 2005 prices) based on enrolment shares for 2013 or latest year. UNESCO data. uis.unesco.org accessed 16/10/2018.
	GNI per female and male for lower secondary, upper secondary and tertiary	GNI per female and male for lower secondary, upper secondary and tertiary with author estimates and scoring 100 for best gender and adjusted for other gender. Source for students UNESCO data.uis.unesco.org accessed 16/10/2018. GNI data for 2017 from UN (2018) Human Development Indices and Indicators Statistical Update.
	India as a destination for migrants male and female	For 2017, India male migrants/male population, and male migrants/total India population, For females female migrants/female population and female migrants/total India population Source: United Nations Migrant Stock origin and destination https://www.un.org/en/development/desa/population/migration. Population data from UN population data https://www.populatiom.un.org/wpp/downlaod/statistical database. Stocks origin and destination accessed 20/10/2018. Author calculations and scoring 100 for best gender and adjusted for the other gender.

(continued)

(continued)

Knowledge Footprint	Metrics	Sources and notes
Knowledge Relationships	Percentage of collaborative papers undertaken by males and females respectively that are domestic collaboration and international collaboration % of papers that are Female-female collaboration and male-male collaboration % of papers that are Joint male-female collaboration with first author female, first author male. Personally knowing an entrepreneur, male (% of male and female adult population) Female invested in business, male invested in business (% of adult population)	For collaborative papers in life sciences, data pertaining to 2008–2009 drawn from Garg and Kumar (2014) Scientometric Profile of Indian scientific output in life sciences with a focus on the contributions of women scientists, Scientometrics 98, 1771–1783. Author scoring 100 for best gender and adjusted for the other gender.Data on knowing an entrepreneur and investing in business drawn from Kelley et al. (2017) Global Entrepreneurship Monitor Women's Entrepreneurship Report 2016–2017. Author scoring 100 for best gender and adjusted for the other gender.
	Emigration of highly educated (ISCED 5 and above) female and male (to OECD countries) % male, % female	OECD Connecting with Emigrants 2015 data pertains to 2010/2011. Author scoring 100 for best gender and adjusted for the other gender.
	Knowledge intensive occupations in US of Indian born males and females	Author calculations and scoring 100 for best gender and adjusted for the other gender based on 2011 data from Migrant Policy online Indian Immigrants in the U.S August 21 2013 Migration Policy Institute. Author determined criteria for knowledge intensive occupations encompassing management, business, finance, IT, other scientists and engineers, social services/legal, education, training and media, health care professionals, service/personal care. https://www.migrationpolicy.org accessed 7/4/2019.
	Received and sent domestic remittances males and females % Indian females and males ownership of business in the U.S by number and value Indian male and female share of Indian migration to US, Indian working age female (20–64) share of Indian migration to US, Indian working age (20–64) male share of Indian migration to U.S. Indian working age migration female share of total Indian female migration in the U.S. Indian male working age migration share of Indian male migration in the U.S	For receiving and sending domestic remittances data World Bank Financial Inclusion Database Global Findex Database.xlsx Demirgüç-Kunt, A, Klapper L, Singer D, Ansar S, Hess J accessed 24/10/2018. Author scoring 100 for best gender and adjusted for the other gender. For data for number of Indian female business/total firms in the US, Number of Indian female owned firms/Total Indian owned firms, Indian female owned businesses/total female owned businesses in the U.S. Comparable analysis done for Indian owned male businesses. Source 2012 Survey of Business Owners statistics for US firms by Industry, Gender, Ethnicity and Race https://www.factfinder.census.gov/faces/tablesaccessed 22/10/2018. Author calculations and scoring of 100 for best gender and adjusted for the other gender. For data on migrationAge-Sex Pyramid of Top Immigrant Origin Groups in the US 2016 Migration Policy Institute Data pertains to 2016 https://www.migrationpolicy.org accessed 22/10/2018 Author calculations and scoring of 100 for best gender and adjusted for other gender.

(continued)

Appendix 2: Gender Knowledge Footprint Methodology

(continued)

Knowledge Footprint	Metrics	Sources and notes
	Country of Origin migration data Indian female migrant stock (abroad)/Indian female population, Indian female migrant stock abroad/total Indian population. Same analysis for males
Inbound tertiary mobility ratios for female and male.
Share of outbound tertiary students male and female
Female share of total international students in India, female knowledge intensive students share of total knowledge intensive international students, female knowledge intensive international students share of female international students, female knowledge intensive students share of female international students. Same analyses replicated for males	Migration data from United Nations United Nations Migrant Stock origin and destination https://www.un.org/en/development/desa/population/migration and population data from UN population data www.population.un.org/wpp/download/statistical database accessed 20/10/2108 Data for 2017 Author calculations and scoring of 100 for best gender and adjusted for the other gender.
Student mobility ratios and share of outbound tertiary mobility data for 2016 or latest year from UNESCO data. uis.unesco.org 16/10/2018. Author calculation and scoring of 100 for best gender and adjusted for the other gender.
For female and male share of total international students in India and in STEM Source: Government of India Ministry of Human Resource and Development AISHE 2017–2018 author calculations based on international enrolments and breakdown by essentially STEM disciplines for knowledge intensive disciplines.
Author calculation and scoring of 100 for best gender and adjusted for the other gender.
Knowledge translation and transformation	Citations per paper, females and males
Women investors by residence, male inventors by residence
Percentage of female established business activity, percentage of male established business activity (% of population),
Percentage of females and males TEA (% of population)
Percentage of female and male opportunity based TEA (% of TEA)
Percentage of female discontinued business, percentage of male discontinued activity (% of population)
Percentage of female and percentage of male TEA self-employed with zero growth
Percentage of males and females TEA expect to hire 6 + employees
Indian female and male share of knowledge intensive services (TEA)	Source: Garg and Kumar (2014) Scientometric Profile of Indian scientific output in life sciences with a focus on the contributions of women scientists, Scientometrics 98, 1771–1783. Author scoring 100 for best gender and adjusted for the other gender.
For gender inventor by residence data Source: Martinez et al. (2016) Identifying the Gender of PCT Inventors WIPO Economic Research Working Paper number 33 November 2016 data is for 2011–2015. Author scoring 100 for best gender and adjusted for the other gender. For data on all gender business activity ie established businesses, TEA, opportunity based TEA, discontinued buiness, employment, growth and TEA knowledge intensive services source:
Kelley et al. (2017) Global Entrepreneurship Monitor Women's Entrepreneurship Report 2016–2017. Author scoring 100 for best gender and adjusted for the other gender.
Author categorisation and calculation of knowledge intensive services as: ICT, Health, Education, Social services; Finance, Professional Services, Administration and Consumer Services. Kelley et al. (2017) Global Entrepreneurship Monitor Women's Entrepreneurship Report 2016–2017. Author calculation and scoring 100 for best gender and adjusted for the other gender.

(continued)

(continued)

Knowledge Footprint	Metrics	Sources and notes
	Estimated Earned Income (PPP$ US), Males and Females Distribution (%) wage and salary earners in India, female and male Rural and Urban, Best Rural and Urban male and female, Best Urban female and best urban male, Best Rural Male and best rural Female, Worst Rural and Urban Male and Female, Worst Urban male and worst urban female, worst rural female and worst rural male High skill employment share of total employment for males and females respectively Medium skilled employment share of total employment males and females respectively Monthly purchasing power males and females Percentage of female and male TEA expecting to have more than 25% exports Productivity of female and male scientists and Impact factor of papers males and females Female and male employment in knowledge intensive industries as a share of total employment for females and males Female and male share of knowledge intensive occupations for females and males Male share of non-teaching staff in Higher Education, Female share of non-teaching staff in Higher Education. Senior most non-teaching Male employment share of senior most employees, and likewise for female share. Senior most male non-teaching share of total male non teaching staff employment and likewise for females. Senior most male non-teaching staff share of total non teaching employment and likewise for females. Employment to population ratio 2017 (% Male, % Female)	Estimated Earned Income from World Economic Forum The Global Gender Gap 2017. Author scoring 100 for best gender and adjusted for the other gender. Wage and salary earners and spatial distribution from Government of India Employment and Unemployment Survey 2015–2016. Author scoring 100 for best gender and adjusted for the other gender. Skill share of employment from ILO May 2018 data https://www.ilo.org accessed 17/10/2018, data pertains to 2017. Author scoring 100 for best gender and adjusted for the other gender. Monthly purchasing power based on proportion of employment by gender in wage and salary bands (mid-point for wages and salary earnings). Data Source: Government of India Ministry of Labour and Employment: Employment-Unemployment Survey 2015–2016. Author calculation and scoring 100 for best gender and adjusted for the other gender. For data on exports by gender source Kelley et al. (2017) Global Entrepreneurship Monitor Women's Entrepreneurship Report 2016–2017. Author scoring 100 for best gender and adjusted for the other gender. Productivity and Impact factors of papers from Garg and Kumar (2014) Scientometric Profile of Indian scientific output in life sciences with a focus on the contributions of women scientists, Scientometrics 98 1771–1783. Author scoring 100 for best gender and adjusted for the other gender Garg et al. with author recalibration. Data pertains to 2008–2009. For gender employment in knowledge intensive industries. Source Government of India Ministry of Labour and Employment Employment-Unemployment Survey 2013–2014. Classification similar to UNCTAD. Author calculations and scoring 100 for best gender and adjusted for the other gender based on determination of classifications according to knowledge inensive manufacturing and services. Classification similar to UNCTAD. For gender employment by occupation. Source Government of India Ministry of Labour and Employment Employment-Unemployment Survey 2015–2016. Author calculation and scoring 100 for best gender and adjusted for the other gender based on determination of classifications according to knowledge intensive occupations. Classification similar to ILO. Data for teaching and non teaching staff by gender in Indian higher education. Source Government of India Ministry of Human Resource and Development AISHE 2017–2018. Senior Most professionals are suggested to be classified as category A (Director and above generally). Author calculations and scoring 100 for best gender and adjusted for the other gender. For data on employment to population ration. Source World Bank https://data.worldbank.org/indicator accessed 29/10/2018. Author scoring 100 for best gender and adjusted for the other gender.

The same data is used for BRIC comparisons by and large. However, note that the following data is not available for BRIC nations except India: spatial distribution of labour market factors; data on international students in knowledge intensive fields; employment of academic and professional (non-teaching staff in Higher Education); data on life sciences papers, citations, collaborations and impact; purchasing power; immigrant labour force composition in the US; knowledge intensive share of employment by industry and by detailed occupation (broad occupation of high skill and medium skill is available and utilised for BRIC); researchers by gender; enrolment in Higher Education by gender by distance mode; Digital Inclusion Index, profile of facebook users, instagram and linkedin.

References

Afridi F, Dinkelman T, Mahajan (2018) Why are fewer married women joining the workforce in rural India? A decomposition analysis over two decades. J Popul Econ 31(3):783–818
Amaral S, Bandyopadhyay S, Sensarma R (2015) Employment programmes for the poor and female empowerment: the effect of NREGS on gender-based violence in India. J Inter-Discip Econ 27(2):199–2018
Amin M, Islam A (2015) Women managers and the gender-based gap in access to education. World Bank group policy research working paper 7269
Ara S (2015) Gender and jobs: evidence from urban labour market in India. Indian J Labour Econ 58:377–403
Asian Development Bank (ADB) Women in the workforce an unmet potential in Asia and the Pacific
Bhalla S, Kaur R (undated) Labour force participation of women in India: some facts, some queries, LSE Asia Research Centre. Working paper 40. Accessed 15 Apr 2019
Biswas C (2017) Spousal violence against working women in India. J Family Violence 32(1):55–67
Chatterjee E, Desai S, Vanneman R (2018) Indian paradox: rising education, declining women's employment. Demogr Res 38:855–878 (Article 31)
Chatterjee U, Murgai R, Rama M (2015) Job opportunities along the rural-urban gradation and female labour force participation in India. World Bank group policy research working paper 7412
Chatterjee U, Murgai R, Rama H (2017) What explains the decline in female labour force participation in India? Ideas of India. https://www.ideasforindia.in/topics/social-identity/what-explains-the-decline-in-female-labour-force-participation-in-india.html. Accessed 14 Apr 2019
Das G (2019) 100 days at Rs 500 per day: Azim Premji's University proposes urban employment guarantee scheme. Business Today, 4 Apr 2019. https://m.businesstoday.in/story/100-days-at-rs-500-per-day-azim-premji-university-proposes-urban-employment-guarantee-scheme/1/332948.html. Accessed 28 Apr 2019
Das S, Jain-Chandra S, Kochhar K, Kumar N (2015) Women working in India: why so few among so many? IMF working paper WP/15/55
Daymard A (2015) Determinants of female entrepreneurship in India. OECD economics department working paper number 1191
Deininger K, Xia F, Jin S, Nagarajan H (2014) Inheritance law reform, empowerment and human capital accumulation, second-generation effects for india. World Bank group policy based working paper 7086
Demirgüç-Kunt A, Klapper L, Singer D, Ansar S, Hess J (2018) World bank financial inclusion database global Findex. 2017 Database.xlsx. Accessed 24 Oct 2018

Desai R, Joshi S (2013) Collective action and community development evidence from self-help groups in Rural India. World Bank development economics vice presidency, partnership, capacity building Unity. Policy research working paper 6547

Dreze J, Sen A (2013) An uncertain glory: India and its contradictions. Princeton University Press, Princeton, NJ

Garg K, Kumar S (2014) Scientometric profile of Indian scientific output in life sciences with a focus on the contributions of women scientists. Scientometrics 98:1771–1783

Garikipati S (2012) Microcredit and women's empowerment: through the lens of time-use data from rural India. Dev Change 43(3):719–750

Ghani E, Kanbur R, O'Connell S (2013a) Urbanisation and agglomeration benefits: gender differentiated impact on enterprise creation in India's informal sector. The World Bank poverty reduction and economic management network. Policy research working paper 6553

Ghani E, Kerr W, O'Connell S (2013b) Political reservation and women's entrepreneurship in India 2013. The World Bank poverty reduction and economic management network. Policy research working paper 6307

Global Entrepreneurship Monitor Consortium (2018) Global entrepreneurship monitor global report 2017/18

Gomes E (2018) EPFO proposes move to create social security cover for all-all you need to know. QRIUS. https://qrius.com/epfo-proposes-social-security-cover-for-all/amp/. Accessed 27 June 2018

Government of India (2019a) Development Mahila Samakhya programme genesis. Ministry of Human Resources Development. www.mhrd.gov.in/mahila-samakhya-programme. Accessed 25 Apr 2019

Government of India (2019b) Development Mahila Samakhya Organogram. Ministry of Human Resources Development. www.mhrd.gov.in/mahila-samakhya-programme. Accessed 25 Apr 2019

Government of India (2019c) Development Mahila Samakhya Programme Agenda. Ministry of Human Resources Development. www.mhrd.gov.in/mahila-samakhya-programme. Accessed 25 Apr 2019

Gupta A (2016) Grassroots innovation, minds on the margin are not marginal minds. Penguin Random House India, Haryana, India

Husain Z, Mukerjee D, Dutta M (2014) Self-help groups and empowerment of women: self selection or actual benefits? J Int Dev 26:422–437

Indian Institute of Management (2014) Mahila Samkhya. A National Rev. Ahmedabad (Ravi J. Matthai, Centre for Educational Innovation)

Intel and Dalberg (2013) Global development advisors: women and the web

Jagannathan R (2018) The jobs crisis in India. MacMillan

Jha J, Menon N (2016) Why it is important to retain an independent. Mahila Samakhya programme. Econ Polit Weekly II(12)

Kalaramadan S (2016) Gender, governance and empowerment in India. Routledge

Kandpal E, Baylis K, Arends-Kuenning M (2013) Measuring the effect of a community-level program on women's empowerment outcomes, evidence from India. The World Bank Development Research Group poverty and inequality, Policy research, Working Paper 6399

Karnik M (2017) MGNREGA's easy jobs may have harmed India's manufacturing sector by luring away skilled factory workers. Quartz, India, 26 Jan 2019. https://qz.com/India878575/mgnregas-easy-jobs-may-have-harmed-indias-manufacturing-sector-by-luring-skilled-factory-workers. Accessed 28 Apr 2019

Kelley D, Baumer B, Brush C, Greene P, Mahdavi M, Majbouri M, Cole M, Dean M, Heavlow R (2017) Global entrepreneurship monitor women's entrepreneurship report 2016–2017

Kumbar V (2013) Some criticised issues of women entrepreneurship in rural India. Eur Acad Res 1(2):185–192

Lahoti R, Swaminathan M (Undated) Economic growth and labour force participation in India. Accessed 15 Apr 2019

Martinez G, Raffo J, Saito K (2016) Identifying the gender of PCT inventors WIPO. Economic research working paper number 33

McKinsey and Company (2018) McKinsey Global Institute. The power of parity: advancing women's equality in Asia Pacific Focus, India

National Institute of Mental Health and Neuro Sciences (NIMHANS) 2016 National mental health survey of India 2015–2016

OECD (2019) Gender portal. https://www.oecd.org/gender/. Accessed 11 Mar 2019

Rowntree O (GSMA) 2018 connected women. The mobile gender gap report

Roy S, Morton M, Bhattacharya S (2016) Hidden human capital: psychological empowerment and adolescent girls' aspirations in India. World Bank group policy research paper 7792

Singh C, Naik G (2018) Financial inclusion after PMJDY: a case study of Gubbi Taluk, Tumkur. Working Paper Number 568. Indian Institute of Management, Bangalore

Sorsa P, Mares J, Didier M, Guimarâes, Rabate M, Tang G, Tuske A (2015) Determination of the low female labour force participation in India. OECD Economics Department working paper number 1207

Terjesen S, Lloyd A (2015) The 2015 female entrepreneurship index. Global entrepreneurship development index

The Association of Academies and Societies of Sciences in Asia (AASSIA) (2015) Women in science and technology in Asia

The Economist (2018a) Why India needs women to work, July 5 2019. https://www.economist.com/leaders/2018/07/05why-India-needs-women-to-work. Accessed 15 May 2019

The Economist (2018b) Job of her own culture and the labour market keep India's women at home, Karputhala, 5 July 2018. https://www.economist.com/briefing/2018/07/05/culture-and-the-labour-market-keep-indias-women-at-home. Accessed 26 Aug 2018

The Economist (2019) How India's men can learn to treat women better, 5 Feb 2019. https://www.economist.com/graphic-detail/2019/02/05/how-indias-men-can-learn-to-treat-women-better. Accessed 9 Feb 2019

The Economist Intelligence Unit (2015) (Report prepared for the British Council) Defined by absence: women and research in South Asia analysing the issue in Afghanistan, Bangladesh, India, Nepal, Pakistan and Sri Lanka

The Wire (2019) Demand for jobs under MGNREGA in 2018–2019 was highest in eight years, 26 Mar 2019. https://thewire.in/labour/mgnrega-jobs-demand-highest-rural-distress

Thompson Reuter Foundation (2018) The world's most dangerous countries for women (2018). www.pol2018.trust.org. Accessed 10 Feb 2019

World Bank (2012) World development report gender equality and development

World Bank (2013) Violence against women and girls: lessons for South Asia

Chapter 6
Conclusion

Abstract This chapter is the concluding chapter. It ends the book with a vision about the sort of knowledge economy and society that the author hopes and envisages for India. This vision centres around India being a truly global player in finding tangible solutions to complex challenges, building an array of capabilities across economy and society, harnessing and linking ideas from everywhere and having institutional structures that meet the needs of the twenty first century.

Keywords Vision · Institutions · Conbundance · Solutions

6.1 Introduction

Imagine an India which is at the epicentre of new medical treatments, linking modern and traditional medicine, as an exemplar of sustainable social housing differentiated by demographic need, having climate resilient cities, being a supplier of highly skilled, creative labour to the world and as a global hub for problem solving entrepreneurs, technologists and everyday innovators. This would be an India with a leading-edge education and research infrastructure, with rapid institutional response as part of a cohesive Enabling State, meshing India's own knowledge with the best of the best from abroad through global value chains founded on knowledge. This is an India where ideas are drawn from far and wide in the country, anywhere, anytime, linking cities with villages, and scientists with local community problem solvers. This would be an India in which empowered females are free, able and encouraged to deploy their innate talents for personal and societal gain.

To some extent, these things are happening, but as we have seen they are patchy, with narrow pockets of capability, interposed with poor performance and uncertain futures. Cases in point include a health system which appears to be in reach only of the nation's most privileged, the lack of basic infrastructure in parts of the country, or an education system which is bereft of high quality or connections with industry and in large measure does not meet current and emerging economic need. Closely associated with these areas of angst is a state which is not, despite various reforms, an enabling one, but rather lurches from one set of measures to another, often in fragmented, ad hoc nature, prone to defensiveness and favouring sectional and particular interests. This is overlayed with institutions whose use by date has well and truly passed.

This book has provided a knowledge economy perspective with which to assess India's performance, perils and prospects. This was done deploying a multifaceted capability and attribute based lens described as the 'E's. This analysis has shown that India, like other developed and developing economies, needs ideas which drive further ideas, aimed at solving real-world economic, environmental and social problems. India can become a winning solutions location and destination. Knowledge is the circuit breaker in a world of physical and material constraint. Knowledge is unbounded and unlimited. Identifying, capturing, leveraging, harnessing and diffusing knowledge, drawing on ideas and know-how from anyone, anywhere, is central. The key role for government is to provide the nurturing, facilitative, supportive and at times leadership roles in this process, backed by enabling institutions.

6.2 Vision for India

Our vision for India has four closely aligned core elements

6.2.1 Enlarging India's Knowledge Footprint

Based on our analysis, India needs to improve its capacity to create, disseminate and diffuse knowledge at home and projecting it abroad, as well as to enhance empowerment. This will mean also being very much alive and open to the world of ideas beyond its shores. Also central to enlarging the Knowledge Footprint, to move it from its current 14th position overall, to inside the top ten, in five years, will be creating greater access and opportunity in knowledge. Opportunity is a prime mover for participation in the knowledge economy.

Enlarging the Knowledge Footprint thus has many dimensions. It is about building on strengths in the services sector, leveraging further India's vibrant diaspora, and nurturing India's growing skills base, while addressing multiple impediments including infrastructure deficiencies, lack of educational opportunity and quality, a manufacturing sector which lags the world's best and pressing issues associated with the digital divide.

6.2.2 Problem Solver

India has the potential and opportunity to be an international and domestic hub for problem-solving at least in the Asian region first, then globally. By this is meant building and linking Indian knowledge with the world's best, in turn exporting know-how. Central to this is the freer flows of ideas in and out of the country. It is also about empowering agents in the economy and society to embrace risk, experiment, trial and test, imagine solutions and different ways of doing things, and to think outside the box. This hinges on being open to new perspectives, insights and tolerate and embrace difference.

In the pursuit of problem-solving, it is also very much about connecting inter-generationally, that is linking traditional knowledge, and the deep and vast culture and heritage of scholarship and inquiry, with modern method of discovery and diffusion. Our suggestion of co-located traditional and modern medical facilities is one example. The blue sky experimental fund that we proposed in chapter four is very much in the vein of problem-solving and giving primacy to discovery.

The other instruments such as NEIF and IdeaBank are to give financial support and expression to the development of entrepreneurship and grass roots innovations respectively. A revamped education and training system as put forward in chapter three would be directed at finding winning solutions to pressing challenges.

6.2.3 Building 'Conbundance' Capabilities

The world and India are experiencing significant constraints. These are: natural resource constraints reflecting the burdens of population pressure and rise of conspicuous consumption among other things, placing pressure on food security, energy, water and waste management, and of course the natural environment, especially the climate; spatial constraints associated with urbanisation and its impacts on liveability, provision of essential services and housing, and the hollowing out of rural areas; time constraints, for some especially, linked to greater demands in the labour force to be faster, more agile and responsive in the context of rapidly changing technologies; lifestyle constraints, often associated with time constraints, which is putting increased pressure on mental and physical health, for example; inequality constraints for those who are have been left behind and are unable to participate in the growing shift towards a knowledge economy, due to lack of skills and opportunity; constraints on personal freedoms that are an unfortunate hallmark of our time as national and individual security concerns prevail; and constraints associated with an explosion of individual centric materialism, and the need for 'time out' and greater reflection, social harmony, building of social capital and spirituality.

A vision for India would seek to develop, build on and link the (potential) *abundance* of knowledge, to address these *constraints (the 'cons')*, hence the term 'conbundance'. These capabilities would be broad based, transferable, adaptable to different contexts, circumstances and needs, and encompass different skill sets, development and deployment of research, new technologies, business models and organisational practices in the spirit of the broad-based innovation approach that we have pursued. If these constraints seem bleak, then the prospects of deploying knowledge to find solutions and address constraints are remedial and uplifting.

Carbon accounting, green finance, resource management and sustainability skills, design and design thinking in its many contexts and domains, data management and analytics, aged and home care capabilities, and a whole raft of broader skills around collaboration, entrepreneurship and empathy are the capabilities of the now and the future. These are the capabilities that India needs to foster, and foster urgently.

6.2.4 Institutions of the Future

This book has made the claim that India's institutions are ossified and in need of renewal, consistent with an Enabling State, and in particular the market adjunct parameter. Future institutions in India, we consider, are those that are responsive to the needs of citizens, connect participants in the economy and society and can attempt to anticipate the future, albeit with its difficulties. The associated terms of a "Vigilant State" and a "Referral State" have been utilised in this book to convey the sorts of roles of the state that are consistent with the knowledge economy.

Institutions of the future are about direct citizen engagement and participation in decision making, promoting collaboration at all levels, and which both enhance and realise aspirations. For example, a high-quality education system, which is relevant to the needs of economy and society in promoting higher value jobs, but which also encompasses notions of 'civil society' and facilitates self and community realisation, represent the way forward.

This book has provided numerous suggestions for revamped institutions including the Commission for Government to clarify public purpose in the context of the knowledge economy, a new form of decentralised planning to identify and unlock knowledge at the city and rural levels, and Collaborate India to foster a stronger partnership ethos across all segments of economy and society. These initiatives would be aligned with extra-parliamentary institutions and mechanisms, to hopefully ensure that parliament works better. Various measures to address the pernicious effects of corruption are put forward.

6.2.5 Returning to the 'E's

At the outset, we introduced the broad notion of 'E's as a set of generic drivers of innovation and knowledge to reach solutions to tangible problems, and as a basis for benchmarking India against other nations.

The vision elements articulated here go hand in hand with these 'E's. Enlarging the Knowledge Footprint is aligned with the engagement and empowerment parameters, while India as a problem solver is about many of the 'E's, notably entrepreneurship, and engagement through exports and trade and the global value chains of knowledge, while conbundance capabilities speak volumes, for example, about education.

Institutions of the future, as we have commented on numerous times, are an essential underpinning of a truly Enabling State.

With reforms, and a collective will, India has the potential, and indeed the historic opportunity, to build on the innate strengths, aspirations and inspiration of its greatest asset—its people.

Printed in the United States
By Bookmasters